Sirach

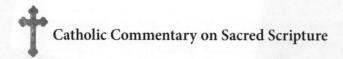 Catholic Commentary on Sacred Scripture

Sirach

André Villeneuve

Baker Academic
a division of Baker Publishing Group
Grand Rapids, Michigan

© 2025 by André Villeneuve

Published by Baker Academic
a division of Baker Publishing Group
Grand Rapids, Michigan
BakerAcademic.com

Printed in the United States of America

Library of Congress Cataloging-in-Publication Data
Names: Villeneuve, André, 1969– author.
Title: Sirach / André Villeneuve.
Description: Grand Rapids, Michigan : Baker Academic, a division of Baker Publishing Group, [2025] | Series: Catholic commentary on sacred scripture | Includes bibliographical references and index.
Identifiers: LCCN 2024027820 | ISBN 9781540965899 (paperback) | ISBN 9781540968692 (casebound) | ISBN 9781493449552 (ebook) | ISBN 9781493449569 (pdf)
Subjects: LCSH: Bible. Ecclesiasticus—Commentaries. | Bible. Ecclesiasticus—Study and teaching. | Wisdom—Biblical teaching.
Classification: LCC BS1765.53 .V55 2025 | DDC 229/.4077—dc23/eng/20240806
LC record available at https://lccn.loc.gov/2024027820

Ecclesiastical approval for printing was granted by the Most Reverend Allen H. Vigneron, Archbishop of Detroit, 17 September 2024, Prot. N. CS24-0047.

Cover art of mosaic from Basilica of Sant'Apollinare in Classe, Ravenna, Italy, showing Abel, Melchizedek, Abraham, and Isaac; De Agostini, A. De Gregorio, Superstock

Baker Publishing Group publications use paper produced from sustainable forestry practices and postconsumer waste whenever possible.

25   26   27   28   29   30   31   7   6   5   4   3   2   1

To my mother,
Loretta Biamonte Villeneuve (1943–2023),
of blessed memory

The man who fears the Lord will do this,
and he who holds to the law will obtain wisdom.
She will come to meet him like a mother,
and like the wife of his youth
she will welcome him. (Sir 15:1–2)

Contents

Illustrations   9

Editors' Preface   11

Abbreviations   15

Introduction to Sirach   17

Outline of Sirach   39

The Prologue of Sirach   43

Book One (1:1–23:28)

Part I (1:1–4:10)   49

Part II (4:11–6:17)   77

Part III (6:18–14:19)   91

Part IV (14:20–23:28)   136

Book Two (24:1–43:33)

Part V (24:1–33:17)   195

Part VI (33:18–38:23)   255

Part VII (38:24–43:33)   283

Book Three (44:1–50:29)

Part VIII (44:1–50:29)   317

The Epilogue of Sirach (51)   356

Suggested Resources   363

Glossary   367

Index of Pastoral Topics   371

Index of Sidebars   373

Illustrations

Figure 1. Map of the Ptolemaic and Seleucid Empires at the time of Sirach   20

Figure 2. Timeline of Ptolemaic and Seleucid rule over Judea   22

Figure 3. The Ben Sira Scroll from Masada   30

Figure 4. Flowchart of Sirach texts and translations   36

Figure 5. The Ten Commandments in Hebrew   58

Figure 6. An ancient Israelite family   68

Figure 7. Model of the Jerusalem temple in the Second Temple period   199

Figure 8. An ancient Jewish wedding   213

Figure 9. Fresco of a *symposion* (banquet)   245

Figure 10. A Jewish scribe at work   287

Figure 11. The high priest ministering in the sanctuary   327

Figure 12. Hezekiah's Tunnel in Jerusalem   344

Figure 13. Priestly blessing   353

Editors' Preface

The Church has always venerated the divine Scriptures just as she venerates the body of the Lord. . . . All the preaching of the Church should be nourished and governed by Sacred Scripture. For in the sacred books, the Father who is in heaven meets His children with great love and speaks with them; and the power and goodness in the word of God is so great that it stands as the support and energy of the Church, the strength of faith for her sons and daughters, the food of the soul, a pure and perennial fountain of spiritual life.

Second Vatican Council, Dei Verbum 21

Did not our hearts burn within us while he talked to us on the road, while he opened to us the Scriptures?

Luke 24:32

The Catholic Commentary on Sacred Scripture Old Testament series aims to serve the ministry of the Word of God in the life and mission of the Church. Since the Second Vatican Council, Catholics have demonstrated an increasing hunger to study Scripture in depth and in a way that reveals its relationship to liturgy, evangelization, catechesis, theology, and personal and communal life. This series responds to that desire by providing accessible yet substantive commentary on the books of the Old Testament, drawn from the best of contemporary biblical scholarship as well as the rich treasury of the Church's tradition. These volumes seek to offer scholarship illumined by faith, in the conviction that the ultimate aim of biblical interpretation is to discover what God has revealed and is still speaking through the sacred text. Central to our approach are the principles taught by Vatican II: first, the use of historical and literary methods to discern what the biblical authors intended to express; second, prayerful theological reflection to understand the sacred text "in accord with the same Spirit by whom it was written"—that is, in light of the content and unity of the whole Scripture, the living tradition of the Church, and the analogy of faith (*Dei Verbum* 12).

The Catholic Commentary on Sacred Scripture is written for those engaged in or training for pastoral ministry and others interested in studying Scripture to understand their faith more deeply, to nourish their spiritual life, or to share the good news with others. With this in mind, the authors focus on the meaning of the text for faith and life rather than on the technical questions that occupy scholars, and they explain the Bible in ordinary language that does not require "translation" for preaching and catechesis. Although this series is written from the perspective of Catholic faith, its authors draw on the interpretation of Protestant and Orthodox scholars and hope these volumes will serve Christians of other traditions as well.

A variety of features are designed to make the commentary as useful as possible. Each volume includes the biblical text of the Revised Standard Version, Second Catholic Edition (RSV-2CE). This translation follows in the English Bible tradition largely embodied in the King James Version and conforms to Vatican guidelines given in *Liturgiam authenticam* (2001). Each unit of the biblical text is followed by a list of references to relevant Scripture passages, Catechism sections, and uses in the Roman Lectionary. The exegesis that follows aims to explain in a clear and engaging way the meaning of the text in its original historical context as well as its perennial meaning for Christians. "Reflection and Application" sections help readers apply Scripture to Christian life today by responding to questions that the text raises, offering spiritual interpretations drawn from Christian tradition or providing suggestions for the use of the biblical text in catechesis, preaching, or other forms of pastoral ministry. "In the Light of Christ" sections illustrate how certain passages prefigure, prophesy, or point forward to Christ and the new covenant.

Interspersed throughout the commentary are Biblical Background sidebars that present historical, literary, or theological information and Living Tradition sidebars that offer pertinent material from the postbiblical Christian tradition, including quotations from Church documents and from the writings of saints and Church Fathers. The Biblical Background sidebars are indicated by a photo of urns that were excavated in Jerusalem, signifying the importance of historical study in understanding the sacred text. The Living Tradition sidebars are indicated by an image of Eadwine, a twelfth-century monk and scribe, signifying the growth in the Church's understanding that comes by the grace of the Holy Spirit as believers study and ponder the word of God in their hearts (see *Dei Verbum* 8).

A glossary is located in the back of each volume for easy reference. The glossary explains key terms from the biblical text as well as theological or exegetical terms, which are marked in the commentary with a cross (†). A list of suggested resources, an index of pastoral topics, and an index of sidebars are included to enhance the usefulness of these volumes. Further resources can be found at the series website, www.CatholicScriptureCommentary.com.

It is our desire and prayer that these volumes be of service so that more and more "the word of the Lord may speed forward and be glorified" (2 Thess 3:1) in the Church and throughout the world.

Mary Healy
Mark Giszczak
Peter S. Williamson

Abbreviations

AB	Anchor Bible	HII	expanded (longer) Hebrew text of Sirach
ACCS:OT	Ancient Christian Commentary on Scripture: Old Testament	KJV	King James Version
		Knox	Knox Bible
ca.	approximately	Lectionary	*The Lectionary for Mass* (1998/2002 USA edition)
Catechism	*Catechism of the Catholic Church* (2nd edition)	MS	manuscript
chap(s).	chapter(s)	NABRE	New American Bible Revised Edition
d.	died		
Douay	Douay-Rheims Bible	NJB	New Jerusalem Bible
DS	Denzinger-Schönmetzer, *Enchiridion Symbolorum, definitionum et declarationum de rebus fidei et morum* (1965)	*NPNF¹*	*Nicene and Post-Nicene Fathers*, First Series
		NPNF²	*Nicene and Post-Nicene Fathers*, Second Series
ESV-CE	English Standard Version, Catholic Edition	NRSV	New Revised Standard Version
		NT	New Testament
fig.	figure	OT	Old Testament
GI	shorter Greek text of Sirach	RSV	Revised Standard Version
GII	longer Greek text of Sirach	RSV-2CE	Revised Standard Version, Second Catholic Edition (2006)
GNT	Good News Translation		
HI	original (shorter) Hebrew text of Sirach	RV	Revised Version

Books of the Old Testament

Gen	Genesis	Judg	Judges	1 Chron	1 Chronicles
Exod	Exodus	Ruth	Ruth	2 Chron	2 Chronicles
Lev	Leviticus	1 Sam	1 Samuel	Ezra	Ezra
Num	Numbers	2 Sam	2 Samuel	Neh	Nehemiah
Deut	Deuteronomy	1 Kings	1 Kings	Tob	Tobit
Josh	Joshua	2 Kings	2 Kings	Jdt	Judith

Esther	Esther	Jer	Jeremiah	Mic	Micah
Job	Job	Lam	Lamentations	Nah	Nahum
Ps(s)	Psalms	Bar	Baruch	Hab	Habakkuk
Prov	Proverbs	Ezek	Ezekiel	Zeph	Zephaniah
Eccles	Ecclesiastes	Dan	Daniel	Hag	Haggai
Song	Song of Songs	Hosea	Hosea	Zech	Zechariah
Wis	Wisdom of Solomon	Joel	Joel	Mal	Malachi
		Amos	Amos	1 Macc	1 Maccabees
Sir	Sirach	Obad	Obadiah	2 Macc	2 Maccabees
Isa	Isaiah	Jon	Jonah		

Books of the New Testament

Matt	Matthew	Eph	Ephesians	Heb	Hebrews
Mark	Mark	Phil	Philippians	James	James
Luke	Luke	Col	Colossians	1 Pet	1 Peter
John	John	1 Thess	1 Thessalonians	2 Pet	2 Peter
Acts	Acts	2 Thess	2 Thessalonians	1 John	1 John
Rom	Romans	1 Tim	1 Timothy	2 John	2 John
1 Cor	1 Corinthians	2 Tim	2 Timothy	3 John	3 John
2 Cor	2 Corinthians	Titus	Titus	Jude	Jude
Gal	Galatians	Philem	Philemon	Rev	Revelation

Introduction to Sirach

In a time when common sense is no longer so common, people today stand in greater need of wisdom than ever. The wisdom books of the Bible, written thousands of years ago, continue to speak to every age, offering timeless principles for living a good life in accordance with God's purposes. The book of Sirach is a treasure trove of such enduring wisdom. Similar in style and content to Proverbs, it offers gems of practical advice for living well, in right relationship with God and neighbor. While originally addressed to Jews living in the †Hellenistic era, it continues to speak to people in every age and culture. As one of the deuterocanonical books in the Catholic Bible, Sirach is also a very Catholic book. Indeed, it has long been known as Ecclesiasticus, "the book of the Church," largely due to its widespread use in the early Church as a handbook of moral training for catechumens.

Title, Author, Date

The book of Sirach was written in Hebrew in Jerusalem at the beginning of the second century BC and translated into Greek by the author's grandson in Egypt around 132 BC. The title of the book according to most Greek manuscripts is "The Wisdom of Jesus the Son of Sirach." This matches the author's self-identification as "Jesus [Hebrew *Yeshua*] the son of Sirach, son of Eleazar, of Jerusalem" in the Greek text of 50:27. Although the Hebrew text of this verse identifies the author as "Simeon, the son of Yeshua, the son of Eleazar, the son of Sira,"[1] tradition has followed the Greek text and the testimony of the author's grandson, who refers to him in the prologue as "my grandfather Jesus."

---

1. A postscript in the Hebrew text of 51:30 also includes this alternate name: "Thus far the words of Simeon, the son of Yeshua, who is called Ben Sira. The Wisdom of Simeon, the son of Yeshua, the son of Eleazar, the son of Sira."

The book is known in Jewish tradition as *Sepher Ben Sira* ("The Book of Ben Sira").[2] In the †Vulgate and in Latin Christian tradition, it has been traditionally known as Ecclesiasticus, but this name has fallen into disuse today because it is easily confused with the book of Ecclesiastes. Today the book is commonly referred to as Sirach—the Greek form of the Hebrew *Sira*—or The Wisdom of Sirach. Scholars typically distinguish the author from the book by referring to the author as Ben Sira and the book as Sirach. We will follow the same convention in this volume.

We know about the author both from the prologue written by his grandson and from several autobiographical remarks sprinkled throughout the book. Ben Sira was a devout Jew, a †sage, and a scribe (38:24; 39:1–11), who "after acquiring considerable proficiency" in Israel's sacred writings set out to write "something pertaining to instruction and wisdom" (prologue). It appears that he acquired his broad learning not only through study but also through extensive travel (34:9–12; 51:13) and a pious life of prayer and devotion to the law (51:13–22). He may have been a renowned teacher and head of an academy for the instruction of youth in Jerusalem (51:23). Yet his goal was not merely to convey "instruction and wisdom" to his students but also to anchor them firmly in the faith and religion of Israel, so that "those who love learning should make even greater progress in living according to the law" (prologue).

Ben Sira lived in Jerusalem and likely wrote his book there shortly after the priestly ministry of "Simon, son of Onias" (50:1–21). This figure is Simeon II, who was high priest in Jerusalem from 219 to 196 BC, near the end of the †Ptolemaic rule over Judea. Ben Sira's vivid depiction of Simon's liturgical ministry in the temple reads like the account of an eyewitness who personally observed the scene. Yet Simon had likely died by the time of the book's writing (50:1). On the one hand, this implies that Ben Sira wrote sometime soon after Simon's death in 196 BC. On the other hand, the book never alludes to the fierce persecution that Antiochus IV Epiphanes unleashed against the Jews in the years following his accession to the throne in 175 BC. This suggests that the book of Sirach was written sometime between 196 and 175 BC, with 190–180 BC being a commonly accepted range.

Ben Sira's grandson informs us in the prologue that his grandfather wrote his book in Hebrew. The grandson later translated the book into Greek after coming to Egypt (most likely Alexandria) "in the thirty-eighth year of the reign of Euergetes." This Euergetes is King Ptolemy VIII Physcon (sometimes numbered VII), who reigned 170–116 BC.[3] These dates indicate that Ben Sira's grandson

2. Babylonian Talmud, *Hagigah* 13a; *Niddah* 16b; *Berakhot* 11b.
3. Ptolemy VIII Euergetes co-reigned over Egypt with his brother Ptolemy VI Philometor from 170 to 164. Euergetes briefly expelled Philometor in 164, but the people of Alexandria drove out Euergetes the following year and reinstated Philometor until his death in 145, during which Euergetes was king of Cyrene. After Philometor's death, Euergetes regained the throne and co-reigned with Cleopatra II and Cleopatra III until his death in 116 BC.

came to Egypt in 132 BC and began translating his grandfather's book shortly thereafter, publishing the work sometime after Euergetes's death in 116 BC.

A little-known alternate prologue, preserved in the King James Bible under the heading "A Prologue Made by an Uncertain Author," provides more information about Jesus Ben Sira and his ancestry. Because it is not original to the text and found in only one Greek manuscript, it is omitted from most modern translations and commentaries.[4] Yet this prologue is very old: it stems from a work traditionally attributed to St. Athanasius (ca. AD 298–373) entitled *Synopsis Scripturae Sacrae*. Although some scholars today view this origin as spurious and date the work to the sixth century, it remains a valuable ancient witness that is worth reprinting here:

> This Jesus was the son of Sirach, and grandchild to Jesus of the same name with him: this man therefore lived in the latter times, after the people had been led away captive, and called home again, and almost after all the prophets. Now his grandfather Jesus, as he himself witnesses, was a man of great diligence and wisdom among the Hebrews, who did not only gather the grave and short sentences of wise men, that had been before him, but himself also uttered some of his own, full of much understanding and wisdom. When as therefore the first Jesus died, leaving this book almost perfected, Sirach his son receiving it after him left it to his own son Jesus, who, having gotten it into his hands, compiled it all orderly into one volume, and called it Wisdom, entitling it both by his own name, his father's name, and his grandfather's; alluring the hearer by the very name of Wisdom to have a greater love to the study of this book. It contains therefore wise sayings, dark sentences, and parables, and certain particular ancient godly stories of men that pleased God; also his prayer and song; moreover, what benefits God had vouchsafed his people, and what plagues he had heaped upon their enemies. This Jesus did imitate Solomon, and was no less famous for wisdom and learning, both being indeed a man of great learning, and so reputed also.[5]

Piecing together the names found in the two prologues and in the text, one arrives at the following genealogy:

1. Jesus Eleazar (author's grandfather)
2. Sirach (author's father)
3. **Jesus, son of Sirach (the book's author)**
4. Unnamed (author's son)
5. Unnamed Greek translator and author of the prologue (author's grandson)

---

4. The alternate prologue is found in MS 248, one of the most important textual witnesses for the longer Greek text.

5. *The New Cambridge Paragraph Bible with the Apocrypha: King James Version*, rev. ed. (Cambridge: Cambridge University Press, 2011), 117. Translation modified.

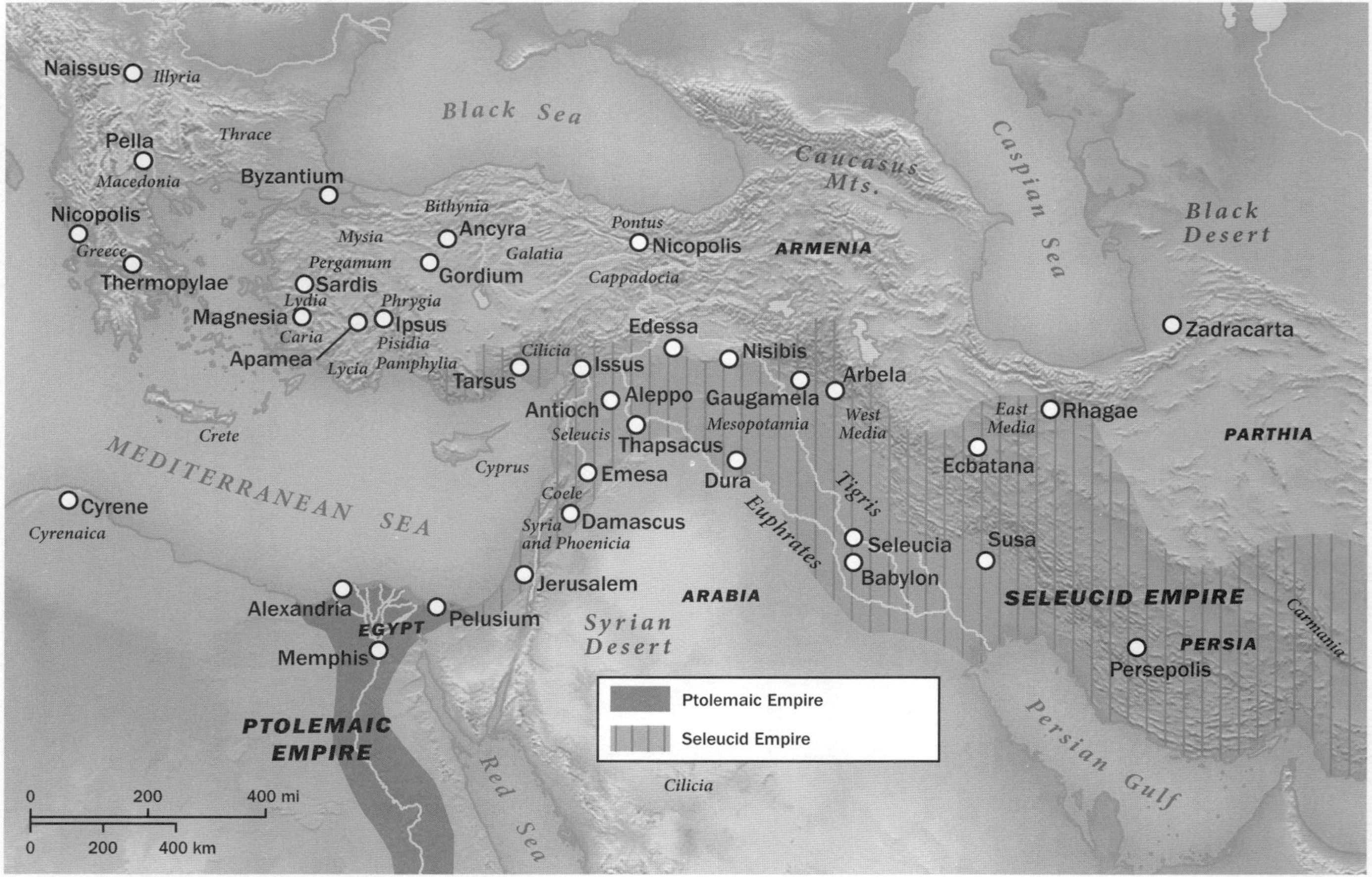

Figure 1. Map of the Ptolemaic and Seleucid Empires at the time of Sirach

Historical Context

Alexander the Great's conquest of the Persian Empire in 334–330 BC transformed the ancient Near East and ushered in the †Hellenistic period—the period of Greek rule and influence over the land of Israel. After Alexander's death in 323, his four generals carved up his vast empire. Ptolemy I Soter ruled over Egypt, and Seleucus I ruled over Syria. Due to its strategic position as a passageway between Africa and Asia, Judea soon became a battleground between the †Ptolemies and the †Seleucids. The Ptolemies ruled over the area from 301 to 198 BC. This was a period of relative peace and stability for the Jews. Many sought better economic opportunities and resettled in Greek colonies around the Mediterranean. This voluntary dispersion in the Hellenistic world became known as the Jewish †Diaspora. As Greek became the lingua franca of the Mediterranean world, the Jews of the Diaspora learned the language and adopted Greek customs and ideas. It is during the Ptolemaic period, around 250 BC, that the Hebrew Scriptures were translated into Greek in Alexandria, producing the Septuagint. Yet despite the proliferation of the Greek language and culture, the Jews were by and large able to preserve their faith and customs under Ptolemaic rule.

During the Fifth Syrian War (202–198 BC), the Seleucids, led by Antiochus III the Great, defeated the Ptolemaic army at Panias in 198 BC, establishing their control over the region and marking the end of the Ptolemaic rule over Judea. The Seleucid reign over the Jews began peaceably under Antiochus III and his son Seleucus IV Philopator (187–175). It was probably during this period that Ben Sira authored his book. Onias III was high priest, and the book of 2 Maccabees speaks of him in glowing terms: "The holy city was inhabited in unbroken peace and the laws were very well observed because of the piety of the high priest Onias and his hatred of wickedness" (2 Macc 3:1).

Nevertheless, the growing influence of Greek culture (†Hellenism) was posing increasingly great challenges to Jewish society. The Seleucids promoted an aggressive policy of Hellenization, imposing Greek culture and mores upon the peoples under their rule. Many Jews embraced the Greek way of life, while others—including Ben Sira—perceived it as a threat to the Jewish religion and culture and set out to resist it. Indeed, the pressure of Hellenization would soon escalate into a full-fledged persecution against the Jews, probably a short time after Sirach was written.

The book of Sirach thus appears to be, at least in some respects, a defense of Judaism against the rising challenges of Hellenism in the early second century BC. The author attempts to counter the rising influence of Greek thought by insisting that true wisdom is found not in Greek philosophy but rather in Israel and in the observance of the †Torah. He drives home this point by closely integrating Israel's salvation history into his wisdom teachings (see the section titled "Sirach within the Bible," below).

Date	Ptolemies	Seleucids	Israel	High Priest
220 BC	Ptolemy IV (221–204)	Antiochus III (223–187)	**Ptolemaic Rule**	Simon II (219–196) (Sir 50:1–21)
210				
200	Ptolemy V (204–180)		Fifth Syrian War (202–198) **Seleucid Rule (198)**	Onias III (196–175)
190		Seleucus IV (187–175)		
180	Ptolemy VI (180–164)	Antiochus IV (175–164)	**Ben Sira writes his book (ca. 180)**	Jason (175–171)
170	Ptolemy VIII (170–164)	Antiochus V (164–161)	Persecution of the Jews (168) Maccabean Revolt (167–142) Judas Maccabeus (ca. 166–160)	Menelaus (171–163)
160	Ptolemy VI (163–145)	Demetrius I (162–150)		Alcimus (162–159)
150	Ptolemy VIII (145–116)	Alexander Balas (150–145) Demetrius II (145–138)	Hasmonean Kingdom (142)	Jonathan Maccabeus (152–142)
140		Antiochus VII (138–129)		Simon Maccabeus (142–134)
130		Demetrius II (129–126)	**Ben Sira's grandson translates the book of Sirach (ca. 132)**	John Hyrcanus I (134–104)
120				

Figure 2. Timeline of Ptolemaic and Seleucid rule over Judea around the time Sirach was written

Yet ironically, Ben Sira is not entirely immune to the influences of Hellenism and other Gentile sources of wisdom. Although his primary influence is certainly the Hebrew Bible, he also credits much of his learning and experience of the world to his travels abroad (34:9–12), and he encourages his disciples to do the same (39:4). Ben Sira does not have a problem borrowing from Greek ideas when these confirm the truth found in Judaism and in the Jewish Scriptures. Scholars have noted many parallels between Sirach and the Greek lyric poet Theognis, and (to a lesser degree) with writers such as Euripides, Xenophon, Hesiod, Homer, and Sophocles. Some identify traces of Stoic and Epicurean philosophies in his theology. According to Stoicism, the universe is ruled by the divine Logos (word or rationality) that is immanent (present) within it. To live well, people must reflect the Logos by conforming themselves to nature and reason. Thus, by obeying the natural laws of the cosmos, humans achieve harmony with the universe and attain a form of wisdom. Some find points of contact with Stoicism in Sirach's ideal of human dignity (41:14–42:8), in the unity of the world (43:27) or of the human race (36:1–4). Others discern in Sirach hints of Epicureanism, which sought a balanced life ruled by reason, free of bodily pain and inner disquiet (14:11–16; 30:21–25; 31:27–29). Still others see Hellenistic features in Sirach's association of virtue with knowledge and wickedness with folly, his adoption of Greek customs pertaining to banquets and medical practices, and his use of philosophical arguments to defend divine justice.[6]

Genre, Structure, Literary Features

Like Proverbs, Sirach is a compilation of wisdom texts intended to serve as a handbook of moral behavior. Although its materials are organized in larger thematic units than Proverbs, it remains difficult to identify a clear structure in such a long book that is primarily composed of wisdom poems, moral exhortations, and words of advice for leading a good life. Nevertheless, the book can be divided into three main divisions (chaps. 1–23; 24–43; 44–50), framed by the prologue and an epilogue (chap. 51). The Greek text includes headings that confirm this basic division: "The Praise of Wisdom" at 24:1, and "Praise of Our Fathers" at 44:1. Some commentators divide the book into five parts, paralleling the structure of the Pentateuch, where each part consists of a doctrinal introduction followed by practical teachings (1:1–16:23; 16:24–23:27; 24:1–32:13; 32:14–42:14; 42:15–50:29).[7] Still others divide the book into eight major parts, each beginning with a poem on wisdom.[8] The present commentary organizes the contents of the book by combining its three main divisions (Books One, Two, Three) with its eight major parts (Parts I–VIII):

Prologue	Book Two (24–43)
Book One (1–23)	Part V (24:1–33:17)
Part I (1:1–4:10)	Part VI (33:18–38:23)
Part II (4:11–6:17)	Part VII (38:24–43:33)
Part III (6:18–14:19)	Book Three (44–50)
Part IV (14:20–23:28)	Part VIII (44:1–50:29)
	Epilogue (51)

6. On the relationship between Ben Sira and non-Jewish literature, see Patrick W. Skehan and Alexander A. Di Lella, *The Wisdom of Ben Sira*, AB (New York: Doubleday, 1987), 46–50; James L. Crenshaw, "The Book of Sirach," in *The New Interpreter's Bible*, ed. Leander E. Keck (Nashville: Abingdon, 1994), 5:624–26; Richard J. Clifford, *The Wisdom Literature*, Interpreting Biblical Texts (Nashville: Abingdon, 1998), 117.

7. J. Gavigan, B. McCarthy, and T. McGovern, eds., *The Navarre Bible: Wisdom Books* (New York: Scepter, 2004), 383–84.

8. Skehan and Di Lella, *Wisdom of Ben Sira*, xiii–xvi.

Sirach's literary features closely resemble those found in Proverbs. The entire book is written in poetic form, of which the most common feature is †parallelism—a pair of lines where the second completes the thought of the first. In a synonymous parallelism, the second line repeats and confirms the first using different words (e.g., 1:17). In a synthetic parallelism, the second line clarifies or develops the thought of the first (12:3; 35:1). In an antithetic parallelism, the second line expresses the opposite of the first, often highlighting the contrast between wise and foolish behavior (21:22).

The most common literary genre within the book is the *mashal*—a broad Hebrew term meaning "proverb," "aphorism," or "maxim." The *mashal* is a brief, often catchy, and witty statement that typically expresses a widely recognized truth or self-evident observation about life that the hearer is expected to acknowledge as true or binding.

One common type of *mashal* is the saying—a sentence, based on experience, that is either observational or didactic. An observational saying does not prescribe how to act; it is a truth statement that observes reality "the way it is" and reminds readers of the laws and principles that govern human existence (6:14; 14:17). A didactic saying, by contrast, implies a good course of action and a bad one, though it stops short of commanding the former or prohibiting the latter (3:26–29). Sirach uses those extensively, including "good" sayings (13:24), "better" sayings (10:27; 19:24), numerical sayings (25:1; 26:28), "abomination" sayings (13:20), "blessed" sayings (14:1–2, 20), and their counterpart, "woe" sayings (2:12–14).

A second type of *mashal* is the instruction or admonition. Expressed in the imperative, often authoritatively addressing the reader as "my son" (or some other paternal address), it is a command, either positive (3:8) or negative (3:10), calling for a certain course of action and often reinforced by warnings, admonitions, promises of rewards, or other motivating clauses (35:12–13).

Less frequently, a *mashal* can also be expressed in the form of rhetorical questions (10:19) or apostrophe—a direct rhetorical address to a person or a personified thing (41:1–2; 47:14–21).

Yet the literary richness of Sirach is not limited to the *mashal*. The book also includes wisdom poems (1:1–10; 24:1–23), prayers (22:27–23:6; 36:1–17), hymns of praise (42:15–43:33; 51:1–12), disputations (16:17), didactic compositions (16:24–17:14; 39:12–35), autobiographical narratives (33:16–17; 51:13–30), and the "rewritten Bible" form, which revisits, adapts, or expands known biblical narratives (44:1–50:24).

In short, by virtue of its breadth of content and variety of literary forms, Sirach is a rich book that has as much to offer to modern readers as it did to its original audience.[9]

9. On the literary forms in Sirach, see Skehan and Di Lella, *Wisdom of Ben Sira*, 21–30; Alexander A. Di Lella, "Wisdom of Ben-Sira," in *Anchor Bible Dictionary*, ed. David Noel Freedman (New York: Doubleday, 1992), 6:938–39; Crenshaw, "Book of Sirach," 613–20.

Theological Themes

Sirach is a long book. It covers so many topics in its fifty-one chapters that it is virtually impossible to summarize them under a few headings. Nevertheless, we can identify a few key themes and golden threads that underlie the book's theology.

Wisdom

At the heart of the book lies the pursuit of wisdom. But what is wisdom, and how is it found? The problem of wisdom's elusiveness has been raised before (Job 28:20–28). Wisdom is indeed difficult to define, and Ben Sira never provides a clear definition of the term. We might define Sirach's wisdom as *the practical knowledge and skills necessary to live a good and successful life in accordance with God's purpose.* Given that "wisdom" is a feminine noun in both Hebrew (*hokhmah*) and Greek (*sophia*),[10] she is personified as a woman, as in other books (Sir 24:1–2; Prov 8:1–36; 9:1–6; Wis 8:2–3). Ben Sira discloses her identity by means of wisdom poems (opening each of the eight parts of the book) that reveal her transcendent nature, and collections of practical exhortations and maxims that teach men how to acquire her through right thinking, right speaking, and right acting. Sirach's teachings on wisdom reveal the following characteristics.

(a) Her Origin

Wisdom originates from God; she is the word that came forth from his mouth at creation (24:3). Although she has a beginning—she was "created before all things" (1:4, 9)—she will never cease to exist (24:9).

(b) Her Role in Creation and History

God created the universe in and through Wisdom. She thus plays an active role in God's creative work. She sustains the world, having been "poured out" upon "all his works" (1:9; 24:3–6; compare Prov 8:22–31), and she steadfastly guides human history—especially Jewish history (16:24–18:14; 39:12–35; 42:15–50:24)—toward what is good and true.

(c) Her Nature

Wisdom is never equated with pure intellectual knowledge. Although study is necessary to acquire her, she is described in terms that are more relational and practical than speculative. She is personified as a wife and mother (4:11–19; 6:18–31; 14:20–15:8), and men are invited to enter into a loving relationship with her. This is not a sentimental romantic relationship, however, but one of

---

10. Wisdom is also a feminine noun in Latin (*sapientia*).

"tough love" and strict discipline whereby she trains her followers to live a life of integrity and righteousness. Through this formative relationship, she grants her followers the ability to distinguish between good and evil and to choose the good so that they may live in right relationship with God and lead a blessed life.

(d) Her Acquisition

Wisdom is a gift from God; he bestows her freely upon those who love him (1:10). Yet humans must do their part to acquire her: they must have the fear of the Lord, which Ben Sira calls the "beginning," "full measure," "crown," and "root" of wisdom (1:11–20). This disposition must translate into concrete action: the person who fears the Lord must pursue Wisdom with dedication and have both the willingness and the humility to submit to her discipline, even at the cost of great effort (4:17; 6:24–25), by studying the law and keeping God's commandments (1:26).

(e) Her Rewards

Although the pursuit of wisdom is difficult, she turns out to be well worth the effort in the end. To those who find her she grants fruits and desirable goods, knowledge and glory (1:16–19), divine life, blessing, and love (4:11–14), rest, joy, a strong protection, a glorious robe, and a crown of gladness (6:28–31). Souls remain thirsty when they refuse to draw near to her (51:24).

Torah and Commandments

Ben Sira identifies Wisdom with "the book of the covenant of the Most High God, the law which Moses commanded us" (24:23). More than the earlier wisdom books, such as Proverbs, Job, and Ecclesiastes, Ben Sira emphasizes the close relationship between Wisdom and †Torah. This does not imply a legalistic view of wisdom, for the Hebrew term *torah* means not so much "law" as "teaching" or "instruction" on how to live a good and godly life. The identification of Wisdom with the Torah implies the preexistence of the Torah and its divine, eternal character. This idea would later become a common teaching in rabbinic Judaism: the rabbis believed that although the Torah was *revealed* to Israel at Mount Sinai during the exodus, its existence preceded the creation of the world[11] and would endure forever (Bar 4:1). It is no wonder, then, that for Ben Sira "he who holds to the law will obtain wisdom" (15:1).

Retribution

Like Proverbs, Sirach subscribes to the classic theology of retribution as expressed in the book of Deuteronomy: pursuing wisdom by obeying God's

---

11. Midrash Genesis Rabbah 8.

commandments brings blessings and prosperity (Deut 28:1–14); despising wisdom by disobeying the commandments leads to curses and misery (28:15–68). Every person has the freedom and responsibility to choose good over evil (Sir 15:11–20). Writing from the perspective of the late Old Testament period, Ben Sira has no clear concept of life after death—apart from the idea that the just live on through their good name, memory, and descendants (30:4–5; 37:26; 41:12–13). He believes that divine retribution takes place in this life, that death is final, and that †Hades is the destination of the deceased. Thus, a man must make the best of the few days he has on earth to establish his legacy (14:11–19; 38:16–23; 41:1–4)—though two prayers for the "revival of bones" (46:12; 49:10) seem to point toward the hope of a future resurrection.

Temple Liturgy

Despite Wisdom's universal presence at every time and place in the cosmos, she "sought a resting place" where she might lodge at a specific moment in history (24:7). Seemingly unsatisfied with her cosmic universality, she came down, as it were, to dwell in Israel, in Jerusalem, and in the sanctuary on Mount Zion, where she ministers before God (24:8–12). Wisdom is thus present and active in the liturgy of the Jewish temple, which itself recalls the garden of Eden (24:13–17). Many verbal parallels between chapters 24 and 50 also indicate that Wisdom is present in the ministry of the high priest (50:1–24). Ben Sira's reverence for the temple service is further seen in his exhortation to honor the priests (7:29–31) and the sacrifices they offer (34:18–20). Although he tends to spiritualize some cultic requirements, so that keeping the Torah, performing acts of kindness, and acting justly are equivalent to offering sacrifices (35:1–3), he never treats the latter as dispensable but affirms their importance as integral to Israel's worship (35:4–11).

Prayer

The quest for wisdom is never an entirely secular pursuit but one grounded in the fear of the Lord. Accordingly, it must be constantly supported by prayer. Ben Sira exhorts his readers to petition God for mercy (21:1; 28:2–4; 39:5), wise counsel (37:15), healing (38:9, 13–14), and, of course, wisdom (51:13). Moreover, the wisdom seeker must keep God's commandments if he or she wishes to be heard (3:5). Offering praises to God is an even higher form of prayer (17:10; 39:14–15; 43:30). The book includes three lengthy prayers: a petition asking God for control of one's thoughts, words, and desires (22:27–23:6), a supplication for the redemption of Zion (36:1–17), and a psalm of thanksgiving (51:1–12).

Life in Society

Ben Sira's moral teachings cover a wide range of situations and topics. Above all, he exhorts his readers (who in his day were primarily men) to live virtuously through the various challenges of life in society. Among the topics he treats, we find advice on honoring one's parents (3:1–16), humility and pride (3:17–28; 7:16–17; 10:26–11:6), generosity and almsgiving (3:30–4:10; 29:1–20), wealth and poverty (10:30–31; 11:10–28; 13:1–14:19; 31:1–11), lending and borrowing (29:1–20), self-mastery and controlling the tongue (19:4–17; 20:1–8; 23:7–15), food and banquets (31:12–32:13; 37:27–31), leadership (9:17–10:18), strength of character (27:4–10; 27:30–28:12), diligence and hard work (40:28–30), true and false friendship (6:5–17; 9:10–16; 11:29–12:18), relationships with women (9:1–9; 25:13–26:27; 42:9–14), raising and disciplining children (30:1–13; 42:9–14), servants and slaves (33:24–31), sickness and health (38:1–15), and life and death (14:11–19; 38:16–23; 41:1–4).[12]

Sirach within the Bible

Ben Sira is thoroughly versed in the traditions of the Hebrew Bible. As his grandson notes in the prologue, he composed his own work "after devoting himself especially to the reading of the law and the prophets and the other books of our fathers, and after acquiring considerable proficiency in them." This proficiency is evident throughout his work. In contrast to older wisdom books such as Job, Proverbs, and Ecclesiastes, which rarely recall Israel's history, Ben Sira frequently draws from the Old Testament to connect his wisdom with Israel's religious traditions and heroes of the faith. Thus, he recalls the creation account (15:14; 39:16), the garden of Eden (24:25–27), Adam (33:10; 40:1) and Eve (25:24), the fallen angels (16:7), the flood (40:10), Lot and Sodom and Gomorrah (16:8; 39:23), the law of Moses (24:23), the tabernacle (24:10, 15), the Israelites in the wilderness (16:9–10; 38:5), and Zion (24:10; 36:13–15). His praise of Israel's ancient heroes of the faith (chaps. 44–50), in particular, provides the most complete overview of salvation history in the Bible. Beginning with Enoch, it surveys the patriarchs, the exodus, the conquest, the judges, the period of the kingship, the prophets, and the †postexilic leaders up to the days of Simon the high priest.

Ben Sira also draws freely from earlier wisdom books, both in their doctrinal content and literary forms. He is most indebted to Proverbs, which he frequently alludes to, adapts, and develops for his own purposes. Compare, for example, the treatment of the origin of wisdom in both books (Prov 8:22; Sir 1:4), the connection between wisdom and the fear of the Lord (Prov 1:7; Sir 1:14), folly

---

12. Michael Phua, "Sirach, Book of," in *Dictionary of the Old Testament: Wisdom, Poetry & Writings*, ed. Tremper Longman III and Peter Enns (Downers Grove, IL: IVP Academic, 2008), 723–24. See also the Index of Pastoral Topics.

as falling into a self-dug pit (Prov 26:27; Sir 27:25–26), the refining power of suffering (Prov 17:3; Sir 2:5), the imperative to trust the Lord (Prov 3:5–6; Sir 2:6–9), and the virtue of humility (Prov 3:34; Sir 3:18).

To a lesser extent, Sirach also shares points of contact with the books of Baruch and Tobit. Like Sirach, Baruch asserts that wisdom is found in the †Torah: she is manifest when Israel observes the commandments and forsaken when the nation disobeys them (Bar 3:9–4:4). Like Sirach, Tobit highlights the value of acts of piety, Torah observance, and personal prayer as expressions of wisdom and devotion to God. Both books address themes such as honoring parents (Tob 4:3; Sir 3:12), praising generosity and condemning stinginess (Tob 4:7; Sir 14:9–10), and being merciful to the righteous but not to sinners (Tob 4:17; Sir 12:4).[13]

Although Sirach is not quoted in the New Testament, several passages seem to allude to it. Jesus echoes Sirach in his teachings on forgiveness (Matt 6:14; Sir 28:2), on gathering heavenly treasures (Matt 6:19; Sir 29:12), and on how God will repay people for their earthly deeds (Matt 16:27; Sir 35:19). Most notably, Jesus's invitation to take on his yoke, which is easy, and bear his burden, which is light (Matt 11:28–30), evokes Wisdom's summons to submit to her bonds and bear her yoke (Sir 6:24–26; 51:26–27). His promise to the Samaritan woman that "whoever drinks of the water that I shall give him will never thirst" (John 4:13–14) also reads like a response to Wisdom's assertion that "those who drink me will thirst for more" (Sir 24:21). Generally, the personification of Wisdom in Sirach is a fitting preparation for the revelation of Jesus as Wisdom incarnate (John 1:1–18), and her role in creation prefigures Christ's identity as the "firstborn of all creation," through whom all things were made (Col 1:15–20; Heb 1:1–2).

The New Testament book that displays the closest parallels with Sirach is the Epistle of James. James echoes Sirach on topics such as double-mindedness (Sir 1:28; 2:12; James 1:6, 8), facing temptations (Sir 2:1; 15:11–20; James 1:2–4, 13–15), being quick to hear (Sir 5:11; James 1:19), the mirror as a reflection of the soul (Sir 12:11; James 1:23), controlling the tongue (Sir 28:12–26; James 3:1–12), humility (Sir 3:18; James 1:9), pride (Sir 10:7; James 4:6), and true wisdom (Sir 19:20–25; James 3:13–18).[14]

Canonicity

Although Ben Sira seems at times to claim divine inspiration for himself (24:30–34; 39:6–11), and his grandson situates him in the tradition of "the law and the

---

13. Skehan and Di Lella, *Wisdom of Ben Sira*, 40–45; R. J. Coggins, *Sirach*, Guides to Apocrypha and Pseudepigrapha (Sheffield: Sheffield Academic, 1998), 62–68.

14. G. H. Box and W. Oesterley, "The Book of Sirach," in *Apocrypha of the Old Testament*, ed. R. H. Charles (Oxford: Clarendon, 1913), 1:294–96; Phua, "Sirach, Book of," 726–27.

prophets and the other books of our fathers" (prologue), the book did not achieve canonical status in the Jewish Bible, probably because of its late date of composition and the traces of †Hellenistic influence in its theology.

Nevertheless, the inclusion of Sirach in the Septuagint and the existence of multiple Hebrew and Greek versions indicate that the book was viewed as sacred

Figure 3. The Ben Sira Scroll from Masada

in some ancient Jewish communities. Scrolls found at Masada and Qumran, in which Sirach is written stichometrically—a common practice in sacred writings, where each verse is written over a full line divided into two columns—also seem to confirm its early sacred status.

Even after Sirach was excluded from the Jewish canon by noted second-century Rabbi Akiba,[15] the book remained popular among Jews. The books of 2 Enoch, the Psalms of Solomon, the †Talmud, and †Midrash all show traces of its influence. It is quoted some eighty-two times in rabbinic writings, sometimes introduced by the formula "it is written," an expression usually reserved for quoting the canonical Scriptures.[16] Sirach is even quoted several times by the great tenth-century rabbi Saadia Gaon.

The canonicity of Sirach was also disputed in the early Church. Sirach 4:31 is quoted as authoritative Scripture in the *Didache* 4.5 and the *Epistle of Barnabas* 19.9, but it is excluded from the first known Christian list of biblical books, attributed to Melito of Sardis (d. 180).[17] In the East, several Fathers quote Sirach and refer to it as "Scripture," yet they tend to exclude it from the Old Testament canon. Clement of Alexandria (d. 220) frequently quotes Sirach and refers to it as "Scripture," yet he places Sirach among the "disputed Scriptures."[18] Origen (d. 254) speaks of Sirach as "authoritative Scripture," "the Divine Word," or "Holy Scripture" but counts only the twenty-two books of the Hebrew canon as Old Testament Scriptures.[19] St. Athanasius (d. 373) adopts

---

15. Akiba even forbade the reading of the noncanonical books (including Sirach) under pain of losing one's part in the world to come (Mishnah, *Sanhedrin* 10:1; †Tosefta, *Yadayim* 2:5; Jerusalem Talmud, *Sanhedrin* 28a; Babylonian Talmud, *Sanhedrin* 100b).

16. Babylonian Talmud, *Hagigah* 13a; *Niddah* 16b.

17. Eusebius, *Ecclesiastical History* 4.26.

18. Eusebius, *Ecclesiastical History* 6.13.

19. Eusebius, *Ecclesiastical History* 6.25. The Jewish canon traditionally includes 24 canonical books—the same as the 39 books of the Protestant canon by combining 1–2 Samuel, 1–2 Kings, Ezra–Nehemiah,

the same approach, occasionally referring to Sirach as "Holy Scripture" but counting only the twenty-two Hebrew books as inspired, and Sirach among other books "not indeed included in the Canon, but appointed by the Fathers to be read by those who newly join us, and who wish for instruction in the word of godliness."[20]

In the West, most Fathers viewed Sirach as canonical. Tertullian (d. 220), St. Cyprian of Carthage (d. 258), Methodius of Olympus (d. 311), and Hilary of Poitiers (d. 368) all quote the book liberally, often referring to it as "Scripture" or with the expression "it is written." The notable exception is St. Jerome, who, after listing the books of the Hebrew canon, states that all other books—including the book of Jesus the son of Sirach—"must be placed amongst the Apocryphal writings" and "are not in the canon."[21] Yet like the Greek Fathers, Jerome often quotes from the Apocrypha with the standard introductory formula used for the canonical books, "as it is written." By contrast, St. Augustine (d. 430) firmly places Sirach in the canon. Of the books of Wisdom and Sirach, he writes: "They are to be reckoned among the prophetical books, since they have attained recognition as being authoritative."[22]

Early Church synods at Hippo (AD 393) and Carthage (397) included Sirach in the canon of Scripture, the latter counting it as one of the "five books of Solomon" (with Proverbs, Ecclesiastes, Song of Songs, and Wisdom). This decision was confirmed at the Council of Carthage of 419. Sirach's canonical status thereafter remained uncontested until the Protestant Reformation, when Martin Luther and the other Reformers relegated it to the Apocrypha and adopted the shorter Hebrew Bible as the Protestant canon of the Old Testament. In response, the Council of Trent reaffirmed at its fourth session (1546) the status of Sirach among the canonical books of Scripture.

In Catholic Bibles, the book of Sirach is placed last among the Old Testament wisdom books. Sirach is also accepted as canonical in the Eastern Orthodox and Oriental Orthodox Churches.

1–2 Chronicles, and the twelve minor prophets. The most ancient authorities, such as Origen and the Jewish historian Josephus (*Against Apion* 1.38–40), count only 22 books—perhaps because Ruth was attached to Judges and Lamentations to Jeremiah.

20. Athanasius, *Festal Letters* 39.7 (*NPNF*[2] 4:552). Cyril of Jerusalem (d. 386), Gregory of Nazianzus (d. 389), and Epiphanius (d. 404) also limit the canon of the Old Testament to the twenty-two Hebrew books, while John Chrysostom (d. 407) does quote from Sirach as "divine Scripture." John of Damascus (d. 750) speaks of Sirach as "virtuous and noble, but not counted" among the books of the Old Testament canon (*Exposition of the Orthodox Faith* 4.17 [*NPNF*[2] 9:90]). On the status of Sirach in the early Eastern Church, see W. O. E. Oesterley, *The Wisdom of Jesus the Son of Sirach or Ecclesiasticus* (Cambridge: Cambridge University Press, 1912), lxxviii–lxxx.

21. *Preface to the Books of Samuel and Kings* (*NPNF*[1] 6:490).

22. *On Christian Doctrine* 2.8 (*NPNF*[2] 2:539). Likewise, John Cassian (d. 450) and Cassiodorus (d. 570) recognize Sirach as canonical. On the status of Sirach in the early Western Church, see Oesterley, *Wisdom of Jesus the Son of Sirach*, lxxx–lxxxii.

Sirach as Sacred Scripture

Reading Sirach as Sacred Scripture—as an inspired book offering timeless wisdom to all people at all times—poses some challenges. Some of Ben Sira's teachings are so embedded in his culture that they are not always applicable to our own day (e.g., his advice concerning dinner parties, or that unmarried women should avoid married women). More significantly, some of his advice comes across as harsh and even contrary to Christian teaching (e.g., his views on women, children, slaves, and corporal punishment). These views are often troubling, shocking, and even scandalous to the modern reader.

Can Christians still read the difficult passages of Sirach as the word of God that, like the rest of Scripture, communicates "divinely revealed realities" written "under the inspiration of the Holy Spirit"?[23] Indeed they can, if guided by the following principles:

1. The life experience on which Ben Sira draws is from the culture of his own time and place—the second-century BC Jewish world—not that of all cultures. His advice therefore must be adapted and applied to different cultural settings in an analogous rather than a literal manner. This requires wisdom in the interpreter, guided by the Holy Spirit, to apply correctly (Catechism 110).

2. The reader must be aware of the literary genres and devices used in Sirach (Catechism 110). For example, the book uses hyperboles and exaggerations to emphasize certain points—a technique that is common throughout the Bible, even in the teachings of Jesus.[24] Thus, Sirach's most shocking statements should not necessarily be taken literally. Instead, the reader must attempt to discern what timely principles the author intends to communicate via hyperboles and exaggerations for rhetorical effect.

3. Although all Scripture is inspired, we can distinguish different levels of inspiration and authority between books—even within the Old Testament. Not all books directly communicate divine speech. Whereas the †Torah (the Pentateuch) is the divinely revealed law given to Israel, and the prophets convey divine oracles (often introduced by the words "thus says the Lord") urging Israel to be faithful to God's covenant and law, the wisdom books function differently. Rather than directly communicating divine speech (apart from allusions to earlier Scriptures), they draw inferences from human experience. Rather than focusing on obedience to the covenant or the attainment of eternal life, they often focus on living well and achieving successful outcomes in this life. The teachings of wisdom books such as Proverbs and Sirach are thus not invariable rules

23. *Dei Verbum* 11; Catechism 105.
24. See Matt 5:27–30; 18:6; Luke 14:26.

or moral absolutes (like the Ten Commandments). They must be read in light of other books of Scripture and *require wisdom from the interpreter* to be understood and applied.

4. Like the rest of the Old Testament, the teachings of Sirach are incomplete, reflecting an earlier stage of divine revelation. Although these books "bear witness to the whole divine pedagogy of God's saving love" and are "a storehouse of sublime teaching on God and of sound wisdom on human life," they still "contain matters imperfect and provisional" (Catechism 122) to be fulfilled later in the incarnation, death, and resurrection of the Messiah, and in the teachings of the New Testament and of the Church. Consequently, Christian readers must interpret Sirach in the light of the fuller revelation of the New Covenant. In some cases, New Covenant revelation develops Sirach's teaching (for example, his limited understanding of the resurrection) or even overturns it (for example, his recommendation of divorce).

Applying these principles to Sirach's most difficult passages—on his treatment of women—the following points must be kept in mind:

1. The passages about women must take into account their cultural conditioning (Catechism 110). Sirach, like all books of Scripture, is written within a cultural context that did not fully value or recognize the dignity of women. Written by a man to other men about seeking and living according to wisdom, it is thus limited to a male perspective and does not generally take into account the perspective of women. In this discourse, often reflecting human fallenness and sin, the intra-male conversation about problems with women sometimes leads to unflattering generalizations, just as women sometimes make unflattering generalizations about men.

2. The passages about women seem to be largely a rhetorically forceful exhortation to young men to choose their wives carefully and to beware of being deceived by superficial qualities like beauty. A poorly chosen spouse can lead to a lifetime of unhappiness. A wife's vice or virtue can have an enormous influence on her husband, for evil or for good. But this also applies in the other direction: a husband's vice or virtue can make his wife either miserable or happy. These passages should be read from this broader perspective. Women readers can apply this teaching to themselves in an analogous manner. For example, the "dejected mind," "gloomy face," and "wounded heart" caused by "an evil wife" (25:23) can also be equally caused by an evil husband.

3. Though inspired, Ben Sira's teachings on women do not directly communicate divine speech. While presupposing the previous (relatively

sparse) teachings of the Torah, Prophets, and Writings on women and on marriage, they still reflect the limited perspective and experience of a Jew from the †Second Temple period who does not yet benefit from the teachings of the gospel. Ben Sira balances his negative comments to some degree by extolling the great value of a virtuous wife and by his portrayal of Wisdom as a noble lady. Yet sometimes his statements require contextualizing and balancing with truths from other texts of Scripture.[25]

4. The passages about women must be read not only in light of the whole canon of Scripture but also in light of Christian tradition and the teachings of the Magisterium, which proclaim the equal dignity of women and men and decry the many ways that women have been devalued and disrespected.[26] Moreover, the gospel offers a radically new and transcendent understanding of marriage that surpasses and even supersedes Sirach's advice.[27]

By keeping these interpretive principles in mind, the Christian reader can approach Sirach as an inspired book of Sacred Scripture while remaining aware of the author's limited second-century BC perspective—not yet perfected by the teachings of the gospel and of the Church.

The Text of Sirach

Anyone who reads a few translations of Sirach side by side will quickly notice significant discrepancies between them, including added or omitted verses and different verse numbers across translations. These differences point to the complicated history of the text, which involves many ancient manuscripts, written in several languages, that at times differ considerably from one another. Although these differences do not substantially alter Sirach's message and theology, they do pose some challenges in terms of identifying and transmitting the most authentic text. Translators and editors of modern Bibles are faced with a choice: Should they prioritize the earliest and most original text, or should they favor expanded texts that are more theologically developed and have been historically more authoritative in Christian tradition? We will sketch this textual history here only in its broadest outline.

We know from the prologue that Ben Sira wrote his book in Hebrew, and his grandson translated the work into Greek. St. Jerome (ca. 347–420) was familiar

---

25. For example, "From a woman sin had its beginning, and because of her we all die" (25:24) needs to be balanced by Rom 5:12, 17–19.

26. See Gal 3:28; Catechism 1938, 2387; John Paul II, *Mulieris Dignitatem* (1988).

27. See the Reflection and Application section for 25:13–26:27 on p. 217.

with the Hebrew text in his own day; it is also quoted in the †Talmud and other early rabbinic texts. Yet because the book was excluded from the Jewish canon of Scripture, the Hebrew text was eventually lost.

Given the disappearance of the Hebrew text, the Greek version remained the primary text of Sirach throughout history. Yet the Greek text has come down to us in two forms: a shorter text (GI), which is the grandson's translation of the original Hebrew text (HI), and a longer Greek text (GII) including some three hundred additional lines, apparently derived from an expanded Hebrew text (HII):

Hebrew I (original) → Greek I (shorter)

Hebrew II (expanded) → Greek II (longer)

While the shorter Greek text is preserved in the major manuscripts of the Septuagint, the longer text is preserved in just a few Greek manuscripts but also attested in the most important ancient translations, such as the *Vetus Latina* or Old Latin (ca. AD 200), the Syriac Peshitta (ca. AD 200), and the Syro-Hexapla (AD 617).

The Old Latin is an expanded translation from the Greek that reflects both GI and GII, with numerous additions of its own. It is preserved in the †Vulgate: St. Jerome, who did not regard Sirach as canonical, did not retranslate it but rather adopted the existing Old Latin text. For this reason—and because of its important role as the authoritative canonical text in the Catholic tradition—the Vulgate remains an important textual witness of the expanded text (as reflected in the RSV-2CE).

The Syriac is a translation of a Hebrew parent text (perhaps a fusion of HI and HII), though the translator (who may have been Jewish or Christian) also incorporates passages from the longer Greek text (GII) and what appear to be expansions of his own. The Syro-Hexapla is another, distinct Syriac version translated from the Greek text of the Septuagint in Origen's Hexapla.[28] Both Syriac versions are important witnesses to the expanded GII text.

Together with other ancient (but less important) versions such as the Coptic, Ethiopic, Armenian, Georgian, Slavonic, Arabic, and Palestinian-Christian Aramaic, these were the main textual witnesses of Sirach until the end of the nineteenth century. Between 1896 and 1900, long fragments of the Hebrew text were discovered in the Cairo Synagogue Geniza (a storeroom for discarded manuscripts). More Hebrew fragments were discovered in Qumran and Masada in the twentieth century, so that a little over two-thirds of the Hebrew text has now been recovered.[29] These archaeological finds have confirmed the existence of

---

28. The Hexapla was a parallel six-column arrangement of the Hebrew text and Greek translations of the Old Testament compiled by the Church Father Origen (third century AD).

29. The major sections of Sirach currently extant in Hebrew are the following: 3:8–16:26; 18:32–19:2; 20:5–7, 13, 22–23, 30–31; 21:22–23, 26; 22:11–12, 21–22; 25:8, 13, 17–24; 26:1–3, 13–17; 30:11–34:1; 35:9–38:27; 39:15–51:30 (some individual verses within these sections are still missing). See Skehan and

Sirach: Texts and Translations

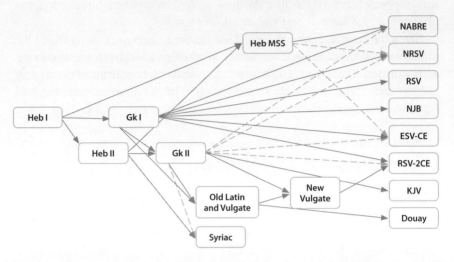

Figure 4. Flowchart of Sirach texts and translations

different editions of the Hebrew text. In many instances, the Hebrew manuscripts agree with the Greek, Latin, and Syriac texts; in other instances, they disagree.

To summarize, the textual witnesses attest that Sirach exists in a shorter text (considered more original) and a longer text (considered to be a later expansion). The Vulgate generally follows the longer Greek version, adding further expansions of its own. Yet the 1979 New Vulgate (upon which the translation used in this commentary, the RSV-2CE, is largely based) sometimes diverges from the Vulgate in order to follow the Greek text more closely (e.g., 3:10, 24).

This state of affairs explains the considerable variations among modern English translations. While older Protestant translations (e.g., KJV) follow the longer Greek text (GII) and older Catholic translations (e.g., Douay, Knox) follow the Vulgate, more recent translations (e.g., RV, RSV, NJB) rely primarily on the shorter Greek text (GI)—resulting in omissions of some verses from GII or their placement in footnotes. Other modern translations (e.g., NRSV, ESV-CE) also follow GI while incorporating more material from GII and the Hebrew manuscripts. The NABRE stands out in prioritizing the Hebrew text wherever it exists and is clear enough. The RSV-2CE—which the present volume follows—is eclectic: it sometimes follows the shorter Greek text (1:12, 18, 21; 24:18, 24), sometimes the longer Greek text (1:5, 7; 3:19), and sometimes the New Vulgate (4:17–18; 24:1–3, 8, 12, 20).

Di Lella, *Wisdom of Ben Sira*, 51–53; Pancratius C. Beentjes, *The Book of Ben Sira in Hebrew: A Text Edition of All Extant Hebrew Manuscripts and a Synopsis of All Parallel Hebrew Ben Sira Texts* (Atlanta: Society of Biblical Literature, 1997), 181–83. See also the Index of Passages compiled by Joshua A. Blachorsky available at https://www.bensira.org/.

In the present commentary, "literally" refers to the Greek text. Additions specific to the Vulgate are marked *in italics*. Unless otherwise noted, translations of the Hebrew text are this author's translation, based on the translation by Benjamin H. Parker and Martin G. Abegg.[30]

A list of textual variants—as reflected in modern English translations based on the original Hebrew text, the shorter and longer Greek texts, and the Latin and Syriac texts of Sirach—is posted online at https://www.catholiccommen taryonsacredscripture.com/sirach/.

Relevance for the Christian Life

Living wisely is living well. Acquiring wisdom, therefore, helps one to navigate through all situations of life, whether this be flourishing among family and friends, succeeding in business and trade, dealing with good and bad leaders, relating to the poor and the powerful, or coping with sickness and death. Yet wisdom is about much more than living a successful, worldly life. More importantly, wisdom concerns living according to God's purposes.

The Christian life is not only concerned with believing the right things. It is also about acting in a certain way. Orthodoxy must be translated into orthopraxy. Wisdom gives one both the ability to recognize what is the true and highest good of human existence, and the will to pursue that good. For the Christian, the highest good is loving God and neighbor (Matt 22:35–40). In many ways, Ben Sira's wisdom teachings provide practical ways by which we can live out the two greatest commandments. They also reflect God's character, the image of the One who is eternal wisdom.

Although nearly 2,200 years old, the book of Sirach continues to convey invaluable wisdom lessons for today's Christian readers. Although some of his advice—most notably his views on women, children, and slaves—reflects the cultural context of his time and should be interpreted and applied in light of the New Testament and teachings of the Church, his instruction remains as relevant and beneficial for life in the twenty-first century AD as it was in the second century BC. The wisdom of Ben Sira teaches the art of living well, communicating principles of a law for humanity that transcends all ages, places, and cultures.

---

30. The Hebrew manuscripts of Sirach, along with Parker/Abegg's translations, are available at https://www.bensira.org/, a site dedicated to the ancient and medieval Hebrew manuscripts of Sirach developed by Gary A. Rendsburg and Jacob Binstein from the Department of Jewish Studies at Rutgers University.

Outline of Sirach

Prologue
Book One (1–23)
  I. Part I (1:1–4:10)
      A. The Divine Origin of Wisdom (1:1–10)
      B. The Fear of the Lord: The Beginning and End of Wisdom
         (1:11–30)
      C. Trusting God amid Trials (2:1–18)
      D. Honoring Father and Mother (3:1–16)
      E. Humility and Pride (3:17–31)
      F. Almsgiving and Justice (4:1–10)
  II. Part II (4:11–6:17)
      A. Lady Wisdom's Motherly Discipline (4:11–19)
      B. On Shame and Timely Speech (4:20–31)
      C. Against Presumption, Deceptive Speech, and Unruly Passions
         (5:1–6:4)
      D. Authentic Friendship (6:5–17)
 III. Part III (6:18–14:19)
      A. Lady Wisdom's Discipline as Path to Joy (6:18–37)
      B. Do Good, Avoid Evil (7:1–17)
      C. On Domestic Life: Duties to Family, Priests, and the Poor
         (7:18–36)
      D. Prudence in Relating to Others (8:1–19)
      E. Relationships with Women, Friends, Sinners, and Neighbors
         (9:1–18)
      F. On Rulers, Pride, Honor, and Humility (10:1–11:1)
      G. On Deceptive Appearances and Trusting in God's Providence
         (11:2–28)

H. Discerning Friends from Enemies (11:29–12:18)

I. Beware of the Rich and Powerful (13:1–14:2)

J. Using Wealth Wisely: On Stinginess and Liberality (14:3–19)

IV. Part IV (14:20–23:28)

A. Courting Lady Wisdom (14:20–15:10)

B. Human Free Will and Divine Justice (15:11–16:23)

i. On the Origin of Good and Evil (15:11–20)

ii. The Fate of Sinners (16:1–23)

C. God's Wisdom, Justice, and Mercy (16:24–18:14)

i. In His Creation of Man (16:24–17:14)

ii. In His Rewards and Punishments (17:15–18:14)

D. Prudence and Integrity in Words and Deeds (18:15–19:17)

i. Give Graciously, Plan Cautiously (18:15–29)

ii. Exercise Temperance, Avoid Gossip (18:30–19:17)

E. True and False Wisdom (19:18–30)

F. Wisdom in Silence and Speech (20:1–31)

i. When to Talk; Gain and Loss (20:1–17)

ii. Appropriate and Inappropriate Talk (20:18–32)

G. The Wise and the Foolish (21:1–22:18)

i. Sin's Deceptive Path (21:1–28)

ii. The Fool's Wayward Path (22:1–18)

H. Preserving Friendship (22:19–26)

I. Self-Control over Thoughts, Words, and Deeds (22:27–23:28)

i. Prayer for Self-Control; Sinful Speech (22:27–23:15)

ii. Sexual Sins; Adultery and Its Consequences (23:16–28)

Book Two (24–43)

V. Part V (24:1–33:17)

A. Lady Wisdom's Hymn of Praise (24:1–34)

i. From Heaven to Earth (24:1–18)

ii. Wisdom's Feast (24:19–34)

B. Wisdom in Interpersonal Relations (25:1–12)

C. On Good and Evil Women (25:13–26:27)

i. The Wicked Wife (25:13–26)

ii. The Virtuous Wife; the Wicked Wife; the Headstrong Daughter (26:1–18)

iii. Calling Men to Sexual Integrity (26:19–27)

D. Honesty and Integrity in Dealing with Others (26:28–27:15)

E. Offenses against Friendship (27:16–28:26)

i. Betrayal, Deceit, and Anger (27:16–28:7)

ii. Strife and Slander (28:8–26)

    F. Lending and Borrowing; Almsgiving and Guaranteeing Loans (29:1–20)

    G. On Living Independently and Raising Children (29:21–30:13)

    H. Health and Gladness of Heart, Not Wealth, Lead to a Happy Life (30:14–31:11)

    I. Proper Etiquette with Food and Wine at Banquets (31:12–32:13)

    J. Fearing the Lord, Keeping the Law, and Trusting in Divine Providence (32:14–33:17)

VI. Part VI (33:18–38:23)

    A. Maintaining Independence and Disciplining Slaves (33:18–31)

    B. Do Not Trust in Dreams; Travel and Fear of the Lord (34:1–17)

    C. True Worship: Worthy Sacrifices, Virtuous Life, and Humble Prayer (34:18–35:20)

    D. Prayer for National Deliverance (36:1–17)

    E. On Choosing a Wife, Friends, and Counselors (36:18–37:15)

    F. On Wisdom and Restraining One's Appetites (37:16–31)

    G. On Physicians, Sickness, and Death (38:1–23)

VII. Part VII (38:24–43:33)

    A. Manual Trades and the Wisdom of the Scribe (38:24–39:11)

    B. Praise of God, Creator of All (39:12–35)

    C. Life's Sorrows and Joys End in Death (40:1–41:13)

        i. Human Sorrow and Joy (40:1–30)

        ii. Death (41:1–13)

    D. Good and Bad Shame; Fathers and Daughters (41:14–42:14)

    E. God's Wondrous Work of Creation (42:15–43:33)

        i. The Heavens (42:15–43:12)

        ii. The Earth (43:13–33)

Book Three (44–50)

VIII. Part VIII (44:1–50:29)

    A. Praise of Israel's Forefathers (44:1–15)

    B. The Early Patriarchs: Enoch, Noah, Abraham, Isaac, and Jacob (44:16–23)

    C. Heroes of the Exodus (45:1–26)

        i. Moses (45:1–5)

        ii. Aaron and Phinehas (45:6–26)

    D. From Conquest to Kingdom: Joshua, Caleb, the Judges, and Samuel (46:1–20)

    E. The Davidic Kingdom (47:1–11)

    F. Solomon and the Divided Kingdom (47:12–25)

    G. The Northern Kingdom of Israel: Elijah and Elisha (48:1–16)

H. The Southern Kingdom of Judah: Hezekiah and Isaiah (48:17–25)
I. King Josiah and the Prophets; Recalling Ancient Heroes (49:1–16)
J. Simon the High Priest (50:1–24)
K. Judah's Neighbors; Author's Postscript (50:25–29)

Epilogue (51)
A. Prayer of Thanksgiving (51:1–12)
B. Psalm of Praise
C. The Author's Search for Wisdom (51:13–30)

The Prologue of Sirach

The prologue of Sirach, written by Ben Sira's grandson in excellent †*Koine* Greek, stylistically resembles classical Greek historical introductions (see Luke 1:1–4). It consists of three long, elegant sentences that correspond to the three paragraphs of the RSV-2CE. In these sentences, Ben Sira's grandson explains (1) the reasons why his grandfather composed his book, (2) the shortcomings of his own Greek translation of the original Hebrew text, and (3) the context of and reasons why he set out to translate the book.

Whereas many great teachings have been given to us through the law and the prophets and the others that followed them, on account of which we should praise Israel for instruction and wisdom; and since it is necessary not only that the readers themselves should acquire understanding but also that those who love learning should be able to help the outsiders by both speaking and writing, my grandfather Jesus, after devoting himself especially to the reading of the law and the prophets and the other books of our fathers, and after acquiring considerable proficiency in them, was himself also led to write something pertaining to instruction and wisdom, in order that, by becoming conversant with this also, those who love learning should make even greater progress in living according to the law.

You are urged therefore to read with good will and attention, and to be indulgent in cases where, despite our diligent labor in translating, we may seem to have rendered some phrases imperfectly. For what was originally expressed in Hebrew does not have exactly the same sense when translated into another language. Not only this work, but even the law itself, the prophecies, and the rest of the books differ not a little as originally expressed.

When I came to Egypt in the thirty-eighth year of the reign of Euergetes and stayed for some time, I found opportunity for no little instruction. It seemed highly necessary that I should myself devote some pains and labor to the translation of the following book, using in that period of time great watchfulness and skill in order to complete and publish the book for those living abroad who wished to gain learning, being prepared in character to live according to the law.

OT: Deut 4:6
NT: Luke 24:44; 2 Thess 2:15
Catechism: the permanent value of the Old Testament, 121–23

Ben Sira's grandson begins his prologue by emphasizing the connection between his grandfather's book and the Hebrew Scriptures.[1] The Jews already have access to **many great teachings** in **the law and the prophets and the others that followed them.** This is the earliest known mention of the tripartite division of the Hebrew Bible, which Jews call the *Tanakh*—an acronym for the law (†*Torah*), prophets (*Nevi'im*), and writings (*Ketuvim*) (see Luke 24:44). It is thanks to these sacred writings that Israel has acquired **instruction** (Greek *paideia*; Hebrew *musar*)—that is, education, learning, or discipline—**and wisdom** (Greek *sophia*; Hebrew *hokhmah*) (see Deut 4:6). Ben Sira did not write his book for specialists. His desire is not only that **the readers**—namely, the professional scribes able to read the Scriptures in their original language—may **acquire understanding** but that the same scribes **who love learning** may **help the outsiders**—the Jews of the †Diaspora or even Gentiles—by passing on orally, by **speaking,** and in **writing** the wisdom that they have acquired (see 2 Thess 2:15). The translator's **grandfather Jesus** (or Yeshua) Ben Sira, far from being a religious innovator, was well-versed in Israel's Scriptures and built upon them as he composed his own work. By **devoting himself** to the study of **the law and the prophets and the other books,** he acquired **considerable proficiency in them.** Only after gaining this expertise did he feel **led**—perhaps the translator means by God or the Holy Spirit—to also **write something pertaining to instruction and wisdom**—the same *paideia* and *sophia* that Israel gained through the study of the Torah, prophets, and writings. The ultimate goal of his work is not mere intellectual erudition but a more devout Torah observance, so that the same lovers of learning, by reading and **becoming conversant** with the book of Sirach, may **make even greater progress in living according to the law**—the essential expression of devotion to God for religious Jews. The ideal of raising up many disciples dedicated to observing the Torah and faithfully passing on its teachings was common in ancient Judaism—anticipating how Jesus trained his own disciples to pass on his teachings to others.[2]

The translator then urges his readers—the Jews living in Egypt—not only to read his grandfather's book **with good will and attention** but also to kindly bear

1. Though now part of the canonical text, the prologue lacks chapter and verse numbering because it was not part of Ben Sira's original text.
2. Mishnah, *Avot* 1:1; Matt 28:19–20; 2 Tim 2:2.

with the shortcomings of his own translation. Speaking in the editorial "we," he confesses that despite his **diligent labor in translating**, he has surely **rendered some phrases imperfectly** from Hebrew to Greek. As the Italian saying goes: "*traduttore, traditore*"—a translator is a traitor, and every translation is a betrayal of the true meaning of the original. This is surely the case when translating **what was originally expressed in Hebrew**—a concise, vivid, and pictorial language that focuses on action and observation—into **another language** like Greek—a precise, rich, and complex language that excels at arguments, descriptions, and nuances of meaning. The considerable difference between the two languages leads Ben Sira's grandson to critique not only his own work of translation but even the Septuagint—the Greek translation of the Jewish Bible, begun just a few generations before Ben Sira's lifetime—as differing **not a little** from the original Hebrew.

In the third sentence, Ben Sira's grandson provides context for his own work. He informs the reader that he **came to Egypt**, presumably from Judea**, in the thirty-eighth year of the reign of Euergetes**—that is, Ptolemy VIII (or VII) Physcon, who reigned from 170 to 116 BC (see "Title, Author, Date" in the introduction, pp. 17–19). Hence the grandson arrived in Egypt in 132 BC and **stayed for some time**. The Greek seems to imply that his stay in Egypt synchronized with Euergetes's reign—that is, he stayed until the king's death (116 BC). Ben Sira's grandson found there **opportunity for no little instruction**, by studying or teaching in the Jewish community of Egypt, likely Alexandria. Sometime later, he became convinced that he should **devote some pains and labor** to the translation of his grandfather's book. The **great watchfulness and skill** he invested to translate, **complete and publish** the book implies that he spent many sleepless nights at his labor. He concludes the prologue by informing his readers that he translated his grandfather's book **for those living abroad**—namely, for the Greek-speaking Jews living outside the land of Israel—who **wished to gain** (or "love") **learning** and were already **prepared in character** and well-disposed **to live according to the law**.

Book One

Sirach 1:1–23:28

Part I

Sirach 1:1–4:10

Wisdom is mysterious and elusive. In every age, thinkers have pursued her by seeking answers to perennial questions: What is wisdom? Where is she found? How does one attain her? The ancient Greek philosopher Aristotle considered wisdom (*sophia*) to be an intellectual virtue, or "intuitive reason combined with scientific knowledge."[1] He distinguished *sophia* from practical wisdom or prudence (*phronēsis*), which gives man the ability to "deliberate well about what is good and expedient for himself."[2] Biblical wisdom includes both these intellectual and practical aspects. We have defined it above as "the practical knowledge and skills necessary to live a good and successful life in accordance with God's purpose" (p. 25). Sirach 1 introduces the intellectual and practical dimensions of wisdom: wisdom is a divine gift that only God knows and possesses (1:1–10), which he grants not primarily to the intellectually gifted but "to those who love him" (1:10). Ben Sira then outlines the practical first steps toward attaining wisdom: she is found by fearing the Lord; avoiding unrighteous anger, pride, and hypocrisy; and keeping God's commandments (1:11–30). A first collection of practical tips follows on how to live wisely: Wisdom seekers must trust God and remain steadfast in the midst of trials and temptations (2:1–18). They must honor their father and mother (3:1–16), humble themselves and avoid pride (3:17–31), and be generous to the poor and needy (4:1–10).

I.A. The Divine Origin of Wisdom (1:1–10)

[1]All wisdom comes from the Lord
and is with him for ever.

1. Aristotle, *Nicomachean Ethics* 6.7 (1141a), in *The Works of Aristotle*, vol. 9, ed. W. D. Ross (Oxford: Clarendon, 1925).
2. Aristotle, *Nicomachean Ethics* 6.5 (1140a; Ross, *Works of Aristotle*).

²The sand of the sea, the drops of rain,
and the days of eternity—who can count them?
³The height of heaven, the breadth of the earth,
the abyss, and wisdom—who can search them out?
⁴Wisdom was created before all things,
and prudent understanding from eternity.
⁵The source of wisdom is God's word in the highest heaven,
and her ways are the eternal commandments.
⁶The root of wisdom—to whom has it been revealed?
Her clever devices—who knows them?
⁷The knowledge of wisdom—to whom was it manifested?
And her abundant experience—who has understood it?
⁸There is One who is wise, *the Creator of all*,[3]
the King greatly to be feared, sitting upon his throne, *and
ruling as God.*
⁹The Lord himself created wisdom *in the holy spirit*;
he saw her and apportioned her,
he poured her out upon all his works.
¹⁰She dwells with all flesh according to his gift,
and he supplied her to those who love him.

OT: Job 12:13; 28:12–28; Prov 2:6; 8:22–23
NT: John 1:1–2; James 1:5; 3:13–18
Catechism: wisdom, gift of the Holy Spirit, 1831; moral law, work of divine wisdom, 1950, 1978

1:1   Ben Sira begins with a poem on wisdom's origins. Wisdom is not only an intellectual virtue but also a divine gift: since **all wisdom comes from the Lord**, only God truly knows her and can bestow her upon others (1 Kings 3:9; Wis 9:1–4). For Ben Sira, this rules out the possibility of attaining a type of "secular wisdom" divorced from faith in God. Catholic tradition similarly distinguishes between wisdom as an intellectual virtue and wisdom as a gift of the Holy Spirit (see the sidebar "From Natural to Divine Wisdom," p. 53). That wisdom remains with the Lord **for ever** implies that she will endure until the end of time. Having been *created* by God (1:4, 9), she has a beginning but will never have an end.

1:2–3   Two sets of rhetorical questions and metaphors describe the vast realm of wisdom: as no one can count **the sand of the sea, the drops of rain, and the days of eternity,** no one except God can measure wisdom's scope. As no one can search out **the height of heaven, the breadth of the earth, the abyss,** no one except God **can search** out wisdom's height, breadth, and depth. The realm of wisdom encompasses the entire creation.

1:4   **Wisdom was created before all things**. Christian tradition distinguishes between *uncreated* wisdom—the eternal *Logos* or "Word" who was with the

---

3. The biblical text in italics is the text of the RSV-2CE deriving specifically from the Latin Vulgate (also found in the older Douay-Rheims translation but absent from most other English versions).

Created and Uncreated Wisdom

LIVING
TRADITION

The New Testament teaches that Christ is the wisdom of God (1 Cor 1:24; Col 2:3). At the time of the Arian heresy in the fourth century, Arian heretics claimed that since wisdom was "created," according to some Old Testament texts (Prov 8:22; Sir 1:4, 9; 24:3), this meant that Christ had also been created. In response, Church Fathers such as St. Hilary of Poitiers (ca. 315–67) and St. Augustine (354–430) argued that a distinction must be made between created wisdom and Christ, the uncreated wisdom of God:

> There is a wisdom born before all things, and again there is a wisdom created for particular purposes. The wisdom which is from everlasting is one, the wisdom which has come into existence during the lapse of time is another.[a]

> Wisdom was created before all things—not certainly that Wisdom that is clearly coeternal and equal to you, our God, his Father, and by whom all things were created (John 1:3) and in whom, as the Beginning, you created heaven and earth (Gen 1:1). Rather, truly, it was that wisdom that has been created, namely, the intellectual nature that, in the contemplation of light, is light. For this is called wisdom, although it is created. But as great as the difference is between the Light that enlightens and that which is enlightened, so great is the difference between the Wisdom that creates and that which has been created.[b]

a. Hilary of Poitiers, *On the Trinity* 1.35, in J. Robert Wright, ed., *Proverbs, Ecclesiastes, Song of Solomon*, ACCS:OT 9 (Downers Grove, IL: InterVarsity, 2005), 67.

b. Augustine, *Confessions* 12.15.20, in Sever J. Voicu, ed., *Apocrypha*, ACCS:OT 15 (Downers Grove, IL: InterVarsity, 2010), 179.

Father in the beginning (Christ)—and *created* wisdom, the intellectual virtue that humans can acquire, which is a participation in uncreated divine wisdom. While other biblical books speak of the first kind of wisdom, identifying it with God's creative word or intelligence (Ps 33:6; Prov 3:19), Ben Sira's wisdom is of the latter kind. Although present at creation, she had a beginning. The Greek text of Prov 8:22 also speaks of wisdom as "created," while the Wisdom of Solomon conceives of her as an uncreated emanation of God (Wis 7:25).

The source of wisdom is God's word (Greek *logos*) **in the highest heaven**. 1:5 The term *logos*, pointing to God's eternal intellect and wisdom, prefigures the revelation of the eternal Logos who was with God in the beginning and became flesh in Jesus Christ (John 1:1, 14). Yet **her ways**, by which she is revealed in this life, are found in **the eternal commandments**—the precepts of the †Torah, which are frequently identified with wisdom.[4] Wisdom's existence before creation and her identification with the Torah imply that the latter also preceded

4. Sir 1:26–27; 15:1; 21:11; 24:23; 34:8; Bar 3:9; 4:1.

creation. Although the Torah was revealed to Israel at Mount Sinai (Exod 20), in fact the divine law existed eternally in the mind of God.[5]

1:6–7   Four additional rhetorical questions inquire about various facets of wisdom, implying that they are inaccessible to the unaided human mind. As in 1:2–3, the implied answer is "no one but God." **The root of wisdom**—the origin from which she springs—**to whom has it been revealed?** Ben Sira later discloses that her root is the fear of the Lord (1:20). No one knows **her clever devices** but God. The same is true for **the knowledge of wisdom** and **her abundant experience**. Man can partake of them only insofar as God chooses to reveal them.[6]

1:8   Ben Sira answers the rhetorical questions posed in 1:2–3, 6–7. Only **One is** truly **wise**—God, *the Creator of all, the King* (†Vulgate), because he alone truly knows and possesses wisdom. The fact that he alone is **greatly to be feared** points to a central theme of wisdom literature—that the fear of the Lord is the beginning of wisdom (1:14). The image of the Lord **sitting upon his throne** (Ps 47:8; Isa 6:1; Rev 4:9–10) demonstrates that he is *ruling as God* (Vulgate) over the universe.

1:9   Ben Sira reasserts the created nature of wisdom (1:4), adding that **the Lord himself created wisdom**. The Vulgate specifies that he created her *in the holy spirit*. The close relationship between the Lord, wisdom, and the Holy Spirit foreshadows the revelation of the Trinity—with the caveat that Jesus, the eternal Logos, is God's *uncreated* wisdom. God **saw her and apportioned** or measured **her**, and like a liquid flowing everywhere, **poured her out upon all his works**, implying that she is present throughout all creation (Rom 1:20).

1:10   Wisdom **dwells with all flesh**. The fact that she dwells with humans hints at her human traits. God grants her to men **according to his gift** of grace: she is available to all but not received equally by all. The Lord **supplied her** especially **to those who love him**, as commanded to Israel in the great commandment of the †*Shema* (Deut 6:5). The pursuit of wisdom is not only an intellectual endeavor but a matter of the heart—a type of courtship. One must love God and wisdom to gain her and grow in her (Sir 2:15–16; 4:14; Prov 8:17; Wis 6:12).[7]

Reflection and Application (1:1–10)

How do we become wise—is wisdom innate, †acquired, or †infused? Does wisdom increase with age or experience? Do we gain wisdom through study, or is it a gift from God? Does wisdom require faith, or can non-Christians and

5. Sir 1:5 is found in the longer Greek text (GII) and the Latin Vulgate (RSV-2CE, ESV-CE). The shorter Greek text (GI) omits it (RSV, NRSV, NABRE, NJB).

6. Sir 1:7 is found in GII and the Latin Vulgate (RSV-2CE, ESV-CE). GI omits it (RSV, NRSV, NABRE, NJB).

7. GII makes an even stronger connection between loving God and finding wisdom, adding to the end of the verse: "Love of the Lord is glorious wisdom; to those to whom he appears he apportions her, that they may see him" (NRSV footnote; compare ESV-CE footnote).

From Natural to Divine Wisdom

LIVING TRADITION

Christian tradition, drawing from both classical Greek philosophy and the Bible, distinguishes two types of wisdom: an †acquired intellectual virtue and an †infused gift of the Holy Spirit. On the one hand, wisdom is the greatest of the intellectual virtues and the highest form of knowledge, which judges all things, considers the Supreme Cause (God), and directs all the other intellectual virtues.[a] Because this form of wisdom is acquired by human effort, all people can attain it to some extent. On the other hand, wisdom is also an infused "spiritual gift which enables one to know the purpose and plan of God; one of the seven gifts of the Holy Spirit" (Isa 11:2).[b] Only those in communion with God can possess this supernatural gift of wisdom. Pope John Paul II, drawing from St. Thomas Aquinas, explains the distinction between the two types of wisdom:

> [St. Thomas perceived] the role of the Holy Spirit in the process by which knowledge matures into wisdom.... Aquinas was keen to show the primacy of the wisdom which is the gift of the Holy Spirit and which opens the way to a knowledge of divine realities. His theology allows us to understand what is distinctive of wisdom in its close link with faith and knowledge of the divine. This wisdom ... presupposes faith and eventually formulates its right judgement on the basis of the truth of faith itself: "The wisdom named among the gifts of the Holy Spirit is distinct from the wisdom found among the intellectual virtues. This second wisdom is acquired through study, but the first 'comes from on high.'...This also distinguishes it from faith, since faith accepts divine truth as it is. But the gift of wisdom enables judgement according to divine truth."[c]

In other words, the wisdom "from on high" (James 3:17) that is a gift of the Holy Spirit presupposes faith, which assents to divine truth, enabling the wise person to judge reality according to this divine truth. The gift of wisdom also presupposes charity and thus cannot coexist with mortal sin; it can be received only by a soul in a state of grace.[d]

a. Thomas Aquinas, *Summa Theologiae* I-II q. 66 a. 5.
b. Catechism, glossary.
c. John Paul II, *Fides et Ratio* 44 (1998); Thomas Aquinas, *Summa Theologiae* II-II q. 45 a. 1 ad 2.
d. Thomas Aquinas, *Summa Theologiae* II-II q. 45 a. 4.

---

atheists also find wisdom? Students of wisdom are often dismayed at wisdom's elusiveness. She seems obscure, intangible, fleeting.

The pursuit of wisdom is not limited to the Judeo-Christian tradition but is also attested in classical texts such as Confucius's *Analects*, Aesop's *Fables*, the *Babylonian Theodicy*, the Egyptian *Instruction of Amenemope*, and Aristotle's *Nicomachean Ethics*. Given that the word "philosophy" (*philo-sophia*) means "love of wisdom," one could argue that all philosophical works in some way reflect the pursuit of wisdom.

These non-Christian works point toward the attainment of *wisdom as an intellectual virtue*, which includes the practical knowledge and skills to live a good life. Yet they cannot reach the *divinely infused wisdom that is a gift of the Holy Spirit*. Sirach instructs us how to obtain *both*: to grow in wisdom, we must (a) practice the virtue of wisdom by conforming our thoughts, words, and actions to God's commandments; and (b) humbly ask God for the gift of wisdom, in faith and without doubting (James 1:5–6).

I.B. The Fear of the Lord: The Beginning and End of Wisdom (1:11–30)

[11]The fear of the Lord is glory and exultation,
   and gladness and a crown of rejoicing.
[12]The fear of the Lord delights the heart,
   and gives gladness and joy and long life.
[13]With him who fears the Lord it will go well at the end;
   on the day of his death he will be blessed.

[14]To fear the Lord is the beginning of wisdom;
   she is created with the faithful in the womb.
[15]She made among men an eternal foundation,
   and among their descendants she will be trusted.
[16]To fear the Lord is wisdom's full measure;
   she satisfies men with her fruits;
[17]she fills their whole house with desirable goods,
   and their storehouses with her produce.
[18]The fear of the Lord is the crown of wisdom,
   making peace and perfect health to flourish.
[19]He saw her and apportioned her;
   he rained down knowledge and discerning comprehension,
   and he exalted the glory of those who held her fast.
[20]To fear the Lord is the root of wisdom,
   and her branches are long life.

[22]Unrighteous anger cannot be justified,
   for a man's anger tips the scale to his ruin.
[23]A patient man will endure until the right moment,
   and then joy will burst forth for him.
[24]He will hide his words until the right moment,
   and the lips of many will tell of his good sense.
[25]In the treasuries of wisdom are wise sayings,
   but godliness is an abomination to a sinner.
[26]If you desire wisdom, keep the commandments,
   and the Lord will supply it for you.

²⁷**For the fear of the Lord is wisdom and instruction,**
    and he delights in fidelity and meekness.
²⁸**Do not disobey the fear of the Lord;**
    do not approach him with a divided mind.
²⁹**Be not a hypocrite in men's sight,**
    and keep watch over your lips.
³⁰**Do not exalt yourself lest you fall,**
    and thus bring dishonor upon yourself.
The Lord will reveal your secrets
    and cast you down in the midst of the congregation,
because you did not come in the fear of the Lord,
    and your heart was full of deceit.

OT: Deut 10:12–13; Job 28:28; Ps 111:10; Prov 9:10; 14:29; Eccles 12:13
NT: Matt 19:16–19; John 14:15; 15:10; Acts 9:31; James 1:8; 1 John 5:3
Catechism: fear of the Lord as gift of the Holy Spirit, 1831; anger as passion, 1765; pride and wrath as capital
    sins, 1866; commandments as way to life, 2052–82

Having established the divine origins of wisdom, Ben Sira now describes how **1:11–13**
people may find her. The indispensable posture of the heart to attain wisdom is a
reverent **fear of the Lord**—mentioned at least ten times in this section (1:11–30).
The fear of the Lord is the source of the best things in life, such as **glory and
exultation, and gladness and a crown of rejoicing**, and a **long life**. It also
promises protection **at the end** of life and blessedness at the moment of **death**.

The wisdom books frequently assert that **to fear the Lord is the beginning** **1:14**
of wisdom.[8] Fearing the Lord by adopting an attitude of deep reverence toward
him and avoiding evil is thus the essential first step toward becoming wise. Yet
the fact that wisdom is **created with the faithful in the womb** implies that she
is a divine gift, imparted to the righteous even before they are born (Jer 1:5–6).

Long ago, wisdom **made among men an eternal foundation** (literally,[9] "she **1:15**
made her nest among human beings as an eternal foundation," ESV-CE), establishing a permanent residence with them. Wisdom's dwelling among humans
anticipates the moment when the eternal Logos "became flesh and dwelt among
us" (John 1:14). Because she has proven herself faithful **among their descendants** in every generation, Ben Sira is confident that she can and **will be trusted**.

To fear the Lord is wisdom's full measure—that is, her goal or end. Those **1:16–17**
who fear the Lord grow in wisdom; the more they increase in wisdom, the more
they are filled with the fear of the Lord, predisposing them to further growth
in wisdom. **She satisfies** (literally, "inebriates," NRSV, ESV-CE, NABRE) **men
with her fruits**—implying that she is like a tree and a source of delight to
those who find her. Ben Sira later develops the metaphor of wisdom as a "tree
of life" (24:13–17; compare Prov 3:18), indicating that the path to wisdom is

8. Job 28:28; Ps 111:10; Prov 1:7; 9:10.
9. Unless otherwise noted, "literally" refers to the Greek text.

the path back to the life lost when Adam and Eve ate the fruit of the tree of the knowledge of good and evil. The life-giving "fruit" of wisdom contrasts with the fruit of knowledge, which seemed "desirable to make one wise" (Gen 3:6) but brought only death. Wisdom "feeds" her followers (Prov 9:1–6): **she fills the whole house** of those who fear the Lord **with desirable goods, and their storehouses with her produce**, granting them both material prosperity and spiritual blessings.

1:18   **The fear of the Lord** is also **the crown** or garland **of wisdom**—the culmination of her quest. Wisdom seekers do not discard the fear of the Lord once they have attained wisdom: they become, rather, more humbly aware that everything they have is a gift. As the crown of wisdom, the fear of the Lord leads them to love God above all things and grants them **peace**—*shalom*, implying safety, prosperity, well-being, and wholeness—**and perfect health** of both body and soul (Prov 3:8).

1:19   God distributes wisdom according to his purpose: **he saw her and apportioned** or measured **her**, and **he rained down knowledge** and understanding upon humankind. Yet this does not absolve humans from the responsibility to pursue wisdom, cultivate her, and cherish her. The Lord **exalted the glory** or reputation **of those who held her fast** and were determined to grow in her.

1:20–21   Another mark of the **fear** of **the Lord** is that it is **the root** or foundation **of wisdom**. The assertion that **her branches are long life** points back to the analogy of the tree of life (Gen 2:9; Prov 3:18). Thus, wisdom—and those who are wise—must be well rooted in the fear of the Lord to grow the strong branches of a long life and produce her inebriating fruit (Sir 1:16; Ps 1:1–3). Gaining wisdom by fearing the Lord and observing his commandments is thus the equivalent of eating from the tree of life, in contrast to eating from the tree of knowledge, which, through human pride and the violation of God's commandment, deceptively appeared "to make one wise" but ultimately brought death (Gen 2:17; 3:6).[10]

1:22   Having explained the relationship between wisdom and the fear of the Lord, Ben Sira now considers some character flaws that hinder people from acquiring either of these qualities, along with some contrasting virtues. **Unrighteous anger**, or losing one's temper without good reason, **cannot be justified**. It is a symptom of impatience that reflects a lack of trust in God. Succumbing to wrath is particularly dangerous, for if left unchecked **a man's anger tips the scale to his ruin** (literally, "for the weight of his anger is his downfall").

1:23–24   By contrast, **a patient man** exercises self-control and endures hardships without expressing anger, **until the right moment**, when his patience is rewarded and **joy will burst forth for him**—that is, gladness returns to him. The

---

10. GII adds 1:21: **The fear of the Lord drives away sins; and where it abides, it will turn away all anger** (RSV-2CE, NRSV footnotes, ESV-CE).

Climbing from Fear to Wisdom

LIVING TRADITION

The fear of the Lord is essential to the Christian life. Like wisdom, it is one of the seven gifts of the Holy Spirit (Isa 11:2; Catechism 1831). While the fear of the Lord perfects natural human desires by restraining them from an excessive pursuit of pleasures and turning them away from evil, wisdom perfects reason by giving it insights into the knowledge of divine things. The fear of the Lord, therefore, is the foundation not only of wisdom but also of all the other gifts.[a] St. Augustine explains how wisdom reaches down to human beings through the fear of the Lord, and how they, through the fear of the Lord, rise up to wisdom:

> Isaiah the prophet presents us with those seven well-known spiritual gifts. He begins with wisdom and ends with the fear of God, as though he were coming down from the heights to our level. He does this to teach us to climb back up again. Thus, he began from where we want to finish, and he arrived at the point where we should begin. "Here will rest on him," he says, "the Spirit of God, the Spirit of wisdom and understanding, the Spirit of counsel and courage, the Spirit of knowledge and piety, the Spirit of the fear of the Lord." Therefore, just as he descended from wisdom to fear . . . we in the same way must climb from fear to wisdom. We do this not as a matter of pride but in order to progress. "For the fear of the Lord is the beginning of wisdom."[b]

a. Thomas Aquinas, *Summa Theologiae* I-II q. 68 a. 4; a. 7 ad 1; II-II q. 45 a. 3.
b. Augustine, *Sermon* 347.2 (Voicu, *Apocrypha*, 181).

patient person refrains from complaining, knowing to **hide his words** and keep quiet **until the right moment**, when it is appropriate to speak. His self-control eventually earns praise from **the lips of many** who, impressed by his patience, **tell of his good sense** and wisdom.

Wisdom's **treasuries** are storehouses full of valuable goods—**wise sayings** **1:25** (literally, "parables of knowledge") that can enlighten men. Although the righteous abundantly draw from these treasuries, the wicked despise them, for **godliness** or moral excellence **is an abomination to a sinner** intent on remaining in his wicked ways.

Another key to attaining wisdom is to **keep the commandments**. For Sirach's **1:26–27** Jewish readers, wisdom rooted in the fear of the Lord consists not in abstract philosophical speculation but in observing God's precepts revealed in the †Torah. There is a direct correlation between one's observance of the commandments and the measure of wisdom that **the Lord will supply. For the fear of the Lord** is not primarily a feeling or emotion but rather **wisdom and instruction** (i.e., training and discipline). People grow in these qualities in proportion to their observance of the Lord's commandments, accompanied by an inner disposition of **fidelity** (or faith) **and meekness** (or humility)—that is, a receptive attitude open to correction in light of God's word (Prov 15:33).

Figure 5. The Ten Commandments in Hebrew

1:28–29   By exhorting his readers not to **disobey the fear of the Lord**, Ben Sira indicates again that the fear of the Lord is not an emotion but a moral imperative that can be either obeyed or disregarded—whether by failing to observe the commandments or by approaching God **with a divided mind** (literally, "a double heart"), lacking single-minded devotion (see James 1:8; 4:8). Personal integrity is an essential trait of the wise person. Thus, he warns, **be not a hypocrite** by pretending to be better than you actually are, or by speaking in one way and acting in another **in men's sight**. To **keep watch over your lips** means exercising restraint in speech, avoiding boasting, gossiping, or rash words.

1:30   The warning to **not exalt yourself lest you fall** echoes common warnings against pride in Scripture. Hypocrisy often manifests as a tendency to exaggerate one's importance or accomplishments before others. Such deceit, diametrically opposed to the fear of the Lord, eventually brings **dishonor** upon those who aggrandize themselves. One can deceive others only for so long: **the Lord will reveal** the hypocrite's **secrets** so that everything hidden will be revealed—whether in this life, as Ben Sira believes, or in the world to come (see Eccles 12:14; Luke 8:17; 12:2). God will **cast down** and humiliate the proud **in the midst of the congregation** (literally, "the synagogue") because they **did not come in the fear of the Lord**, and their hypocrisy revealed a heart **full of deceit**. Since "pride goes before destruction, and a haughty spirit before a fall" (Prov 16:18), God often exalts the humble and casts down the proud.[11]

11. 1 Sam 2:7; Job 22:29; Ps 147:6; Luke 1:52–53.

Reflection and Application (1:11–30)

If the fear of the Lord is the beginning of wisdom, then we must first acquire this fear in order to gain wisdom. But what is the fear of the Lord, and how do we attain it? We generally see fear as something negative. Fear is a passion or feeling that we cannot produce at will—a recoiling from a perceived or potential evil causing agitation in the mind and soul, or an emotional reaction to something harmful and unwanted (Catechism 1765).

How, then, should we fear God, who is all-good? Though we cannot fear God insofar as he is perfect goodness, we *should* fear him insofar as he is the just judge who administers punishment when we sin against him. This fear of punishment is a *servile fear*, like the fear of a slave before his master. Yet we should also fear God with a *filial fear*, dreading to offend him because he is our loving Father (Catechism 1828).[12] Both types of fear are the beginning of wisdom: servile fear is the first *cause* of wisdom insofar as it restrains us from sinning against God through fear of punishment (Sir 1:21). Filial fear is the first *effect* of wisdom insofar as it prompts us to love God by relating to him in a reverent manner and refusing to offend him. This *filial* fear of the Lord is also a gift of the Holy Spirit.[13]

To grow in the fear of the Lord, therefore, we must adopt an attitude of deep religious reverence, being mindful of both God's goodness and power, while turning away from sin and diligently keeping his commandments (Matt 7:21). We must also ask God in prayer for the gift of the fear of the Lord that is the beginning and foundation of wisdom.

I.C. Trusting God amid Trials (2:1–18)

> [1]My son, if you come forward to serve the Lord,
>   *remain in justice and in fear,*
>   and prepare yourself for temptation.
> [2]Set your heart right and be steadfast,
>   *incline your ear, and receive words of understanding,*
>   and do not be hasty in time of calamity.
> [3]*Await God's patience,* cling to him and do not depart,
>   *that you may be wise in all your ways.*
> [4]Accept whatever is brought upon you,
>   *and endure it in sorrow;*
>   in changes that humble you be patient.
> [5]For gold and silver are tested in the fire,
>   and acceptable men in the furnace of humiliation.

---

12. Thomas Aquinas, *Summa Theologiae* II-II q. 19 a. 1–2.
13. Thomas Aquinas, *Summa Theologiae* II-II q. 19 a. 7–8.

⁶Trust in God, and he will help you;
  hope in him, *and he will* make your ways straight.
Stay in fear of him, and grow old in him.

⁷You who fear the Lord, wait for his mercy;
  and turn not aside, lest you fall.
⁸You who fear the Lord, trust in him,
  and your reward will not fail;
⁹you who fear the Lord, hope for good things,
  for everlasting joy and mercy.
You who fear the Lord, love him,
  and your hearts will be made radiant.
¹⁰Consider the ancient generations and see:
  who ever trusted in the Lord and was put to shame?
Or who ever persevered *in his commandments* and was forsaken?
  Or who ever called upon him and was overlooked?
¹¹For the Lord is compassionate and merciful;
  he forgives sins and saves in time of affliction,
  and he is the shield of all who seek him in truth.

¹²Woe to timid hearts and to slack hands,
  and to the sinner who walks along two ways!
¹³Woe to the faint heart, for it has no trust!
  Therefore it will not be sheltered.
¹⁴Woe to you who have lost your endurance!
  What will you do when the Lord punishes you?
¹⁵Those who fear the Lord will not disobey his words,
  and those who love him will keep his ways.
¹⁶Those who fear the Lord will seek his approval,
  and those who love him will be filled with the law.
¹⁷Those who fear the Lord will prepare their hearts,
  and will humble themselves before him.
¹⁸Let us fall into the hands of the Lord,
  but not into the hands of men;
for as his majesty is,
  so also is his mercy.

OT: Pss 37:3–6; 62:8; Prov 3:5–6; 17:3; Isa 48:10–11
NT: Rom 2:7; 1 Cor 3:13; Heb 12:5–6; James 1:3; 1 Pet 1:7
Catechism: Jesus resisted temptations, 538–40; hope as trust in God's promises, 1817; filial trust in prayer,
  2734–41, 2828–30; resisting temptation, 2846–49
Lectionary: 2:7–11: St. Cajetan, Priest; Common of Holy Men and Women[14]

2:1–2 One who fears the Lord must also trust him steadfastly—especially in times of trial, as God invariably tests the faithful. Ben Sira addresses the reader

14. All Scripture references for the Lectionary readings refer to the RSV-2CE version. The verse numbers may differ in lectionaries that follow other Bible translations (such as the NABRE or NRSV).

affectionately as **my son** (see Prov 1:8, 10; 2:1), viewing him as a young appren-
tice in wisdom, desirous **to serve the Lord**. He exhorts his disciple to **remain
in justice and in fear** of the Lord (†Vulgate) and warns him to **prepare** himself
(literally, "prepare your soul") **for temptation**. The Greek word for "temptation"
(*peirasmos*) does not necessarily imply the temptation to sin; it could refer to
any challenging situation of trial or testing (Catechism 2847). In anticipation
of future trials, Ben Sira encourages his disciple: **Set your heart** on the **right**
course in the service of God **and be steadfast**, persevering with strength and
determination even in the midst of afflictions. *Incline your ear*—that is, listen—
and receive words of understanding as communicated through Ben Sira's own
teachings (Prov 3:5–6). Reflecting his earlier warning against impatient anger
(Sir 1:22–23), Ben Sira advises the reader to **not be hasty**, rash, or imprudent
in time of calamity, when life becomes difficult.

The meaning of *Await God's patience* (Vulgate) is probably better conveyed   2:3–4
in the Douay-Rheims translation: "Wait on God with patience."[15] In times
of trial, the faithful disciple must **cling to him** by exercising faith, hope, and
love, and **not depart** from his commandments. Patiently enduring seasons
of testing will bear fruit so that the disciple *may be wise in all* his *ways*. Seasons of trial provide the best opportunities for spiritual growth (Deut 10:20;
13:4; Josh 22:5). Patience is a key for growing in wisdom (Sir 1:23). **Accept**,
therefore, **whatever** hardship **is brought upon you**, for God has permitted it
for a reason, *and endure it in sorrow* (Vulgate): one who undergoes painful
trials does not have to pretend that all is well. Expressing grief and pain is
a normal part of the human experience. Nevertheless, the right disposition
when going through **changes that humble you** or "times of humiliation"
(NRSV) is to **be patient**, trusting that even the greatest difficulties are part
of God's good providence.

Just as **gold and silver are tested in the fire**—melted so that the precious met-   2:5–6
als are purified and separated from other materials—so are the righteous refined
in the furnace of humiliation: the fire of suffering purifies their character from
sins, vices, and selfishness (Prov 17:3; Wis 3:6; Isa 48:10; 1 Pet 1:7). Yet people
cannot endure trials out of their own strength. Ben Sira reminds his reader:
Trust in God, and he will help you. The Lord is close to those who draw near
to him in the midst of sufferings. Steadfastly relying on God amid tribulations
expresses a strong faith that will reap rewards in the end (Pss 37:3–5; 46:1; Prov
3:5–6). While trusting God in faith focuses on the present, the exhortation to
hope in him points to a future deliverance when God *will* **make your ways
straight** and lead you into the right path of life (Prov 10:17; 12:28). While it is
man's duty to seek the straight path, God rewards an attitude of trust and hope

---

15. All quotations from the Douay-Rheims Bible (hereafter "Douay") are from the Challoner revi-
sion, first published in America in 1790. *The Holy Bible, Translated from the Latin Vulgate* (Bellingham,
WA: Logos Bible Software, 2009).

by assisting him in that task and straightening the paths before him (Tob 4:19; Ps 5:8; Prov 3:6; Isa 45:13). This journey requires perseverance: *Stay in fear of him, and grow old in him* (Vulgate). The one who seeks wisdom must persevere, fearing God all his life until he reaches old age.

2:7–9   Ben Sira addresses those **who fear the Lord** with three exhortations in the imperative. First, they must patiently **wait for his mercy**, trusting that he will reveal it in due time. Ben Sira reminds them to **turn not aside**, away from the Lord's straight path, **lest** they **fall** into temptation or sin. Second, those **who fear the Lord** must **trust in him**; by making a firm act of faith amid tribulations they can be assured that their **reward will not fail**. Third, those **who fear the Lord** must **hope for good things** to come—namely, **everlasting joy and mercy**. The longer Greek text and Vulgate add a fourth exhortation: *You who fear the Lord, love him, and your hearts will be made radiant*. Even more than waiting upon the Lord, trusting in him, and hoping in him, loving him is the purest and best response that guarantees superlative joy in return.

2:10   To persuade his readers of the soundness of his advice, Ben Sira invites them to **consider the ancient generations**, reflect on their lives, **and see** how they fared. He considers the condition of the ancients via three rhetorical questions on God's faithfulness that are a variation on the theme: Does the Lord ever forsake the righteous? Although one may be tempted to answer "yes" when undergoing intense suffering (Ps 22:1; Job), Ben Sira insists that the answer is "no," for the Lord constantly reveals his salvation in Israel's history (Exod 34:6; Pss 22:4–5; 37:25). The first question is **who ever trusted in the Lord and was put to shame?** The implied answer is "no one." The faithful often pray to God that they may not be put to shame (Pss 25:2–3; 31:1; 71:1); Scripture confidently replies that they "shall never be ashamed" (Ps 34:5), even in "evil times" (Ps 37:19; compare Isa 50:7). In his second question, Ben Sira asks: **Who ever persevered in his commandments and was forsaken?** The implied answer is again "no one." According to the psalmist, fixing one's eyes on the Lord's commandments is the sure way not to be put to shame (Ps 119:6, 80). The third question is: **Who ever called upon him and was overlooked?** Again, the implied answer is "no one." The Scriptures repeatedly assert that "all who call upon the name of the LORD shall be delivered" (Joel 2:32).[16]

2:11   The Lord delivers his people because he is **compassionate and merciful**— two of his defining attributes (Exod 34:6; Pss 103:8; 145:8). God manifests his kindness in that he graciously **forgives sins and saves** when his children call upon him, especially **in time of affliction** (see Pss 37:39–40; 103:3). The Vulgate adds: *and he is the shield* or guardian *of all who seek him in truth*. By living in the truth, the faithful place themselves under the Lord's protection (Sir 51:2; Pss 33:20; 84:9; 144:2).

---

16. 2 Sam 22:4; Pss 18:3; 50:15; 55:16; Jer 29:12; Rom 10:13.

In sharp contrast to the three assurances promised to those who fear the   2:12–14
Lord, Ben Sira utters three woes against unfaithful people. Paradoxically, while
those who fear the Lord are bold, courageous, and strong, those who do not
fear him are timid, cowardly, and fickle. Uttering a **woe** against someone, while
not exactly a curse, anticipates misery and misfortune to fall upon that person
as the direct consequence of his or her own actions. Those with **timid** or cowardly **hearts** lack the courage and determination to persevere in the fear of the
Lord; **slack hands** denote laziness and sluggishness in performing one's duties.
The sinner who walks along two ways is likely someone who is duplicitous,
double-minded, or hypocritical (1:28–30). Ben Sira pronounces a second **woe**
(2:13) against **the faint heart** who is careless and indolent, slothful in pursuing truth and neglectful of his spiritual duties so that he has **no trust** or faith.
In contrast to the faithful, whom God protects, this feeble person **will not be
sheltered** in times of trouble. A third **woe** (2:14) is directed against those **who
have lost** their **endurance** and failed to persevere in waiting for the Lord's
mercy (2:7). Ben Sira rhetorically asks these fickle people: **What will you do
when the Lord punishes you** when his reckoning comes?—implying that they
will be utterly powerless on the day of judgment. By pronouncing these woes
against the cowardly, Ben Sira implicitly summons his readers to be strong and
courageous in the face of adversity, following the example of those described
in the next three verses.

Ben Sira turns again to **those who fear the Lord**, offering another series of   2:15–17
three statements. In contrast to the faint and feeble, they are strong and steadfast
in their faith, for they **will not disobey his words**. **Those who love him will
keep his ways** precisely by obeying his words. Verse 15 employs a synonymous
†parallelism, in which both halves of the verse convey the same meaning in different terms. This idea is reiterated in the second statement: **Those who fear
the Lord** will also **seek his approval** or seek to please him; they **love him** and
keep his ways by meditating constantly on **the law** (Ps 1:2). In his third statement, Ben Sira states that **those who fear the Lord will prepare their hearts**
to receive God's words and always be ready to do his will. Moreover, they **will
humble themselves before him**—an essential way to express the fear of the
Lord and a prerequisite for attaining wisdom.

Throughout the chapter, Ben Sira contrasts those who fear the Lord with   2:18
those who do not. As noted above, while the fear of the Lord produces courageous people, lacking the fear of the Lord produces cowards. Every person must
choose their fear. Those who fear the Lord are humble, yet bold and confident
before men—like David before Goliath (1 Sam 17:26–54) and the apostles before
the Sanhedrin (Acts 4:5–31). Those who do not fear the Lord are arrogant, yet
fearful and cowardly before men—like King Saul before Samuel (1 Sam 15:24)
and the corrupt chief priests before the crowds (Luke 20:19). It is far better to
fall into the hands of the Lord than into those **of men** (see 2 Sam 24:14); for

while **his majesty** expects much of those who follow him, **his mercy** overlooks their failures and shortcomings.

Reflection and Application (2:1–18)

Suffering is an inescapable part of life in a fallen world. Yet we can adopt very different attitudes toward suffering. For those in the world, without God and without faith, suffering is often intolerable—sometimes so intolerable that it must be eliminated at all costs, even by eliminating the sufferer. The fear of suffering often drives the so-called culture of death, which advocates for killing by abortion or euthanasia those who suffer or cause suffering to others.

For a devout Jew like Ben Sira, suffering is not entirely bad but serves a purpose: it can and must be tolerated, for it acts as a "refining fire" that purifies one's character. Human experience confirms that suffering can make one less selfish and more empathetic toward the suffering of others.

For the Christian, suffering takes on an even deeper meaning in light of Christ. Although it remains a painful reality—the tragic consequence of the fall that was not originally part of God's plan—it also has redemptive value: "By his passion and death on the cross Christ has given a new meaning to suffering: it can henceforth configure us to him and unite us with his redemptive Passion" (Catechism 1505). Thanks to this hope, as the apostle Paul writes, "we rejoice in our sufferings, knowing that suffering produces endurance, and endurance produces character, and character produces hope, and hope does not disappoint us, because God's love has been poured into our hearts through the Holy Spirit who has been given to us" (Rom 5:3–5).

I.D. Honoring Father and Mother (3:1–16)

¹**Listen to me your father, O children;**
   and act accordingly, that you may be kept in safety.
²**For the Lord honored the father above the children,**
   and he confirmed the right of the mother over her sons.
³**Whoever honors his father atones for sins,**
   and preserves himself from them.
When he prays, he is heard;
   ⁴**and whoever glorifies his mother is like one who lays up**
      treasure.
⁵**Whoever honors his father will be gladdened by his own**
      children,
   and when he prays he will be heard.
⁶**Whoever glorifies his father will have long life,**

and whoever obeys the Lord will refresh his mother;
⁷he will serve his parents as his masters.
⁸Honor your father by word and deed,
that a blessing from him may come upon you.
⁹For a father's blessing strengthens the houses of the children,
but a mother's curse uproots their foundations.

¹⁰Do not glorify yourself by dishonoring your father,
for your father's dishonor is no glory to you.
¹¹For a man's glory comes from honoring his father,
and it is a disgrace for children not to respect their mother.
¹²O son, help your father in his old age,
and do not grieve him as long as he lives;
¹³even if he is lacking in understanding, show forbearance;
and do not despise him *all the days of his life.*
¹⁴For kindness to a father will not be forgotten,
and against your sins it will be credited to you
—*a house raised in justice to you.*
¹⁵In the day of your affliction it will be remembered in your favor;
as frost in fair weather, your sins will melt away.
¹⁶Whoever forsakes his father is like a blasphemer,
and whoever angers his mother is cursed by the Lord.

OT: Exod 20:12; Lev 19:3; Deut 5:16
NT: Matt 15:4; Eph 6:2–3; James 5:20; 1 Pet 4:8
Catechism: the fourth commandment, 2197–200; duties of children toward parents, 2214–18
Lectionary: 3:2–6, 12–14: Feast of the Holy Family

Ben Sira now turns to the duties of children to their parents, in a commentary   3:1–2
on the fourth commandment of the †Decalogue: "Honor your father and your
mother" (Exod 20:12; Deut 5:16). Parents not only give life to their children;
they are also their primary teachers and educators. Because parents reflect
God as co-creators of their children, holding authority over them in God's
ordering of society, children owe them honor and respect. Ben Sira addresses
his disciples again with a paternal tone: **Listen to me your father, O children**.
As a †sage and teacher of wisdom he considers them his spiritual sons. They
are to **act accordingly**, in conformity to his instructions, so that they **may be
kept in safety**—literally, "that you may be saved"—not in the sense of gaining eternal life in heaven but in the sense of being protected from dangers in
order to live a safe, prosperous, and happy life on earth. The assertion that **the
Lord honored the father above the children** and **confirmed the right of the
mother over her sons** implies that parents have authority over their children,
and children have responsibilities toward their parents (Catechism 2218). The
verse also indicates that even in Ben Sira's patriarchal society, a mother had
authority over her sons.

Honoring God by Honoring Parents

LIVING TRADITION

Catholic tradition follows the division of the Ten Commandments established by St. Augustine. According to this view, the first three commandments (concerning the love of God) were written on the first tablet, and the other seven (concerning the love of neighbor) on the second tablet (Catechism 2066–67). Thus, in Catholic tradition, the commandment to "honor your father and mother" is the fourth commandment—or the first concerning the love of neighbor—which opens the second tablet of the †Decalogue (Catechism 2197).

Jewish tradition divides the commandments differently. While the first tablet also contains the commandments pertaining to the love of God and the second those pertaining to the love of neighbor, Judaism lists *five* commandments on each tablet. The commandment to honor father and mother is the *fifth* commandment, written on the *first* tablet, suggesting that it primarily pertains to the *love of God*.[a] As the Catechism teaches, "The divine fatherhood is the source of human fatherhood; this is the foundation of the honor owed to parents" (Catechism 2214; compare Eph 3:14–15). Parents give life to their children and teach them God's laws on his behalf, for God has vested parents with his own authority (Catechism 2197). Procreation, therefore, is a form of creation, and honoring one's parents is equivalent to honoring God. Thus, "respect for parents (*filial piety*) derives from *gratitude* toward those who, by the gift of life, their love and their work, have brought their children into the world and enabled them to grow in stature, wisdom, and grace" (Catechism 2215). Conversely, those who are disrespectful to their earthly parents also disrespect their heavenly Father (Sir 3:16). Justice toward God (the virtue of religion) is naturally founded on justice toward one's parents (the virtue of piety) (Catechism 1807).

a. The order of the commandments in Jewish tradition is as follows. Pertaining to the love of God: (1) belief in one God; (2) prohibition of idolatry; (3) do not take the name of God in vain; (4) remember the Sabbath; (5) honor father and mother. Pertaining to the love of neighbor: prohibitions against (6) murder; (7) adultery; (8) theft; (9) bearing false witness; (10) coveting.

3:3–5   The †Torah stipulates that the Israelites must offer blood sacrifices to atone for their sins (Lev 4:1–6:7; 16:11–22). Yet Ben Sira makes a startling claim here: **Whoever honors his father atones for sins**. He holds that observing the commandments and performing acts of kindness—especially toward one's father—can serve as a substitute for sacrifices and is efficacious in obtaining forgiveness (Sir 3:14–15, 30; 28:2). The idea that acts of mercy have atoning power eventually became a mainstream teaching in Judaism and Christianity. From a Christian perspective, although all atonement ultimately derives from Christ's sacrifice,[17]

17. Rom 3:23–25; 1 John 2:2; 4:10; Catechism 615–16.

the Bible also teaches that "love covers a multitude of sins" (1 Pet 4:8; compare Prov 10:12; James 5:20). **Whoever glorifies his mother** parallels "whoever honors his father." One who does so **is like one who lays up** a **treasure** of merit before God through his good deeds. **Whoever honors his father will be gladdened by his own children** expresses the classic doctrine of retribution, which teaches that a man reaps what he sows. If he brings joy to his parents by honoring them, he will reap the same from his own children. **When he prays he will be heard**, for the Lord "hears the prayer of the righteous" (Prov 15:29).

Observing the fourth commandment carries specific benefits: the one who   **3:6–7** **glorifies** or honors **his father will have long life**. This echoes the Torah's promise: "Honor your father and your mother, that your days may be long in the land which the LORD your God gives you" (Exod 20:12; see also Deut 5:16). As St. Paul writes, "This is the first commandment with a promise" (Eph 6:2; see also *Catechism* 2200). The close correlation between honoring one's parents and honoring God is seen in Ben Sira's next statement: **whoever obeys the Lord will refresh** or "bring rest to" **his mother**, giving her no cause for embarrassment or worry. The idea that a child should **serve his parents as his masters** may seem shocking to modern readers. The Greek is even stronger, stating that children must serve their parents as slaves serve their masters, obeying them faithfully and without question. Although the reference to slavery is archaic and should be read in light of the Church's universal condemnation of slavery (*Catechism* 2414), it remains true that "filial respect is shown by true docility and *obedience*" (*Catechism* 2216; see also Prov 6:20–22; 13:1). The fourth commandment still requires that "as long as a child lives at home with his parents, the child should obey his parents in all that they ask of him when it is for his good or that of the family" (*Catechism* 2217; see also Eph 6:1; Col 3:20).

Ben Sira exhorts the reader: **Honor your father by word and deed**, in every-   **3:8–9** thing you do and say, so that **a blessing from him may come upon you**. A father's blessing in Scripture implies more than a benevolent feeling or good wish. As seen in the next verse, it is efficacious, bringing about what is spoken through faith in God's power (Gen 9:26–27; 27:27–29; 48:15–16). The contrast between **a father's blessing** and **a mother's curse** does not imply that it is the father's job to bless his children and the mother's job to curse them. The †parallelism emphasizes the power of the words spoken by either of one's parents. By honoring them, children earn their good favor and blessing, ensuring that their own future homes and families will be well established.

These verses address conflicts or possible rivalries between a father and his   **3:10–11** son. Ben Sira warns the son: **Do not glorify yourself** or try to increase your own reputation **by dishonoring** or belittling **your father**. Self-aggrandizement at another's expense is never praiseworthy—all the more when it concerns one's parents, **for your father's dishonor is no glory to you**. On the contrary, a son should feel ashamed if he sees his father dishonored. Concern for family solidarity

Figure 6. An ancient Israelite family

should dismiss any temptation to engage in intrafamilial rivalries. **For a man's glory comes from honoring his father**: the degree to which a father is honored carries over to his children, who are blessed in proportion to the honor they have shown him. This reflects the fourth commandment's promise that honoring one's father and mother leads to a long and blessed life (Deut 5:16; Prov 17:6; Eph 6:2–3). Conversely, **it is a disgrace for children not to respect their mother** (literally, "a mother in dishonor is a disgrace to her children"). Again, the parallelism does not imply that children owe different levels of honor to their father and mother; both must be honored with equal respect (Prov 15:20; 23:22; 30:17).

3:12–13   In the ancient world, children were expected to care for their aging parents, with whom they often shared close quarters. Physical and mental illness would have rendered this task difficult and burdensome. Nevertheless, Ben Sira exhorts his reader: **O son, help your father** and look after him **in his old age** as he becomes weaker. The Catechism quotes this verse in its exposition of the fourth commandment, reminding adult children that they must give their parents "material and moral support in old age and in times of illness, loneliness, or distress"

(Catechism 2218). Honoring one's father also means to **not grieve him** or cause him sorrow **as long as he lives. Even if he is lacking in understanding**, or "if his mind fails" (NRSV) due to senility or dementia, **show forbearance** by being patient and kind with him **and do not despise him** as long as he lives.

Ben Sira returns to the idea that good works are efficacious in overcoming   **3:14–15**
sins (3:3). Though he states in the passive voice that **kindness to a father will not be forgotten, and against your sins it will be credited to you**, it is evident that God is the one who will remember the son's kindness and will "credit" it against his sins. **In the day** of his **affliction** or in times of distress, the Lord will extend mercy to the son based on the merits he gained by extending mercy to his aging father, so that **as frost in fair weather,** his **sins will melt away**.

Ben Sira underlines the gravity of violating the fourth commandment: offenses   **3:16**
against one's parents are offenses against God himself, because he has set them as his representatives in each family. He who **forsakes his father**, therefore, **is like a blasphemer** who reviles God and holds him in contempt. Likewise, **whoever angers his mother** by disrespecting or disobeying her **is cursed by the Lord**. Again, the parallelism does not intend to single out one offense against the father and another against the mother; both must be equally respected. The Catechism adopts the biblical premise that we should honor and respect our parents, not only because we owe them life but also because God has vested them with his authority and entrusted them with the task of handing on to us the knowledge of God (Catechism 2197).

Reflection and Application (3:1–16)

St. Paul writes that a great evil, already prevalent in his own day, will also be widespread in the "last days": disobedience to parents (Rom 1:30; 2 Tim 3:1–2). Arguably, this phenomenon is visible all around us today. The breakdown of the family has had a devastating impact on our society, and children have been its first victims. Learning to honor one's parents does not come naturally to children growing up in a fallen world. They must be taught respect and obedience by word and example. This is why Paul, after asking the Ephesian children to obey their parents in the Lord, reminds their fathers to "bring them up in the discipline and instruction of the Lord" (Eph 6:1–4). As the Catechism says, the respect of children for their parents "is nourished by the natural affection born of the bond uniting them" (Catechism 2214). This is all the more important because "the family is the *original cell of social life*," where children first "learn moral values, begin to honor God, and make good use of freedom." Thus, "family life is an initiation into life in society" (Catechism 2207) and "a *domestic church*," the first experience of a community of faith, hope, and charity called to reflect the communion of love of the Father, Son, and Holy Spirit (Catechism 2204–5). Sirach

3:1–16 is of such importance for family catechesis that it is always read as the first reading on Holy Family Sunday (between Christmas and New Year's Day).

I.E. Humility and Pride (3:17–31)

[17]My son, perform your tasks in meekness;
  then you will be loved more than a giver of gifts.
[18]The greater you are, the more you must humble yourself;
  so you will find favor with God.
[19]There are many who are noble and renowned,
  but it is to the humble that he reveals his mysteries.
[20]For great is the might of the Lord;
  he is glorified by the humble.
[21]Seek not what is too difficult for you,
  nor investigate what is beyond your power.
[22]Reflect upon what has been assigned to you,
  and do not be curious about many of his works,
  for you do not need *to see with your eyes* what is hidden.
[23]Do not meddle in what is beyond your tasks,
  for matters too great for human understanding have been
    shown you.
[24]For their hasty judgment has led many astray,
  and wrong opinion has caused their thoughts to slip.

[26]A stubborn mind will be afflicted at the end,
  and whoever loves danger will perish by it.
[27]A stubborn mind will be burdened by troubles,
  and the sinner will heap sin upon sin.
[28]The affliction of the proud has no healing,
  for a plant of wickedness has taken root in them,
  though it will not be perceived.
[29]The mind of the wise man will ponder *the words of the wise,*
  and an attentive ear is the wise man's desire.
[30]Water extinguishes a blazing fire:
  so almsgiving atones for sin.
[31]Whoever repays favors gives thought to the future;
  at the moment of his falling he will find support.

OT: Ps 131:1; Prov 11:2; 16:18–19; 29:23; Sir 10:1–11:1; Isa 57:15; Mic 6:8
NT: Matt 11:29; 23:12; Luke 18:9–14; Phil 2:3–11; James 4:6–10; 1 Pet 5:5–6
Catechism: pride as capital sin, 1866; humility as poverty of spirit, 2546; humility, foundation of prayer, 2559
Lectionary: 3:17–18, 20, 28–29: 22nd Sunday in Ordinary Time (Year C); 3:17–24: Common of Holy Men and Women

3:17–18 Ben Sira now begins a discourse on humility and pride. The wisdom literature closely associates humility with the fear of the Lord. While pride leads to disgrace and destruction, humility and the fear of the Lord lead to wisdom, honor, and abundant life (Prov 11:2; 15:33; 18:12; 22:4). Accordingly, Ben Sira exhorts his reader to perform his tasks **in meekness**, for the humble person is **loved more than a giver of gifts**. People tend to appreciate an unpretentious and modest disposition more than someone who gives lavishly but boastfully. Pride is a vice that tends to grow with worldly success. All the more, **the greater you are,** or the higher your status in society, **the more you must humble yourself** (Hebrew: "humble your soul from all the great things of the world"). In this way, **you will find favor with God**, and he will be pleased with you. The New Testament often develops this theme.[18]

There is no reason to envy the **many who are noble and renowned**, for **it is**   3:19–20
to the humble that the Lord **reveals his mysteries** and teaches them his ways so that they may know him and live a full life (Ps 25:9; Zeph 3:12).[19] Ben Sira contrasts the vain power of the noble with the great **might of the Lord.** While they obscure the power of God in their arrogance, **he is glorified by the humble** as they recognize and manifest his glory and power, fearing him with humility and lowliness (Pss 25:14; 33:17–18; 147:10–11; Matt 11:25).

Ben Sira turns from praising humility to warning against intellectual pride.   3:21
His readers may have been tempted to pursue wisdom in the Greek philosophy that increasingly permeated Jewish culture. Yet they should not seek things that are **too difficult** to understand, nor **investigate** philosophical speculations or ideas that are **beyond** their **power** (Hebrew: "that which is hidden from you")— for this is an exercise in futility and "unhappy business" (Eccles 1:13; see also Ps 131:1). In the New Testament, St. Paul also warns against undue curiosity for idle philosophical ideas that do not lead to Christ (Col 2:8).

A better course of action is to **reflect upon what has been assigned** or "com-   3:22–23
manded" **to you**. Seekers of wisdom should meditate on the commandments of the †Torah rather than waste their time on lofty speculative ideas. They should not be unduly *curious about many of* God's *works*, for God has left many mysteries **hidden** in creation that cannot be known and therefore do not need to be probed. Christian tradition considers undue curiosity about futile or frivolous things a vice, in contrast to the studiousness that seeks the knowledge of divine things.[20] Verse 23 repeats the exhortation, so that the two verses form a †chiasm: In verse 22, Ben Sira offers a positive command ("reflect") followed by a negative one ("do not be curious"). In verse 23 he reverses the order, beginning with a negative command (**do not meddle** in vain things), followed by an implicit invitation to investigate the **matters too great for human understanding** that God has revealed in the Torah (Isa 64:4; 1 Cor 2:9).

18. Matt 20:26–27; Luke 1:50–53; Phil 2:3; James 4:6, 10; 1 Pet 5:5–6.
19. Sir 3:19 is from the longer Greek text (GII); it is omitted from most other translations or relegated to the footnotes.
20. Thomas Aquinas, *Summa Theologiae* II-II qq. 166–67.

3:24–25   Ben Sira continues to warn his reader against philosophical brooding: **For their hasty judgment**, or perhaps "speculation" (ESV-CE), "conceit" (NRSV), or "vain opinion" (KJV), **has led many astray** from the ways of the Lord. There are consequences to holding a **wrong opinion**: this has **caused their thoughts to slip**, obscuring their understanding and impairing their judgment. The longer Greek text adds the rather obscure verse 25: **If you have no eyes you will be without light; if you lack knowledge do not profess to have it** (RSV-2CE footnote). Just as a blind person should not pretend to see light, so a person without knowledge should not try to fool others by pretending to be wise. The Hebrew states this more succinctly: "Without the pupil of the eye, light is missing; without knowledge, wisdom is missing" (NABRE).

3:26–27   **A stubborn mind** (literally, "a hard heart")—that is, an obstinate person who is unwilling to listen and be corrected—**will be afflicted at the end**, perhaps alluding to the "hard heart" of Pharaoh during the exodus (Exod 7:14). Moreover, **whoever loves danger will perish by it**—in other words, whoever refuses correction and plays with fire will get burned. Having a "hard heart" or stubborn mind is diametrically opposed to having the fear of the Lord and wisdom. It is the height of foolishness. Ben Sira repeats for emphasis: **A stubborn mind** or hard heart **will be burdened** or weighed down **by troubles, and the sinner will heap sin upon sin**. Resisting correction intractably is a sure path to accumulating sins. If sins are not kept in check through repentance and conversion, they inevitably increase and multiply, unleashing divine curses and ultimately leading to self-destruction (Deut 28:15–68).

3:28–29   Precisely because of his resistance to correction, **the affliction of the proud has no healing**. His misery is self-inflicted because he does not fear the Lord and will not repent (Prov 12:3). Pride is compared to a poisonous, deep-rooted weed that corrupts people at the deepest level and makes them virtually irreformable: **for a plant of wickedness has taken root in them**—in contrast to the righteous, who are firmly planted like strong trees (Pss 1:3; 92:12–14; Matt 7:17–19). The †Vulgate adds: *though it will not be perceived*. Even though pride is the deadliest of sins, it is also the most subtle, for it easily goes unnoticed in the inattentive soul. Having concluded his invective against the proud, Ben Sira returns to **the mind of the wise** (literally, "the wise heart"). In contrast to the "hard heart," the wise heart seeks to be instructed by others. It gladly ponders *the words of the wise* (Hebrew, Latin), or "a parable" (Greek)—that is, any form of wisdom saying. The **attentive ear** points to **the wise man's desire** to learn from the wisdom of others (Matt 13:9).

3:30–31   Ben Sira introduces the topic of almsgiving (developed in 4:1–10) by means of a †parallelism: **Water extinguishes a blazing fire: so almsgiving atones for sin**. Here is a remedy to the problem of sin's propagation (3:27): if sin is like fire, spreading rapidly and burning everything in its path, almsgiving is like the water that puts it out. This confirms the idea that good works have atoning power: like honoring one's father, almsgiving is an efficacious work that atones for sin (3:3, 14–15). **Whoever repays favors gives thought to the future.** The Hebrew expresses this more poetically: "The deeds of the one who is good will meet him on his ways." Good deeds such as giving alms or acting kindly are stored, as it were, in a "treasury of merits" that God can recall at an opportune time, so that especially **at the moment of his falling** the righteous man **will find support.** Kindness is a wise investment that will pay dividends in the future (Tob 4:7–11; 14:10–11; Prov 19:17).

Reflection and Application (3:17–31)

Humility is an essential virtue for attaining wisdom. Indeed, it is the only proper attitude that a person can have before God. The word derives from the Latin *humilitas*, which comes from *humus*—the earth beneath us. Thus, the humble, well aware of their imperfections, maintain a modest opinion of themselves and willingly submit to God and others in the fear of the Lord. The humble person remains aware of his flaws, conscious that he has a limited perspective on life and might well be mistaken in his views. This unpretentious disposition makes him docile and teachable, and thus able to grow in wisdom. For this reason, Christian tradition sees humility as the "queen of virtues." Although other virtues, such as faith, hope, and charity, are objectively greater, humility in some sense holds the first place because it removes pride and makes people receptive to divine grace.[21] By contrast, those who are pretentious or arrogant, believing they know better than everyone else, cannot be wise. This is why pride—the excessive love of one's own excellence—is considered the worst of sins, for it shuts the human heart to divine grace (10:1–11:1).

I.F. Almsgiving and Justice (4:1–10)

> ¹**My son, deprive not the poor of his living,**
>   **and do not keep needy eyes waiting.**
> ²**Do not grieve the one who is hungry,**
>   **nor anger a man in want.**
> ³**Do not add to the troubles of an angry mind,**
>   **nor delay your gift to a beggar.**
> ⁴**Do not reject an afflicted suppliant,**
>   **nor turn your face away from the poor.**
> ⁵**Do not avert your eye from the needy,**
>   **nor give a man occasion to curse you;**

---

21. Thomas Aquinas, *Summa Theologiae* II-II q. 161 a. 5 ad 2.

⁶for if in bitterness of soul he calls down a curse upon you,
  his Creator will hear his prayer.

⁷Make yourself beloved in the congregation;
  bow your head low to a great man.
⁸Incline your ear to the poor,
  and answer him peaceably and gently.
⁹Deliver him who is wronged from the hand of the wrongdoer;
  and do not be fainthearted in judging a case.
¹⁰Be like a father to orphans,
  and instead of a husband to their mother;
  you will then be like a son of the Most High,
  and he will love you more than does your mother.

OT: Exod 22:22–24; Lev 19:9–10; Deut 10:18; 15:7–11; Tob 4:7–11; Amos 8:4–6
NT: Matt 5:42; 6:2–4; 19:21; 25:31–46; Luke 12:33; James 1:27
Catechism: love for the poor, 2443–49; almsgiving as penance, 1434; as act of religion, 1969; the family's responsibility in taking care of the poor, 2208

4:1–2   With his familiar paternal address **my son**, Ben Sira begins a new speech on the responsibility of the wise toward the poor. The pursuit of wisdom is never divorced from concrete, virtuous action toward others. He illustrates this with five pairs of negative admonitions on how not to treat the poor (4:1–6), followed by four pairs of positive exhortations encouraging the wise man to be generous (4:7–10). **Deprive not the poor of his living** is literally "do not rob the life of the poor." Almsgiving is not just an optional act of kindness but a grave moral obligation: the †Torah commands Israel to help the poor (Lev 19:9–10; Deut 15:7–11), so withholding alms from them is the equivalent of robbing them. Ben Sira urges the reader to **not keep needy eyes waiting** for help, but to assist the poor without delay. Cold-hearted indifference can **grieve the one who is hungry** and add to his plight. A lack of compassion toward human suffering can **anger a man in want** against the inequalities and injustices of society.

4:3–4   Those who are better off should not **add to the troubles of** a person with **an angry mind** (literally, "angry heart") who is disappointed at his lot in life, by withholding or delaying a **gift to a beggar**. By giving promptly and cheerfully, the generous person alleviates not only the beggar's hunger but also restores some measure of hope and joy in him (Prov 3:28; 2 Cor 9:7). One should **not reject an afflicted suppliant**, a poor person who explicitly asks for help, as this only adds insult to injury. The injunction to not **turn your face away from the poor** is an invitation to imitate God, who does not hide his face from the afflicted but hears and helps them (Tob 4:7; Ps 22:24; Matt 5:42).

4:5–6   **Do not avert your eye from the needy** reiterates the thought of the previous verse with a synonymous †parallelism. One should not give the destitute an **occasion to curse** those who lack compassion. Ben Sira imagines a scene where a beggar asks for alms, the passerby ignores the request, and the beggar **in bitterness of soul** curses him in return. The miserly, uncompassionate person bears some responsibility if the poor person **calls down a curse** upon him (Prov 28:27). Even more unsettling is the thought that **his Creator will hear his prayer**. God hears the cry of the poor when they ask him for justice; he may even punish those who afflict them (Exod 22:22–23), for "He who oppresses a poor man insults his Maker" (Prov 14:31; 17:5).

Ben Sira now turns to the right conduct, not only toward the poor but also 4:7–8 toward people of importance, as well as those who are oppressed, orphans, and widows. One who acts kindly toward all will be **beloved in the congregation** or "synagogue." **Bow your head low** is a way of showing deference to **a great man**—that is, a person of authority—resuming the theme of humility treated in 3:17–24. **Incline your ear to the poor**, acknowledging them and listening to their requests, stands in contrast to the uncharitable person who turns away from them (4:5). One should not only provide material assistance to a poor man but also **answer him peaceably and gently** (Hebrew: "return him peace"), treating him with dignity and kindness.

The just person should not only refrain from committing injustice but also 4:9 take an active role in opposing it whenever possible. He should **deliver him who is wronged** from his oppressors, perhaps in a situation brought for judgment before members of the community similar to a modern case set before a jury (Dan 13:44–64). The wise should **not be fainthearted in judging a case** (see Ps 82:2–4); it takes a strong person to resist pressures and judge impartially and fairly.

Society is an extended family. Thus, the wise man should be **like a father to** 4:10 **orphans**, caring for them as his own children, and take the place of **a husband to their mother**, not that he should marry her but should take care of her by being *like* a husband to her. This solidarity reflects God's fatherly love and care of every member of society, so that the one who imitates his compassion is **like a son of the Most High**. This expression, rare in the Old Testament, is sometimes used to refer to Jesus in the Gospels (Mark 5:7; Luke 1:32; 8:28)—he who most perfectly reflected the heart of the Father for his people. God's concern for the downtrodden is such that **he will love you more than does your mother** if you care for them. This description of God's love as loyal, unconditional motherly love is rare but not unheard of in the Bible (Isa 49:15; 66:13). It also sets the stage for the following poem, where wisdom is depicted as a loving mother.

Reflection and Application (4:1–10)

The practice of giving alms is frequently commanded in Scripture as an imitation of God's gratuitous love. Inspired by the Beatitudes and Jesus's own poverty, "the Church's love for the poor . . . is a part of her constant tradition" and mission (Catechism 2444). Pope John Paul II defined the "preferential option for the poor" as an outstanding way of exercising Christian charity: the Church, in imitation of Christ, must especially embrace those most in need— namely, "the hungry, the needy, the homeless, those without medical care and, above all, those without hope of a better future."[22] Pope Benedict XVI echoed the same concern, writing that "love for widows and orphans, prisoners, and the sick and needy of every kind, is as essential to [the Church] as the ministry of the sacraments and preaching of the Gospel."[23]

Almsgiving is an act of mercy that extends beyond simply giving money to the poor. Traditionally, it has been taken to encompass the seven corporal works of mercy—namely, feeding the hungry, giving drink to the thirsty, clothing the naked, sheltering the homeless, visiting the sick, visiting the imprisoned, and burying the dead (Catechism 2447).[24] Six of these derive from Matthew's depiction of the last judgment (Matt 25:31–46), while the seventh is from Tobit 1:16–20; 12:12. Jesus teaches that the nations will be judged according to how they carried out the works of mercy to the poor and needy.

Almsgiving is also a way of expressing interior penance (Catechism 1434) and an act of religion (Catechism 1969). Christians should give alms generously for all these reasons, but perhaps especially because by doing so they imitate God's love for the poor, and by being merciful to others they are promised God's mercy in return (Matt 5:7).

---

22. John Paul II, *Sollicitudo Rei Socialis* (Vatican City: Libreria Editrice Vaticana, 1987), 42; see also *Centesimus Annus* (Vatican City: Libreria Editrice Vaticana, 1991), 57.

23. Benedict XVI, *Deus Caritas Est* (Vatican City: Libreria Editrice Vaticana, 2005), 22.

24. Thomas Aquinas, *Summa Theologiae* II-II q. 32 a. 2.

Part II

Sirach 4:11–6:17

The second major part of the book begins with a second poem praising Wisdom. In chapter 1, she was introduced in her cosmic grandeur as the first of God's creation (1:1–10). Here, she is personified as a mother who loves her children, exercising "tough love" and disciplining them so that they may grow into wise adults, able to serve God and ready to receive his blessings (4:11–19). Following this poem, Ben Sira turns to practical advice, demonstrating how Wisdom instructs her children. This begins with a treatment of shame, along with a reflection on the appropriate time to speak and the importance of always telling the truth (4:20–31). Ben Sira then turns to a series of warnings against presumption, duplicitous speech, and unruly passions (5:1–6:4), followed by the first of several speeches on friendship (6:5–17).

II.A. Lady Wisdom's Motherly Discipline (4:11–19)

> ¹¹Wisdom *breathes life into* her sons
>   and gives help to those who seek her.
> ¹²Whoever loves her loves life,
>   and those who seek her early
>   *will win the Lord's good favor.*
> ¹³Whoever holds her fast will obtain glory,
>   and the Lord will bless the place she enters.
> ¹⁴Those who serve her will minister to the Holy One;
>   the Lord loves those who love her.
> ¹⁵He who obeys her will judge the nations,
>   and whoever gives heed to her will dwell secure.
> ¹⁶If he has faith in her he will obtain her;
>   and his descendants will remain in possession of her.

> ¹⁷For she will walk with him *in disguise,*
> and at first she will put him to the test;
> she will bring fear and cowardice upon him,
> and will torment him by her discipline
> until he holds her in his thoughts,
> and she trusts him.
> ¹⁸Then she will come straight back to him *and strengthen him,*
> she will gladden him and will reveal her secrets to him,
> *and store up for him knowledge*
> *and the discernment of what is right.*
> ¹⁹But if he goes astray she will forsake him,
> and give him over *into the hands of his foe.*

OT: Prov 3:11–18; Wis 8:16–17
NT: Matt 7:13–14; 16:24; Heb 12:5–11
Catechism: wisdom as gift of the Holy Spirit, 1831; self-mortification, 1734, 1804, 2015

4:11–12   Wisdom *breathes life into* her sons follows the †Vulgate, alluding to God's creation of man (Gen 2:7) and portraying Wisdom as "a breath of the power of God" (Wis 7:25–26). It is more evocative than the Greek ("Wisdom exalts her sons," ESV-CE) or Hebrew ("Wisdom teaches her sons"; compare NRSV, NABRE). All versions portray Wisdom as a loving yet demanding mother who gives life to her children and raises them to spiritual maturity by teaching them the right way to live. Wisdom is often depicted as a source of life in other books (Prov 3:16–18; 8:35; Wis 8:16–17). Her relational aspect shines through in the affirmation that **whoever loves her loves life.** Pursuing Wisdom is much more than acquiring knowledge or acting in a certain way to attain worldly success. It is primarily a matter of the heart. While elsewhere the love for Wisdom is described as spousal (Prov 8:17), here it is compared to the love of a child for its mother. Those who are disciplined enough to **seek her early** in the morning—presumably through prayer and study—are promised that they *will win the Lord's good favor* (Latin) or "will be filled with joy" (Greek, ESV-CE).

4:13–14   **Whoever holds her fast,** as a child holds fast to its mother, **will obtain glory** and honor from God, **and the Lord will bless the place** where Wisdom **enters** (Hebrew: "they shall abide in the blessing of the Lord," NABRE). The pursuit of Wisdom requires discipline; it involves serving her with devotion and diligence. While this is a demanding task, it carries benefits and rewards: **Those who serve her** are promised that they **will minister** (literally, "perform a liturgical ministry") **to the Holy One.** Serving Wisdom is viewed as an act of worshiping God. Because he is honored by those who devotedly serve Wisdom, **the Lord loves those who love her.**

4:15–16   **He who obeys** Wisdom by diligently following her teachings will **judge the nations:** this suggests that the one who is wise will be able to lead others and rule over them (Wis 3:8; 1 Cor 6:2; Rev 3:21). He will also **dwell secure,** living in confidence, or in Wisdom's "innermost chambers" (Hebrew, NABRE). The reader is exhorted to have **faith** in Wisdom: by remaining faithful to her and entrusting himself to her, **he will obtain her,** or more literally "inherit her." The idea that a person can communicate wisdom to **his descendants** so that they may also **remain in possession of her** points to an ancient Jewish view of family catechesis, where wisdom (like other virtues) is passed on from parents to children, from generation to generation.

The pursuit of Wisdom is difficult, especially in the beginning. At first, she is **4:17** not particularly attractive; indeed, she is hard to recognize, for she walks with the disciple *in disguise* (Hebrew, Latin) or "on tortuous paths" (Greek, ESV-CE, NRSV), putting him **to the test** through rigorous discipline and severe trials. Wisdom's training may resemble that of a tough drill sergeant more than that of a tender mother. It is so severe that it can **bring fear and cowardice** upon the student and **torment him by her discipline,** tempting him to give up. Yet if he is strong and **holds her** steadfastly **in his thoughts** while persevering through the trials, he will prove himself worthy and in this way will gain her trust. The idea that wisdom is acquired through discipline is a common theme not only in the wisdom books (Prov 3:11–12; 12:1; 13:24; 29:17) but throughout the whole Bible.[1]

Once the student has proven himself, Wisdom reveals her true colors. She **4:18–19** removes her disguise and quickly returns to *strengthen him*, **gladden him**, **reveal her secrets to him,** and—the Vulgate adds—*store up for him knowledge and the discernment of what is right*. In other words, to acquire wisdom one must first acquire faithfulness and strength of character through testing. On the other hand, Wisdom will not pursue the one who fails the test and **goes astray** by wandering away from the path of her discipline, giving in to discouragement and losing faith. She not only will **forsake him,** leaving him to his own devices, but also will **give him over** *into the hands of his foe* (Latin) or "of his downfall" (Greek, ESV-CE). In short, the path of Wisdom, harsh and demanding at first, ultimately grants strength, joy, and life; while the path of foolishness, pleasant and easy at first, ultimately turns into weakness, distress, and death (Matt 7:13–14).

Reflection and Application (4:11–19)

Wisdom's way of relating to her disciples—at first hiding herself through harsh trials and only later revealing herself after they have proven the worthiness of their character—reveals an important principle about the spiritual life. Spiritual growth does not consist in first "figuring things out" and then changing one's way of life accordingly. Obedience to the Lord's word comes first; understanding of the truth follows—not vice versa. As Jesus says, "If you continue in my word, you are truly my disciples, and you will know the truth, and the truth

---

1. Deut 8:5; Job 5:17; Ps 94:12; 1 Cor 11:32; Heb 12:5–11.

will make you free" (John 8:31–32). Jesus's words "you are my friends if you do what I command you" (John 15:14) echo those of Lady Wisdom.

The spiritual life alternates between times of desolation—periods of aridity and trials when God seems distant—and times of consolation when the Lord manifests his presence through increased love and joy. While times of desolation are difficult, they are indispensable for our spiritual growth, for they provide us with unique opportunities to exercise patience and perseverance. By remaining faithful to God in the midst of trials, we demonstrate our faithfulness to him and show ourselves to be worthy of wisdom.

II.B. On Shame and Timely Speech (4:20–31)

20Observe the right time, and beware of evil;
    and do not bring shame on yourself.
21For there is a shame which brings sin,
    and there is a shame which is glory and favor.
22Do not show partiality, to your own harm,
    or deference, to your downfall.
23Do not refrain from speaking at the crucial time,
    and do not hide your wisdom.
24For wisdom is known through speech,
    and education through the words of the tongue.
25Never speak against the truth,
    but be mindful of your ignorance.
26Do not be ashamed to confess your sins,
    and do not try to stop the current of a river.
27Do not subject yourself to a foolish fellow,
    nor show partiality to a ruler.
28Strive even to death for the truth
    and the Lord God will fight for you.

29Do not be reckless in your speech,
    or sluggish and remiss in your deeds.
30Do not be like a lion in your home,
    nor be a faultfinder with your servants.
31Let not your hand be extended to receive,
    but withdrawn when it is time to repay.

OT: Gen 2:25; 3:7; Exod 20:16; Pss 51:6; 119:160
NT: Matt 5:33–37; John 8:32; 14:6; 17:17–19; 2 Thess 2:9–13
Catechism: not bearing false witness, 2464–513

4:20   Wisdom—or the lack thereof—is revealed through speech. What we say, when we say it, and how we say it reveals much about who we are. Ben Sira explains the connections between wisdom, speech, sin, and shame. First, **observe the right time,** and be aware of your circumstances before speaking. There is "a time to keep silence, and a time to speak" (Eccles 3:7). One must **beware of evil**— likely a caution against *doing* evil more than against evil persons—because it is by sinning that one brings **shame** on oneself, for shame is a consequence of sin (Gen 2:25; 3:7). While it can denote a personal sense of guilt before God, shame is often associated with damage to one's public reputation manifesting as disgrace, dishonor, or social rejection (Pss 31:17; 35:26).

Still, Ben Sira does not see shame as an absolute evil but makes a distinction between "bad shame" and "good shame." "Bad shame" is **shame which brings sin**. Indeed, sin and shame are often caught in a vicious circle: not only does sin cause shame, but a deep sense of shame can drive a person into a spiral of despair, blocking the path to repentance and leading to more sin. "Bad shame" could also refer to being ashamed of practicing one's faith, speaking the truth, or standing for what is right. Yet there is also **a shame which is glory and favor**: this "good shame" could refer to being ashamed of committing sins—a posture rooted in the fear of the Lord that leads to repentance and conversion (4:26). Put simply, "bad shame" is to be ashamed of what is good and true; "good shame" is to be ashamed of what is evil and false. Thus, we call "shameless" a person who lacks "good shame" and is not ashamed of committing evil (41:14–42:8). **4:21**

The injunction to **not show partiality** or favoritism implies that this is also a shameful act, a sin against truth. God is an impartial judge (Sir 35:16; Deut 10:17), and he calls his people to exercise the same fairness (Lev 19:15; Ps 82:2; Prov 18:5; Sir 42:1). Favoritism causes **harm**, not only to the person discriminated against, but even more so to the one guilty of showing unjust **deference**, for this will ultimately lead to his **downfall**. **4:22**

Silence is golden—but not always. In certain situations, the wise should **not refrain from speaking**, especially **at the crucial time** when their wisdom is needed—whether or not it is welcome. The wise must **not hide** their **wisdom** out of false modesty, for God has given them wisdom to help and edify others. The wise, therefore, must speak out at the opportune time to instruct, counsel, exhort, or admonish, always in defense of justice and truth (4:9; Prov 15:23; 2 Tim 4:2). **For wisdom is known through speech**, or "in word" (Greek *logos*). Acting rightly is not enough: for wisdom to be shared with others, it must be communicated through human language. All **education**—or "discipline" (Greek *paideia*)—is passed on from teacher to student **through the words of the tongue**. **4:23–24**

Never speak against the truth—for falsehood is incompatible with both wisdom and God, who is truth (Ps 119:160; John 14:6). Accordingly, walking in truth is essential to remaining in God's presence and serving wisdom (Ps 15:1–2); **but be mindful of your ignorance** so as not to speak rashly, lest your words later prove false. The wise, who fear the Lord, have the humility to recognize that their knowledge is always limited. **4:25**

4:26   **Do not be ashamed to confess your sins** or, following the Hebrew, "repent of iniquity" (Lev 5:5; Num 5:7). Being ashamed to confess one's sins is a form of "bad shame" (4:21). Far from humility, this reluctance reveals a combination of pride and despair—two of the gravest sins that block the way to reconciliation with God. By contrast, the wise humbly and promptly confess their sins. The metaphorical injunction to **not try to stop the current of a river** may suggest that trying to conceal one's sins from God is as futile as attempting to stop a river's current.

4:27–28   The wise person is humble but not a doormat. Ben Sira exhorts him, **Do not subject yourself** or "prostrate your soul" (Hebrew) **to a foolish fellow**. He should neither allow fools to dominate him nor **show partiality to a ruler** by giving preferential treatment to people of authority (James 2:1). Ben Sira advocates for truth-telling in the strongest terms: the wise man should **strive even to death for the truth**. This is the witness of the martyrs, who are willing to give their lives for truth. For Ben Sira's contemporaries, this meant defending the Jewish faith despite the increasing pressure of Hellenization. Many Jews would soon face martyrdom under the persecution of Antiochus Epiphanes (2 Macc 6:18–7:42), leading to the Maccabean revolt against the Greeks. Yet even in such dire situations Ben Sira encourages his readers not to be afraid, for if they fight for truth, **the Lord God will fight** for them (see Exod 14:14).

4:29–30   If the wise person is often obligated to speak (4:23–24), he must **not be reckless** or boastful in his **speech**, speaking rashly while being **sluggish** or negligent in his **deeds**. It is better to be slow to speak and quick to act. Actions speak louder than words (James 1:19–25). Continuing on the topic of speech, Ben Sira addresses the domineering personality who roars **like a lion** at his wife and children at **home** and is **a faultfinder**, suspicious of his **servants**, quick to criticize and oppress them. Such behavior contradicts the meekness required of the wise person (3:17–20).

4:31   This verse, addressing avarice and greed, serves as a fitting transition to the next section on presumption and arrogance. It warns the reader against extending a hand **to receive** money or other benefits only to withdraw it **when it is time to repay**. Avarice goes hand in hand with foolishness, while generosity is a hallmark of the wise (4:1–10; Acts 20:35).

Reflection and Application (4:20–31)

Ben Sira's forceful exhortation "Never speak against the truth" (4:25) sounds countercultural in our age of postmodernism, relativism, and "fake news," when there is an acute skepticism regarding truth. Many still echo Pilate's existential question, "What is truth?" (John 18:38). It is not necessary to write a philosophical treatise to answer this question. The best way to witness to truth is by living truthfully. Since God is truth, his people are called to live in the truth (Catechism

2465), showing themselves "true in deeds and truthful in words, and in guarding against duplicity, dissimulation, and hypocrisy" (Catechism 2468). Living truthfully is not optional, for as the †Decalogue stipulates, "You shall not bear false witness against your neighbor" (Exod 20:16). So-called white lies can easily lead to larger deceptions. If lies are not kept in check and renounced, the person who lies becomes a liar, and liars often start believing their own lies. A society permeated by lies can neither function nor survive. According to St. Paul, the defining mark of ungodliness and wickedness is *suppressing truth* about God and *exchanging it for a lie* (Rom 1:18, 25). The ultimate lie—denying God's providence and relying solely on human wisdom—leads to debased passions and a debased mind, improper conduct, and ultimately death (Rom 1:26–32). It is all the more important for disciples of wisdom to regularly examine their consciences and ensure that they are living their lives in honesty, authenticity, and truth.

II.C. Against Presumption, Deceptive Speech, and Unruly Passions (5:1–6:4)

¹Do not set your heart on your wealth,
  nor say, "I have enough."
²Do not follow your inclination and strength,
  walking according to the desires of your heart.
³Do not say, "Who will have power over me?"
  or *"Who will bring me down because of my deeds?"*
  for God will surely punish you.

⁴Do not say, "I sinned, and what happened to me?"
  for the Most High is slow to anger.
⁵Do not be so confident of atonement
  that you add sin to sin.
⁶Do not say, "His mercy is great,
  he will forgive the multitude of my sins,"
for both mercy and wrath are with him,
  and his anger rests on sinners.
⁷Do not delay to turn to the Lord,
  nor postpone it from day to day;
for suddenly the wrath of the Lord will go forth,
  and at the time of punishment you will perish.

⁸Do not depend on dishonest wealth,
  for it will not benefit you in the day of calamity.
⁹Do not winnow with every wind,
  nor follow every path:
  the double-tongued sinner does that.

¹⁰Be steadfast in your understanding,
  and let your speech be consistent.
¹¹Be quick to hear,
  and be deliberate in answering.
¹²If you have understanding, answer your neighbor;
  but if not, put your hand on your mouth.
¹³Glory and dishonor come from speaking,
  and a man's tongue is his downfall.

¹⁴Do not be called a slanderer,
  and do not lie in ambush with your tongue;
for shame comes to the thief,
  and severe condemnation to the double-tongued.
¹⁵In great or small matters do not act amiss,
  and do not become an enemy instead of a friend;
⁶:¹for a bad name incurs shame and reproach:
  so fares the double-tongued sinner.

²Do not exalt yourself through your soul's counsel,
  lest your soul be torn in pieces like a bull.
³You will devour your leaves and destroy your fruit,
  and will be left like a withered tree.
⁴An evil soul will destroy him who has it,
  and make him the laughingstock of his enemies.

OT: Prov 3:5–6; 12:18; 18:21
NT: Matt 12:37; James 1:19; 3:2–10
Catechism: presumption, 2091–92; offenses against truth, 2475–87; avarice, 2536

5:1–2   While continuing his warning against greed, Ben Sira now cautions against the
sin of presumption with eight prohibitions (5:1–8). The connection between
avarice and presumption is obvious: one who sets his **heart on wealth** is trying
to achieve self-sufficiency and autonomy from God. By saying, "**I have enough**
with my material goods," the avaricious person implies, "I don't need God or
his provision." It is no surprise that Scripture frequently warns against the love
of money (Ps 52:7; Matt 6:24; Luke 12:15; 1 Tim 6:17). The thought of following **your inclination** (literally, "your soul") **and strength, walking according
to the desires of your heart** sounds like the advice of many a commencement
speaker—yet Ben Sira rejects it. Following one's "heart" without the guidance of
wisdom and the other virtues is often nothing more than being driven by one's
passions and instincts—and a recipe for disaster. The †Torah explicitly warns
"*not* to follow after your own heart and your own eyes, which you are inclined
to go after wantonly" (Num 15:39; compare Prov 3:5–6).

5:3–4   Ben Sira asks two rhetorical questions: **Who will have power over me?** (i.e.,
"I am my own master") and *Who will bring me down because of my deeds?*

(†Vulgate) (i.e., "No one will tell me what to do"). These questions express the arrogance of those who think they are accountable to no one—not even to God. Yet **God** continues to reign even over the wicked and **will surely punish** them in due time (16:17–23). By saying, **"I sinned, and what happened to me?"** the presumptuous man assumes that he can commit transgressions with impunity and get away with it because God **the Most High is slow to anger** (Exod 34:6; Num 14:18) and will forgive him. Yet God will execute judgment upon all sinners (Eccles 8:11–13).

Jews were **confident** of obtaining **atonement** and forgiveness through the **5:5–6** offering of blood sacrifices (Exod 30:10). Yet the offerings prescribed in Leviticus provided forgiveness only for sins committed *unintentionally* (Lev 4:2, 13, 22, 27; Num 15:22–29). There was no atonement for iniquities committed *intentionally* or "with a high hand"; the sinner had "reviled the LORD" and was to be "cut off from among his people" (Num 15:30–31). Thus, one who sins presumptuously adds **sin to sin**. To those who boast that God's **"mercy is great, he will forgive the multitude of my sins,"** St. Paul might reply: "Are we to continue in sin that grace may abound? By no means!" (Rom 6:1–2). God reveals both his **mercy and wrath**, the former to the penitent and the latter to the impenitent, for **his anger rests on sinners** who continually transgress his law with impunity (Sir 16:11; Wis 11:9; Isa 60:10; Rom 2:4–5). Awareness of God's mercy should lead us not to presumption but to repentance (Rom 2:4).

All the more should the sinner **not delay to turn to the Lord** in genuine **5:7–8** repentance. No one should **postpone** repentance **from day to day**, for no one knows when **the wrath of the Lord** will be revealed. For presumptuous sinners, this will be not a time of mercy but a **time of punishment** when they **will perish**. In an †*inclusio* tying the end of this section with its beginning (5:1), Ben Sira returns to the topic of presumptuous reliance on money, warning in verse 8 that **dishonest wealth** will be of no use **in the day of calamity**—the "day of the Lord," when his judgment is manifest (see Prov 10:2; 11:4; Ezek 7:19; Matt 6:19–21).

Ben Sira now turns to the question of prudence, integrity, and consistency **5:9** in speech. He has a particular aversion toward those whose words are fickle or duplicitous. He warns the reader to **not winnow with every wind**: Farmers winnow grain by throwing it into a breeze that blows away the husks while the edible grain falls back to the ground. Winnowing with every changing wind would result in the husks falling back into the grain, undoing the work. Likewise, a person trying to **follow every path** will get nowhere, like the **double-tongued sinner** who tries to please everyone by speaking duplicitously: he scatters his words without purpose and cannot be trusted.

What we say reflects how we think. Therefore, the first step toward speak-**5:10–11** ing with integrity is to be **steadfast in your understanding** and be a person of conviction, able to discern right from wrong. **Let your speech be consistent** (literally, "let your word be one") and be reliable in what you say. **Be quick to**

Do Not Sin Presumptuously

LIVING TRADITION

Jewish tradition warns against the temptation to continue sinning while presumptuously relying on God's mercy: "If a man said, 'I will sin and repent, and sin again and repent,' he will be given no chance to repent. [If he said,] 'I will sin and the Day of Atonement will effect atonement,' then the Day of Atonement effects no atonement."[a]

Christian tradition agrees. As one Church Father says, "We should repent soon because the more we delay our repentance, the more chance death has to lead us to damnation instead of salvation."[b] In the words of St. Paul, *now* is the day of salvation and the day to accept God's grace (2 Cor 6:1–2), for "the day of the Lord will come like a thief in the night" (1 Thess 5:2).

a. Mishnah, *Yoma* 8:9, in Herbert Danby, trans., *The Mishnah* (Oxford: Oxford University Press, 1933), 172.

b. Fulgentius of Ruspe, *On the Forgiveness of Sins* 2.5, in Sever J. Voicu, ed., *Apocrypha*, ACCS:OT 15 (Downers Grove, IL: InterVarsity, 2010), 205.

hear and attentive to what others say; **be deliberate in answering** (literally, "in patience utter an answer"), having the discipline not to answer rashly before thinking through what is the right thing to say (1:23–24; Prov 18:13; James 1:19).

5:12–13   When someone speaks, consider **if you have understanding**, genuine insight or wisdom to share, in which case it is right to **answer your neighbor**. Otherwise, it is best to **put your hand on your mouth**—an idiom meaning to remain silent out of respect for the speaker (Job 40:4; Prov 30:32; Mic 7:16). Several biblical authors warn about the power of the tongue to do good or evil (Prov 12:18; 18:21; Matt 12:37; James 3:2–10). The words we speak bring either **glory** or **dishonor**: they can build or destroy a reputation—either of the person spoken of or of the person speaking. Ben Sira seems to think especially of the latter when he adds that **a man's tongue is his downfall**. Foolish, imprudent words spoken at the wrong time—especially in the age of social media—can permanently ruin a person's reputation.

5:14   Ben Sira exhorts the reader to watch his words lest he develop the reputation of being **a slanderer** (Hebrew: a "two-faced" person). Malicious gossip, or speaking evil of others in their absence, is even worse than speaking carelessly. Ben Sira depicts this metaphorically as lying **in ambush with your tongue** like a predator waiting for the opportunity to attack a victim. By saying that **shame comes to the thief**, he seems to equate slander with "stealing" someone's good reputation. This is a reprehensible action that brings **severe condemnation to the double-tongued** or deceitful person. By saying one thing with his mouth while thinking another in his heart, he proves himself to be unworthy of trust.

Given the power of words, one should be vigilant in both **great or small**   5:15–6:1
matters to **not act amiss**—literally, "not remain ignorant" (Hebrew: "do no
harm"). Duplicity creates antagonistic relationships with others so that one
risks becoming **an enemy instead of a friend**. Once a person has tarnished his
own reputation and made for himself a **bad name**, he can no longer be trusted
and draws only **shame and reproach**.

The injunction to **not exalt yourself through your soul's counsel** in the   6:2
Greek text is obscure; perhaps it cautions the reader against rising up in pride
or anger (or lust). The Hebrew, "Do not fall into the hand of your soul," sounds
like a warning against giving in to unruly passions (NRSV: "Do not fall into the
grip of passion"). Those who get carried away by a hot temper or uncontrolled
lust lose control of themselves. Ben Sira illustrates this vividly as the soul being
torn in pieces by unruly passions **like a bull** that wreaks havoc around it.

Ben Sira develops the same point with a different metaphor of the soul as a   6:3–4
tree. The person with raging passions will **devour** his own **leaves** and **destroy**
his fruit, leaving the soul barren and fruitless like a **withered tree**, in contrast
to the wise person who is like a tree that "yields its fruit in its season" (Ps 1:3).
The person with an **evil soul**, who lacks self-mastery and is driven by his passions, tends to act erratically and foolishly. Such a person earns no respect but
becomes **the laughingstock of his enemies**.

Reflection and Application (5:1–6:4)

The Catechism explains that there are two kinds of presumption: "Either
man presumes upon his own capacities (hoping to be able to save himself
without help from on high), or he presumes upon God's almighty power or
his mercy (hoping to obtain his forgiveness without conversion and glory
without merit)" (Catechism 2092). In both cases, presumption is a sin against
hope, which acknowledges that one cannot fully respond to divine love by one's
own powers. The hopeful person must have *both* a confident trust in God's
mercy *and* an appropriate fear of offending him and incurring punishment
(Catechism 2090).

II.D. Authentic Friendship (6:5–17)

> [5]**A pleasant voice multiplies friends** *and softens enemies,*
>   **and a gracious tongue multiplies courtesies.**
> [6]**Let those that are at peace with you be many,**
>   **but let your advisers be one in a thousand.**
> [7]**When you gain a friend, gain him through testing,**
>   **and do not trust him hastily.**

⁸For there is a friend who is such at his own convenience,
    but will not stand by you in your day of trouble.
⁹And there is a friend who changes into an enemy,
    and will disclose a quarrel to your disgrace.
¹⁰And there is a friend who is a table companion,
    but will not stand by you in your day of trouble.
¹¹In prosperity he will make himself your equal,
    and be bold with your servants;
¹²but if you are brought low he will turn against you,
    and will hide himself from your presence.
¹³Keep yourself far from your enemies,
    and be on guard toward your friends.
¹⁴A faithful friend is a sturdy shelter:
    he that has found one has found a treasure.
¹⁵There is nothing so precious as a faithful friend,
    and no scales can measure his excellence.
¹⁶A faithful friend is an elixir of life;
    and those who fear the Lord will find him.
¹⁷Whoever fears the Lord directs his friendship aright,
    for as he is, so is his neighbor also.

OT: Pss 41:9; 55:12–13; Prov 17:17; 18:24; 19:4
NT: John 13:18; 15:13–15
Catechism: chaste friendship, 2347

6:5–6   Ben Sira begins the first of several discourses on friendship—a topic of great interest to him.[2] Good friendships are essential to a good life. One must therefore choose friends wisely, for not everyone who claims to be a friend is sincere. On the one hand, it is good to speak with a **pleasant voice** (literally, "a sweet throat"), kindly and gently to all. The affable, courteous person **multiplies friends** and, the †Vulgate adds, *softens enemies* (in contrast to the "double-tongued sinner" who multiplies enemies, 6:1–4). **A gracious tongue** that speaks well of others (in contrast to the slanderer who lies in ambush with his tongue, 5:14) **multiplies courtesies** that others extend to him in return, or "multiplies those who wish you well" (Hebrew). It is good, therefore, to have many friendly acquaintances who **are at peace with you**. Yet the close **advisers** that you trust should be few—**one in a thousand**, says Ben Sira hyperbolically.

6:7–8   How should people choose their friends? **Through testing,** says Ben Sira. Just as Lady Wisdom tests the loyalty of her followers (4:17), so you should test the loyalty and worthiness of character of an acquaintance by considering how he (or she) acts in difficult or uncomfortable situations. Until then, you should **not trust him hastily** until he has demonstrated his trustworthiness (19:4).

2. Sir 9:10–16; 12:8–13:1; 19:13–17; 22:19–26; 27:16–21; 37:1–6.

Ben Sira now warns against false friends. The "fair-weather friend" is friendly **at his own convenience** (literally, "in his time") when he has something to gain from the friendship, but he disappears **in your day of trouble**, when you are in difficulty and he no longer benefits from your company (Prov 18:24).

Even worse is the case when a presumed **friend** becomes hostile and **changes**   6:9–10 **into an enemy** (Pss 41:9; 55:12–13; John 13:18). True friends are able to vigorously disagree while still respecting each other and keeping the disagreement to themselves. A false friend, however, will turn to gossip and slander and **disclose a quarrel** to others, exposing you to **disgrace**. Friends typically enjoy eating and drinking together. The false friend will readily take advantage of hospitality offered to him and be a willing **table companion**, but again (echoing v. 8), **will not stand by you in your day of trouble** (see Prov 19:4).

Verses 11 and 12—forming an antithetic †parallelism—reveal the false friend's   6:11–13 duplicity. In good times, when you enjoy **prosperity**, **he will make himself your equal** (literally, "he will be as you") and even make himself at home, being **bold with your servants** and ordering them around. In hard times, however, when **you are brought low** (Hebrew: "if evil overtakes you") through illness, financial hardship, or some other adversity, the fair-weather friend will show no interest in sharing your afflictions and **will hide himself** from you. In other words, when life is good, he says, "What is yours, is mine," but when life gets tough, "What is yours, is yours." The theme of the righteous man abandoned by his friends in his hour of greatest need is common in Scripture (Job 19:19; Ps 41:9; Mark 14:50). Thus, one should approach all people with prudence and caution: while **enemies** should be avoided altogether, one should even be **on guard** toward **friends** until they have proven themselves trustworthy.

Following his warning against false friends, Ben Sira now praises the value   6:14–15 of a true friend. **A faithful friend is a sturdy shelter** who protects those whom he or she loves from threats and harm. As much as the fair-weather friend is to be avoided, the loyal friend is to be cherished as **a treasure**—rare, **precious**, and immensely valuable—like wisdom (Prov 8:18). That **no scales can measure his excellence** means that his worth cannot be weighed: it is more than money can buy.

The **faithful friend** is also **an elixir of life**—that is, "life-saving medicine"   6:16–17 (NRSV) or "a bundle of life" (Hebrew). The life-giving power of friendship alludes to the identity of wisdom as a "tree of life" (Prov 3:18) and implies that wisdom is found in good friendships, since both contribute to human well-being. We see another connection between friendship and wisdom in their correlation with the fear of the Lord: just as those who fear the Lord find wisdom (Sir 1:14), so **those who fear the Lord will find** a faithful friend. Both friendship and wisdom are gifts from God to those who fear him. Yet one who **fears the Lord** does not simply find faithful friends as a reward for his piety. The fear of the Lord also **directs his friendship aright** so that he pursues wisdom in friendships and learns how to be a loyal friend to others. He understands that **as he is, so is his neighbor also**. By loving his neighbor as himself (Lev 19:18; Matt 19:19), the one who fears the Lord establishes himself as a faithful friend.

Reflection and Application (6:5–17)

Many young people today long for authentic friendship. Yet many have also been burned by false friends who may have taken advantage of them or did not have their best interests in mind. Like Ben Sira, the ancient Greek philosopher Aristotle valued friendship. He wrote that "without friends, no one would choose to live, though he had all other goods."[3] Yet what is it that people love in friendship? Aristotle determined that people love what is useful, pleasant, or good in their friends. Accordingly, there are three types of friendships: friendship of utility, friendship of pleasure, and friendship of virtue. Friends of utility "love" their friends because they are useful. Friends of pleasure "love" their friends because it is enjoyable to be around them. Obviously, a person who loves his friends for the sake of utility or pleasure does not really love *them*; he "loves" them only insofar as they are useful or pleasant to *himself*. Such friendships are typically short-lived, for if one party ceases to be useful or pleasant, the other ceases to love him.[4] Aristotle's friends of utility or pleasure look a lot like Ben Sira's fair-weather friend.

On the other hand, friends who love each other for their own sake and not for any kind of gain are true friends. This is friendship for the good, or friendship of virtue. Such a friendship is rare but long-lasting and even permanent. As Prov 17:17 notes, "A friend loves at all times." This means that while evil persons may be temporary "friends" of utility or pleasure (because they gain some mutual advantage), only good people can be true and lasting friends, because true friendship desires the true good of the other.

Rabbinic tradition expresses the same idea: "If love depends on some [transitory] thing, and the [transitory] thing passes away, the love passes away too; but if it does not depend on some [transitory] thing it will never pass away."[5]

---

3. Aristotle, *Nicomachean Ethics* 8.1 (1155a), in *The Works of Aristotle*, vol. 9, ed. W. D. Ross (Oxford: Clarendon, 1925).
4. Aristotle, *Nicomachean Ethics* 8.3 (1156a; Ross, *Works of Aristotle*).
5. Mishnah, *Avot* 5:16 (Danby, *Mishnah*, 457).

Part III

Sirach 6:18–14:19

In his third poem on wisdom, Ben Sira revisits the idea that wisdom initially appears harsh to the uninitiated and that pursuing her requires great effort at first; yet she proves to be well worth it in the end (6:18–37). He offers miscellaneous advice for right conduct toward God and neighbor in public life, largely communicated in the form of negative admonitions ("do not . . . ") and based on the fundamental principle "do good, avoid evil" (7:1–17). He then turns to private life, offering counsel on household management, including a man's duties to his friends, family, and servants, as well as to priests and the poor (7:18–36). Nineteen other negative admonitions follow on relating prudently to the rich and powerful, sinners and penitents, the elderly and the deceased, and the wise and the foolish (8:1–19). Further advice is then offered on relationships with women, friends, sinners, and acquaintances (9:1–18). He also discusses wise leadership: Good leaders must rule with the awareness that they are subject to God's rule. Vices such as lack of discipline, anger, and pride must be diligently avoided, for they have led to the demise of many rulers and governments (10:1–11:1). The wise person should also avoid making hasty judgments based on the appearances of things either seen or heard (11:2–9), and should trust in God's providence in financial matters (11:10–28). More advice follows on how to discern friends from enemies (11:29–12:18), on dealing cautiously with the rich and powerful (13:1–14:2), and on using wealth wisely and liberally (14:3–19).

III.A. Lady Wisdom's Discipline as Path to Joy (6:18–37)

> [18]My son, from your youth up choose instruction,
>   and until you are old you will keep finding wisdom.
> [19]Come to her like one who plows and sows,
>   and wait for her good harvest.

For in her service you will toil a little while,
    and soon you will eat of her produce.
²⁰She seems very harsh to the uninstructed;
    a weakling will not remain with her.
²¹She will weigh him down like a heavy testing stone,
    and he will not be slow to cast her off.
²²For wisdom is like her name,
    and is not manifest to many.

²³Listen, my son, and accept my judgment;
    do not reject my counsel.
²⁴Put your feet into her chains,
    and your neck into her collar.
²⁵Put your shoulder under her and carry her,
    and do not fret under her bonds.
²⁶Come to her with all your soul,
    and keep her ways with all your might.
²⁷Search out and seek, and she will become known to you;
    and when you get hold of her, do not let her go.
²⁸For at last you will find the rest she gives,
    and she will be changed into joy for you.
²⁹Then her chains will become for you a strong protection,
    and her collar a glorious robe.
³⁰Her yoke is a golden ornament,
    and her bonds are a cord of blue.
³¹You will wear her like a glorious robe,
    and put her on like a crown of gladness.

³²If you are willing, my son, you will be taught,
    and if you apply yourself you will become clever.
³³If you love to listen you will gain knowledge,
    and if you incline your ear you will become wise.
³⁴Stand in the assembly of the elders.
    Who is wise? Cling to him.
³⁵Be ready to listen to every narrative,
    and do not let wise proverbs escape you.
³⁶If you see an intelligent man, visit him early;
    let your foot wear out his doorstep.
³⁷Reflect on the statutes of the Lord,
    and meditate at all times on his commandments.
It is he who will give insight to your mind,
    and your desire for wisdom will be granted.

OT: Prov 1:2–7; 3:11–12; 4:9, 13
NT: Matt 7:13–14; 11:29–30; Heb 12:5–11
Catechism: way of the cross, 2015; education of children, 2223

The fatherly address **My son** marks the beginning of a new unit. A child is not   6:18–19
normally wise **from youth**. Wisdom is a habit that is formed slowly after years
spent in restraining one's passions, fostering a virtuous life, and studying God's
law. Yet a child can **choose instruction** (Greek *paideia*)—education, training,
or discipline—to set out early in life on the path to find **wisdom**. Still, one
never "graduates" in this pursuit. The diligent disciple continues to discover her
until **old** age (literally, "until gray hairs"). The search for wisdom is a lifelong
quest. Like a farmer who **plows and sows** in the fields, then patiently waits
for a **good harvest**, one who pursues wisdom must **toil a little while** at her
service through diligent study and character formation until he can **eat of her
produce**—that is, enjoy the benefits she yields. This requires a long process of
growth and maturity.

Ben Sira returns to the topic of wisdom's rigor (4:17). She seems **harsh to**   6:20–22
the uninstructed—that is, her demands seem too difficult to the undisciplined.
Indeed, she is not for the faint of heart: **a weakling** (literally, "one with no
heart") who lacks determination and courage **will not remain with her** very
long. The feeble man cannot bear the weight of her discipline and perceives
her as **a heavy testing stone**; unable to bear this burden, he is eager to **cast her
off**. **For wisdom** (Hebrew: "discipline") **is like her name**: this obscure saying
is based on a Hebrew pun. In Hebrew the word for "discipline" (*musar*) also
means "withdrawn" or "far removed." Thus, wisdom or discipline seems distant,
far removed and is **not manifest to many** because few are willing to submit
themselves to her demands.

Listen, my son marks yet another unit. Ben Sira encourages his disciple not   6:23–26
to be daunted by wisdom's discipline but to follow his **counsel** and persevere
through the challenges of following her. The committed disciple must submit
to wisdom as a slave submits to a master, or as an animal submits to its yoke
(51:26). The image of **feet** bound by **chains**, of the **neck** restrained by a **collar**,
and of the **shoulder** carrying wisdom illustrates the need to willingly accept
her **bonds**—the discipline of her commandments. If you desire to find wisdom,
you must **come to her with all your soul, and keep her ways with all your
might**. This echoes the commandment of the †*Shema*, exhorting Israel to love
God "with all your soul and with all your might" (Deut 6:5).

Having emphasized the struggle involved in pursuing wisdom, Ben Sira now   6:27–28
assures his readers that the pursuit is well worth it. She will not always remain
so elusive but **will become known** to the one who perseveres in seeking her,
revealing herself and even *giving* herself to him so that he can lay **hold of her**.
When this occurs, he must **not let her go** lest he lose her again (Prov 4:13; Song
3:4). The words **at last** reaffirm that the long struggle in searching for wisdom
is not perpetual: the disciple who labors to find will finally know her as she
really is. He will **find the rest she gives**, while the pain caused by her previously
harsh demeanor **will be changed into joy** (see Matt 11:29).

6:29–31 These verses complete the imagery of 6:24–25. Signs of slavery and bondage are transformed into symbols of strength and beauty. Wisdom's **chains** no longer bind but provide **strong protection**—or a "sturdy shelter" like the faithful friend (6:14). **Her collar** no longer restrains but turns into a **glorious robe**—like the robe of the high priest (50:11). Her **yoke** and **bonds** no longer evoke slavery but have changed into a **golden ornament** and royal **cord of blue**—recalling the tassels worn by Jews to remind them of God's commandments (Num 15:38–39). The metaphor of "wearing wisdom" **like a glorious robe** (Sir 27:8) and putting her on **like a crown of gladness** (1:11; 15:6; Prov 4:9; 16:31) indicate that the persevering and disciplined wisdom seeker will enjoy the glory of the priesthood and splendor of royalty.

6:32–33 No one can be compelled to become wise. In this new unit, Ben Sira emphasizes how every disciple must freely choose to seek wisdom. This is expressed by the repeated use of conditional clauses: Only **if you are willing** will you **be taught**, disciplined, and educated. Only **if you apply yourself** (literally, "if you give over your soul") and put your mind and heart to it can you **become clever**. Only **if you love to listen** will you grow in **knowledge** and wisdom (Prov 8:32–33).

6:34–35 Yet not every discourse is of equal value. It is best to keep company with **the assembly of the elders**—wiser, older people with more life experience, or people in authority. The disciple should **cling** to the wise person and his teachings as a man clings to his wife (Gen 2:24). While the Hebrew says that the disciple should be disposed to **listen to every narrative**, the Greek specifies "every godly discourse" (NRSV), or the speech spoken by godly people. One should not miss the opportunity to learn **wise proverbs**—short, memorable utterances—caught in conversations with the wise.

6:36–37 The search for wisdom should not be compartmentalized or restricted to the classroom. The disciple must be proactive and determined to pursue her in the company of the wise at every hour of the day. Ben Sira expresses this dedication hyperbolically, with the disciple seeking out **an intelligent man** by visiting him **early** in the morning and wearing out **his doorstep**. Ben Sira concludes this section by returning to the ultimate, divine source of wisdom: the †Torah. To find wisdom the disciple must **reflect on the statutes of the Lord** (Hebrew: "reflect on the fear of the Most High") and **meditate at all times on his commandments** (see Ps 1:2). Paradoxically, after encouraging his students to invest so much effort in the pursuit of wisdom, he adds that acquiring wisdom is ultimately *not* only the result of human effort but primarily a gift from God. It is God, ultimately, who will **give insight** to the human **mind** (Hebrew; Greek: he will "strengthen your heart," ESV-CE) and grant a person's **desire for wisdom**. The attainment of wisdom depends on human effort cooperating with divine grace (Catechism 2022).

Reflection and Application (6:18–37)

The idea that wisdom first appears as a heavy yoke and only later bestows her rewards to those who have the courage to bear her discipline is echoed in other Jewish and Christian texts. Rabbinic tradition also portrays the †Torah as a yoke. Willingly taking on the yoke of the Torah frees one from the yoke of secular rule and worldly cares: "Whoever accepts upon himself the yoke of Torah will be relieved from the yoke of government and the yoke of worldly concerns; but whoever throws off the yoke of Torah from himself will be burdened with the yoke of government and the yoke of worldly concerns."[1] According to the †Talmud, the Torah grants protection and health to whoever occupies himself with it, because it is an "elixir of life to the whole of Israel's body, 'and healing to all his flesh' (Prov 4:22)."[2]

Jesus also employs the yoke metaphor to describe both the demands of Christian discipleship and the freedom that it offers, assuring those who take on his yoke: "You will find rest for your souls. For my yoke is easy, and my burden is light" (Matt 11:29–30). While some choices appear easy at first but eventually lead to destruction, the hard path of following Christ through discipline and self-denial ultimately leads to life (Matt 7:13–14).

III.B. Do Good, Avoid Evil (7:1–17)

¹Do no evil, and evil will never befall you.
  ²Stay away from wrong, and it will turn away from you.
³My son, do not sow the furrows of injustice,
  and you will not reap a sevenfold crop.

⁴Do not seek from the Lord the highest office,
  nor the seat of honor from the king.
⁵Do not assert your righteousness before the Lord,
  nor display your wisdom before the king.
⁶Do not seek to become a judge,
  lest you be unable to remove iniquity,
lest you be partial to a powerful man,
  and thus put a blot on your integrity.
⁷Do not offend against the public,
  and do not disgrace yourself among the people.

⁸Do not commit a sin twice;
  even for one you will not go unpunished.

---

1. Mishnah, *Avot* 3:5. *The Mishnah: A New Integrated Translation and Commentary*, 2007, https://www.echok.com/mishnah/nezikin_vol_2/Avot3.pdf.
2. Babylonian Talmud, *Erubin* 54a. All quotes from the Babylonian Talmud are from Jacob Neusner, *The Babylonian Talmud: A Translation and Commentary* (Peabody, MA: Hendrickson, 2011); here, 3:264.

⁹Do not say, "He will consider the multitude of my gifts,
  and when I make an offering to the Most High God he will
  accept it."
¹⁰Do not be fainthearted in your prayer,
  nor neglect to give alms.

¹¹Do not ridicule a man who is bitter in soul,
  for there is One who abases and exalts.
¹²Do not devise a lie against your brother,
  nor do the like to a friend.
¹³Refuse to utter any lie,
  for the habit of lying serves no good.
¹⁴Do not prattle in the assembly of the elders,
  nor repeat yourself in your prayer.

¹⁵Do not hate toilsome labor,
  or farm work, which were created by the Most High.
¹⁶Do not count yourself among the crowd of sinners;
  remember that wrath does not delay.
¹⁷Humble yourself greatly,
  for the punishment of the ungodly is fire and worms.

OT: Pss 34:14; 37:27
NT: Luke 1:51–53; 1 Pet 3:11
Catechism: doing good and avoiding evil, 1706; human authority and governance, 1897–904; participation in public life, 1913–17

7:1–3   Doing good and avoiding evil (Pss 34:14; 37:27; 1 Pet 3:11) is the most basic precept of the moral life, inscribed by God on the human heart and echoed in every person's conscience. By following this law, one reflects the image of God and expresses the dignity of the human person.[3] Ben Sira expresses here the classic law of retribution: **Do no evil, and evil will never befall you.** Of course, life does not always quite work that way. While Scripture promises blessings to those who obey God's law and threatens curses to those who disobey it (Deut 28; Prov 10:16; 12:14), it is also full of laments asking God why the just suffer and the wicked prosper (Job 21:7–13; Jer 12:1–2). Though it is true that evil men may flourish for a time, they are eventually consumed by their own wickedness (Ps 37:14–15). And while the just cannot avoid suffering, God can use this suffering for good (Gen 50:20; Rom 8:28). Thus, the first priority of the righteous should be to **stay away from wrong.** Although they can still suffer evil from others (Eccles 8:14), by avoiding wickedness they are able to guard themselves from the more dangerous moral evil (Luke 12:4–5), so that by resisting it, it will **turn away** from them (James 4:7; 1 Pet 5:8–10). Ben Sira makes the same

---

3. *Gaudium et Spes* 16; Catechism 1706.

point in verse 3 with a metaphor of sowing and reaping evil (Job 4:8; Prov 22:8; Hosea 10:12; Gal 6:8). He warns against sowing in **the furrows of injustice**. The furrows—strips of earth that have been turned by the plow—here symbolize situations where only injustice can grow. One should stay clear of such fields, lest one reap **a sevenfold crop** of trouble and woes.

Ben Sira now cautions his readers against vanity or conceit, urging them **7:4–5** instead to pursue humility (Prov 3:34; James 4:6; 1 Pet 5:5). He discourages the pursuit of political power, even when asking **the Lord** for **the highest office**, or **the king** for a **seat of honor**. Although those who seek positions of influence may couch their motivation in altruistic or noble terms, often a thirst for power lurks behind this desire. The righteous should seek to serve others rather than rule over them (Matt 20:21–28). Verse 5, which follows the same parallel structure as verse 4, warns against boasting of one's **righteousness before the Lord** or one's **wisdom before the king**. God will not be convinced of our own goodness, because "no man living is righteous" before him (Ps 143:2; see also Job 9:20; Ps 14:3; Eccles 7:20). Likewise, showing off before human rulers is incompatible with wisdom.

The exhortation to avoid the wrong kind of ambition is extended to the **7:6–7** legal realm. One should not **seek to become a judge** (Hebrew: "a ruler"), for not everyone has the moral strength to **remove iniquity** and put an end to injustice. A judge who lacks inner strength is vulnerable to being **partial to a powerful man** and may be corrupted by receiving bribes or favoring people of influence, thus putting **a blot** on his **integrity**. Any offense **against the public** and the common good would **disgrace** the judge's reputation **among the people**.

Ben Sira returns to the topic of presumption. Some think that they can **7:8–10** **commit a sin twice**—that is, over and over—presuming that by bringing a **multitude of gifts** or **an offering** to **God**, he will accept these as atonement and overlook their offenses. As stated earlier (5:4–7), such a presumptuous attitude only stores up God's wrath, for no sin goes unpunished. The Lord does not look kindly on sacrifices offered without a contrite spirit (Ps 51:16–17; Prov 21:27; Isa 1:11–16; Amos 5:21–24). For this reason, it is all the more important to **not be fainthearted in your prayer** but to pray—presumably here a prayer of confession and repentance (Mark 11:24; Luke 18:1–14; James 1:6)—with earnestness, perseverance, and faith, while continuing to **give alms**, since these have the power to atone for sins (Sir 3:30).

The topic shifts back to interpersonal relationships. The wise person should **7:11** not **ridicule** or mock **a man who is bitter in soul**, humiliated by poverty or adverse circumstances. For the Lord is the **One who abases and exalts**: he bestows either adversity or prosperity on each person and is able to reverse the situation at any time (2 Sam 22:28; Ps 147:6; Luke 1:51–53). Thus, as Proverbs says, "He who mocks the poor insults his Maker" (Prov 17:5).

Torah Study and Work

LIVING TRADITION

Ben Sira's respect for manual work is reflected in the rabbinic writings: "Excellent is the study of the Law together with worldly occupation, for toil in them both puts sin out of mind. But all study of the Law without [worldly] labour comes to naught and brings sin in its train."[a] The †Talmud adds: "Anyone who does not teach his son a trade is as though he trains him to be a gangster."[b] As valuable as religious study may be in itself, it must be balanced with work (2 Thess 3:10–12).

a. Mishnah, *Avot* 2:2, in Herbert Danby, trans., *The Mishnah* (Oxford: Oxford University Press, 1933), 447.
b. Babylonian Talmud, *Qiddushin* 29a (Neusner, *Babylonian Talmud*, 12:127).

7:12–13   Having already advocated for speaking the truth (4:25, 28) and avoiding duplicity (5:14), Ben Sira now plainly warns against lying, particularly against a **brother** or **friend**. St. Paul makes a similar point: "Let every one speak the truth with his neighbor, for we are members one of another" (Eph 4:25). The wise disciple should avoid lying altogether, not only because it is an offense against the eighth commandment (Exod 20:16), but because a **habit of lying** leads to a life of deceit, which never serves any **good**. See the Reflection and Application section for Sir 4:20–31 (p. 82).

7:14–15   Still on the topic of controlling one's tongue, a wise person should **not prattle** or engage in idle chatter **in the assembly of the elders** (6:34). Neither should one **repeat** oneself in vain repetition in **prayer**, advice found elsewhere in Scripture (Eccles 5:2; Matt 6:7). A good antidote to idle talk is manual work, which Ben Sira holds in high esteem—even for the scholar. One should **not hate toilsome labor, or farm work** because these **were created by the Most High**—likely an allusion to Gen 2:15, where God entrusts the task of tilling the ground to Adam, or to Gen 3:17–19, where this work becomes a heavy burden after the fall.

7:16–17   **Do not count yourself among the crowd of sinners** does not mean "do not consider yourself a sinner" but rather means "do not join the company of sinners"—for divine **wrath** and judgment will not be postponed indefinitely. Ben Sira concludes this section on arrogance and presumption by proposing the contrary virtue to those vices: **Humble yourself greatly**, or do not think too highly of yourself, **for the punishment of the ungodly is fire and worms** (see Acts 12:23). This points to the corruption of the body after death and likely alludes to Isa 66:24, which depicts the bodies of the wicked as given over to worms and fire—a terrifying image that would eventually become identified with eternal damnation (Jdt 16:17; Mark 9:47–48).

Reflection and Application (7:1–17)

Ben Sira's warning not to seek positions of power (7:4–6) strikes at one of the deepest temptations of the fallen human heart: the prideful ambition to "be like God, knowing good and evil" (Gen 3:5)—which often comes with a drive to *determine* what is good and evil on the basis of one's own opinions and desires, and sometimes to impose this arbitrary morality upon others. St. John calls "pride of life" (1 John 2:16) the perennial ambition to "be like God," but "without God, before God, and not in accordance with God" (Catechism 398).

C. S. Lewis warns that one of the permanent mainsprings of human action is the desire to be part of some privileged "Inner Ring" of society. Being a member of this Ring grants not only privileges of "power, money, liberty to break rules, avoidance of routine duties, evasion of discipline" but also a "delicious sense of secret intimacy" in the knowledge that one belongs to the exclusive, select few who know better than all the rest.[4] Lewis suggests that of all passions, "the passion for the Inner Ring is most skillful in making a man who is not yet a very bad man do very bad things."[5]

When Jesus resisted the devil's temptation to throw himself down from the pinnacle of the temple, refusing to tempt God by asserting his divine power over the laws of nature (Luke 4:9–12), he rejected the pride of life and the temptation of the Inner Ring. Instead, having been born under the law (Gal 4:4), he humbly took the form of a servant and became obedient unto death (Phil 2:5–8) for the sake of our salvation. All the more should his disciples not seek positions of power out of selfish ambition or conceit, but "in humility count others better than yourselves," with each one looking "not only to his own interests, but also to the interests of others" (Phil 2:3–4).

III.C. On Domestic Life: Duties to Family, Priests, and the Poor (7:18–36)

> [18]Do not exchange a friend for money,
>   or a real brother for the gold of Ophir.
> [19]Do not deprive yourself of a wise and good wife,
>   for her charm is worth more than gold.
> [20]Do not abuse a servant who performs his work faithfully,
>   or a hired laborer who devotes himself to you.
> [21]Let your soul love an intelligent servant;
>   do not withhold from him his freedom.

---

4. C. S. Lewis, "The Inner Ring," in *The Weight of Glory* (New York: HarperCollins, 1980), 151.
5. Lewis, "Inner Ring," 154.

²²Do you have cattle? Look after them;
  if they are profitable to you, keep them.
²³Do you have children? Discipline them,
  and make them obedient from their youth.
²⁴Do you have daughters? Be concerned for their chastity,
  and do not show yourself too indulgent with them.
²⁵Give a daughter in marriage; you will have finished a great task.
  But give her to a man of understanding.

²⁶If you have a wife who pleases you, do not cast her out;
  but do not trust yourself to one whom you detest.
²⁷With all your heart honor your father,
  and do not forget the birth pangs of your mother.
²⁸Remember that through your parents you were born;
  and what can you give back to them that equals their gift to you?

²⁹With all your soul fear the Lord,
  and honor his priests.
³⁰With all your might love your Maker,
  and do not forsake his ministers.
³¹Fear the Lord and honor the priest,
  and give him his portion, as is commanded you:
the first fruits, the guilt offering, the gift of the shoulders,
  the sacrifice of sanctification, and the first fruits of the holy things.

³²Stretch forth your hand to the poor,
  so that your blessing may be complete.
³³Give graciously to all the living,
  and withhold not kindness from the dead.
³⁴Do not fail those who weep,
  but mourn with those who mourn.
³⁵Do not shrink from visiting a sick man,
  because for such deeds you will be loved.
³⁶In all you do, remember the end of your life,
  and then you will never sin.

OT: Lev 19:18; Deut 5:16; 24:14
NT: Eph 5:21–6:9; Col 3:18–4:1
Catechism: the domestic church, 1655–58; family and society, 2207–13; filial piety, 2214–18

7:18–19   A close **friend** (6:15) is like a **real brother** and has priceless value. One should **not** trade such a friendship **for money** or any other material benefit, even the famed **gold of Ophir** (a place of uncertain location known for its fine gold; 1 Kings 9:28; Ps 45:9; Isa 13:12). Likewise, **do not deprive yourself of a wise and good wife**; or following the Hebrew, "do not dismiss" (NRSV) or "depart from" (ESV-CE) a wise and good wife, for finding her is like finding wisdom (Prov 18:22; 31:10), and **her charm**—her gracious character (NABRE, NJB)—**is worth more than gold** or "better than jewels" (Hebrew) (see Prov 31:10).

The †Torah commands the Israelites to release their Hebrew servants after six years (Exod 21:2; Deut 15:12) and be kind to all slaves (Deut 24:14). Ben Sira goes beyond this injunction, not only advising his readers not to **abuse a faithful servant** or dedicated **hired laborer** but also instructing them to **love an intelligent servant** (the Hebrew adds "as your soul"), in addition to granting him **his freedom** at the fitting time (Philem 10–16).
7:20–21

Ben Sira offers more advice pertaining to domestic life, approaching four topics (cattle, children, daughters, wives) with the question "**Do you have . . . ?**" (vv. 22–26). Those who own **cattle** should **look after them**, in conformity with the Torah's instructions to treat animals kindly (Deut 22:4; 25:4; Prov 12:10; 27:23). Good fathers should **discipline** their **children** (as wisdom does, Sir 4:17) and **make them obedient** (literally, "bend their necks") **from their youth**—a recurring topic in wisdom literature (30:1–13; Prov 23:13).
7:22–23

Ben Sira also urges fathers of **daughters** to be **concerned for their chastity** (literally, "their body") by protecting them and their virginity until marriage. A father should not be **too indulgent with them** (literally, "and do not let your face shine on them"). While this advice may sound harsh, it is perhaps intended for the wayward daughters of 26:10–12; 42:9–14 and is an expression of wise parenting. A father in Ben Sira's day was responsible for giving his **daughter in marriage**; he advises entrusting her to a **man of understanding**, in contrast to other possible qualities, such as wealth, social status, or physical appearance.
7:24–25

The advice to **not cast out** (or divorce) a **wife who pleases you** (literally, "a wife according to your soul") seems self-evident. In Hebrew the command is more sweeping: "Do you have a wife? Do not abhor her." By contrast, a man should not **trust** one whom he detests (literally, "a hated wife"; see Deut 21:15–17), either because she has proven herself untrustworthy or because he cannot count on her loyalty.
7:26

Verses 27–30 echo the †*Shema* (Deut 6:4–5), which enjoins Israel to love God **with all your heart . . . soul . . . might**. Applying the same language to parents, priests, and ministers implies that they act as God's representatives and are due a corresponding honor (see the sidebar "Honoring God by Honoring Parents," p. 66). Ben Sira briefly revisits the commandment to honor your father and your mother (3:1–16; Exod 20:12; Deut 5:16). **Honor your father** is literally "give glory to your father." **Do not forget the birth pangs of your mother** reminds the reader that she suffered much to bring him into the world (Gen 3:16). Children exercise the virtue of piety when they **remember** that they owe a debt of gratitude to their **parents** for giving them life, a **gift** that no one will ever be able to fully repay (Catechism 2215).
7:27–30

The sphere of concern is expanded from household management to include the Lord's priests and ministers, who mediate his presence to the society and family. The wise person should not only **fear the Lord** with reverence and awe but also **honor his priests** (Hebrew: "sanctify his priests," i.e., regard them as holy)—the descendants of Aaron who ministered and offered sacrifices in the Jerusalem temple. Still echoing the *Shema*, verse 30 parallels verse 29 with the same structure and thought: **With all your might love your Maker** or "the one who made you." The commandment to **not forsake his ministers** alludes to the obligation to provide financially for priests and Levites as mandated by the law (Num 18:8–19; Deut 12:19; 18:1–5).

7:31   The Torah commands Israelites to **give** to priests and Levites a **portion** of their harvests and sacrifices. This includes the **first fruits** of their harvest (Num 18:13; Deut 18:4), the meat of **the guilt offering** made in atonement for sins (Lev 7:1–7), **the gift of the shoulders** or heave offering (Deut 18:3), **the sacrifice of sanctification** (possibly the grain offering, Lev 2:1–16), and **the first fruits of the holy things** (the priest's portion described in Num 18:8–11).

7:32–33   One who manages his household well should also **stretch forth** his **hand** to give generously to **the poor** (3:30–4:10) so that his **blessing may be complete**, as God promises to bless those who give generously (Deut 14:28–29). The Greek of verse 33 (**Give graciously to all the living**) is difficult. It means something like "a gift has grace before all living"—that is, every living person appreciates a gift. One should also not **withhold kindness from the dead** but be gracious to the deceased. Probably what is in view is revering their memory, granting them a dignified burial, and comforting those who mourn their passing.

7:34–35   Being present with those who **weep** when they have experienced loss is a noble act of charity; so is the act of showing sympathy by mourning **with those who mourn** (Rom 12:15). Jewish custom provides for seven days of mourning for the dead (Sir 22:12). Likewise, one should not hesitate to visit **a sick man**. Visiting the sick is one of the corporal works of mercy and an excellent way of fulfilling the commandment to "love your neighbor as yourself" (Lev 19:18). Not only are **such deeds** as described in Sir 7:18–35—extended to friends, servants, animals, children, wives, parents, priests, ministers, the poor, the living, and the dead—praiseworthy in themselves, but the person who diligently carries them out **will be loved** by God and by all. From a Christian perspective, these works of mercy exemplify the golden rule of doing unto others what you would like done to you (Matt 7:12; 25:37–40).

7:36   In a final motivating statement, Ben Sira reminds the reader: **In all you do** (or "in all your words"), **remember the end of your life** (literally, "your last things"), **and then you will never sin**. This is the classic *memento mori* ("remember that you die") saying—a reminder of the inevitability of death. An ancient Jewish tradition makes the same point: "Consider three things and you will not come to sin. Know from where you came, and to where you are going, and before Whom you will have to give an account and reckoning."[6]

Reflection and Application (7:18–36)

By extending familial relations beyond spouse and children to also include friends, servants, animals, priests, and the poor, Ben Sira anticipates the concept of the *family as the domestic church*. Christian families are called to be not insular bubbles closed in on themselves but rather "islands of Christian life in an unbelieving world" and "centers of living, radiant faith" (Catechism 1655–56). Just as Ben Sira promotes harmonious relationships not only in the families of his day but also in all levels of society, so Christians today have the grace and responsibility to make the family "a school of deeper humanity" by showing care and love for the little ones, the sick, and the aged; by serving one another; and by sharing goods, joys, and sorrows in a spirit of sacrifice.[7] Ben Sira upholds the biblical view that, as the "first and vital cell of society," the family has "vital and organic links with society" and is its very foundation.[8] By valuing one's friends, cherishing one's spouse, treating well one's workers, disciplining one's children, honoring one's parents and priests, being generous to the poor, mourning with those who mourn, and visiting the sick, Christian families not only apply Ben Sira's teachings. They also build and develop society through their service of love toward God and neighbor, thus becoming "the most effective means for humanizing and personalizing society."[9]

III.D. Prudence in Relating to Others (8:1–19)

> [1]**Do not contend with a powerful man,**
>   **lest you fall into his hands.**
> [2]**Do not quarrel with a rich man,**
>   **lest his resources outweigh yours;**
> **for gold has ruined many,**
>   **and has perverted the minds of kings.**
> [3]**Do not argue with a chatterer,**
>   **nor heap wood on his fire.**
>
> [4]**Do not jest with an ill-bred person,**
>   **lest your ancestors be disgraced.**

6. Mishnah, *Avot* 3:1. *The Mishnah: A New Integrated Translation and Commentary*, https://www.echok.com/mishnah/nezikin_vol_2/Avot3.pdf. See the Reflection and Application section for 41:1–13 (pp. 300–301).

7. *Gaudium et Spes* 52; John Paul II, Apostolic Constitution *Familiaris Consortio* 21.

8. John Paul II, *Familiaris Consortio* 42 (1981).

9. John Paul II, *Familiaris Consortio* 43.

⁵Do not reproach a man who is turning away from sin;
   remember that we all deserve punishment.
⁶Do not disdain a man when he is old,
   for some of us are growing old.
⁷Do not rejoice over any one's death;
   remember that we all must die.
⁸Do not slight the discourse of the sages,
   but busy yourself with their maxims;
because from them you will gain instruction
   and learn how to serve great men.
⁹Do not disregard the discourse of the aged,
   for they themselves learned from their fathers;
because from them you will gain understanding
   and learn how to give an answer in time of need.

¹⁰Do not kindle the coals of a sinner,
   lest you be burned in his flaming fire.
¹¹Do not get up and leave an insolent fellow,
   lest he lie in ambush against your words.
¹²Do not lend to a man who is stronger than you;
   but if you do lend anything, be as one who has lost it.
¹³Do not give surety beyond your means,
   but if you give surety, be concerned as one who must pay.

¹⁴Do not go to law against a judge,
   for the decision will favor him because of his standing.
¹⁵Do not travel on the road with a foolhardy fellow,
   lest he be burdensome to you;
for he will act as he pleases,
   and through his folly you will perish with him.
¹⁶Do not fight with a wrathful man,
   and do not cross the wilderness with him;
because blood is as nothing in his sight,
   and where no help is at hand, he will strike you down.
¹⁷Do not consult with a fool,
   for he will not be able to keep a secret.
¹⁸In the presence of a stranger do nothing that is to be kept secret,
   for you do not know what he will divulge.
¹⁹Do not reveal your thoughts to every one,
   lest you drive away your good luck.

OT: Lev 19:32; Prov 6:1–5; 15:1, 18; 26:20–22; 29:22
NT: Col 3:8; James 1:19; 3:5–6
Catechism: prudence, 1806; conversion and society, 1886–89

Not all the counsel of wisdom books like Sirach is about morality; some wisdom is simply practical, tips on how to avoid problems and succeed in life. This section of Sirach contains much advice of that kind. Counsels like these are not moral absolutes but rather advice that needs to be weighed and applied with wisdom.

In life, we must choose our battles. While some are worth fighting, others **8:1–3** cannot be won and are best avoided. Ben Sira advises to **not contend with a powerful** or influential **man** because he will surely win and inflict harm upon you if **you fall into his hands**. Likewise, it is futile to **quarrel with a rich man**, for his financial **resources** give him a marked advantage over his opponent. He can use his wealth to pervert justice by bribery and ruin you, **for gold has ruined many** in the past and even **perverted the minds of kings** whose hearts were swayed by the love of gain. It is also pointless to **argue with a chatterer** who only talks and never listens. Disputing with him only heaps **wood on his fire** and gives him still more to talk about (28:8–12; Prov 26:20–22; James 3:5–6).

The wise person should avoid displaying a superior attitude when dealing **8:4–5** with less fortunate people and should conduct himself with humility and nobility of character. **Do not jest**, ridicule, or make fun of **an ill-bred** or uneducated **person, lest your ancestors be disgraced** by his unseemly response. Neither should you **reproach** a repentant **man who is turning away from sin**, for **we all deserve punishment**. The Hebrew reads: "Remember that we are all guilty" (NJB; compare NABRE). A rabbinic saying echoes this principle: "If one was a repentant [sinner], one must not say to him, 'Remember your former deeds.'"[10]

No one should **disdain** the elderly. Scripture often commands us to honor **8:6–7** them (3:12; 25:4–6; Lev 19:32; Wis 4:8–9) for, as Ben Sira adds with a touch of humor, **some of us are growing old**. Neither should one **rejoice over any one's death**—even if this person is a rival or an enemy, or you have something to gain such as an inheritance. For in the end, **we all must die**. The passing of every person should soberly remind us of our own death (Sir 7:36). As the †Vulgate adds, we do not wish *that others should rejoice at our death* (Douay, 8:8).

While verses 4–7 caution readers against looking down on those who seem **8:8** inferior, verses 8–9 warn them not to overlook or ignore those who are wiser. **Do not slight** or disregard **the discourse of the sages**. One should learn to recognize those who are wise and pay attention to **their maxims** or proverbs (6:34–36). Then as now, it is customary for people in the Middle East to sprinkle their speech with proverbs and short wisdom sayings, so that those who listen may **gain instruction** (or "learn discipline") and social skills to **serve great men** or "stand before princes" (Hebrew).

This verse continues the thought initiated in verse 6 on the elderly while **8:9** following the same parallel structure as verse 8. The **discourse of the aged**, like that of the †sages, is to be held in high regard, **for they themselves learned from their fathers**: wisdom is passed down from generation to generation (Deut 4:9;

---

10. Mishnah, *Baba Metzia* 4:10. *The Mishnah: A New Integrated Translation and Commentary*, https://www.echok.com/mishnah/PDFs/Bava%20Metzia%204.pdf.

Oral Law and Apostolic Tradition

BIBLICAL
BACKGROUND

The idea that wisdom is passed down from generation to generation is preserved in the Jewish concept of the Oral Law. The †Mishnah—the oldest compilation of Jewish Oral Law—attests to this idea of transmission going back to Moses: "Moses received the Law from Sinai and committed it to Joshua, and Joshua to the elders, and the elders to the Prophets; and the Prophets committed it to the men of the Great Synagogue."[a] This idea anticipates the Catholic concept of apostolic tradition, by which Christ entrusted his teachings to his apostles, who passed them on to their successors: "What you have heard from me before many witnesses entrust to faithful men who will be able to teach others also" (2 Tim 2:2).[b]

a. Mishnah, *Avot* 1:1 (Danby, *Mishnah*, 446).
b. *Dei Verbum* 7–8; Catechism 75–79.

11:18–19; Job 8:8–10). Why **gain understanding** haphazardly by trial and error when you could learn from the wisdom of the more experienced **how to give an answer in time of need** (Job 12:12)?

8:10–11   In 8:10–19 Ben Sira returns to the topic of not provoking those who can inflict harm (8:1–3). He warns readers not to **kindle the coals of a sinner**, either by approving of his misdeeds or (following the Vulgate; see Douay) by rebuking him, **lest you be burned** in the **fire** of his sin or anger or be tempted to sin yourself. The warning to **not get up and leave an insolent fellow** seems counterintuitive. A more accurate translation may be "Do not rise up to argue" against him, which is close to the Latin: "Do not stand against the face of an injurious person" (Douay, 8:14). In other words, avoid unnecessary conflict with such a person **lest he lie in ambush** to trap you in your words or provoke you into saying something that he could use against you.

8:12–13   Ben Sira now offers advice on lending. It is ill-advised to **lend to a man who is stronger than you** because it may be very difficult to enforce repayment of the debt. If you choose to do so, **be as one who has lost it** because there is no guarantee that the borrower will repay you (Prov 22:7). Giving **surety** occurs when a person wants to borrow money, but the lender requests that someone else cosign, guaranteeing to repay the loan if the borrower fails to do so (Sir 29:14–20; Prov 6:1–5; 11:15; 22:26–27). If you decide to cosign, **do not** commit to an amount **beyond your means**, because you may have to **pay** back the entire loan.

8:14   **Do not go to law** or litigate **against a judge**; this would be like appealing to someone's friends to decide against him. **The decision** in court will surely **favor him** due to **his standing**, and you will have no chance of winning.

Ben Sira next advises on choosing **travel** companions wisely. Travel in the   8:15
ancient world was slow and dangerous. Keeping company with a **foolhardy fellow** (Hebrew: "a cruel man") while on the road was imprudent; such a person
would likely **be burdensome**, and his recklessness would overwhelm you with
trouble. A travel companion lacking self-control acts foolishly **as he pleases**;
if he takes life-threatening risks, he will endanger you as well, and you may
perish with him.

Avoid quarreling with a quick-tempered, **wrathful man** (see Prov 15:18; 26:21;   8:16
29:22). **Do not cross the wilderness with him** may be taken literally; or it may
be a metaphorical way of saying, "Avoid finding yourself alone with him," for
he may resort to violence even to the point of shedding **blood**: when no one is
around and **no help is at hand**, he may well **strike you down** and murder you.

The last three verses of this section deal with discretion when confiding in   8:17–19
others. The wise person should consider carefully to whom he will reveal his
thoughts. Certainly, he should **not consult with a fool**, for a person who lacks
wisdom and prudence is unable to **keep a secret**. A clever Hebrew pun is lost
in translation in verse 18: "Before a stranger [*zar*] make no secret [*raz*]." Do not
reveal anything confidential when a **stranger** is present, whether in public or
private, for **you do not know what he will divulge** and repeat to others. Finally,
do not reveal your thoughts (literally, "your heart") **to every one** (8:19) or more
broadly "to anyone." One should speak discreetly not only in the presence of
fools and strangers but in all circumstances. "Thinking aloud" is rarely a good
idea unless you are in the company of a few trustworthy friends, lest someone
present use your words against you and **drive away your good luck** (Hebrew:
"the good").

Reflection and Application (8:1–19)

How should I relate to others? When should I speak, and when should I remain silent? Whom should I befriend? Which activities are fruitful, and which
are frivolous? Which battles are worth fighting, and which are best avoided?
Answering these questions calls for the virtue of *prudence*. The Catechism defines
prudence as "the virtue that disposes practical reason to discern our true good
in every circumstance and to choose the right means of achieving it" (Catechism
1806). Following Aristotle, St. Thomas Aquinas calls prudence "right reason applied to action."[11] It is known as "the charioteer of the virtues," because it guides
the other virtues and the judgment of conscience so that we are able to choose
the good and avoid evil. Exercising prudence requires engaging its various parts

11. Thomas Aquinas, *Summa Theologiae* II-II q. 47 a. 2; compare Catechism 1806. Quotations from
the *Summa* are taken from *Summa Theologica*, trans. Fathers of the English Dominican Province (New
York: Benziger Bros., 1948).

by drawing upon various abilities and virtues. These include *memory* (drawing from past experience), *understanding* (having a good grasp of reality), *docility* (being willing to learn from others), *shrewdness* (quickly estimating what is right in any situation), *reason* (thinking rightly), *foresight* (anticipating potential future consequences of my actions), *circumspection* (perceiving what is most suitable here and now), and *caution* (avoiding any potential evil that may arise out of my decision).[12] A prudent person is able to quickly and intuitively consider these dimensions while navigating the many decisions of life.

III.E. Relationships with Women, Friends, Sinners, and Neighbors (9:1–18)

> [1]Do not be jealous of the wife of your bosom,
>   and do not teach her an evil lesson to your own hurt.
> [2]Do not give yourself to a woman
>   so that she gains mastery over your strength.
> [3]Do not go to meet a loose woman,
>   lest you fall into her snares.
> [4]Do not associate with a woman singer,
>   lest you be caught in her intrigues.
> [5]Do not look intently at a virgin,
>   lest you stumble and incur penalties for her.
> [6]Do not give yourself to harlots
>   lest you lose your inheritance.
> [7]Do not look around in the streets of a city,
>   nor wander about in its deserted sections.
> [8]Turn away your eyes from a shapely woman,
>   and do not look intently at beauty belonging to another;
> many have been misled by a woman's beauty,
>   and by it passion is kindled like a fire.
> [9]Never dine with another man's wife,
>   nor revel with her at wine;
> lest your heart turn aside to her,
>   and in blood you be plunged into destruction.
>
> [10]Forsake not an old friend,
>   for a new one does not compare with him.
> A new friend is like new wine;
>   when it has aged you will drink it with pleasure.
>
> [11]Do not envy the honors of a sinner,
>   for you do not know what his end will be.

---

12. Thomas Aquinas, *Summa Theologiae* II-II q. 49 a. 1–8.

[12]Do not delight in what pleases the ungodly;
    remember that they will not be held guiltless as long as they live.

[13]Keep far from a man who has the power to kill,
    and you will not be worried by the fear of death.
But if you approach him, make no misstep,
    lest he rob you of your life.
Know that you are walking in the midst of snares,
    and that you are going about on the city battlements.

[14]As much as you can, aim to know your neighbors,
    and consult with the wise.
[15]Let your conversation be with men of understanding,
    and let all your discussion be about the law of the Most High.
[16]Let righteous men be your dinner companions,
    and let your glorying be in the fear of the Lord.
[17]A work will be praised for the skill of the craftsmen;
    so a people's leader is proved wise by his words.
[18]A babbler is feared in his city,
    and the man who is reckless in speech will be hated.

OT: Prov 2:16; 5:3–14; 7:4–27; 13:14–20; 22:11; 24:1
NT: Matt 5:8, 28; 1 Cor 6:18; 1 Tim 5:1–2
Catechism: chastity, 2337–59; purity of heart, 2517–27

Ben Sira now offers advice concerning relationships with women (9:1–9). The   9:1–2
advice is written from a male perspective, but much of the advice applies to both
sexes. **Do not be jealous** or suspicious **of the wife of your bosom** is a Hebrew
idiom for "the wife you love." Groundless jealousy not only brings no benefits;
it can even promote the realization of the thing feared. Distrusting your wife
could **teach her an evil lesson to your own hurt** (Hebrew: "lest you teach her
to do evil against you," NABRE)—that is, it could make her jealous as well,
resulting in a breakdown of trust between spouses. On the other hand, **do not
give yourself** (literally, "your soul") **to a woman**—especially one of questionable morals, as described in the following verses. If you let her dominate you,
she will gain **mastery over your strength** as Delilah did with Samson (Judg
16:4–21) and, the Latin adds, you will be *confounded* (see Douay). This would
be the mark of a weak man.

    The next five verses warn against sexual temptations, each time with a com-   9:3
mand followed by consequences for violating it ("do not . . . lest . . ."). The reader
is warned not to **go to meet a loose woman** (Hebrew: "a strange woman"; Prov
2:16; 5:3; 7:5)—that is, a prostitute or adulteress—lest one become tempted and
fall into her snares, trapped by her deceptive charms (Prov 7:22–23; Eccles 7:26).
The appeal of the strange woman enticing a man into a trap contrasts with the
chains and bonds of wisdom that ultimately bring freedom (Sir 6:24–25, 29–30).

Beauty and Corrupt Will

LIVING
TRADITION

Commenting on Gen 6:2 ("The sons of God saw that the daughters of men were fair; and they took to wife such of them as they chose"), St. John Chrysostom explains that the cause of these sinful, illegitimate unions was not the beauty of the women but the perverted will of the "sons of God":

> Was beauty the cause of sin? It could never be so. In fact, beauty is the work of the wisdom of God. And a work of God could never become the cause of wickedness. What is it then? Having seen them with evil intentions—that is the result of a corrupt will. Therefore also a wise man exhorted: "Do not gaze on the beauty of others" (Sir 9:8).[a]

a. John Chrysostom, *Homilies on Hosea* 3.4, in Sever Voicu, ed., *Apocrypha*, ACCS:OT 15 (Downers Grove, IL: InterVarsity, 2010), 221.

9:4–5   One should also not **associate with a woman singer** ([†]Vulgate: a *dancer* [see Douay]). Women who sang publicly were considered morally suspect in ancient Israel (Isa 23:16)—the equivalent of a "loose woman." Here the danger of being **caught in her intrigues** suggests succumbing to seduction. The Vulgate reads instead: *and do not listen to her, lest you perish by the force of her charms* (compare Douay). To avoid the near occasion of sin, a man should not even **look intently at a virgin** or a young, unmarried woman (Job 31:1), **lest** he **stumble** into sexual sin with her and subsequently incur **penalties for her**: the [†]Torah stipulates that a man who had relations with an unmarried woman had to pay a fine to her father and marry her (Exod 22:16–17; Deut 22:28–29).

9:6–7   The wisdom books often warn men to stay away from **harlots** (e.g., Prov 5:3–14; 6:26; 23:27), not only because of the gravity of sexual sin but also because they may **lose** their **inheritance** by squandering their money through an immoral lifestyle (compare Luke 15:30), or perhaps as the consequence of divine punishment. A man should not **look around in the streets** where prostitutes are found but should avoid those places (Prov 7:7–12).

9:8   **Turn away your eyes from a shapely** (Hebrew: "graceful") **woman**. Ben Sira encourages again the discretion of the eyes. By turning one's gaze away from the **beauty** of a woman **belonging to another**—that is, another man's wife or daughter—a man guards his imagination from lust (Matt 5:28). That **many have been misled** in this way is to put blame not on **a woman's beauty** but on the corrupt heart of a man who looks upon her with lust and, instead of controlling his **passion,** allows it to be **kindled like a fire.**

9:9   Undue familiarity can also be an occasion of sin. A man should **never** wine and **dine with another man's wife**—an imprudent situation that could lead his

heart to **turn aside to her** with the desire to commit adultery, and so he would **be plunged into destruction**. Adultery can ruin a person; it can lead to death—metaphorically (Prov 7:21–27) or literally. Not only does the Torah stipulate the death penalty for adultery (Lev 20:10; Deut 22:22; John 8:4–5); adulterers also expose themselves to the betrayed husband's vengeance.

Ben Sira now turns to interactions between men (9:10–18). Since it takes   **9:10** time to build trust between companions, an **old**, long-lasting **friend** should be valued more than a **new one** who has not yet proven himself trustworthy. Once the friendship **has aged**, like a good wine, **you will drink it with pleasure** and cherish it (6:5–17; 37:1–6).

Why do the wicked prosper? It is a perennial temptation to **envy** the successes   **9:11–12** and **honors of a sinner** (see Job 21:7–18; Ps 73:3–12; Prov 3:31–32). Yet no one knows **what his end will be**: his prosperity is only temporary, and he will reap in time punishment for his sins (Sir 16:6–14; Pss 37:1–2; 73:18–19). Therefore, the wise man should not **delight in** the vain honors that **the ungodly** pursue, because **they will not be held guiltless as long as they live**. Literally, "they will not be declared innocent until †Hades"—they will not escape judgment indefinitely.

Keep far from a powerful or violent **man who has the power to kill** (8:1;   **9:13** Prov 20:2). Yet if you cannot avoid him, be cautious and **make no misstep, lest he rob you of your life** by murdering you or causing you some other harm. Ben Sira describes being in the presence of such a volatile person as **walking in the midst of snares** and **on the city battlements**. In modern idiom, this would be like walking through a minefield, vulnerable and in full view of the enemy.

The advice to **aim to know your neighbors** means taking stock of them so   **9:14–16** that you may know which ones are wise (v. 14), devout (v. 15), or righteous (v. 16). It is good to **consult with the wise** (see 6:34) and not with fools (8:17; Prov 13:20); to converse with **men of understanding** who love to discuss **the law of the Most High**—the ultimate source of wisdom (Sir 19:17; 24:23; Ps 1:2); and to dine with **righteous men** who glory in **the fear of the Lord**—the beginning, root, and crown of wisdom (Sir 1:14–20).

The last two verses of this chapter contrast a good leader's wisdom with a   **9:17–18** rambler's folly. Just as the quality of **a work** of art proves **the skill of the crafts-men**, so the speech of a **leader** demonstrates wisdom. But **a babbler** who speaks vainly and accomplishes nothing is not respected but only **hated** by all.

Reflection and Application (9:1–18)

Ben Sira's advice to avoid compromising situations that could lead to sexual temptations remains today more relevant than ever. He understands human weakness and its proneness to the "lust of the flesh" (1 John 2:16). The petition "lead us not into temptation" in the Lord's Prayer implies a *decision of the heart* to stay clear of morally risky situations called "near occasions of sin" and to exercise vigilance, which is "custody of the heart" (Catechism 2848–49). "Blessed are the pure in heart, for they shall see God" (Matt 5:8). In a sexualized culture, the purity of heart and holiness that are so essential to see the Lord (Heb 12:14) must be actively cultivated by the virtue and gift of chastity, by purity of intention, by purity of vision (including feelings and imagination), and by prayer (Catechism 2520). Ben Sira's counsel on relationships between men and women also presupposes the virtue of *modesty*, an integral part of the virtue of temperance, which protects the intimate center of the person through appropriate dress, speech, and conduct (Catechism 2521–24).

III.F. On Rulers, Pride, Honor, and Humility (10:1–11:1)

¹A wise magistrate will educate his people,
　　and the rule of an understanding man will be well ordered.
²Like the magistrate of the people, so are his officials;
　　and like the ruler of the city, so are all its inhabitants.
³An undisciplined king will ruin his people,
　　but a city will grow through the understanding of its rulers.
⁴The government of the earth is in the hands of the Lord,
　　and over it he will raise up the right man for the time.
⁵The success of a man is in the hands of the Lord,
　　and he confers his honor upon the person of the scribe.

⁶Do not be angry with your neighbor for any injury,
　　and do not attempt anything by acts of insolence.
⁷Arrogance is hateful before the Lord and before men,
　　and injustice is outrageous to both.
⁸Sovereignty passes from nation to nation
　　on account of injustice and insolence and wealth.
⁹How can he who is dust and ashes be proud?
　　for even in life his bowels decay.
¹⁰A long illness baffles the physician;
　　the king of today will die tomorrow.
¹¹For when a man is dead,
　　he will inherit creeping things, and wild beasts, and worms.
¹²The beginning of man's pride is to depart from the Lord;
　　his heart has forsaken his Maker.
¹³For the beginning of pride is sin,
　　and the man who clings to it pours out abominations.
Therefore the Lord brought upon them extraordinary afflictions,
　　and destroyed them utterly.
¹⁴The Lord has cast down the thrones of rulers,
　　and has seated the lowly in their place.

¹⁵The Lord has plucked up the roots of the nations,
  and has planted the humble in their place.
¹⁶The Lord has overthrown the lands of the nations,
  and has destroyed them to the foundations of the earth.
¹⁷He has removed some of them and destroyed them,
  and has extinguished the memory of them from the earth.
¹⁸Pride was not created for men,
  nor fierce anger for those born of women.

¹⁹What race is worthy of honor? The human race.
  What race is worthy of honor? Those who fear the Lord.
What race is unworthy of honor? The human race.
  What race is unworthy of honor? Those who transgress the
    commandments.
²⁰Among brothers their leader is worthy of honor,
  and those who fear the Lord are worthy of honor in his eyes.
²²The rich, and the eminent, and the poor—
  their glory is the fear of the Lord.
²³It is not right to despise an intelligent poor man,
  nor is it proper to honor a sinful man.
²⁴The nobleman, and the judge, and the ruler will be honored,
  but none of them is greater than the man who fears the Lord.
²⁵Free men will be at the service of a wise servant,
  and a man of understanding will not grumble.
²⁶Do not make a display of your wisdom when you do your work,
  nor glorify yourself at a time when you are in want.
²⁷Better is a man who works and has an abundance of everything,
  than one who goes about boasting, but lacks bread.
²⁸My son, glorify yourself with humility,
  and ascribe to yourself honor according to your worth.
²⁹Who will justify the man that sins against himself?
  And who will honor the man that dishonors his own life?
³⁰A poor man is honored for his knowledge,
  while a rich man is honored for his wealth.
³¹A man honored in poverty, how much more in wealth!
  And a man dishonored in wealth, how much more in poverty!

^{11:1}The wisdom of a humble man will lift up his head,
  and will seat him among the great.

OT: Prov 8:15–16; 16:18; 28:15–16; 29:2; Wis 6:1–11; Sir 3:17–31
NT: Luke 1:51–52; Rom 11:20; 13:1–2; James 4:6–10; 1 Pet 5:5–6
Catechism: pride as capital sin, 1866; authority and political rule, 1897–1904

A **magistrate** or judge—the Hebrew term refers to anyone who exercises lead-   10:1–3
ership—must not only be wise (Prov 8:15–16) but also **educate** or discipline

(Greek *paideuō*) **his people** by teaching them to live virtuously and by setting the example with a **rule** that is **well ordered**, just, and dependable. The character of a ruler is important because his subordinates and subjects tend to follow his example: the competence of a **magistrate** is often seen in **his officials**, and the quality of a city's **ruler** is reflected in its **inhabitants** (Prov 29:12). Thus, an **undisciplined** or reckless **king will ruin his people** (see Prov 28:15–16; 29:2), while **a city will grow** strong and prosper when ruled by intelligent and competent rulers.

10:4–5   The focus shifts from human rulers to the divine Ruler, who delegates his authority to men. These two verses share a similar parallel structure: both the *global* **government of the earth**, over which he raises up **the right man** as leader, and the *personal* **success** (Hebrew: "government") of that **man** are **in the hands of the Lord**. If he governs wisely, the Lord **confers his honor** upon **the scribe** (Greek and Latin texts; see 39:1–11) or, more fittingly, upon the "lawgiver" (Hebrew text, NRSV).

10:6   Weaknesses and sins that undermine good leadership are now addressed. First, **do not be angry** (Hebrew: "return evil") **with your neighbor for any** (or "every") **injury** committed against you. A wise person should have the patience and maturity to overlook and forgive the minor faults of others (Lev 19:17–18; Matt 18:21–22). He should also avoid **acts of insolence** (Hebrew: "do not walk in the way of pride"), such as insulting or humiliating a neighbor who has offended him.

10:7–8   **Arrogance** or pride **is hateful before the Lord** and **men**, not only because it is diametrically opposed to the fear of the Lord and wisdom, but also because it is the root of all other sins, including **injustice**. For this reason, **sovereignty passes from nation to nation**. Political regime changes are not accidents of history but occur **on account of injustice and insolence and wealth**—that is, the greedy pursuit of material gain (Hebrew: "on account of violence and pride"). This is the national outworking of the proverb "Pride goes before destruction, and a haughty spirit before a fall" (Prov 16:18). Ben Sira may have in mind the recent political takeover of Judea by the †Seleucids over the †Ptolemies (198 BC).

10:9–11   Meditating on one's mortality serves as a good antidote to pride. **How can** anyone created out of **dust and ashes** and destined to return to dust (17:32; Gen 2:7; 3:19) **be proud**, when **even in life** the body is subject to **decay**? **A long illness baffles the physician**, and he is powerless when faced with a terminal disease. Even the most powerful **king of today will die tomorrow**, eventually decaying and becoming food for insects, predators, or **worms** like all other mortals.

10:12–13   Ben Sira now considers the **beginning** and essence of pride: pride arises when a person forsakes the fear of the Lord and instead chooses to **depart from the Lord**—a foolish choice given that God is **his Maker** and the one who sustains his life. The phrase **For the beginning of pride is sin** suggests that sin is the

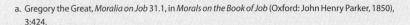

Pride: The Cause of All Sins

LIVING TRADITION

St. Gregory the Great explains how the devil brought sin into the world through pride, and how God provided the remedy to pride in Christ's humility, manifest when he became man:

> The devil, through envy, inflicted the wound of pride on healthy man in Paradise; in order that he, who had not received death when created, might deserve it when elated. But since it is competent for Divine power not only to make good things out of nothing, but also to refashion them from the evils which the devil had committed, the humility of God appeared among men as a remedy against this wound inflicted by the proud devil, that they who had fallen through imitation of their haughty enemy might rise by the example of their humbled Creator. Against, therefore, the haughty devil, God appeared among men, having been made a humble Man.[a]

a. Gregory the Great, *Moralia on Job* 31.1, in *Morals on the Book of Job* (Oxford: John Henry Parker, 1850), 3:424.

source of pride, implying that "even the first stage of pride is sinful" or "pride has its beginning in sin." The Latin reverses this with the more standard statement "Pride is the beginning of all sin," while the Hebrew reads, "For sin is a reservoir of insolence, a source which runs over with vice" (NABRE). The three versions together illustrate a vicious circle: Sin engenders pride, which in turn leads to more sin, so that **the man** who stubbornly **clings to** pride **pours out abominations**, and the fruit of his life is detestable to God. **Therefore**, since pride manifests a sinful rebellion against God, God has inflicted **extraordinary afflictions** on arrogant rulers and **destroyed them utterly**.

These two verses reiterate the same concept in parallel form: God humili- **10:14–15** ates the arrogant by casting down powerful **rulers** and plucking up **the roots** of proud **nations**, replacing them with the **lowly** and **humble**—a theme found throughout the Bible (1 Sam 2:7–8; Ps 147:6; Luke 1:52).

Ben Sira further emphasizes the severity of divine judgment: **The Lord has** **10:16–18** **overthrown** prideful **nations, destroyed them**, and **removed them** until nothing remained. Even their **memory** was **extinguished from the earth** so that they were forgotten by future generations (Deut 32:26). Ben Sira likely has in mind the fate of proud nations that once oppressed Israel, such as Egypt (Exod 7–12), Assyria (612 BC), Babylon (539 BC), and Persia (331 BC). In a concluding statement, Ben Sira reminds readers that **pride** and **fierce anger** were **not created for men** but are vices that grievously distort human nature and stray from God's plan for humanity.

10:19–21   Prideful people seek honor but are unworthy of it. **What race,** then (or "whose offspring"), **is worthy of honor?** By rhetorical repetition, Ben Sira asserts that **the human race** (or "human offspring") is **worthy of honor** if they **fear the Lord,** but **unworthy** if they **transgress the commandments** of the law. This implies that fearing the Lord is lived out by keeping the commandments. Just as **brothers** (men who are of equal status) should **honor** their **leader,** so a good leader should honor **those who fear the Lord.**[13]

10:22–24   Yet fearing the Lord is not merely a means to attain worldly honor. Those who are wise, whether **the rich, the eminent,** or **the poor,** recognize that their greatest **glory is** not human praise but **the fear of the Lord** itself, as it is the very gateway to wisdom. People focused on appearances may be tempted to **despise an intelligent man** because he is **poor,** or to **honor a sinful man** because he is wealthy, influential, or famous. This is neither **right** nor **proper.** Even though **the nobleman, judge,** and **ruler** are **honored** due to their social standing, they have less merit in God's eyes **than the man who fears the Lord.** We must resist the perennial temptation to idolize celebrities on the basis of outward appearance and instead seek to be like the Lord, who looks at the heart (1 Sam 16:7).

10:25   Ancient societies were strongly hierarchical: free citizens ruled over servants, who had very few rights. Yet Ben Sira makes a stunning statement: wisdom is so honorable that even **free men** with enough **understanding** would willingly place themselves **at the service of a wise servant** without grumbling (Prov 17:2). People should be honored on the basis of their fear of God and their wisdom, not their social standing.

10:26–27   Wisdom encompasses not only knowledge and virtue but also technical and professional skills. Yet one should not **make a display** of it while at **work;** neither should a person draw excessive attention to his troubles when he is **in want.** True wisdom is humble and modest. **Better is a man who** diligently **works** and prospers than an idle braggart **who goes about boasting** but goes hungry (Prov 12:9). Actions speak louder than words.

10:28–29   While Ben Sira warns against pride, he also cautions against false humility. With his usual fatherly address **my son,** he makes a paradoxical statement: **Glorify yourself with humility.** It is perfectly possible to have a healthy yet modest self-regard. Quietly ascribing **to yourself honor according to your worth** and accomplishments is not the same as boasting. On the other hand, a person with undue low self-esteem who self-deprecates and thinks of himself as worthless is not humble, but **sins against himself** and **dishonors his own life** (see the Reflection and Application section for 3:17–31, p. 73).

10:30–11:1   Continuing the thought of verse 23, while **a poor man** can be **honored for his knowledge**—a lasting good more precious than gold (Prov 8:10)—**a rich**

13. GII adds v. 21: **The fear of the Lord is the beginning of acceptance; obduracy and pride are the beginning of rejection** (RSV-2CE footnote).

man is often **honored** solely **for his wealth**—a fleeting good that can enslave him and be lost or stolen. Thus, a knowledgeable **man honored in poverty** is rightly honored and will be even **much more** honored **in wealth**; but a rich man who is **dishonored** would be even more despised if he were poor. Wealth increases the honor of the wise, and poverty the dishonor of the foolish. For this reason, **the wisdom of a humble** or poor **man will lift up his head** with a healthy self-confidence; those who recognize his wisdom **will seat him among the great**, for Wisdom exalts those who embrace her (Prov 4:8).

Reflection and Application (10:1–11:1)

Pride is the inordinate love of one's own excellence. It is "undue self-esteem or self-love, which seeks attention and honor and sets oneself in competition with God."[14] Because its essence is the refusal to be subject to God's rule, it directly opposes the fear of the Lord and the virtue of humility (which recognizes humanity's subjection to God). Christian tradition considers pride to be *the most grievous* and *beginning of all sins*, because it constitutes an aversion from God and contempt of him.[15] While pride is often counted among the seven capital or deadly sins, St. Gregory the Great sets it apart as the "queen of vices" that conquers the heart of a person and delivers it to the seven capital sins—from which Christ delivers us by granting the seven gifts of the Holy Spirit.

> For when pride, the queen of sins, has fully possessed a conquered heart, she surrenders it immediately to seven principal sins, as if to some of her generals, to lay it waste. And an army in truth follows these generals, because, doubtless, there spring up from them importunate hosts of sins. . . . For pride is the root of all evil, of which it is said, as Scripture bears witness, *Pride is the beginning of all sin* [Sir 10:15 †Vulgate]. But seven principal vices, as its first progeny, spring doubtless from this poisonous root, namely, vainglory [vanity], envy, anger, melancholy [acedia or sloth], avarice, gluttony, lust. For, because He grieved that we were held captive by these seven sins of pride, therefore our Redeemer came to the spiritual battle of our liberation, full of the spirit of sevenfold grace.[16]

III.G. On Deceptive Appearances and Trusting in God's Providence (11:2–28)

> [2]**Do not praise a man for his good looks,
> nor loathe a man because of his appearance.**

14. Catechism, glossary.

15. Thomas Aquinas, *Summa Theologiae* II-II q. 162 a. 1–7.

16. Gregory the Great, *Moralia on Job* 31.45.87 (in *Morals on the Book of Job*, 3:489); compare Thomas Aquinas, *Summa Theologiae* II-II q. 162 a. 8.

³The bee is small among flying creatures,
 but her product is the best of sweet things.
⁴Do not boast about wearing fine clothes,
 nor exalt yourself in the day that you are honored;
for the works of the Lord are wonderful,
 and his works are concealed from men.
⁵Many kings have had to sit on the ground,
 but one who was never thought of has worn a crown.
⁶Many rulers have been greatly disgraced,
 and illustrious men have been handed over to others.

⁷Do not find fault before you investigate;
 first consider, and then reprove.
⁸Do not answer before you have heard,
 nor interrupt a speaker in the midst of his words.
⁹Do not argue about a matter which does not concern you,
 nor sit with sinners when they judge a case.

¹⁰My son, do not busy yourself with many matters;
 if you multiply activities you will not go unpunished,
and if you pursue you will not overtake,
 and by fleeing you will not escape.
¹¹There is a man who works, and toils, and presses on,
 but is so much the more in want.
¹²There is another who is slow and needs help,
 who lacks strength and abounds in poverty;
but the eyes of the Lord look upon him for his good;
 he lifts him out of his low estate
¹³and raises up his head,
 so that many are amazed at him.

¹⁴Good things and bad, life and death,
 poverty and wealth, come from the Lord.
¹⁷The gift of the Lord endures for those who are godly,
 and what he approves will have lasting success.
¹⁸There is a man who is rich through his diligence and self-denial,
 and this is the reward allotted to him:
¹⁹when he says, "I have found rest,
 and now I shall enjoy my goods!"
he does not know how much time will pass
 until he leaves them to others and dies.
²⁰Stand by your covenant and attend to it,
 and grow old in your work.

²¹Do not wonder at the works of a sinner,
 but trust in the Lord and keep at your toil;

> for it is easy in the sight of the Lord
> > to enrich a poor man quickly and suddenly.
> ²²The blessing of the Lord is the reward of the godly,
> > and quickly God causes his blessing to flourish.
> ²³Do not say, "What do I need,
> > and what prosperity could be mine in the future?"
> ²⁴Do not say, "I have enough,
> > and what calamity could happen to me in the future?"
> ²⁵In the day of prosperity, adversity is forgotten,
> > and in the day of adversity, prosperity is not remembered.
> ²⁶For it is easy in the sight of the Lord
> > to reward a man on the day of death according to his conduct.
> ²⁷The misery of an hour makes one forget luxury,
> > and at the close of a man's life his deeds will be revealed.
> ²⁸Call no one happy before his death;
> > a man will be known through his children.

OT: 1 Sam 16:7; Ps 127:1–2; Prov 28:20; Eccles 6:1–3
NT: Matt 7:1–5; Luke 12:16–21; James 2:1–9; Rev 20:12
Catechism: divine providence, 302–14

Appearances are deceiving (1 Sam 16:7; Isa 53:2). Since true worth is not vis-   **11:2–3**
ible to the naked eye, one should not praise a person's **good looks, nor loathe**
him or her on the basis of their **appearance** (see James 2:1–9). The example of
the bee illustrates this principle: though **small** and apparently insignificant, it
produces honey, **the best of sweet things**.

Clothing, in particular, does not reflect a person's true quality. Thus, one   **11:4**
should **not boast about wearing fine clothes**. It is foolish to **exalt yourself**
when **you are honored** on account of your attire, for that honor, like clothing,
can easily be stripped away. The Hebrew text describes an opposite situation:
"Do not mock the one who wears only a loin-cloth, or scoff at a person's bitter
day" (NABRE). Since God is not fooled by external appearances and looks at the
heart, his **works** are **wonderful** and **concealed from men**, as when he reverses
and overturns a person's status in society.

Many powerful **kings** (or "tyrants") have been toppled from their thrones   **11:5–6**
and **have had to sit on the ground**, while previously unknown people have
been raised from obscurity to kingship and have **worn a crown**—such as David
(1 Sam 16:1–13). **Many rulers have been greatly disgraced** by their fall, losing not only their power but also their freedom: though previously **illustrious**
and honored, some were captured and **handed over to others** as prisoners or
slaves (2 Kings 25:1–7).

Just as one should avoid rash judgment based on the appearance of things   **11:7–9**
seen, one must also exercise caution before passing judgment on things *heard*.
Even ancient societies understood principles of justice that are now universally

recognized. Thus, **do not find fault** in a person suspected of wrongdoing **before you investigate** (see Matt 7:1–5); **first consider** impartially the matter at hand **and then reprove** the person only if the suspicion proves true. One is to be presumed innocent until proven guilty. For a judgment to be fair, one must not **answer** hastily or **interrupt a speaker** before giving that person a fair hearing (Sir 5:11–12; Prov 18:13). Yet many arguments that do not **concern you** are best avoided altogether. One should not **sit with sinners when they judge a case**—that is, one should not participate in a judgment when the judges are unjust, or in disputes between sinners (Ps 1:1; Luke 12:13–15).

11:10–11   The address **My son** marks the beginning of a new unit, now on providence and trusting God in financial and professional matters (11:10–28). Particularly relevant for twenty-first-century readers is Ben Sira's advice against overcommitment: it is ill-advised to **busy yourself with many matters**. To needlessly **multiply activities** is not only ineffective but even blameworthy. One who multitasks excessively risks dissipating his soul and falling into sin (26:29–27:3; 31:5–7; Prov 28:20), for which he **will not go unpunished** (or "will not be held blameless"). **If you** relentlessly **pursue** wealth or worldly success, you will constantly run but **not overtake**, and you will never reach the finish line; nor will **fleeing** help you **escape** the burden of your responsibilities. This serves as a warning against workaholism: the person who ceaselessly **works, and toils, and presses on** finds neither satisfaction nor peace in the end but remains **so much the more in want**. Finding life balance was a challenge then, just as it is now.

11:12–13   By contrast, one who is **slow and needs help**, or weak and poor, draws the kindness and mercy of **the Lord**. God **lifts him out** of his lowly condition and **raises up his head** to a position of honor, granting him prosperity to the amazement of **many**. Success does not depend solely on one's own efforts; the Lord can grant it gratuitously to those who trust in him (Pss 31:16; 127:1–2; Eccles 5:18–19).

11:14–16   All aspects of human existence, **good things and bad, life and death, poverty and wealth come from the Lord**, who is sovereign over creation (Catechism 304). This raises a theological problem: Is God the author of evil and death? Verses 15–16 address this question:[17] while all good things **come from the Lord, error and darkness were created with sinners** (Hebrew: "*for* sinners"), meaning that error and darkness arise naturally from their own choices. Other Scripture passages clarify that God is not the author of evil, which originates from humanity's free will (Gen 3:1–7), nor of suffering and death, which came into the world as the result of sin (Gen 3:16–19; Wis 2:23–24; Rom 5:12).

---

17. Verses 15–16 are omitted in GI but present in the Hebrew, GII, and Vulgate: **[15]Wisdom, understanding, and knowledge of the law come from the Lord; affection and the ways of good works come from him. [16]Error and darkness were created with sinners; evil will grow old with those who take pride in malice** (RSV-2CE footnote).

Despite the presence of evil in the world, **the Lord** generously grants his 　11:17–19
gifts to **those who are godly**, and his favor grants them **lasting success**. If an
avaricious **man**, on the other hand, enriches himself and hoards wealth even
through diligence and self-denial, he misuses these virtues and his **reward**
might not be what he expects. When he finally finds **rest**, he does not know
whether he will ever live to **enjoy** his **goods**: he may leave them **to others** if he
dies unexpectedly. Although it is wise to prepare for one's financial future (Prov
6:6–8), one should also live well now, using wealth to bless others (Sir 14:3–10;
Eccles 6:1–3; Luke 12:16–21).

Stand by your covenant could refer to God's covenant with Israel; or it could 　11:20–21
be a more pragmatic exhortation to respect one's commitments (Hebrew: "stand
by your task") and **attend** to duties with care so that you may **grow old in your
work** well done. **Do not wonder at the works of a sinner** or envy his success,
even if it seems undeserved, **but trust in the Lord** and continue your labor
faithfully and diligently. Since poverty and wealth come from **the Lord**, he can
reverse anyone's fortunes and **enrich a poor man** at any moment.

The blessing of the Lord—including material benefits—**is the reward of the** 　11:22–24
godly, who fear and obey him, even if this promise does not exclude seasons
of hardship (compare Job). **God causes his blessing to flourish** at the right
time (Prov 10:22). Therefore, one should not be greedy, constantly seeking to
increase one's **prosperity**. Nor should one be presumptuous, saying, "**I have
enough**" with a smug sense of security, imagining that wealth serves as a shield
from any future **calamity**. God is able to withdraw his blessing as quickly as he
is able to bestow it (11:22).

Although it is human nature to be immersed in our present concerns, these 　11:25–26
are quickly forgotten when our condition changes. The Greek expresses this
simply and elegantly: **In the day of** good things, bad things are **forgotten**;
in the day of bad things, good things are **not remembered**. Past fortunes
or misfortunes are unreliable indicators of divine favor or wrath. Since both
prosperity and adversity are fleeting, these should be of little concern to the
wise. **The Lord** may allow temporary chastisements upon the righteous and
prosperity upon the wicked because he will **reward** each one at their last hour,
on the day of death according to his conduct and his works (35:19; Prov
24:12; Matt 16:27; Rom 2:6). Like most other Old Testament authors, Ben Sira
did not have a clear concept of life after death, so he looks for the fulfillment
of divine justice in this present life, even at the last hour, perhaps expecting
that the righteous will die content and at peace, and the wicked will die in
disgrace and anxiety.

The misery of one's last **hour** at the time of death **makes one forget luxury** 　11:27–28
and the pleasures of the past. **At the close of a man's life**, the worthiness or un-
worthiness of **his deeds will be revealed**, and he will become aware of his legacy,
whether for good or evil (Luke 12:2). Therefore, **call no one happy** or blessed (Matt

5:2–11) **before his death**, for the fleeting pleasures of life are a poor indicator of a person's ultimate happiness, and one does not know how life will turn out until it is complete. The Greek text adds: **a man will be known through his children**—that is, people will recognize his true worth by the character of his children, or possibly the children will share in his rewards or punishments (Exod 20:5–6). The Hebrew reads instead "by how he ends a person becomes known" (NRSV).

Reflection and Application (11:2–28)

Ben Sira warns against judging others on the basis of outward appearances. Yet throughout his book he constantly judges between right and wrong behavior. This distinction sheds light on one of Jesus's most misunderstood sayings: "Judge not, that you be not judged" (Matt 7:1). Today, these words are often interpreted as if Jesus were discouraging all moral judgments so that no one should presume to judge the rightness or wrongness of any action or lifestyle. Recast into postmodern slogans such as "Live and let live," or "Don't impose your values on me," "Judge not" has become a license for moral relativism. Of course, this is not at all what Jesus had in mind. As an orthodox Jew and indeed, as the *Author* of the †Torah, Jesus fully endorsed its authority, teaching that observing the commandments is the path to eternal life (Matt 5:17–20; 19:17–19). He accepted the biblical view that some acts are good and others are evil (Ps 37:27), and that we must diligently pursue the good and purge the evil from among us (1 Cor 5:13), as the former leads to life and the latter to death (Deut 28:1–68). Jesus constantly confronts evil in the Gospels (Matt 12:34–39). By teaching us to pray, "Deliver us from evil," he implies that we must rightly judge what is evil.

What, then, does Jesus mean by "judge not"? Like Ben Sira, Jesus asks us to refrain from judging people on the basis of *external appearances*, which do not reflect one's moral character, or from assuming we understand their *intentions* or *dispositions*, because we cannot look into a person's heart. We must first judge ourselves before judging others (Matt 7:3–5). Yet this does not mean that we should turn a blind eye to blatant sins or injustices: "If your brother sins against you, go and tell him his fault" (Matt 18:15). We bear responsibility for the sins of others, not only when we participate in or approve of them but also when we fail to hinder them when we have an obligation to do so (Catechism 1868; compare Ezek 3:18). Thus, while the wise should not judge external appearances or inner dispositions, they must indeed judge the moral quality of words and actions, lifestyles and public policies, for God "filled their hearts with understanding, and showed them good and evil" (Sir 17:7).

III.H. Discerning Friends from Enemies (11:29–12:18)

²⁹Do not bring every man into your home,
   for many are the wiles of the crafty.
³⁰Like a decoy partridge in a cage, so is the mind of a proud man,
   and like a spy he observes your weakness;
³¹for he lies in wait, turning good into evil,
   and to worthy actions he will attach blame.
³²From a spark of fire come many burning coals,
   and a sinner lies in wait to shed blood.
³³Beware of a scoundrel, for he devises evil,
   lest he give you a lasting blemish.
³⁴Receive a stranger into your home and he will upset you with
      commotion,
   and will estrange you from your family.

¹²:¹If you do a kindness, know to whom you do it,
   and you will be thanked for your good deeds.
²Do good to a godly man, and you will be repaid—
   if not by him, certainly by the Most High.
³No good will come to the man who persists in evil
   or to him who does not give alms.
⁴Give to the godly man, but do not help the sinner.
   ⁵Do good to the humble, but do not give to the ungodly;
hold back his bread, and do not give it to him,
   lest by means of it he subdue you;
for you will receive twice as much evil
   for all the good which you do to him.
⁶For the Most High also hates sinners
   and will inflict punishment on the ungodly.
⁷Give to the good man, but do not help the sinner.

⁸A friend will not be known in prosperity,
   nor will an enemy be hidden in adversity.
⁹A man's enemies are grieved when he prospers,
   and in his adversity even his friend will separate from him.
¹⁰Never trust your enemy,
   for like the rusting of copper, so is his wickedness.
¹¹Even if he humbles himself and goes about cringing,
   watch yourself, and be on your guard against him;
and you will be to him like one who has polished a mirror,
   and you will know that it was not hopelessly tarnished.
¹²Do not put him next to you,
   lest he overthrow you and take your place;
do not have him sit at your right,
   lest he try to take your seat of honor,

and at last you will realize the truth of my words,
>	and be stung by what I have said.
¹³Who will pity a snake charmer bitten by a serpent,
>	or any who go near wild beasts?
¹⁴So no one will pity a man who associates with a sinner
>	and becomes involved in his sins.
¹⁵He will stay with you for a time,
>	but if you falter, he will not stand by you.

¹⁶An enemy will speak sweetly with his lips,
>	but in his mind he will plan to throw you into a pit;
an enemy will weep with his eyes,
>	but if he finds an opportunity his thirst for blood will be
>	insatiable.
¹⁷If calamity befalls you, you will find him there ahead of you;
>	and while pretending to help you, he will trip you by the heel;
¹⁸he will shake his head, and clap his hands,
>	and whisper much, and change his expression.

OT: Prov 19:4; 25:21–22; 26:22–28
NT: Matt 5:43–47; Luke 6:27–28; Rom 12:20; 1 Cor 15:33
Catechism: respect for the human person, 1929–33

11:29–31 Hospitality is a noble virtue, and people of good character are naturally inclined to trust their guests. Nevertheless, wise people must be cautious to **not bring every** person into their **home**—the sanctuary of the family. Not everyone is honest; **many are the wiles of the crafty** who may take advantage of a good person's hospitality. **Like a decoy partridge in a cage**, set to lure and capture other birds, so **the mind of** an arrogant person seeks to trap you; **like a spy he observes your weakness**, or "watches for your downfall." Like a predator **he lies in wait** to ambush and malign you, ready to exploit even your **good** deeds for **evil** purposes or to find fault and **blame** in **worthy actions**.

11:32–34 Just as **a spark of fire** can set alight **many burning coals**, so **a sinner** who **lies in wait to shed blood** is capable of harming many people. Great evils often begin with small actions. A wise person, therefore, must not play with fire: **beware of a scoundrel** who continually **devises evil** plans to exploit others; if you associate with him, he may **give you a lasting blemish** and inflict on you permanent harm. Ben Sira thus concludes his advice on prudent hospitality: exercise careful discernment before receiving **a stranger into your home**; if he turns out to be the scoundrel described here, he will likely stir up trouble in your household and may even **estrange you from your family**.

12:1 Ben Sira also advises discernment when exercising generosity. Since everyone has limited resources, we must choose wisely how to use them for the benefit of others. **If you do a kindness** (literally, "if you do good"), **know to whom**

you do it and ensure that the recipient of your generosity is worthy of it, so that **you will be thanked for your good deeds**. This does not necessarily mean that you will gain from your own generosity, but that it will not be wasted and will bear good fruit.

Ben Sira holds that one should **do good**, not indiscriminately to everyone but only to **a godly man**. The giver **will be repaid** for his kindness, **if not by** its recipient, then **certainly by** God **the Most High**, who renders to each according to his or her works (11:26; Prov 24:12). In contrast, **no good will come to the man who persists in evil**. The Hebrew is quite different and better fits the context: "No good comes to those who give comfort to the wicked, nor is it an act of mercy that they do" (NABRE). This idea is expanded upon in 12:4–7.

12:2–3

Give to the godly man, but do not help the sinner—a directive that refers not to every person who has ever sinned but to those who "persist in evil" without repenting (12:3). Ben Sira's strict view, that acts of kindness should be extended only to the righteous, contrasts with teachings found in both the Old and the New Testament (Prov 25:21–22; Matt 5:43–47; Rom 12:20). His rationale is that doing **good to the humble** and withholding aid **to the ungodly** is an act of justice. As an ancient Jewish commentary explains: "Do not do good to an evil person, and evil shall not befall you; and if you do good to an evil person, you have done evil."[18] By giving **bread** (i.e., food) to an evil man, you risk subsidizing his evil. He will not necessarily repent after benefiting from acts of kindness but may continue to do evil and even attempt to **subdue you** with the resources you have given him. Feeding a wicked man makes him stronger, enabling him to return **twice as much evil** for **the good which you do to him.**

12:4–5

The wise should not be generous to habitual, unrepentant sinners because God **the Most High also hates** them. This is a shocking statement. Does God really hate certain people? God certainly hates evil, and he calls the wise to do the same (Ps 97:10; Amos 5:14–15; Rom 12:9). Thus, God "hates" the wicked insofar as they do evil, though not in their nature as reflecting his image and likeness, for God still desires that they repent and be saved (Rom 5:8; 1 Tim 2:4). Nevertheless, if they do not repent, for the sake of justice he **will inflict punishment on the ungodly** (see 2 Pet 2:4, 9). This explains Ben Sira's rationale to **give to the good man** but not to the habitual **sinner** (see the Reflection and Application section below, p. 127).

12:6–7

Ben Sira returns to the topic of identifying a true friend from a false one (6:5–13). **A friend will not be known in prosperity**: when all is well, it is difficult to tell who your true friends are. In times of **adversity**, however, it becomes easier to distinguish a real friend from **an enemy** who feigned friendship in good times

12:8–9

---

18. Midrash Qoheleth [Ecclesiastes] Rabbah 5:10, in Harry Freedman and Maurice Simon, eds., *Midrash Rabbah* (London: Soncino, 1939).

but was actually **grieved** and envious of your prosperity (Hebrew: "When one is successful even an enemy is friendly," NABRE). Yet in **adversity** your self-serving, false **friend will separate from** you and disappear (Prov 19:4). An ancient Jewish proverb makes the same point: "They appear as friends when it is in their own interest [to do so], but they do not stand by the person in his time of need."[19]

12:10–11   **Never trust your enemy: his wickedness** is **like the rusting** or corrosion **of copper.** Ancient bronze mirrors corroded and became tarnished with time, so that one could no longer see clearly unless they were frequently polished. Likewise, an enemy can put on a false display of humility, **cringing** or bowing to you (Prov 26:24). Do not be duped, and **be on your guard against him.** Be toward such a person as **one who has polished a mirror**, alert and able to see false friends as they truly are.

12:12   **Do not** let down your guard and allow your enemy to sit **next to you** as if he were a friend, for he will inevitably exploit this closeness at your expense, seek to **overthrow you,** and **take your seat of honor.** If this occurs, you will **realize the truth** of these warnings and will **be stung** with regret at not having paid them more heed.

12:13–15   No one **will pity a snake charmer** or someone who goes **near wild beasts**, because they foolishly place themselves in dangerous situations that are likely to harm them (Eccles 10:11). Similarly, **no one will pity a man who associates with a grave sinner**, either because he risks becoming complicit in the sinner's transgressions, or because he foolishly exposes himself to falling into similar sins. "Bad company ruins good morals" (1 Cor 15:33). The sinner may be a friend of convenience **for a time,** but when adversity comes and **you falter, he will not stand by you.** He will flee because he has nothing more to gain from the friendship (Sir 12:9).

12:16   Of course, **an enemy** cannot be trusted: he says one thing, speaking **sweetly with his lips**, while thinking another (27:23). **In his mind** or heart he plans **to throw you into a pit**—a figure of speech illustrating his intention to destroy you. Though he may feign to **weep with his eyes**, pretending to share your sorrows, in reality he harbors an **insatiable** violence and **thirst for blood** in his heart; he will not be satisfied until he **finds an opportunity** to harm or even kill you (Prov 26:22–28).

12:17–18   If misfortune or **calamity befalls you**, your enemy will be **there**, ready to exploit your position of weakness. Though he may pretend **to help you**, in fact **he will trip you by the heel** and attempt to destroy you. Only then will he drop all pretense: **he will shake his head** in mockery (Ps 22:7), **clap his hands** with malicious joy (Lam 2:15), **whisper** scornfully (Ps 41:7), and **change his expression**, unmasking his true intentions.

19. Mishnah, *Avot* 2:3. *The Mishnah: A New Integrated Translation and Commentary*, https://www.echok.com/mishnah/nezikin_vol_2/Avot2.pdf.

Reflection and Application (11:29–12:18)

Ben Sira's advice to "give to the good man, but do not help the sinner" (12:7) is difficult. Do these words still apply to Christians today? Does the gospel not command us to "give to him who begs from you" (Matt 5:42), and "if your enemy is hungry, feed him" (Rom 12:20)? Exegetes and theologians have grappled with this apparent contradiction, pointing out that these evangelical teachings are not moral absolutes but must be applied with spiritual discernment.

The Fathers of the Church also addressed these questions. St. Augustine comments: "Execute mercy to the wicked, but not because he is wicked. Do not receive the wicked, in so far as he is wicked, that is, do not receive him because you have an inclination and love for his iniquity."[20] Thus, extending mercy to sinners can be permissible and even praiseworthy as long as this help does not support their sin (for example, giving money to a drunkard knowing that he will use it to buy more alcohol). Similarly, St. Gregory the Great writes: "He who gives his bread to one that is indigent, though he is a sinner, not because he is a sinner but because he is a human being, does not in truth nourish a sinner but a poor righteous person, because what he loves in him is not his sin but his nature."[21] In other words, as St. Thomas Aquinas says, "We ought not to help a sinner as such, that is by encouraging him to sin, but as man, that is by supporting his nature."[22]

III.I. Beware of the Rich and Powerful (13:1–14:2)

[1]Whoever touches pitch will be defiled,
    and whoever associates with a proud man will become like
        him.
[2]Do not lift a weight beyond your strength,
    nor associate with a man mightier and richer than you.
How can the clay pot associate with the iron kettle?
    The pot will strike against it, and will itself be broken.
[3]A rich man does wrong, and he even adds reproaches;
    a poor man suffers wrong, and he must add apologies.
[4]A rich man will exploit you if you can be of use to him,
    but if you are in need he will forsake you.
[5]If you own something, he will live with you;
    he will drain your resources and he will not care.

20. Augustine, *Expositions of the Psalms* 102.13, in Sever J. Voicu, ed., *Apocrypha*, ACCS:OT 15 (Downers Grove, IL: InterVarsity, 2010), 239.
21. Gregory the Great, *Pastoral Rule* 3.20 (Voicu, *Apocrypha*, 239–40).
22. Thomas Aquinas, *Summa Theologiae* II-II q. 32 a. 9 (trans. Fathers of the English Dominican Province [New York: Benziger Bros., 1948]).

⁶When he needs you he will deceive you,
 he will smile at you and give you hope.
He will speak to you kindly and say, "What do you need?"
⁷He will shame you with his foods,
 until he has drained you two or three times;
 and finally he will deride you.
Should he see you afterwards, he will forsake you,
 and shake his head at you.
⁸Take care not to be led astray,
 and not to be humiliated in your feasting.
⁹When a powerful man invites you, be reserved;
 and he will invite you the more often.
¹⁰Do not push forward, lest you be repulsed;
 and do not remain at a distance, lest you be forgotten.
¹¹Do not try to treat him as an equal,
 nor trust his abundance of words;
for he will test you through much talk,
 and while he smiles he will be examining you.
¹²Cruel is he who does not keep words to himself;
 he will not hesitate to injure or to imprison.
¹³Keep words to yourself and be very watchful,
 for you are walking about with your own downfall.

¹⁵Every creature loves its like,
 and every person his neighbor;
¹⁶all living beings associate by species,
 and a man clings to one like himself.
¹⁷What fellowship has a wolf with a lamb?
 No more has a sinner with a godly man.
¹⁸What peace is there between a hyena and a dog?
 And what peace between a rich man and a poor man?
¹⁹Wild donkeys in the wilderness are the prey of lions;
 likewise the poor are pastures for the rich.
²⁰Humility is an abomination to a proud man;
 likewise a poor man is an abomination to a rich one.

²¹When a rich man totters, he is steadied by friends,
 but when a humble man falls, he is even pushed away by friends.
²²If a rich man slips, his helpers are many;
 he speaks unseemly words, and they justify him.
If a humble man slips, they even reproach him;
 he speaks sensibly, and receives no attention.
²³When the rich man speaks all are silent,
 and they extol to the clouds what he says.
When the poor man speaks they say, "Who is this fellow?"
 And should he stumble, they even push him down.

²⁴Riches are good if they are free from sin,
   and poverty is evil in the opinion of the ungodly.
²⁵A man's heart changes his countenance,
   either for good or for evil.
²⁶The mark of a happy heart is a cheerful face,
   but to devise proverbs requires painful thinking.

¹⁴:¹Blessed is the man who does not blunder with his lips
   and need not suffer grief for sin.
²Blessed is he whose heart does not condemn him,
   and who has not given up his hope.

OT: Prov 8:21; 10:15; 12:27; 28:20; Eccles 9:16
NT: Matt 6:24; 19:23–24; Luke 6:20, 24; 1 Tim 6:10; James 5:1–6
Catechism: all bow before wealth, 1723; the idolatry of money, 2113, 2424

Ben Sira now advises on how to relate to the rich and powerful (13:1–8). Just   **13:1–2**
as someone who **touches pitch**—a thick, black, and sticky substance derived
from petroleum—is **defiled**, so one who **associates with a proud man** (Hebrew:
"scoffer") will also be defiled and **become** proud **like him** (see 1 Cor 15:33). As
lifting a heavy **weight beyond your strength** can cause injury, so associating
with a man mightier and richer than you can be harmful. The modest person
is like a **clay pot**, and the rich and powerful like an **iron kettle**. If the two **associate**, the latter will eventually bump against the former and break it. The
Hebrew adds: "Or why should the rich associate with the poor?"

If **a rich man does wrong**, being emboldened by his wealth and power and   **13:3**
unafraid of retribution, he sometimes **adds reproaches** and boasts about his
deeds, or becomes indignant as if he himself has been wronged. By contrast, **a
poor man** is helpless when he **suffers wrong**, so that he must even **add apologies**
to the one who has harmed him—as if he, and not the rich man, were at fault.

Like the false friend and enemy (12:8–9, 16–17), the corrupt **rich man will**   **13:4–6**
exploit you (Hebrew: "enslave you," NABRE) as long as you are useful to him
but will **forsake you** and leave you helpless in your hour of need. As long as
you **own something** of value **he will live with you**—not literally move in with
you but remain close to you—to unscrupulously **drain your resources**. He will
deceive and flatter you, **smile at you and give you hope** that he is a trusted
friend, speaking **kindly** to you and asking, **"What do you need?"** as though he
were genuinely disposed to help you.

The rich man, seeking to gain control over you, will even **shame you with his**   **13:7–8**
foods, extending hospitality and obliging you to return his invitations until you
overspend yourself into ruin. Afterward, he will maliciously **deride you, forsake
you, and shake his head** in mockery **at you** (12:18). **Take care**, therefore, not
to be deceived and **led astray** by the rich man's wealth, or **humiliated in your
feasting** (Hebrew and Latin: "in your folly").

13:9–10   Ben Sira turns his attention to dealing with politically powerful people (13:9–14). **When a powerful man invites** or summons **you, be reserved** (Hebrew: "keep your distance," NABRE), and do not rush to respond, so that **he will invite you** more insistently (Luke 14:10). A modest person should neither **push forward** and assert himself too aggressively, **lest** he **be repulsed** and rebuffed, nor shyly **remain at a distance, lest** he **be forgotten**.

13:11–14   One should not grow overly familiar with an influential person, however friendly he may be. **Do not try to treat him as an equal** (Hebrew: "Do not venture to be free" with him, NABRE), **nor trust his abundance of** affable **words**, but approach him with deference and respect. There may be an ulterior motive to his friendliness. He may be testing you **through much talk**, trying to put you at ease; he may be attempting to catch you off guard **while he smiles** to gather information that he could use against you. **Cruel is he**—presumably the same powerful man—**who does not keep** your **words to himself** but turns them against you, even to the point of injuring or imprisoning you. Therefore, be discreet: **keep** your **words to yourself and be very watchful** when speaking around rich or powerful men, for you tread on precarious ground, and anything you say could lead to **your own downfall**.[23]

13:15–16   Ben Sira emphasizes the stark differences between the rich and the poor, whom he views almost as distinct species (13:15–26). Just as **every creature loves its** own kind, so **every person** is drawn to like-minded people. Just as **living beings** (Greek and Hebrew: "all flesh") **associate** with animals of the same **species**, so a person naturally **clings to one like himself**. The text evokes the creation of Eve, called "a helper fit" for Adam, who would "cling" to her and become "one flesh" with her (Gen 2:18, 24). Wise men seek friends among the wise, not among fools (Sir 6:16–17), and they marry wise women rather than undisciplined ones (25:8).

13:17–18   There is no **fellowship** between **a wolf** and **a lamb**, not just because they are different but because the wolf poses a mortal threat to the lamb. Likewise, **a sinner** not only has nothing in common **with a godly man**; the former is spiritually hazardous to the latter due to his corrupting influence (Matt 7:15). Similarly, there is no **peace between a hyena and a dog**; the latter guards the flocks from the former, and the two are natural enemies. Likewise, there can be no **peace between a** greedy, predatory **rich man and a** vulnerable **poor man**.

13:19–20   This idea is illustrated in a third analogy from the animal world: as **wild donkeys** are **the prey** of voracious **lions**, so **the poor are pastures** or feeding grounds **for the rich** (see Pss 34:10; 35:17). The two are utterly incompatible. As **humility is an abomination to a proud man**, who cannot appreciate its virtue, so **a poor man is an abomination to a rich one**, who fails to see the simplicity of poverty or anticipate its blessedness as revealed in the gospel (Luke 6:20).

23. GII adds verse 14: **When you hear these things in your sleep, wake up! During all your life love the Lord, and call on him for your salvation** (RSV-2CE footnote).

There is a vast difference in how the rich and poor man are treated. **When a** **13:21–22** **rich man totters** and is about to fall, either literally or metaphorically—that is, he finds himself in difficulty—he can count on **friends** eager to help him; **but when a humble** (Hebrew: "poor") **man falls** or is in trouble, **he is even pushed away by friends** and left without help, because he is unable to repay favors done to him. This contrast extends to matters of speech. **If a rich man slips** with his tongue and **speaks unseemly** or offensive **words**, his many **helpers** eagerly rise to his defense to **justify him** and cover up for him (Hebrew: "though his words are corrupt, they are perceived as beautiful"). No such benefit of the doubt is granted to a **humble** (or "poor") **man**: if he **slips**, people are quick to **reproach him**; even when **he speaks sensibly**, no one takes him seriously, and he **receives no attention**.

When the rich man speaks all are silent and listen to him attentively. **13:23** No matter what he says, **they extol** his words **to the clouds** and praise him extravagantly—though his credibility often stems from his wealth and not from the wisdom of his words. By contrast, few listen to or even acknowledge **the poor man** when he **speaks**; they **push him down** even if he has something valuable to say (Eccles 9:16).

Despite his harsh critique of the rich man, Ben Sira does not see wealth as **13:24** inherently evil. Though **riches** can be detrimental to one's spiritual life (Prov 28:20; Matt 19:23–24; 1 Tim 6:10), they **are good if they are free from sin**—that is, gained honestly. In contrast, the ungodly perceive **poverty** as **evil** because they recognize worth only in material wealth. While poverty may sometimes signal God's disfavor or curse (Deut 28:47–48; Prov 22:16), it can also be the result of laziness (Prov 6:6–11), worthless pursuits (28:19), idle talk (14:23), drunkenness and gluttony (23:21), or pleasure seeking (21:17). Nonetheless, poverty is not necessarily a mark of God's disfavor and can even be a blessing in disguise (Luke 6:20). Ben Sira's caution about wealth remains relevant to our age, for the tendency to overvalue wealth remains as common as in ancient times. Yet his caution should be balanced with Jesus's commandment not only to "love your neighbor as yourself" but to love all people, including your enemies (Lev 19:18; Matt 5:43–48)—the wealthy included.

A person's happiness depends not on wealth but on the **heart**—the seat of **13:25–26** understanding and will, the "depths of one's being" (Catechism 368)—and it is reflected in a **cheerful face** (see Prov 15:13; Eccles 8:1). But Ben Sira adds a qualification about a limit to happiness in his own line of work: **to devise proverbs requires painful thinking**!

In contrast to the one who speaks carelessly (13:22), the prudent speaker **14:1–2** who **does not blunder with his lips**, living innocently and avoiding the sting of remorse **for sin**, is counted as **blessed**. This blessed life without regrets is found not among the rich and powerful but in a **heart** that **does not condemn**, a clear conscience, and a steadfast **hope**.

III.J. Using Wealth Wisely: On Stinginess and Liberality (14:3–19)

³Riches are not seemly for a stingy man;
   and of what use is property to an envious man?
⁴Whoever accumulates by depriving himself, accumulates for others;
   and others will live in luxury on his goods.
⁵If a man is mean to himself, to whom will he be generous?
   He will not enjoy his own riches.
⁶No one is meaner than the man who is grudging to himself,
   and this is the retribution for his baseness;
⁷even if he does good, he does it unintentionally,
   and betrays his baseness in the end.
⁸Evil is the man with a grudging eye;
   he averts his face and disregards people.
⁹A greedy man's eye is not satisfied with a portion,
   and mean injustice withers the soul.
¹⁰A stingy man's eye begrudges bread,
   and it is lacking at his table.

¹¹My son, treat yourself well, according to your means,
   and present worthy offerings to the Lord.
¹²Remember that death will not delay,
   and the decree of Hades has not been shown to you.
¹³Do good to a friend before you die,
   and reach out and give to him as much as you can.
¹⁴Do not deprive yourself of a happy day;
   let not your share of desired good pass by you.
¹⁵Will you not leave the fruit of your labors to another,
   and what you acquired by toil to be divided by lot?
¹⁶Give, and take, and beguile yourself,
   because in Hades one cannot look for luxury.
¹⁷All living beings become old like a garment,
   for the decree from of old is, "You must surely die!"
¹⁸Like flourishing leaves on a spreading tree
   which sheds some and puts forth others,
so are the generations of flesh and blood:
   one dies and another is born.
¹⁹Every product decays and ceases to exist,
   and the man who made it will pass away with it.

OT: Lev 19:18; Tob 4:7–11; Prov 3:27–28; Eccles 2:24; 6:2; 9:7–10
NT: Matt 6:19–21; James 5:1–6
Catechism: avarice, 2445, 2536, 2547; generosity, 1832, 1937, 2407

14:3–5   Ben Sira now discusses the proper use of wealth. Though **riches** are good when "free from sin" (13:24), they are unseemly **for a stingy** (Hebrew: a "small heart") or **envious** (Hebrew: "evil-eyed") person who spends neither on others nor even on himself. He argues that the hoarder who **accumulates** wealth **by depriving himself** only **accumulates** riches **for others** to inherit after he dies. Those who follow him **will live in luxury** on the money he so carefully saved (11:19; 14:15; Eccles 6:2)! **If a man is mean to himself** by being stingy, **to whom will he be generous?** (literally, "the one who is evil to himself, to whom will he be good?"). **He will not enjoy his own riches**: this type of thriftiness is not the same as self-denial for the benefit of others.

No one is meaner than one **who is grudging to himself** (compare Prov **14:6–7** 11:17). A miser is even worse than a self-indulgent person who does not give to others so he can enjoy his own goods, for his self-indulgence at least brings him some joy (Eccles 2:24); but the miser deprives himself of all happiness. **This is the retribution for his baseness**: stinginess is its own punishment. **Even if he** occasionally **does good, he does it unintentionally**, almost by accident, for he has lost the habit of generosity. He cannot conceal his true intentions for long, and **in the end** his evil nature is exposed.

Evil is the man with a grudging eye—a selfish person who resents helping **14:8–10** others; **he averts his face**, avoiding eye contact to avoid those in need (contrast 4:4–5; Tob 4:7–11). **A greedy**, covetous **man's eye is not satisfied with a portion**; he always craves more than he has. For **injustice withers the soul** and saps his vitality. The Hebrew reads: "He who takes the portion of his neighbor loses his own." The Latin is even more vivid: "*The eye of the covetous man is insatiable in his portion of iniquity: he will not be satisfied till he consume his own soul, drying it up*" (Douay). **A stingy man's eye** (literally, "an evil eye"—a Hebrew idiom for a stingy person, Sir 31:13; Matt 6:22–23) **begrudges bread**—that is, he will not even put enough food on **his** own **table**. The Hebrew adds a proverb that reinforces the point: In contrast to the stingy man, "the generous multiplies bread to increase. Even a dry well flows upon his table."

The fatherly address **My son** marks a new topic. Having condemned stin- **14:11** giness, Ben Sira now explains how to make good use of wealth. First, **treat yourself well** (literally, "be good to yourself"), **according to your means** and what you can afford, **and present worthy offerings to the Lord**. In this section on making generous use of one's resources, Ben Sira may have the two great commandments in mind: love the Lord your God, and love your neighbor as yourself (Deut 6:5; Lev 19:18; Matt 22:37–39). To love one's neighbor well, one must begin by loving oneself and avoid excessively harsh forms of asceticism.

Remember that death will not delay: it is inevitable and may come sooner **14:12–13** rather than later (7:36), for **the decree** (or "covenant") **of** †**Hades**—the moment of your death—**has not been shown to you**. Hades (Hebrew *Sheol*) is the under-world and abode of the dead (17:27; 21:10; Ps 16:10; Isa 28:15). There was not yet a clear doctrine of life after death in the Old Testament prior to the book of Wisdom (Wis 3:1–5). Since your time on earth is limited, **do good to a friend**

(Hebrew: "to one who loves you") **before you die**, and **give to him** generously
and according to your ability while you still can (Prov 3:27–28).

14:14–15   The same consideration of life's brevity invites one to live joyfully. Echoing
the teaching of Ecclesiastes, Ben Sira advises to **not deprive yourself of a happy
day** but enjoy God's good gifts while they last (Eccles 7:14; 9:7–10). Do not let
your share of desired good pass by you, missing the opportunity to make the
best of your life. Otherwise, you will **leave the fruit of your labors to another**,
with your hard-earned possessions **divided by lot** to your heirs after you die
(Sir 11:19; 14:4; Ps 49:10).

14:16–17   **Give** generously to others, therefore, **and take** the blessings that come your
way. **Beguile yourself** or "enjoy life," for **in Hades**—the world of the dead—
one cannot look for luxury. In the Old Testament period, it was believed that
rewards and punishments were meted out in this life, not in the next. This
perspective changes in the New Testament; thus, Christians must read Sirach
"in the light of Christ crucified and risen" (Catechism 129), and in view of his
revelation of heaven and hell (Matt 5:3, 19–20; 6:19–21). **All living beings** (literally, "all flesh") **become old** and wear out **like a garment** (see Ps 102:26; Isa
50:9), **for the decree** or "covenant" (Greek) **of old** that God established in the
garden of Eden—the penalty for eating of the tree of the knowledge of good
and evil—**is, "You must surely die"** (see Gen 2:17).

14:18–19   Human life is as precarious and passing as the **flourishing leaves** that sea-
sonally fall and sprout anew. So are the mortal **generations of flesh and blood**
(17:31; 1 Cor 15:50): **one dies and another is born** (Isa 34:4; 40:6–8). **Every
product** or work made by human hands eventually **decays and ceases to exist**—
including **the man who made it**. All the more must one make the best of what
has been entrusted to us in this life.

Reflection and Application (14:3–19)

Is wealth good or bad? On the one hand, traditional biblical wisdom asserts
that wealth is a sign of God's favor. It is God who grants people the power to
acquire wealth (Deut 8:18), who makes some poor and others rich (1 Sam
2:7), and who grants riches and honor to those who love him (1 Chron 29:12;
2 Chron 1:12; Prov 8:21). Wealth is a reward for diligence (Prov 12:27) and a
"strong city" (10:15).

Yet paradoxically, wealth comes with many dangers. Many have been led
astray by the love of money, such as Achan (Josh 7:20–21), Gehazi (2 Kings
5:19–27), the rich young ruler (Matt 19:22–23), and Judas Iscariot (Matt 26:14–
15). It is foolish to trust in riches, for they cannot protect one in times of need
(Pss 52:7; 62:10), and no one can take them at death (Prov 11:4; 27:24; Luke
12:16–21; James 5:1–3). One cannot serve two masters—God and mammon

(Matt 6:24)—because care for riches chokes the seed of the kingdom (Luke 8:14) and makes it much harder to enter it (18:24–25). For these reasons, Scripture calls the love of money the "root of all evils" (1 Tim 6:10). Avarice (or covetousness) is known as one of the seven capital or deadly sins because it leads to other vices such as treachery, fraud, falsehood, perjury, restlessness, violence, and insensibility to mercy.[24]

Nevertheless, wealth can be used well through the virtue of liberality, by honoring the Lord with it (Prov 3:9), giving to the poor (Prov 19:6; Luke 12:33), fostering friendships (Prov 19:4), or providing for one's family (1 Tim 5:8) (see the Reflection and Application section for 29:1–20, p. 233).

---

24. Thomas Aquinas, *Summa Theologiae* II-II q. 118 a. 8.

Part IV

Sirach 14:20–23:28

Part IV begins with a fourth poem on the pursuit of wisdom, in which Ben Sira emphasizes the determination necessary to find her (14:20–27) and the benefits she grants to those who do (15:1–10). He then considers the questions of human sin, free will, responsibility, the origin of evil (15:11–20), and God's punishment of sinners (16:1–23). This is followed by a reflection on God's wisdom, justice, and mercy in his creation of man (16:24–17:14). Because God repays all human actions with rewards or punishments, all must forsake their sins and turn to God (17:15–32), the benevolent judge (18:1–14). Ben Sira also urges people to exercise prudence in words and deeds by giving gifts graciously, engaging in self-examination, restraining their appetites, and avoiding gossip (18:15–19:17). The wise person distinguishes between true and false wisdom (19:18–30), knows when to choose between silence and speech (20:1–31), avoids sin's deceptive paths (21:1–22:18), preserves valuable friendships (22:19–26), and seeks God's help to control thoughts, words, and deeds (22:27–23:28).

IV.A. Courting Lady Wisdom (14:20–15:10)

> ²⁰**Blessed is the man who meditates on wisdom**
> **and who reasons intelligently.**
> ²¹**He who reflects in his mind on her ways**
> **will also ponder her secrets.**
> ²²**Pursue wisdom like a hunter,**
> **and lie in wait on her paths.**
> ²³**He who peers through her windows**
> **will also listen at her doors;**
> ²⁴**he who encamps near her house**
> **will also fasten his tent peg to her walls;**

²⁵he will pitch his tent near her,
>   and will lodge in an excellent lodging place;
²⁶he will place his children under her shelter,
>   and will camp under her boughs;
²⁷he will be sheltered by her from the heat,
and will dwell in the midst of her glory.

^{15:1}The man who fears the Lord will do this,
>   and he who holds to the law will obtain wisdom.
²She will come to meet him like a mother,
>   and like the wife of his youth she will welcome him.
³She will feed him with the bread of understanding,
>   and give him the water of wisdom to drink.
⁴He will lean on her and will not fall,
>   and he will rely on her and will not be put to shame.
⁵She will exalt him above his neighbors,
>   and will open his mouth in the midst of the assembly;
she will fill him with a spirit of wisdom and understanding,
>   *and clothe him with a robe of glory.*
⁶He will find gladness and a crown of rejoicing,
>   and will acquire an everlasting name.
⁷Foolish men will not obtain her,
>   and sinful men will not see her.
⁸She is far from men of pride,
>   and liars will never think of her.

⁹A hymn of praise is not fitting on the lips of a sinner,
>   for it has not been sent from the Lord.
¹⁰For a hymn of praise should be uttered in wisdom,
>   and the Lord will prosper it.

OT: Ps 1:1–2; Prov 8:34; 9:1–6; Song 2:9; Wis 8:2
NT: John 4:10–15; 1 Cor 2:6–16
Catechism: wisdom is truth, 215–17; Mary, seat of wisdom, 721; praise, 2639–43
Lectionary: 15:1–6: St. Bernard, Abbot and Doctor; St. Albert the Great, Bishop and Doctor; Common of Doctors of the Church

Blessed or happy (14:1–2; Matt 5:3–11) is the one **who meditates on wisdom**:   14:20–21
this is an echo of Ps 1:1–2, which praises the person who meditates on the †Torah
(Sir 6:37; Ps 119:15). One who does so **reasons intelligently** and lucidly. One
who **reflects** in **mind** and heart **on her ways** and steadfastly keeps God's commandments not only finds pleasantness and peace (Prov 3:17; 8:32) but also
ponders **her secrets**—deeper insights that wisdom reveals to those who follow
her persistently (Sir 4:18; 39:3, 7).

    Pursue wisdom like a hunter—with cleverness and determination—**and lie**   14:22–23
in wait with patience and perseverance **on her paths**, where she is found. The

Hebrew suggests pursuing her "like a scout" (NABRE) or "like a spy" (Latin *quasi investigator*), implying the use of shrewdness in pursuing her. The image of peering **through her windows** could develop the spy metaphor but more likely evokes courtship (Song 2:9). A young man eager to pursue Wisdom might even **listen at her doors,** suggesting that Lady Wisdom dwells in a home (Prov 8:34; 9:1).

14:24–25   Wisdom's suitor is so dedicated to winning her that he **encamps near her house,** close **to her walls,** not hesitating to **pitch his tent** and live **near her** as her neighbor. To learn her deeper secrets, it is not enough to pay her an occasional visit; one must **lodge** permanently in the **excellent lodging place** where she abides. The Hebrew describes the seeker as "dwelling in a good dwelling" or "tabernacling in a good tabernacle," evoking Israel's sanctuary in the wilderness, in which God's presence rested (24:10).

14:26–27   The metaphor shifts to present wisdom as a sheltering tree: the wisdom seeker places **his children under her shelter** so that they may find protection in her (Hebrew: "he builds his nest in her leaves"; see NABRE). Sheltered **from the heat** of life's trials beneath her branches, he dwells **in the midst of her glory** (Hebrew: "in her home," NABRE). The theme of wisdom's glory—alluding to the revelation of God's glory at Mount Sinai and in the temple—recurs frequently in Sirach (4:13; 17:13; 42:16–17; 50:11).

15:1–2   Ben Sira describes the rewards that await the wisdom seeker once he attains her. As explained elsewhere (1:11–20; 2:7–17; 19:20; 21:11), one **who fears the Lord** perseveres in his pursuit of wisdom (14:20–27) by observing **the law** and its commandments (1:26; 6:37; 9:15) until he proves himself worthy to **obtain wisdom**. Using a double metaphor, Ben Sira personifies Wisdom coming **to meet him like a** tender **mother** welcoming her cherished son (Wis 7:12; Isa 49:15; 66:13), or **like the wife of his youth** (Greek: "a virgin bride," NJB) eagerly waiting for her beloved husband (Prov 4:6–9; Wis 8:2).

15:3–4   No longer displaying her earlier severity (4:17; 6:20–21), Wisdom prepares a lavish meal for her son or husband, eager to **feed him with the bread of understanding, and give him the water of wisdom to drink.** This scene recalls Lady Wisdom's similar feast in Prov 9:1–6, where she invites her followers to partake of her banquet of insight and understanding, in contrast to Dame Folly's paltry meal of vice and ignorance leading to death in Prov 9:17–18 (also Isa 55:1–2; John 4:10–15; 6:35).[1] Later Jewish literature often refers to the "bread" and "water" (or wine) of the Torah.[2] The one who fears the Lord, strengthened by Wisdom's banquet, **will lean on her and will not fall,** for she is his support and pillar. By relying on her, he is not **put to shame** (Sir 24:22), like Adam and Eve before the fall (Gen 2:25), and in contrast to those who, by sinning and pursuing Folly, are

---

1. In Proverbs, "Lady Folly" or "Dame Folly" is a personification of foolishness and Wisdom's nemesis.
2. Midrash Song of Songs Rabbah 1.2.19; Midrash Genesis Rabbah 70.5; Babylonian Talmud, *Hagigah* 14a.

The Torah Exalts Her Followers

BIBLICAL BACKGROUND

In Sirach and in Jewish tradition, the law is the expression of God's wisdom (24:23), for it teaches how to live in communion with him. Accordingly, just as Wisdom exalts her followers in Sirach, so does the law in rabbinic literature. The †Mishnah thus exhorts its readers: Pursue the †Torah, and the Torah will exalt you.

> Everyone who occupies himself with Torah for its own sake merits many things; not only that, but he makes the entire world worthwhile. He is called beloved friend, a lover of God, a lover of humanity, one who gladdens God, and gladdens humanity. His Torah study clothes him in humility and reverence, and leads him to be righteous, pious, upright, and faithful. It distances him from sin, and draws him near goodness. From him come the benefits of counsel and resourcefulness, of understanding and courage . . . (Prov 8:14). It gives him sovereignty and dominion and discerning judgment. It reveals to him secrets of Torah. He becomes an ever-flowing fountain, a stream that never runs dry. He becomes modest, patient, and forgiving of affronts. It magnifies and exalts him over all creation.[a]

a. Mishnah, *Avot* 6:1, in William Berkson, *Pirke Avot: Timeless Wisdom for Modern Life*, trans. Menachem Fisch (Philadelphia: The Jewish Publication Society, 2010), 213.

covered with shame (Job 8:22; Prov 9:13; Dan 12:2). The image of Wisdom as a loving mother and virgin bride anticipates the Church's identification of the Blessed Virgin Mary as the "Seat of Wisdom" (Catechism 721).

15:5–6   Wisdom **will exalt** the one who fears the Lord to a position of honor and prominence **above his neighbors**, so that he will **open his mouth** and speak wisely in the public forum, as Wisdom does (24:1–2). The †Vulgate adds that *she will fill him with a spirit of wisdom and understanding* (see Isa 11:2) *and clothe him with a robe of glory* (Sir 6:29–31; 45:8; 50:11). He will not only **find gladness** but also reign with **a crown of rejoicing** (1:11) and **acquire an everlasting name**, suggesting that he will be remembered forever (Isa 56:5).

15:7–8   While those who fear the Lord are assured of finding wisdom, she remains hidden from **foolish** and **sinful men**. This confirms that the pursuit of wisdom is not only an *intellectual* quest but also a *moral* and *spiritual* one. The wicked can never attain her, because **she is far** from **pride** (Hebrew: "scoffers") and deceit; **liars never think of her** because her nature is truth, as God himself is truth (4:25, 28; Catechism 216–17).

15:9–10   **A hymn of praise** is the natural response of the just, who pursue wisdom and laud God not only for what he does but for who he is (Catechism 2639). As they recognize God's character—his goodness, mercy, justice, power, and strength—he grants them fitting words to express their praise. Such words are **not fitting on the lips of a sinner**, not only because sinners fail to recognize who God is, but also because their praise would be insincere, given their violation of God's will. Thus, **the Lord** does not grant sinners such a hymn, for it **should be uttered in wisdom** and not in hypocrisy. The Hebrew reads: "But praise is uttered by the mouth of the wise, and its rightful owner teaches it" (NABRE). Praising God is the outward manifestation of the wisdom of the just.

IV.B. (i) Human Free Will and Divine Justice: On the Origin of Good and Evil (15:11–20)

¹¹Do not say, "Because of the Lord I left the right way";
    for he will not do what he hates.
¹²Do not say, "It was he who led me astray";
    for he has no need of a sinful man.
¹³The Lord hates all abominations,
    and they are not loved by those who fear him.
¹⁴It was he who created man in the beginning,
    and he left him in the power of his own inclination.
¹⁵If you will, you can keep the commandments, *they will save you*;
    if you trust in God, you too shall live.
¹⁶He has placed before you fire and water:
    stretch out your hand for whichever you wish.
¹⁷Before a man are life and death, good and evil,
    and whichever he chooses will be given to him.
¹⁸For great is the wisdom of the Lord;
    he is mighty in power and sees everything.
¹⁹The eyes of the Lord are on those who fear him,
    and he knows every deed of man.
²⁰He has not commanded any one to be ungodly,
    and he has not given any one permission to sin.

OT: Gen 1:27, 31; 3:1–7; Deut 11:26–28; 30:15–20
NT: James 1:13–15
Catechism: providence and the scandal of evil, 309–14; the fall and original sin, 385–409; human freedom, 1730–48
Lectionary: 15:16–20: Sixth Sunday in Ordinary Time (Year A)

15:11–13   Ben Sira now considers the question of sin, human free will, and divine justice: Is God responsible for evil? Some may try to excuse their wrongful actions by claiming that God led them to sin, saying, **"Because of the Lord I left the right way"** (Hebrew: "my transgression is from God"), or **"It was he who led me astray."** This view, which may derive from the misinterpretation of some Old Testament passages (Exod 9:12; 2 Sam 24:1; Isa 45:7), is untenable.

The Good and Evil Inclinations

BIBLICAL BACKGROUND

Ben Sira's assertion that God left man "in the power of his own inclination" (Hebrew *yetzer*; Greek *diaboulion*, 15:14) points to a concept that would later become central in Jewish thought. According to rabbinic tradition, God formed two impulses in man, the good inclination (*yetzer hatov*) and the evil inclination (*yetzer hara'*).[a] Although this idea seems to conflict with Christian doctrine, which asserts that "God is in no way, directly or indirectly, the cause of moral evil" (Catechism 311), it may be a metaphorical way of saying that God created man with the freedom to choose between good and evil. The Catholic theological tradition certainly rejects the idea that God "formed" the evil inclination in man. Yet the Catechism adds that God *permits* evil (by giving each person the possibility of choosing it) "because he respects the freedom of his creatures and, mysteriously, knows how to derive good from it" (Catechism 311). The Jewish concept of the *yetzer hara'* is closely related to the Catholic notion of concupiscence—"the movement of the sensitive appetite contrary to the operation of the human reason" (Catechism 2515). Both traditions hold that this inclination toward evil unsettles man's moral faculties and inclines man to commit sins. Yet Christian tradition holds that concupiscence is not formed by God but "stems from the disobedience of the first sin" (Catechism 2515; see also 405).

The *yetzer hara'* is first mentioned in Gen 6:5 ("Every imagination [*yetzer*] of the thoughts of [man's] heart was only evil continually") and Gen 8:21 ("The imagination [*yetzer*] of man's heart is evil from his youth"). In Jewish tradition, it is loosely associated with untamed natural passions (especially sexual desire). In this light, some rabbis teach that there is something redeemable about the *yetzer hara'*, as without it, a man would never build a house, take a wife, or beget children (see 1 Cor 7:9).[b] At the same time, the *yetzer hara'* is also associated with the angel of death and Satan,[c] manifesting itself in traits such as vindictiveness, avarice, anger, and vanity. It tends to grow with a person, so that the greater the person, the greater his or her *yetzer hara'*: at first, it is a mere traveler in the soul (a careless sin); then it becomes a guest (a habitual sin), until it finally makes itself master of the house (an ingrained vice), prevailing over and seeking to kill the person daily.[d] Thus, the *yetzer hara'* must be resisted and overcome. A rabbinic parable on Eccles 9:14–15 depicts the *yetzer hara'* as a great king besieging a little city—the human body and heart. The city is delivered by a poor wise man (the *yetzer hatov*), repentance, and good deeds.[e] Another effective antidote to the *yetzer hara'* is the study and observance of Torah because it orders, guides, and disciplines untamed natural urges.[f] The *yetzer hara'* will no longer have power over man in the age to come.[g] For now, the rabbis interpret the injunction to love God "with all your heart" (Deut 6:5) as an invitation to love him wholly by subordinating both instincts to divine ends and redirecting their inner division toward a wholehearted devotion to God.[h]

In the New Testament, St. Paul identifies the inclination to sin with the rebellion of the "flesh" against the "spirit" (Rom 8:5–13; Gal 5:16–26; Eph 2:3). In contrast to the Jewish idea of "redirecting" the *yetzer hara'* toward good ends, however, Paul teaches that concupiscence or "the flesh" must always be resisted. If God has indeed left man "in the power of his own inclination" or counsel (Sir 15:14; see Catechism 1730), this is so that he may always combat the movements of concupiscence and bring them in line with God's will and commandments—a spiritual battle that can be won only with the aid of God's grace (Catechism 409, 978, 1264).[i]

a. Babylonian Talmud, *Berakhot* 61a; *Qiddushin* 30b.

b. Midrash Genesis Rabbah 9:7.

c. Babylonian Talmud, *Baba Bathra* 16a.

d. Babylonian Talmud, *Sukkah* 52a–b.

e. Babylonian Talmud, *Nedarim* 32b.

f. Babylonian Talmud, *Qiddushin* 30b.

g. Babylonian Talmud, *Sukkah* 52b.

h. Mishnah, *Berakhot* 9:5.

i. See Joseph Jacobs, "Yezer ha-ra," in *The Jewish Encyclopedia*, ed. Isidore Singer (New York: Funk & Wagnalls, 1901–6), 12:602–6. See also Samuel Rosenblatt, "Inclination, Good and Evil," in *Encyclopedia Judaica*, ed. Fred Skolnik and Michael Berenbaum (Detroit: Thomson Gale, 2007), 9:756–57.

God never leads people to sin, **for he will not do what he hates**—namely, sin and evil (Ps 97:10; Prov 8:13; Amos 5:15; James 1:13–15)—and he does not need **a sinful man** to accomplish his purposes. Although he may use the wicked to achieve his ends (Hab 1:5–11), this may turn out to be either for their salvation (Gen 50:20) or for their demise if they persist in rejecting God and his ways (Prov 16:4; Rom 9:22). Just as **the Lord hates all abominations** (Hebrew: "evil and abomination"), so the wise **who fear him** should also love what he loves and hate what he hates by diligently avoiding whatever he has declared to be evil.

15:14   To explain the origin of sin, Ben Sira returns to the Genesis account of creation: God **created man in the beginning** (see Gen 1:27) and made him "very good" (1:31). The Hebrew adds: "and put him into the hand of his kidnapper"— possibly a reference to Satan. Yet the presence of evil in the world cannot be used as an excuse to sin, for God left man **in the power of his own inclination** (Hebrew *yetzer*; see the sidebar "The Good and Evil Inclinations" above), deliberation, and free choice. God endowed Adam and Eve with free will and the capacity to obey him. Yet tempted by the devil, they abused their freedom and deliberately chose to disobey God's commandment (Gen 3:1–7; Catechism 397). In the same way, each person is given the freedom to choose his or her own actions. As the Second Vatican Council expresses it, "God willed that man should be 'left in the hand of his own counsel,' so that he might of his own accord seek his Creator and freely attain his full and blessed perfection by cleaving to him."[3] God created humanity good, but sin came into the world because human

3. *Gaudium et Spes* 17; see also Catechism 1730.

beings abused their free will and strayed from God's will. Thus, evil originates in people, not in God (Rom 5:12).

Ben Sira strongly affirms human free will and personal responsibility: **If you will, you can keep the commandments**. Despite the wound of original sin, man still has "the possibility of choosing *between good and evil*, and thus of growing in perfection or of failing and sinning" (Catechism 1732). This freedom makes people responsible for their acts (Catechism 1734). The RSV-2CE (following the Vulgate) adds that the commandments *will save you*—or more accurately "preserve" or "protect" you (*conservabunt te*) by keeping you on the right track. The statement **if you trust in God, you too shall live** follows the Hebrew (see Hab 2:4).[4] While the law and commandments serve as divine aids guiding man toward salvation, man still needs grace and faith to sustain him (Matt 19:17–21; Gal 5:6; Eph 2:8; James 2:14–26; Catechism 1949).

15:15

Ben Sira presents life's fundamental choice using the symbols of **fire and water** placed before every person. Each individual has the power to shape their own fate and can freely **stretch out** their **hand** to pick either one. Both fire and water are needed for life, but here, fire likely represents destruction, while water stands for life (3:30). These images reflect the choice between **life and death, good and evil** that is central to God's covenant with humanity (Deut 11:26–28; 30:15–20; Jer 21:8). One's destiny is ultimately in one's own hands: **whichever he chooses will be given to him**.

15:16–17

The mysterious interaction between divine providence and human free will reveals the greatness of the Lord's **wisdom**. Although people remain free to choose their destinies, God is still **mighty in power and sees everything**. He looks kindly upon **those who fear him** and **knows every deed of man**, including each person's choices for good or evil. Ben Sira concludes his argument by rebutting again the allegations made in 15:11–12: God is never responsible for moral evil. He never desires anyone **to be ungodly**, nor does he give **any one permission to sin**, but he desires everyone to choose the good. The Hebrew adds: "And he does not show mercy to the one who works vanity or to the one who reveals secret counsel."

15:18–20

Reflection and Application (15:11–20)

Ben Sira makes some startling claims about the commandments. First, he asserts that it is possible to observe them. Second, he seems to attribute salvific power to them (15:15). The law of Moses contains 613 commandments—365 prohibitions and 248 positive mandates.[5] Is it possible to keep them all? And do they have power to save?

---

4. The Greek of 15:15b is difficult. It could be further emphasizing human free will, stating that "to act faithfully is a matter of your own choice" (RSV, NRSV; compare ESV-CE); or it may be simply asserting that by keeping the commandments you will "be faithful to his will" (NJB).

5. Babylonian Talmud, *Makkot* 23b.

At first sight, the New Testament seems to contradict Sirach. St. Paul argues that the "law of sin" in the human heart wages war against the law of God (Rom 7:14–23), making it virtually impossible to consistently keep the commandments and do what is right. Submitting to the law is likened to taking on a "yoke of slavery" (Gal 5:1) that is impossible to bear (Acts 15:10). Those who attempt to rely exclusively on the law are even placed under a curse (Gal 3:10). Thus, even though "the law is holy, and the commandment is holy and just and good" (Rom 7:12), one is justified before God not by the works of the law but by grace through faith (Rom 3:20, 28; Gal 2:16; 3:11; Eph 2:8–9). Christ is the one who saves, not the law.

And yet, several biblical texts indicate that keeping the law is possible (Deut 30:11–14), and that one can be "blameless" before God in regard to the commandments (Pss 18:23–24; 119:1–3; Luke 1:6; Phil 3:6). God's law and precepts are called "perfect," for they revive the soul, make wise the simple, rejoice the heart, and enlighten the eyes (Ps 19:7–10). In this sense, the commandments *guide* us toward salvation, though they are insufficient to attain the fullness of salvation (Catechism 1949). This said, even in Old Testament times, keeping the law did not require attaining an impossible standard of perfection. The Israelite who sinned (and all sinned, Ps 14:3; see also Rom 3:23) could ask God for forgiveness (Pss 19:11–13; 32:1–5; 51:1–17) and obtain atonement by offering sin and guilt offerings (Lev 4:1–6:7). Thus, an ancient Israelite could be righteous before God and "live by his faith" (Hab 2:4) by striving to keep the commandments to the best of his ability while trusting in God's mercy and obtaining forgiveness through repentance and sacrifices whenever he fell short.

How does this apply to Christians today? First, it is important to note that the 613 commandments of the †Torah are not binding on Christians as they originally were on Israel (Acts 15), but are now fulfilled and perfected by the "Law of the Gospel" (Catechism 1967). And yet, "far from abolishing or devaluing the moral prescriptions of the Old Law," the New Law "releases their hidden potential and has new demands arise from them" (Catechism 1968). These demands are expressed in the Church's exposition of the †Decalogue as found in the third part of the *Catechism of the Catholic Church* (Catechism 2083–557).

Still, Ben Sira's principles remain the same: although it is impossible to lead a morally perfect life "by the natural power of free will and without the necessary help of God's grace,"[6] this does not mean that we should not try! Too many people in our time despair of their ability to make good moral choices, perhaps thinking that "I was born this way" or "my depression (or anxiety, or addiction, or upbringing) made me do it." While human freedom is greatly compromised by the wound of original sin, Scripture teaches that human beings can and must

---

6. Overconfidence in a person's ability to live a good life without the help of God's grace is known as the heresy of Pelagianism (Catechism 406).

choose right over wrong, and they always remain responsible for their actions (Catechism 1734).[7]

IV.B. (ii) Human Free Will and Divine Justice: The Fate of Sinners (16:1–23)

¹Do not desire a multitude of useless children,
  nor rejoice in ungodly sons.
²If they multiply, do not rejoice in them,
  unless the fear of the Lord is in them.
³Do not trust in their survival,
  and do not rely on their multitude;
for one is better than a thousand,
  and to die childless is better than to have ungodly children.
⁴For through one man of understanding a city will be filled with
    people,
  but through a tribe of lawless men it will be made desolate.
⁵Many such things my eye has seen,
  and my ear has heard things more striking than these.

⁶In an assembly of sinners a fire will be kindled,
  and in a disobedient nation wrath was kindled.
⁷He was not propitiated for the ancient giants
  who revolted in their might.
⁸He did not spare the neighbors of Lot,
  whom he loathed on account of their insolence.
⁹He showed no pity for a nation devoted to destruction,
  for those destroyed in their sins;
¹⁰nor for the six hundred thousand men on foot,
  who rebelliously assembled in their stubbornness.
¹¹Even if there is only one stiffnecked person,
  it will be a wonder if he remains unpunished.
For mercy and wrath are with the Lord;
  he is mighty to forgive, and he pours out wrath.
¹²As great as his mercy, so great is also his reproof;
  he judges a man according to his deeds.

---

7. Quoting St. Augustine, the Council of Trent condemns the idea that the commandments are impossible to observe and asserts that they can be observed with the help of Christ's grace: "But no one, however much justified, should consider himself exempt from the observance of the commandments; no one should make use of that rash statement forbidden under an anathema by the Fathers, that the commandments of God are *impossible* to observe for a man who is justified. 'For God does not command impossibilities, but by commanding admonishes you both to do what you can do, and to pray for what you cannot do, and assists you that you may be able'; 'whose commandments are not heavy' (1 John 5:3), 'whose yoke is sweet and whose burden is light'" (Matt 11:30)" (DS 1536; see also 1569–70; Catechism 2068, 2072).

¹³The sinner will not escape with his plunder,
   and the patience of the godly will not be frustrated.
¹⁴He will make room for every act of mercy;
   every one will receive in accordance with his deeds.

¹⁷Do not say, "I shall be hidden from the Lord,
   and who from on high will remember me?
Among so many people I shall not be known,
   for what is my soul in the boundless creation?
¹⁸Behold, heaven and the highest heaven,
   the abyss and the earth, will tremble at his visitation.
¹⁹The mountains also and the foundations of the earth
   shake with trembling when he looks upon them.
²⁰And no mind will reflect on this.
   Who will ponder his ways?
²¹Like a tempest which no man can see,
   so most of his works are concealed.
²²Who will announce his acts of justice?
   Or who will await them? For the covenant is far off."
²³This is what one devoid of understanding thinks;
   a senseless and misguided man thinks foolishly.

OT: Gen 18:20–19:28; Wis 3:10–4:6
NT: Matt 16:27; Rom 8:28; 9:22; Rev 22:12
Catechism: particular judgment, 1021–22; final judgment, 1038–41

16:1–2 Having emphasized each person's responsibility for their own sins, Ben Sira now discusses God's punishment of sinners. He begins with ungodly children (16:1–5). Although Scripture consistently views children as a blessing (Gen 15:5; Pss 127:3–5; 128:3–4), it is pointless to **desire** many **children** without a firm commitment to raise them well, lest they grow up to be **useless** and **ungodly**. While parents must love their children unconditionally, they must also train them to grow up in **the fear of the Lord**. A large family is of no advantage if the children turn out to be wicked, as they will leave behind a bitter legacy, and their inheritance will perish (40:15–16; 41:5–6).

16:3 Parents should not place their **trust** in the **survival** of their children or assume they will have a long life, as they may come to an untimely end (Deut 28:15–19; Job 24:24; Ps 55:23; Wis 14:15). Neither should parents **rely on** having a **multitude** of children. As the longer Greek text explains, many ungodly children only bring greater grief: "For you will groan in untimely mourning, and will know of their sudden end."[8] The next clause is somewhat obscure but clarified by the †Vulgate: **for one** *who fears God* **is better than a thousand** *wicked sons* (compare Douay). It is better, therefore, to **die childless** after having

8. NRSV footnote; compare ESV-CE footnote.

lived a virtuous life **than to have ungodly children** who will bring evil into the world (Wis 3:10–4:6).

Godliness is inherently fruitful: through **one man of understanding** (He-   16:4–5
brew: "a solitary childless person who fears the Lord") **a city will be filled with people**—as it was with Abraham, who became the father of a great multitude even though his wife Sarah was initially barren (Gen 15:2–5). Ben Sira may also have in mind the tale of a "poor wise man" who by his wisdom delivered a besieged city (Eccles 9:14–15). By contrast, **a tribe of lawless men**—such as the inhabitants of Sodom—will make a city **desolate**, for its iniquity will draw divine judgment upon it (Gen 18:20–19:28). Ben Sira appeals to his own experience and eyewitness account: he has personally **seen** families that increased in numbers but not in virtue and only left a legacy of godlessness and chaos. He also recalls **striking** accounts from the past when God punished sinners for their wicked deeds (16:6–10).

In an assembly of sinners—such as that of Korah, Dathan, Abiram, and   16:6–8
their followers—a heavenly **fire will be kindled**, as fire consumed those leaders of **a disobedient nation** when they rebelled against Moses and Aaron in the wilderness, and divine **wrath was kindled** against them (45:18–19; Num 16:1–35; Ps 106:18). God **was not propitiated**—that is, he did not forgive **the ancient giants** (Hebrew: "princes of old"), those "mighty men" who unleashed the flood when they **revolted** against God (Gen 6:1–4; Wis 14:6). Nor did he **spare the neighbors of Lot**—the wicked inhabitants of Sodom and Gomorrah who were **loathed** and destroyed because of **their insolence** and pride. Other biblical sources also attribute the sins of Sodom to neglect of the poor and sexual immorality (Gen 19:1–25; Ezek 16:49–50; Jude 7).

The Lord **showed no pity** to the Canaanites, notorious for their immoral   16:9–10
practices and thus doomed **to destruction**; they were dispossessed and **destroyed in their sins** (see Exod 34:11–16; Num 33:51–56; Deut 7:1–2; Wis 12:3–7). Neither did **the six hundred thousand** Israelites of the exodus, who stubbornly rebelled against Moses and God during their wilderness wanderings, escape punishment for their sins (Sir 46:7–8; Exod 12:37; Num 11:21; 14:1–35).

Ben Sira turns from examples of the past to warnings about the future (16:11–   16:11–14
16). Just as it was for the generation of the exodus (Exod 32:9; 33:3–5), so it will be for **stiffnecked** individuals who stubbornly oppose God—they will not go **unpunished**. **Mercy and wrath** are two essential attributes of **the Lord**: with the former, **he is mighty to forgive** those who repent and turn to him, but he also metes out punishment to those who continually resist him (Sir 5:6). **As great as his mercy** is, so are **his reproof** and chastisement severe. **He judges** each person **according to his deeds**—expressing the classic doctrine of retribution (11:26; 12:2; Matt 16:27; Rev 22:12): **the sinner will not escape with** ill-gotten **plunder**, and God will reward **the patience of the godly** for their **every act of mercy**, for he will not overlook a single act of kindness.

16:15–16   The Hebrew, long Greek text, and Syriac add these two verses (omitted from the shorter Greek text and the Latin Vulgate).[9] **The Lord hardened Pharaoh** at the time of the exodus so that the stubborn king of Egypt **did not know** God (Exod 7:3; 9:12; 10:27; 11:10). This was done so that his mighty **works** of delivering Israel from slavery **might be known** to all nations **under heaven**. In this way, **his mercy** was **manifest** not only to Israel but to all **creation**. The lessons of the exodus serve as a stark reminder of God's justice and mercy to Ben Sira's own generation.

16:17   In response to Ben Sira's confidence that God will judge all sin, some might be tempted to think that their own deeds will go unnoticed (16:17–23), saying, **"I shall be hidden from the Lord."** The skeptic foolishly believes that God does not see him **among so many people** in the world and that he will not be noticed, thinking his **soul** is insignificant **in the boundless creation**. By assuming that he is not important to God, or that God is too great, inscrutable, and remote to concern himself with the skeptic's sins, such a person expresses a form of Deism, denying that God is intimately involved in every aspect of his creation (Catechism 285).

16:18–19   The skeptic depicts the supreme power of God over all creation: even **the highest heaven** (literally, "the heaven of heavens"; see Deut 10:14; 1 Kings 8:27), the subterranean **abyss** or "great deep" (Hebrew *tehom*) of primordial waters (Gen 1:2; 7:11), **and the earth will tremble** when God comes to judge the earth (Pss 18:7–8; 97:4–5; Isa 29:6; Joel 2:10). The longer Greek text (GII) adds to verse 18: "The whole world past and present is in his will,"[10] so that even **the mountains** and the earth's **foundations shake with trembling** at the Lord's mere glance.

16:20–21   The Greek text (followed by the RSV-2CE and most other translations) continues the thought of verse 19, asserting that God's works are far removed from human knowledge and activity: **no mind will reflect** on the Lord's supreme power over creation, so that no one **will ponder** his mysterious, awe-inspiring **ways**. Like a violent **tempest** that people cannot see until it is suddenly upon them, so most of the Lord's **works** remain **concealed** from the human eye until the day of judgment. The Hebrew is quite different, continuing the thought of the skeptic in verse 17 who thinks he can get away with sinning with impunity: "Of me, therefore, he will take no notice; with my ways who will be concerned? If I sin, no eye will see me; if all in secret I act deceitfully, who is to know?" (NABRE). Such sinners mistakenly believe that the universe is so vast that God cannot possibly pay attention to their actions.

---

9. [15]**The Lord hardened Pharaoh so that he did not know him; in order that his works might be known under heaven.** [16]**His mercy is manifest to the whole of creation, and he divided his light and darkness with a plumb line** (Sir 16:15–16, RSV-2CE footnote; compare NRSV, ESV-CE, NABRE footnotes).

10. NRSV footnote; compare ESV-CE.

The skeptic now asks: **Who will announce** God's **acts of justice? Or who**   16:22
has the patience to **await them** indefinitely to see whether God is, in fact, just?
To the skeptic, **the covenant** between God and his people, and the promise of
just retribution for man's deeds, seems **far off**: he wonders whether it will even
come to pass, believing that God is slow in fulfilling his promises. The longer
Greek text and Vulgate add: "and a scrutiny for all comes at the end"[11]—further
emphasizing how God's judgment seems distant to the skeptic.

Ben Sira dismisses the words of the skeptic (16:17–22) as those spoken by   16:23
one devoid of understanding; only **a senseless and misguided man thinks
foolishly** enough to suppose that God will overlook both sins and good deeds.
The truth of each person's relationship with God, along with their most secret
deeds, will be revealed at the last judgment (Wis 4:20–5:23; Dan 7:10; Mal 3:18;
1 Cor 4:5; Catechism 678; 1039). Moreover, each person will be "rewarded im-
mediately after death in accordance with his works and faith" at the particular
judgment (Catechism 1021; see also Luke 16:22–23; Heb 9:27).

IV.C. (i) God's Wisdom, Justice, and Mercy: In His Creation of Man (16:24–17:14)

> [24]Listen to me, my son, and acquire knowledge,
>   and pay close attention to my words.
> [25]I will impart instruction by weight,
>   and declare knowledge accurately.
>
> [26]The works of the Lord have existed from the beginning by his
>   creation,
>   and when he made them, he determined their divisions.
> [27]He arranged his works in an eternal order,
>   and their dominion for all generations;
> they neither hunger nor grow weary,
>   and they do not cease from their labors.
> [28]They do not crowd one another aside,
>   and they will never disobey his word.
> [29]After this the Lord looked upon the earth,
>   and filled it with his good things;
> [30]with all kinds of living beings he covered its surface,
>   and to it they return.
>
> [17:1]The Lord created man out of earth,
>   *and made him into his own image;*
> [2]he turned him back into earth again,
>   but clothed him in strength like his own.

---

11. NRSV footnote; compare ESV-CE.

³He gave to men few days, a limited time,
   but granted them authority over the things upon the earth.
⁴He placed the fear of them in all flesh,
   and granted them dominion over beasts and birds.
⁶He made for them discretion, with a tongue and eyes and ears;
   he gave them a mind for thinking,
   and filled them with *the discipline of discernment.*
⁷*He created in them the* knowledge *of the spirit;*
   he filled their hearts with understanding,
   and showed them good and evil.
⁸He placed the fear of him into their hearts,
   showing them the majesty of his works.
⁹He made them glory in his wondrous deeds,
   ¹⁰that they might praise his holy name,
   to proclaim the grandeur of his works.
¹¹He bestowed knowledge upon them,
   and allotted to them the law of life.
¹²He established with them an eternal covenant,
   and showed them *his justice and* his judgments.
¹³Their eyes saw his glorious majesty,
   and their ears heard the glory of his voice.
¹⁴And he said to them, "Beware of all unrighteousness."
   And he gave commandment to each of them concerning his
   neighbor.

OT: Gen 1:27; 2:7; 3:19
NT: 1 Cor 11:7
Catechism: man, the image of God, 356–61, 1701–15

16:24–25   The fatherly address **Listen to me, my son** marks the beginning of a new section. In response to the skeptic who thinks that God is too far removed to care about each person's deeds (16:17–23), Ben Sira urges his disciple to **acquire knowledge** and **pay close attention** (literally, "set your heart") to the master's **words** and **instruction**, which **accurately** explain how the Lord's wisdom permeates every detail of creation.

16:26–28   Reflecting on the **works** that **the Lord** created **from the beginning**, Ben Sira recalls the first chapter of Genesis, which describes how God **determined** the **divisions**, realms, boundaries, and functions of everything he made. God **arranged his works**—referring here to the sun, moon, and stars—**in an eternal order**, so that **their dominion** over day and night would endure as long as the present universe (Gen 1:14–18; Ps 136:8–9). That the heavenly bodies **neither hunger nor grow weary**, nor **cease from their labors**, points to the enduring stability of the created order (Isa 40:26; Jer 31:35–36). The galaxies and planetary systems **do not crowd one another** but follow their course with extraordinary regularity. As part of a fine-tuned, well-ordered system, they

never disobey the Creator's **word** and order of creation (Pss 104:19; 148:5–6), unlike humans, who have the capacity to abuse their free will and stray away from his good purposes.

After creating the heavenly bodies, **the Lord looked upon the earth** that **16:29–30** he had made **and filled it with his good things**—such as the sea creatures and birds created on the fifth day of creation (Gen 1:20–23)—and the **living beings** that **covered its surface**—the land animals created on the sixth day (Gen 1:24–25). All of these **return** to the earth when they die (Sir 40:11; Ps 104:24–30; Eccles 3:20).

Ben Sira turns from God's creation of the universe to his creation of human- **17:1–2** kind and the gifts he bestowed on all humanity (17:1–10)[12] and specifically on Israel (17:11–14). Drawing from the first two chapters of Genesis, Ben Sira recalls that **the Lord created man out of earth** (Gen 2:7) *and made him into his own image* and likeness (Gen 1:26–27). This double allusion to Genesis points to human nature as a union of matter and spirit, body and soul (Catechism 362). Although God **turned him back into earth** after man sinned and became subject to death (Gen 3:19; Ps 146:4; Catechism 400), God still **clothed him in strength like his own**, delegating his authority, glory, and honor to humankind (Ps 8:5; 1 Cor 11:7).

Since the fall, God allotted humans **a limited time** to live (18:9–10; Gen **17:3–5** 6:3; Job 14:1–2; Ps 90:10), yet he still **granted them authority** to rule over **the earth** (Gen 1:26–28; Ps 8:6–8; Wis 9:2–3). **He placed the fear of them in all** living beings (Gen 9:2), granting them **dominion over beasts and birds**. Human dominance over the animal kingdom and mastery over nature through science and technological achievement reflect the unique gifts that God has given to the human race. The longer Greek text adds verse 5.[13] To enable people to rule over creation, the Lord not only gave them **five operations**—the senses of sight, hearing, smell, taste, and touch that humans share with animals. He also granted them **the gift of mind** or intelligence (Greek *nous*)—that is, the psychological faculty of understanding, thinking, and deciding—as well as the gift of **reason** (Greek *logos*), which Ben Sira views as **the interpreter of his operations**, which enables humans to process rationally what they perceive through the senses.

Rationality is what sets humans apart from all other animals. The Lord gave **17:6–7** them **discretion** (Greek *diaboulion*, translated as "inclination" in 15:14)—that is, counsel or deliberation enabling them to discern, make, and express rational

12. No Hebrew text is extant for this section. The text of the manuscripts is in disarray, resulting in different verse numbers between modern English translations. The RSV-2CE generally follows the Latin Vulgate.

13. **They obtained the use of the five operations of the Lord; as sixth he distributed to them the gift of mind, and as seventh reason, the interpreter of his operations** (Sir 17:5, RSV-2CE footnote; compare NRSV, ESV-CE, NABRE footnotes).

decisions by means of the senses, using the **tongue** to speak, **eyes** to see, and **ears** to hear. God also **gave them a mind** (literally, "heart") **for thinking** and understanding. The †Vulgate adds that he **filled them with** *the discipline of discernment* so that they could make good decisions, granted them **knowledge of the spirit** (perhaps meaning "spiritual knowledge"), *filled their hearts with* **understanding,** and revealed to them the difference between **good and evil**. This seems to allude to the fall of Adam and Eve. While in their state of innocence Adam and Eve intuitively knew the good, they obtained the knowledge of good and evil when they ate of the forbidden fruit in the garden of Eden (Gen 2:17; 3:5, 22).

17:8–10   God **placed the fear of him into their hearts:**[14] as people contemplate **the majesty of his works** and the greatness of his creation revealed to them, they are drawn to fear him and grow in wisdom. **He made them glory in his wondrous deeds**[15] so that, as they recognize his goodness in the magnificence of creation, they **praise his holy name** and **proclaim the grandeur of his works** in worship and adoration. Sirach, like Rom 1:19–20, teaches that human beings are able to see God's greatness in creation and thus should honor and praise him for it. However, Sirach focuses on the positive response of some human beings, while Romans addresses the Gentile world that rejected this revelation and instead worshiped idols.

17:11–13   While God gave knowledge to all people, **he bestowed** a special kind of **knowledge upon** his people Israel by endowing them with **the law of life—** the †Torah given at Mount Sinai, which is a source of life (24:23–29; 45:5; Deut 28:1–14; 30:16; Bar 4:1). As expressed in ancient Jewish tradition, "One who has acquired words of Torah acquires life in the World to come"[16]—that is, one who hears the word of God, understands it, and applies it to his or her life bears great fruit for the kingdom of God (Matt 13:23). This idea finds its supreme fulfillment in the person of Jesus, who, as the Incarnate Word (Greek *Logos*), is also the "Incarnate Torah" (see John 1:14; 5:39–40). At Mount Sinai, the Lord **established with** Israel **an eternal covenant** (Exod 19:5–6; Deut 5:1–5); by giving them the law, he **showed them** *his justice and* **his judgments**. The Israelites **saw his glorious majesty** when he appeared to them in thunder and lightning, fire and smoke, and they **heard the glory of his voice** when he spoke to Moses and to all the people (Sir 45:5; Exod 19:16–20:18; 24:15–17).

17:14   God said to Israel at Sinai, in effect, **"Beware of all unrighteousness"**—that is, of sins prohibited by the Torah, such as idolatry and Sabbath violation. Thus,

14. Follows a few Greek manuscripts and the New Vulgate. Most Greek manuscripts read: "He set his eye upon their hearts" (ESV-CE).

15. Verse 9—an addition from GII—is placed here according to a few Greek manuscripts, followed by the New Vulgate. Verse 9 follows v. 10 in some translations (NRSV) or is relegated to a footnote (ESV-CE).

16. Mishnah, *Avot* 2:7. *The Mishnah: A New Integrated Translation and Commentary*, https://www.echok.com/mishnah/nezikin_vol_2/Avot2.pdf.

he gave commandment not just collectively to the entire nation but also **to each** individual **concerning his neighbor** by prohibiting murder, adultery, theft, bearing false witness, and coveting (Exod 20:1–20). Israel's obedience to the Torah is the standard by which their faithfulness to the covenant is measured.

IV.C. (ii) God's Wisdom, Justice, and Mercy: In His Rewards and Punishments (17:15–18:14)

[15]Their ways are always before him,
    they will not be hidden from his eyes.
[17]He appointed a ruler for every nation,
    but Israel is the Lord's own portion.
[19]All their works are as the sun before him,
    and his eyes are continually upon their ways.
[20]Their iniquities are not hidden from him,
    and all their sins are before the Lord.
[22]A man's almsgiving is like a signet with the Lord,
    and he will keep a person's kindness like the apple of his eye.
[23]Afterward he will arise and repay them,
    and he will bring their recompense on their heads.
[24]Yet to those who repent he grants a return,
    and he encourages those whose endurance is failing,
    and he has appointed to them the lot of truth.

[25]Turn to the Lord and forsake your sins;
    pray in his presence and lessen your offenses.
[26]Return to the Most High and turn away from iniquity,
    and hate abominations intensely.
Know the justice and the judgments of God,
    and stand firm in the lot that is set before you,
    in prayer to God, the Almighty.
[27]Who will sing praises to the Most High in Hades,
    as do those who are alive and give thanks?
Tarry not in the waywardness of the ungodly,
    and give thanks before death.
[28]From the dead, as from one who does not exist, thanksgiving
        has ceased;
    he who is alive and well sings the Lord's praises.
[29]How great is the mercy of the Lord,
    and his forgiveness for those who turn to him!
[30]For all things cannot be in men,
    since a son of man is not immortal.
[31]What is brighter than the sun? Yet its light fails.
    So flesh and blood devise evil.

³²He marshals the host of the height of heaven;
  but all men are dust and ashes.

¹⁸:¹He who lives for ever created the whole universe;
  ²the Lord alone will be declared righteous.
⁴To none has he given power to proclaim his works;
  and who can search out his mighty deeds?
⁵Who can measure his majestic power?
  And who can fully recount his mercies?
⁶It is not possible to diminish or increase them,
  nor is it possible to trace the wonders of the Lord.
⁷When a man has finished, he is just beginning,
  and when he stops, he will be at a loss.
⁸What is man, and of what use is he?
  What is his good and what is his evil?
⁹The number of a man's days is great if he reaches a hundred
  years.
¹⁰Like a drop of water from the sea and a grain of sand
  so are a few years in the day of eternity.
¹¹Therefore the Lord is patient with them
  and pours out his mercy upon them.
¹²He sees and recognizes that their end will be evil;
  therefore he grants them forgiveness in abundance.
¹³The compassion of man is for his neighbor,
  but the compassion of the Lord is for all living beings.
He rebukes and trains and teaches them,
  and turns them back, as a shepherd his flock.
¹⁴He has compassion on those who accept his discipline
  and who are eager for his judgments.

OT: Ps 8; Zech 1:3–4; Mal 3:7
NT: Matt 4:17; Luke 5:32; 24:47; Acts 2:38; Rom 11:32; Rev 2:5
Catechism: conversion and penance, 1427–60; works of mercy, 2447; mercy and sin, 1846–48

17:15–16   Ben Sira previously admonished the skeptics who think that God is not concerned with their actions (16:17–23). This skepticism is foolish, because God reigns over the whole universe (16:26–30), over all humanity (17:1–10), and especially over Israel, to whom he gave the law as an expression of his justice (17:11–14). He now counters the same skeptics who deny that God will repay every human action with rewards or punishments (17:15–24). **Their ways are always before him**, for the Lord is constantly aware of people's actions. The longer Greek text adds verse 16 and part of verse 17.[17] Although

17. GII adds: ¹⁶Their ways from youth tend toward evil, and they are unable to make for themselves hearts of flesh in place of their stony hearts. ¹⁷For in the division of the nations of the whole earth . . . (Sir 17:16–17, RSV-2CE footnote).

everyone remains free to choose good or evil, fallen human nature inclines people **toward evil** from an early age, leaving them prone to sin (Gen 6:5; 8:21). Even Israelites, who have the †Torah as their guide, **are unable to make for themselves**, without the help of divine grace, **hearts of flesh** able to love God and neighbor **in place of their stony hearts** hardened by sin (Ezek 11:19; 36:26).

For in the division of the nations of the whole earth[18] established after the flood (Gen 10), the Lord **appointed a ruler for every nation**, meaning either a civil or perhaps an angelic ruler (Deut 32:8–9; Dan 10:13–21). Yet unlike the other nations, **Israel is the Lord's own portion** and treasured possession (Exod 19:5; Deut 7:6; Ps 135:4). The longer Greek text adds verse 18.[19] Because Israel is God's **first-born** (see Exod 4:22), **he brings up** the nation **with discipline** as an expression of his love (Prov 3:12). By shining **the light of his love** on Israel, **he does not neglect** his chosen people but manifests his bountiful providence toward them (Deut 31:6–8).

17:17–18

All human **works are as the sun before him**—as visible as they are in broad daylight (17:15; 23:19; Ps 94:11). Contrary to the claims of the skeptic (Sir 16:22), God always considers **their ways** so that none of **their iniquities** is **hidden from him**. Everyone's good deeds, but also **their sins**, are in plain sight **before the Lord**. Verse 21 (an addition from GII)[20] emphasizes the Lord's kindly providence over his judgment: because he is **gracious and knows his creatures,** he has not **abandoned them, but spared them**. God does not only keep track of evildoing; he also watches over his people and extends mercy whenever they turn to him (Deut 31:6–8; Ps 103:13–14; Wis 11:23–24).

17:19–21

The righteous are identified by their **almsgiving**, which is **like a signet with the Lord**—that is, "a work of justice pleasing to God" (Catechism 2447). A signet or "seal" was a signature ring that carried an engraved mark of identification (49:11; Song 8:6). The Lord remembers **a person's kindness** and good deeds like the precious **apple** (pupil) **of his eye** (see Deut 32:10; Ps 17:8; Zech 2:8), just as people value their eyesight as something very precious. **Afterward**, in the end, **he will arise** on the day of judgment and **repay** those skeptics who think that God does not act (Sir 16:22); **he will bring their recompense** or punishment upon them according to their works, so all will receive what they deserve (Ps 7:16; Jer 23:19; Ezek 22:31).

17:22–23

Yet to those who have failed to live righteously in the past but then **repent** (Greek *metanoeō*) of their sins, God **grants a return** to himself, to the covenant, and to a good life (Ezek 33:11). In every act of repentance, God's grace

17:24

---

18. An addition from GII (RSV-2CE footnote).

19. GII adds: **whom, being his first-born, he brings up with discipline, and allotting to him the light of his love, he does not neglect him** (Sir 17:18, RSV-2CE footnote).

20. GII adds: **But the Lord, who is gracious and knows his creatures, has neither left nor abandoned them, but spared them** (Sir 17:21, RSV-2CE footnote).

Repent and Return

BIBLICAL
BACKGROUND

Behind the Greek verb *metanoeō* in 17:24 lies almost certainly the He-brew word *shuv*, which means both "to repent" and "to return."[a] Thus, the act of repenting is an act not just of *turning away* from sin but also of *returning* to where we truly belong, to what is true and good—to God. Repentance is the central message of the prophets (Isa 31:6; Ezek 14:6; Zech 1:3–4; Mal 3:7), of Jesus (Matt 4:17; Luke 5:32; 13:3–5; Rev 2:5), and of the apostles (Acts 2:38; 17:30; 2 Tim 2:25). The Catechism defines repentance as "a radical reorientation of our whole life, a return, a conversion to God with all our heart, an end of sin, a turning away from evil, with repugnance toward the evil actions we have committed" (Cate-chism 1431). One could argue that repentance is the central message of the Bible.

Ancient Jewish tradition extols the power of repentance: "Great is repentance, which brings healing to the world, . . . reaches up to the throne of glory, . . . brings redemption near, . . . lengthens the years of a person; . . . for on account of a single individual who repents, the whole world is forgiven in its entirety."[b] This hyperbolic statement is reminiscent of Jesus's own parables and teachings on repentance—for example, when he says that "there will be more joy in heaven over one sinner who repents than over ninety-nine righteous persons who need no repentance" (Luke 15:7).

a. The text of Sir 17 has not been preserved in any extant Hebrew manuscript.
b. Babylonian Talmud, *Yoma* 86a–b, in Jacob Neusner, *The Babylonian Talmud: A Translation and Com-mentary* (Peabody, MA: Hendrickson, 2011), 5a:338–40.

is at work. As the first agent of repentance, he gently nudges the human soul away from sin and death toward goodness and life (Acts 11:18; 2 Tim 2:25). The Lord **encourages** those who are discouraged or **whose endurance is failing** to continue pursuing righteousness and justice, for *he has appointed to them the lot* of dwelling in his saving *truth* ([†]Vulgate) by calling them to reconciliation and communion with him.

17:25   Because God will judge all sin, Ben Sira calls his reader to repent (17:25–32): **Turn to the Lord and forsake your sins**. Although no Hebrew text is extant for this verse, the original Hebrew word for "turn" or "return" is almost certainly *shuv*, which also means "repent" (see the sidebar "Repent and Return"). Thus, turning to the Lord implies renouncing sin and returning to the "place" where one truly belongs (Ps 90:3; Mal 3:7). To **pray in his presence** perhaps means to "pray in the temple" or "pray in earnest." **Lessen your offenses** may be an encouragement to come to prayer with the right disposition; or it may describe the outcome of earnest prayer.

17:26   **Return to the Most High and turn away from iniquity** is a [†]parallelism that repeats the first half of verse 25. GII adds: **for he will lead you out of darkness**

to the light of health,[21] emphasizing the role of divine grace in the process of conversion and healing. One who repents and returns to God must **hate abominations intensely**—just as the Lord does (15:13). The rest of the verse is an addition from the Vulgate: *Know the justice and the judgments of God, and stand firm* with patience *in the lot that is set before you,* whether in joy or in suffering, always persevering *in prayer to God, the Almighty.*

Ben Sira asks rhetorically: **Who will sing praises to the Most High in** †**Hades?**   17:27–28 Hades (Hebrew *Sheol*) is the dark abode of the dead in Old Testament times, where it was believed that no one could praise God (Pss 6:5; 30:9; Isa 38:18–19). From the Old Testament's perspective, before Israel learned about life after death, only **those who are alive** can praise and thank God. Thus (the Vulgate adds), *tarry not in the waywardness of the ungodly,* who in their self-centeredness are unable to turn their hearts and souls toward heaven; instead, seize the day *and give thanks before death.* While in Old Testament times it was believed that this life offered the only chance to thank and praise God, the New Testament reveals that the saints will praise God forever in heaven (Rev 7:9–12; 19:5–8). Yet from Ben Sira's perspective, it is as if **the dead** did **not exist**. For them, **thanksgiving has ceased**; only those who are **alive and well** are able to sing **the Lord's praises**. The wise, therefore, must not miss this opportunity to give thanks as long as they are alive.

Ben Sira continues to call his readers to repentance, reminding them of **the**   17:29–32 **mercy of the Lord**, who is ever willing to extend **his forgiveness** to **those who turn to him** with a contrite heart (Pss 86:5; 103:8; 145:7–9). Not **all things**, such as mercy and forgiveness, are within human reach, for we are **not immortal** and thus cannot grasp the extent of God's mercy. Although nothing **is brighter than the sun**, even **its light fails** and is darkened by night or an eclipse; how much more are **flesh and blood** (human nature) darkened when men **devise evil** (see Job 25:4–6)? If God **marshals the host of heaven**, ruling over and judging heavenly powers such as the sun, moon, and stars, as well as the angelic hosts with which they were often associated (Isa 24:21; 34:4), how much more will he judge **all men** who are but **dust and ashes** (see Gen 18:27)?

Ben Sira continues to contrast God's majesty (18:1–7) with man's smallness   18:1–3 (18:8–10) and then considers the Lord's role as the righteous and benevolent judge of humanity (18:11–14). Because the eternal God **created the whole universe**, he alone is found **righteous**—that is, true and wise in all things. The longer Greek text adds[22] that **there is no other beside him**, for he is the only true God (1 Sam 2:2; Isa 45:21); **he steers the world** and governs the universe **with the span of his hand** (see Isa 40:12). All elements of creation **obey his**

---

21. Sir 17:26, RSV-2CE footnote.
22. GII adds: **and there is no other beside him;** [3]**he steers the world with the span of his hand, and all things obey his will; for he is king of all things, by his power separating among them the holy things from the profane** (Sir 18:2–3, RSV-2CE footnote).

will; for he is king who rules over all things, and by his power he separates and distinguishes holy things from the profane—not good things from evil, but rather things set apart and consecrated to God for his service from those used for common purposes (Lev 10:10; Ezek 22:26).

18:4–7   To none has the Lord given the ability to proclaim his works, comprehend the grandeur of his mighty deeds, measure his majestic power, or fully recount the countless times when he manifested his infinite mercies (1:3; 42:17; Job 9:10; Ps 145:3). No one can diminish or increase them, for he has acted perfectly in every situation; nor is it possible to trace the wonders of the Lord that he has accomplished in human history. Anyone who believes he has finished recounting these wonders and merciful deeds (Ps 77:12–13) is really just beginning, and when he stops recounting them, he remains perplexed by his inability to understand God's works.

18:8   In contrast to God's supreme majesty and power, Ben Sira asks: What is man, and of what use is he? The human person is insignificant compared to his Maker (Pss 8:4; 144:3). What is his good and what is his evil? is a perplexing question that surely does not deny or downplay the morality of human actions, which is strongly affirmed throughout the entire book. Perhaps it expresses man's confusion in discerning good from evil without the guidance of God's law, for apart from it he often does not know what is truly good for him.

18:9–10   Human insignificance is also evident in short lifespans, for a man's age is considered great if he reaches a hundred years. Yet this is barely a moment from God's perspective (Ps 90:10). GII adds "but the death of each one is beyond the calculation of all,"[23] for no one knows the day when it will come. As insignificant as a drop of water and a grain of sand are the few years of human life when considered from the standpoint of eternity (Sir 1:2; Ps 90:3–6).

18:11–12   Precisely because people are so fragile and short-lived, the Lord is patient with them. Because he wants them to live, he pours out his mercy upon them. Because he recognizes that their end will be evil, painful, and grievous when they die, he grants them abundant forgiveness throughout their lives, even up to the moment of death.

18:13–14   A person tends to show compassion to his neighbor, who is close to him. By contrast, the Lord is compassionate to all living beings (literally, "all flesh"), even when demonstrating "tough love" as he rebukes and trains and teaches them (see Wis 12:19–22; 2 Macc 6:12–16). He turns them back to himself in repentance, as a shepherd tends his flock, using a stick to guide stray sheep to stay with the herd (Ps 23; Ezek 34:11–16; John 10:11–18). Although the Lord extends his mercy to all, he has compassion especially on those who accept his discipline and exercise the fear of the Lord by eagerly observing his judgments and precepts.

23. Sir 18:9, NRSV footnote.

Reflection and Application (16:24–18:14)

It is no secret that the present generation is going through a profound crisis of faith. This is a *theological* crisis insofar as it involves a widespread forgetfulness of who God is, but also an *anthropological* crisis because the loss of faith has led to a pervasive confusion about who *the human person* is. This is evident in manifold ways: Many couples choose to cohabitate without getting married; others would rather have pets than children. Many think it is morally permissible to end the life of the most vulnerable through abortion or euthanasia. Some believe their identity is defined by their sexual attractions, or that they can change their gender at will. Still others no longer accept the male-female duality of the sexes, holding that numerous genders exist on an ever-expanding "nonbinary" spectrum.

This breakdown of traditional societal structures points to a profound identity crisis: *modern people have forgotten who they are.* If they do not know who they are and think they are only animals, then everything becomes permissible.

In response, the Bible asserts that "God created man in his own image, . . . male and female he created them" (Gen 1:27). This truth has significant implications for the moral life. It means that, unlike other animals, man is a rational being, capable of knowing and loving his Creator and sharing in his life (Catechism 356). It means that humans possess infinite dignity and worth and are capable of self-knowledge, self-possession, and self-gift for the sake of entering into communion with God and others (Catechism 357). It means that humans are a union of body and soul, and that what they do with their bodies is not morally indifferent (Catechism 362). It means that the male-female duality is not an arbitrary social construct but a good reality willed by God, who created man and woman for each other so that they could bring forth new life and cooperate in his work of creation (Catechism 369–72). Finally, the reality of sin means that not every human instinct, desire, or attraction is good. On the contrary, the concupiscence that is deeply ingrained in fallen human nature tends to pull people "downward" toward their animal nature and away from their divine purpose (Catechism 405). Repentance is God's call to turn away from base, animalistic impulses and "return" to our identity as adopted children, created in the image and likeness of God.

IV.D. (i) Prudence and Integrity in Words and Deeds: Give Graciously, Plan Cautiously (18:15–29)

> ¹⁵**My son, do not mix reproach with your good deeds,**
>   **nor cause grief by your words when you present a gift.**
> ¹⁶**Does not the dew assuage the scorching heat?**
>   **So a word is better than a gift.**

¹⁷Indeed, does not a word surpass a good gift?
Both are to be found in a gracious man.
¹⁸A fool is ungracious and abusive,
and the gift of a grudging man makes the eyes dim.

¹⁹Before you speak, learn,
and before you fall ill, take care of your health.
²⁰Before judgment, examine yourself,
and in the hour of visitation you will find forgiveness.
²¹Before falling ill, humble yourself,
and when you are on the point of sinning, turn back.
²²Let nothing hinder you from paying a vow promptly,
and do not wait until death to be released from it.
²³Before making a vow, prepare yourself;
and do not be like a man who tempts the Lord.
²⁴Think of his wrath on the day of death,
and of the moment of vengeance when he turns away his face.
²⁵In the time of plenty think of the time of hunger;
in the days of wealth think of poverty and need.
²⁶From morning to evening conditions change,
and all things move swiftly before the Lord.

²⁷A wise man is cautious in everything,
and in days of sin he guards against wrongdoing.
²⁸Every intelligent man knows wisdom,
and he praises the one who finds her.
²⁹Those who understand sayings become skilled themselves,
and pour forth apt proverbs.

OT: Num 30:2; Prov 6:6–11; Eccles 5:4
NT: Matt 6:22–23; Luke 1:28
Catechism: examination of conscience, 1454; conscience, 1776–94; prudence, 1806

18:15–18 With the fatherly address **My son**, Ben Sira opens a new section. Having reflected on God's mercy, he now encourages the reader to imitate the Lord by giving graciously: **do not mix reproach with your good deeds** by casting blame or accusations, **nor cause grief** by adding uncharitable **words** of criticism **when you present a gift** with the wrong intention or attitude. As **the dew** provides relief from **the scorching heat** (43:22), so a kind **word is better than a gift**, for it brings joy and encouragement to its recipient. Both are **found in a gracious man**. In the Gospel of Luke, the same Greek term for "gracious" (*kecharitomenos*) is used when the angel Gabriel calls Mary "full of grace" (Luke 1:28). Ancient Jewish tradition confirms these principles on gracious giving: "Any one who gives a penny to the poor is blessed with six blessings, and anyone who speaks to him in a comforting manner is blessed with eleven."[24] But unlike the wise man who gives cheerfully (2 Cor 9:7) in imitation of God (James 1:5), **a fool is ungracious and abusive**, giving grudgingly and with reproach (Sir 20:14–15). His gift **makes the eyes dim** or "waste away" (ESV-CE)—perhaps when the receiver is humiliated by his cruel words. The expression may also refer to the eyes of the grudging giver, drawing on the Hebraism "to have a bad eye," which means to be selfish and stingy (Matt 6:22–23).

The wise person must exercise prudence and be prepared for all situations by taking proper precautions (18:19–29). Ben Sira offers this advice with a series of injunctions on preparedness, beginning with "before . . .": **Before you speak** on any topic, **learn** about it so you can speak knowledgeably; **before you fall ill, take care of your health,** for prevention is the best medicine. The same principle applies to the health of the soul: **Before** the coming of God's **judgment, examine yourself,** for a good examination of conscience is the first step toward repentance; if you do so, when the Lord comes to judge you **in the hour of visitation**—that is, at the moment of sickness or death (16:18)—**you will find forgiveness**. *[18:19–20]*

Before falling ill—which may at times be a form of divine chastisement (2 Chron 26:20)—**humble yourself** to avoid the punishment that may follow (Sir 2:17; 7:16–17), **and when you are on the point of sinning** (literally, "at the time of sins"), **turn back** or "repent." This exhortation reflects the Hebrew word *shuv*, which means both "return" and "repent" (see the sidebar "Repent and Return," p. 156). It is better to turn back to God *before* sinning (and thus not to sin at all) than to repent *after* sinning. *[18:21]*

One should pay **a vow**—that is, fulfill a solemn promise made to God—**promptly** (Num 30:2; Eccles 5:4). **Do not** postpone this task indefinitely or **wait until** you are close to **death to be released** from your obligation to fulfill it. **Before making a vow**, therefore, **prepare yourself**, consider it carefully, and ensure you have the means to fulfill it in due course. A person who makes a rash vow that he is unlikely to keep **tempts the Lord**—in other words, he puts the Lord to the test (Deut 6:16; Prov 20:25; Matt 4:7) by "tempting God" to punish him if he does not keep his vow. One who leaves promises unfulfilled can expect to encounter God's **wrath on the day of death**. Ben Sira considers one who fails to keep his vows as having turned his back on God. Thus, the day of judgment will be a **moment of vengeance** (requital or retribution) as God **turns away his face** from this person (Deut 31:17–18; Ps 30:7). *[18:22–24]*

In the time of plenty, the wise should **think of the time of hunger** that may follow. This could be an appeal to store up material provisions in **days of wealth** to prepare for times of scarcity (Gen 41:29–36; Prov 6:6–11). Or, since hunger and poverty can sometimes be divine punishments for sin, it may be a reminder *[18:25–26]*

---

24. Babylonian Talmud, *Baba Bathra* 9b (Neusner, *Babylonian Talmud*, 15:34).

not to take God's blessings for granted and to remain faithful to him in days of abundance, lest laxity and sin lead to **poverty and need** (see Deut 8:10–20; 28:33). **From morning to evening**—in the span of a single day—**conditions change** and life can turn around radically (2 Kings 7:1–16; Job 4:19–21); **all things move swiftly before the Lord**: he is able to suddenly turn one's fortune from prosperity to destitution.

18:27–29   **A wise man is cautious in everything**, for prudence—"right reason in action" (Catechism 1806)—is a mark of the wise. When **sin** prevails widely, or when the wise person is tempted to sin, he or she carefully avoids all **wrongdoing** by vigilantly resisting temptation. An **intelligent** person **knows** how to recognize **wisdom** in others; **he praises** and encourages **the one who** pursues her, **finds her**, and lives wisely. **Those who understand sayings** (or are "skilled in words")[25] **become skilled**, clever, and wise, so that they are able to utter their own **apt proverbs** and become a source of wisdom for others.

IV.D. (ii) Prudence and Integrity in Words and Deeds: Exercise Temperance, Avoid Gossip (18:30–19:17)

³⁰Do not follow your base desires,
 but restrain your appetites.
³¹If you allow your soul to take pleasure in base desire,
 it will make you the laughingstock of your enemies.
³²Do not revel in great luxury,
 lest you become impoverished by its expense.
³³Do not become a beggar by feasting with borrowed money,
 when you have nothing in your purse.

¹⁹:¹A workman who is a drunkard will not become rich;
 he who despises small things will fail little by little.
²Wine and women lead intelligent men astray,
 and the man who consorts with harlots is very reckless.
³Decay and worms will inherit him,
 and the reckless soul will be snatched away.

⁴One who trusts others too quickly is lightminded,
 and one who sins does wrong to himself.
⁵One who rejoices in wickedness will be condemned,
⁶and for one who hates gossip evil is lessened.
⁷Never repeat a conversation,
 and you will lose nothing at all.
⁸With friend or foe do not report it,
 and unless it would be a sin for you, do not disclose it;

25. NRSV, NABRE.

⁹for some one has heard you and watched you,
　and when the time comes he will hate you.
¹⁰Have you heard a word? Let it die with you.
　Be brave! It will not make you burst!
¹¹With such a word a fool will suffer pangs
　like a woman in labor with a child.
¹²Like an arrow stuck in the flesh of the thigh,
　so is a word inside a fool.

¹³Question a friend, perhaps he did not do it;
　but if he did anything, so that he may do it no more.
¹⁴Question a neighbor, perhaps he did not say it;
　but if he said it, so that he may not say it again.
¹⁵Question a friend, for often it is slander;
　so do not believe everything you hear.
¹⁶A person may make a slip without intending it.
　Who has never sinned with his tongue?
¹⁷Question your neighbor before you threaten him;
　and let the law of the Most High take its course.

OT: Prov 17:9; 21:17; 23:21; 25:9–10; 31:3–7
NT: Matt 18:15–17; Rom 13:14; Gal 5:16–24; Col 3:5
Catechism: temperance, 1809; offenses against truth and respect for truth, 2475–92

Ben Sira turns to the virtue of self-control or temperance, the cardinal virtue　**18:30–31**
that moderates the attraction of pleasures and natural desires for good things
(Catechism 1809). **Do not follow your base desires** or passions, **but restrain**
even your legitimate **appetites**, lest they dominate your life (Rom 13:14; Gal
5:16–19; Col 3:5). **If you allow your soul** to indulge in **base** passions, your lack
of self-control and excessive self-indulgence will make you appear foolish, and
you will become **the laughingstock of your enemies** (6:4).

One who indulges in **great luxury** runs the risk of becoming **impoverished**,　**18:32–33**
for the cost of living lavishly can lead to financial ruin. The Hebrew expresses
this advice vividly: "Do not rejoice in a little pleasure that will produce twice
as much poverty." Self-indulgence is particularly destructive when it entails
living beyond one's means: it is foolish to **become a beggar** (Hebrew: "a glutton
and a drunkard"; compare NABRE) **by feasting with borrowed money, when
you have** no financial means of your own. As the longer Greek text explains,
by living such a reckless lifestyle "you will be plotting against your own life."²⁶

Ben Sira continues to advise prudence and self-control in matters of passions　**19:1**
and appetites. **A workman who is a drunkard** (Hebrew: "Whoever does this")
will not become rich. Indeed, drunkenness often leads to poverty (Prov 21:17;
23:21). The Hebrew text refers to the previous verse—that is, he who feasts with

26. Sir 18:33, NRSV, ESV-CE footnotes.

borrowed money will not become rich.[27] Likewise, one **who despises small things** will be careless with greater matters as well and **will fail little by little** until his negligence leads him to ruin (Matt 25:14–30).

19:2–3   **Wine and women**—symbolizing drunkenness and sexual immorality—lead not only fools but even **intelligent men astray**, for all are vulnerable to those common temptations (31:25–30; Prov 31:3–7; Hosea 4:11). One who frequents prostitutes is particularly **reckless** and does not think about the consequences of his actions. **Decay and worms**—a metaphor for death—will take possession of him as the ultimate consequence of his foolish actions (Prov 5:5; 7:26–27; Rom 6:23; Gal 6:8), **and the reckless soul** who indulges in such pleasures **will be snatched away** to his demise.

19:4   Ben Sira now advises on speaking wisely and avoiding gossip (19:4–17). **One who trusts others** and believes what they say **too quickly** or uncritically lacks prudence and has a shallow mind. This thoughtless disposition encourages gossip; **one who sins**—for example, by speaking carelessly—**does wrong to himself** (literally, "to his own soul").

19:5–6   **One who rejoices in wickedness** by enjoying malicious talk **will be condemned**—either by God or by other people. The longer Greek text adds:[28] **but he who withstands pleasures** by refusing to listen to gossip **crowns his life**. **He who controls his tongue** and refrains from idle speech lives **without strife**, at peace with others; **one who hates gossip** and does not indulge in it spares himself much **evil**. Alternatively, "whoever repeats gossip is lessened in heart" (Syriac) or "has no sense" (NABRE).

19:7–9   **Never repeat a conversation** (literally, "a word"), and **you will** not **lose** anything that is of value to you, such as your friends or reputation (Prov 17:9; 25:9–10). **With friend or foe do not report** your conversation or speak ill of anyone, **unless it would be a sin for you** to remain silent—for example, by becoming complicit in another's sin or by putting someone in danger. For if someone **has heard you and watched you** as you engaged in gossip, sooner or later **he will hate you** because you have proven yourself untrustworthy. People who hear you gossip will mistrust you, because if you gossip *to* them, you will likely gossip *about* them as well.

19:10–12   **Have you heard a word** or rumor *against your neighbor* ([†]Vulgate, Douay)? Do not repeat it, but **let it die with you**—let it go no further. **Be brave! It will not make you burst!**—says Ben Sira in jest. Fools are unable to restrain themselves from gossiping, imagining that they will explode if they don't repeat rumors they have heard (Job 32:18–19). He describes a **fool** who cannot control his speech as suffering **pangs like a woman in labor**. Just as a woman suffers pain until a child is born, or someone feels the pain of **an arrow stuck in the**

---

27. NRSV, NABRE.
28. GII adds: **but he who withstands pleasures crowns his life. He who controls his tongue will live without strife,** (Sir 19:5–6, RSV-2CE, ESV-CE footnotes; compare NRSV footnote).

flesh of the thigh until it is removed, so the gossiper is in agony until he lets the words out of his mouth.

Ben Sira has exhorted his readers not to engage in gossip. But how should   **19:13–15**
they respond to it? **Question** or "admonish" (NABRE) **a friend** if you hear a rumor that he has done something wrong; **perhaps** the rumor is unfounded and **he did not do it**. First get the facts straight by speaking with him (Matt 18:15–17). If the rumor turns out to be true, then it is better to discuss the matter frankly with him rather than talk behind his back, **so that he may do it no more**. Similarly, **question a neighbor** who has allegedly started a rumor or repeated something inappropriate; **perhaps he did not say it** and the rumor is unfounded or the result of miscommunication. **But if he said it**, admonish him so **that he may not say it again**. Likewise, if you hear an accusation against **a friend**, question him about it, **for often it is slander**—a false rumor spread maliciously about him; **so do not believe everything you hear** nor be too quick to trust everyone (19:4).

Not all gossip is malicious or intentional: anyone **may make** a careless **slip** of   **19:16–17**
the tongue. Correction concerning gossip should be given kindly and charitably, because everyone has **sinned with his tongue** and spoken carelessly at some point. False rumors can stir up anger, either toward the source of the rumor or its object. Yet one should not assume malice but give others the benefit of the doubt. **Question your neighbor** and get the facts straight **before you** reprove or **threaten him, and let the law of the Most High take its course**—a probable reference to Lev 19:17–18, which exhorts one not to take vengeance or bear a grudge against one's brother but to "love your neighbor as yourself," and to Deut 32:35, which assures readers that God's justice will handle wrongs done to them (compare Rom 12:19).[29]

IV.E. True and False Wisdom (19:18–30)

> [20]**All wisdom is the fear of the Lord,**
>   **and in all wisdom there is the fulfilment of the law.**
> [22]**But the knowledge of wickedness is not wisdom,**
>   **nor is there prudence where sinners take counsel.**
> [23]**There is a cleverness which is abominable,**
>   **but there is a fool who merely lacks wisdom.**
> [24]**Better is the God-fearing man who lacks intelligence,**
>   **than the highly prudent man who transgresses the law.**
> [25]**There is a cleverness which is scrupulous but unjust,**
>   **and there are people who distort kindness to gain a verdict.**
> [26]**There is a rascal bowed down in mourning,**
>   **but inwardly he is full of deceit.**

---

29. GII adds: **and do not be angry** (Sir 19:17, RSV-2CE, NRSV footnotes).

²⁷He hides his face and pretends not to hear;
    but where no one notices, he will forestall you.
²⁸And if by lack of strength he is prevented from sinning,
    he will do evil when he finds an opportunity.
²⁹A man is known by his appearance,
    and a sensible man is known by his face, when you meet him.
³⁰A man's attire and open-mouthed laughter,
    and a man's manner of walking, show what he is.

OT: Ps 1:1; Prov 8:5; Wis 1:3–5
NT: Luke 20:23; 1 Cor 3:19; 2 Cor 4:2; 11:3; Eph 4:14
Catechism: prudence, 1806; law and wisdom, 1950–51; truthfulness, 2468–70

19:18–19 The longer Greek text adds two verses introducing the next section on true and false wisdom.³⁰ **The fear of the Lord is the beginning** of being accepted by God, and by seeking **wisdom** one **obtains his love** (4:10–14). The knowledge and observance of **the Lord's commandments is life-giving discipline** or "education for life," for it forms one's character with the habits necessary to live a good life; those who please him **enjoy the fruit of the tree of immortality** (see Prov 3:18). Immortality, or the doctrine of a blessed afterlife, is not typical of most books of the Old Testament, but it is representative of later Old Testament theology (Wis 3:4; 4:1; 6:18–19; 8:13–17) and the New Testament (Rom 2:7; 1 Cor 15:53–54; 2 Tim 1:10).³¹

19:20–21   In contrast to counterfeit forms of wisdom, Ben Sira reiterates the essence of **all** authentic **wisdom**, which is **the fear of the Lord** (1:9–30; 2:7–17; 10:19–20; 21:6), in which **there is the fulfillment of the law** because fearing God is expressed by keeping the commandments (9:15; 15:1; 21:11; 24:23; Bar 4:1). GII adds that in wisdom there is also **the knowledge of his omnipotence**.³² Wisdom is not just a path to a better life; she is also the path to knowing the power of God. Yet obedience is necessary to remain in God's favor: **When a servant** refuses to obey **his master, even if later** he changes his mind and does what was commanded, **he angers** his master, **who supports him**. Likewise with God: the fear of the Lord is expressed not by reluctant or halfhearted obedience but by prompt and willing obedience to his commandments (Matt 21:28–32).

30. ¹⁸The fear of the Lord is the beginning of acceptance, and wisdom obtains his love. ¹⁹The knowledge of the Lord's commandments is life-giving discipline; and those who do what is pleasing to him enjoy the fruit of the tree of immortality (Sir 19:18–19, RSV-2CE, NRSV, ESV-CE footnotes).

31. Some commentators suggest that the mention of immortality in v. 19 is a development of the theology of the afterlife in the longer Greek text that was added by another author after Ben Sira's lifetime. See Patrick W. Skehan and Alexander A. Di Lella, *The Wisdom of Ben Sira*, AB (New York: Doubleday, 1987), 299.

32. GII adds: **and the knowledge of his omnipotence.** ²¹ When a servant says to his master, "I will not act as you wish," even if later he does it, he angers the one who supports him (Sir 19:20–21, RSV-2CE footnote; compare NRSV, ESV-CE footnotes).

The knowledge of wickedness—whether this means knowing about wicked- 19:22
ness, or the knowledge possessed by wicked people—**is not wisdom**, for "wisdom
will not enter a deceitful soul, nor dwell in a body enslaved to sin" (Wis 1:4);
nor is there prudence where sinners take counsel, for their reasoning never
provides sound counsel to follow (Ps 1:1).

Ben Sira begins a series of declarative statements (beginning with "there is") 19:23–24
to clarify the difference between godly wisdom and its counterfeits. **There is
a cleverness** or craftiness (Greek *panourgia*; see 21:12) **which is abominable**
because it is deceptively used to achieve evil ends (21:12). Those who maliciously
use their intelligence imitate the serpent's cunning when he deceived Eve (2 Cor
11:3) and are far worse than **a fool who merely lacks wisdom**. Therefore, it is
better to be a devout, **God-fearing man who lacks intelligence** but keeps God's
commandments than a **highly prudent** or shrewd **man who transgresses the
law**. True wisdom is found not primarily in intellectual capacity but in devotion
and adherence to God and to the †Torah.

Cleverness can be **scrupulous** and meticulous, yet at the same time dishon- 19:25–26
est and **unjust** (see 1 Cor 3:19; 2 Cor 4:2; Eph 4:14). It is found in **people who**
feign and **distort kindness**, misusing it to deceive others and **gain a verdict**—
that is, to win their case—for an ulterior motive or to obtain a personal favor.
Likewise, a hypocritical **rascal bowed down in mourning** may look solemn
by putting on a show of false humility, **but inwardly** he is deceitful and seeks
only to take advantage of others.

The cunning person **hides his face**—that is, he avoids eye contact and **pre-** 19:27–28
tends not to hear or notice you; but after putting you off guard, when **no one**

The Body Reflects the Soul

LIVING
TRADITION

In his *Baptismal Instructions*, St. John Chrysostom (ca. 347–407) comments on Sir 19:30, explaining how one's external appearance reflects
the inner disposition of the soul:

> Let each of our actions be very dignified. As it says, "A person's attire, his
> laughter and his gait reveal who he is" (Sir 19:30). The external posture
> can be a clear image of the condition of the soul; indeed, the movement
> of the members reveals its beauty in a particular way. If we go into the
> town square, let our gait, our serenity and our composure be such as
> to attract the notice of those we encounter, let our eye not roam or our
> feet walk in a disorderly manner, and let our tongue proffer words with tranquil-
> ity and gentleness. In other words, let our entire exterior disposition indicate the
> interior beauty of the soul.[a]

a. John Chrysostom, *Baptismal Instructions* 4.24–26, in Sever J. Voicu, ed., *Apocrypha*, ACCS:OT 15
(Downers Grove, IL: InterVarsity, 2010), 272.

notices, he will take advantage of you. If this sly opportunist **by lack of strength** is temporarily **prevented from sinning, he will do evil when he finds an opportunity** and when you least expect it.

19:29–30   Even if fraudsters mask their true intentions, a man's character is still **known by his appearance.** A wise, discerning person can "read" body and facial language and recognize **a sensible,** trustworthy individual. Although appearances can be deceptive, **a man's attire,** hearty **laughter,** and **manner of walking** may still reveal much about his true character (2 Macc 15:12–13).

IV.F. (i) Wisdom in Silence and Speech: When to Talk; Gain and Loss (20:1–17)

¹There is a reproof which is not timely;
  and there is a man who keeps silent but is wise.
²How much better it is to reprove than to stay angry!
  And the one who confesses his fault will be kept from loss.
⁴Like a eunuch's desire to violate a maiden
  is a man who executes judgments by violence.
⁵There is one who by keeping silent is found wise,
  while another is detested for being too talkative.
⁶There is one who keeps silent because he has no answer,
  while another keeps silent because he knows when to speak.
⁷A wise man will be silent until the right moment,
  but a braggart and fool goes beyond the right moment.
⁸Whoever uses too many words will be loathed,
  and whoever usurps the right to speak will be hated.

⁹There may be good fortune for a man in adversity,
  and a windfall may result in a loss.
¹⁰There is a gift that profits you nothing,
  and there is a gift that brings a double return.
¹¹There are losses because of glory,
  and there are men who have raised their heads from humble
    circumstances.
¹²There is a man who buys much for a little,
  but pays for it seven times over.

¹³The wise man makes himself beloved through his words,
  but the courtesies of fools are wasted.
¹⁴A fool's gift will profit you nothing,
  for he has many eyes instead of one.
¹⁵He gives little and upbraids much,
  he opens his mouth like a herald;
  today he lends and tomorrow he asks it back;

such a one is a hateful man.
¹⁶A fool will say, "I have no friend,
   and there is no gratitude for my good deeds;
   those who eat my bread speak unkindly."
¹⁷How many will ridicule him, and how often!

OT: Prov 10:19; 15:23; 17:28; Eccles 3:7
NT: Matt 18:15–17; Col 4:6; 2 Tim 4:2; Heb 3:13; James 1:19
Catechism: discretion, 2488–89; modesty in silence, 2522

There is "a time to keep silence, and a time to speak" (Eccles 3:7). While it is **20:1**
sometimes appropriate and even necessary to exhort or rebuke someone who
has done wrong (Matt 18:15–17; 2 Tim 4:2; Heb 3:13), an untimely **reproof**
can cause more harm than good. Thus, one **who keeps silent but is wise** in his
restraint discerns carefully the right time to speak.

In a situation of conflict, it is often **better to reprove** your adversary and **20:2–4**
openly address the problem **than to stay angry** and resentful. While trying to
save face or "win the argument" can escalate and worsen the conflict, **one who
confesses his fault** with candor is **kept from loss** or failure and shielded from
embarrassment. The †Vulgate emphasizes the importance of humility in such
situations: *How good it is to show repentance when you are reproved, for so
you will escape deliberate sin!*[33] By contrast, just as a castrated **eunuch's desire
to violate a maiden** is as futile as it is evil, so too one who **executes judgments
by violence** and tries to control others by force will never succeed in doing
what is right.

Wisdom is not always demonstrated by speech. On the contrary, one who **20:5–6**
keeps **silent** is often considered **wise**—whether or not he actually *is* wise (Prov
17:28). Certainly, some people are **detested for being too talkative**, either because they engage in gossip or are unable to engage in an authentic dialogue,
which requires not just talking but also attentive listening. There are good reasons
to remain silent: one person may refrain from speaking because he has nothing
to say; another may exercise restraint **because he knows when to speak** and
waits for the opportune time to give his "word in season" (Prov 15:23).

While the **wise** person knows how to remain **silent until the right moment** **20:7–8**
(James 1:19), **a braggart and fool** who lacks self-awareness and seeks to show
off does not notice when it is best to start or stop talking. The babbler who **uses
too many words** and **usurps the right to speak** by posing as an authority figure
or by constantly interrupting others **will be hated** (see Prov 10:19); many will
avoid conversation with such a person altogether.

Everyone experiences gain and loss in life. Yet things are not always as they **20:9–10**
seem: apparent losses may turn out to be blessings in disguise—and vice versa
(20:9–17). **Good fortune** may be the lot of a person **in adversity**, for times of

33. Sir 20:3 (RSV-2CE footnote). GII places this addition after 20:8 (NRSV, ESV-CE footnotes).

Silent until the Right Moment

In his *Pastoral Rule*, St. Gregory the Great (ca. 540–604) emphasizes the value of speaking discreetly at the right time and on the right occasion.

> Those who notice what is evil in their neighbors, and yet refrain their tongue in silence, withdraw, as it were, the aid of medicine from observed sores and become the cause of death because they would not cure the venom that they could have cured. The tongue, therefore, should be discreetly curbed, not tied up fast. For it is written, "A wise person will hold his tongue until the opportune time" (Sir 20:7).... This is something we need to learn with discretion so that we use our voice in a discreet and fitting time to open the mouth, and at the appropriate time also let silence close it. But those who spend time in much speaking are to be admonished that they vigilantly note from what a state of being they fall away when they flow forth in a multitude of words.[a]

a. Gregory the Great, *Pastoral Rule* 3.14 (Voicu, *Apocrypha*, 273).

trouble sometimes bring unforeseen blessings (Matt 5:2–12). Conversely, **a windfall**—some unexpected good fortune, as when the wind blows fruit off a tree—**may result in a loss** or misfortune. Similarly, the giving of gifts is also unpredictable: you may give **a gift** to another **that profits you nothing** in return, while at other times you may give **a gift that brings a double return**, so that you receive back twice as much as you gave.

20:11–12   While some **losses** are experienced due to a misguided or excessive pursuit of **glory** and honor, people have also risen **from humble circumstances** and lowly origins to places of high honor (1 Sam 2:4–9; Ps 113:7–9; Luke 1:51–53). Business transactions are similarly unreliable: one thinks he has found a bargain—such as a used car—and **buys much for a little** money, but in the end **pays for it seven times over** in maintenance and repairs.

20:13   A **wise** person **makes himself beloved through** few, well-chosen **words**, establishing himself as a person of integrity who utters gracious speech, "seasoned with salt" (Col 4:6). By contrast, people see through the insincere **courtesies** and flatteries **of fools**, which **are wasted** because few believe them.

20:14–15   **A fool's gift will profit you nothing**: he gives only reluctantly and for an ulterior motive, **for he has many eyes instead of one**. This difficult expression may mean "the fool thinks his gift is worth much more than it is, and he expects too much in return." The Syriac reads: "He looks for recompense sevenfold" (NRSV). The fool **gives little and upbraids much**, having little to offer other than criticism; **he opens his mouth** to disparage others **like a herald**—a public announcer shouting news with a loud voice. Unstable and self-serving, **today he lends and tomorrow he asks** for repayment, making himself **hateful** to both God and humans.

Ever lacking in self-awareness, the **fool** fails to consider his actions and instead　20:16–17
feels sorry for himself, saying, **"I have no friend"**—probably a true statement,
but through his own fault. He laments that no one shows him **gratitude** for
his imagined **good deeds**—though he has not really done any—for even **those
who eat** with him at his table **speak unkindly** of him. Ben Sira concludes his
reflections on the self-inflicted misery of the fool with a stinging exclamation:
How many will ridicule him, and how often!

IV.F. (ii) Wisdom in Silence and Speech: Appropriate and Inappropriate Talk (20:18–32)

¹⁸A slip on the pavement is better than a slip of the tongue;
　　so the downfall of the wicked will occur speedily.
¹⁹An ungracious man is like a story told at the wrong time,
　　which is continually on the lips of the ignorant.
²⁰A proverb from a fool's lips will be rejected,
　　for he does not tell it at its proper time.

²¹A man may be prevented from sinning by his poverty,
　　so when he rests he feels no remorse.
²²A man may lose his life through shame,
　　or lose it because of his foolish look.
²³A man may for shame make promises to a friend,
　　and needlessly make him an enemy.

²⁴A lie is an ugly blot on a man;
　　it is continually on the lips of the ignorant.
²⁵A thief is preferable to a habitual liar,
　　but the lot of both is ruin.
²⁶The disposition of a liar brings disgrace,
　　and his shame is ever with him.

²⁷He who speaks wisely will advance himself,
　　and a sensible man will please great men.
²⁸Whoever cultivates the soil will heap up his harvest,
　　and whoever pleases great men will atone for injustice.
²⁹Presents and gifts blind the eyes of the wise;
　　like a muzzle on the mouth they avert reproofs.
³⁰Hidden wisdom and unseen treasure,
　　what advantage is there in either of them?
³¹Better is the man who hides his folly
　　than the man who hides his wisdom.

OT: Exod 23:8; Deut 16:19; Prov 6:16–19; 15:27; 26:7–9
NT: Matt 5:3
Catechism: lying, 2482–87

20:18–20   Ben Sira offers more guidelines on appropriate and inappropriate speech, noting that there are consequences for saying the wrong thing. **A slip on the pavement** leading to a painful fall is still **better** than an imprudent **slip of the tongue**, which can cause significant damage in interpersonal relationships. The **downfall of the wicked** occurs just as **speedily** as a physical fall, presumably because they tend to speak rashly. **An ungracious** or rude person is **like a story told at the wrong time** (literally, "an ungracious man, an untimely tale"). Those who speak too much (20:8) are prone to tell offensive stories or jokes at inappropriate moments, for such things are **continually on** the mind and **lips of the ignorant**. Even **a proverb** that usually commands attention and respect is disregarded when uttered **from a fool's lips**, for he speaks it in an untimely manner rather than **at its proper time** (see Prov 26:7–9).

20:21   Ben Sira holds that a person **may be prevented from sinning by his poverty**. It is not that a poor person cannot sin, but that his material poverty may help him avoid occasions of sin and lead him to the poverty of spirit that draws one near to God (Matt 5:3), so that **when he rests he feels no remorse** or guilty conscience for the sins he did not commit.

20:22–23   Verse 22 is difficult: **A man may lose his life**—perhaps meaning his reputation or self-respect—**through shame** or timidity. This could occur **because of his foolish look** or "posturing" (NABRE), lack of frankness, or failing to resist the foolishness of another. The NJB reads that such a person "courts destruction for the sake of a fool's opinion." A person may also **for shame**— that is, out of weakness—**make promises to a friend** that he is unable to keep, thus becoming **an enemy** when the friend asks him to follow through on his promise.

20:24–26   **A lie** is a grave defect in a person's character (7:13; 25:2; Prov 6:16–19), **continually on the lips** of **ignorant** or undisciplined people who are not ashamed to speak falsehoods. A **habitual liar** is even worse than a **thief**—for if theft is a sin against the property of others (Exod 20:15), lying consists in "stealing the truth" from those to whom it is due, distorting their perception of reality. Thus, the **disposition** or habit **of a liar brings disgrace** and **shame** because he ruins his own credibility and reputation through his falsehoods.

20:27–28   If fools should remain quiet, one **who speaks wisely** achieves success in life, for **a sensible**, prudent person will naturally **please** and impress—whether intentionally or not—those who are influential and powerful, as Joseph did in Egypt and Daniel in Babylon (Gen 41:38–40; Dan 1:17–20). Just as one who **cultivates the soil** reaps a full **harvest**, so one who **pleases great men** wins their goodwill and atones **for injustice**—in other words, he disposes them to overlook or forgive one's misdeeds in due time.

20:29   **Presents and gifts**—that is, bribes—**blind the eyes of the wise**. The †Torah forbids the giving and taking of bribes because they subvert justice and negatively affect even the judgment of the wise (Exod 23:8; Deut 16:19; Prov 15:27;

17:23). **Like a muzzle on the mouth** of a dog that prevents it from barking or biting, so bribes **avert reproofs** and inhibit authorities from correcting others.

Wisdom is meant to be shared with others: **Hidden wisdom** is as useless as an **unseen treasure**—there is no **advantage** to **either of them**, because no one benefits from them. While it is good for the fool to hide **his folly**, the wise person should not hide **his wisdom** when it could be beneficial to others (41:14–15). GII adds verse 32:[34] **Unwearied patience** or persistent endurance **in seeking the Lord,** even if it requires effort, **is better than** trying to be **a masterless charioteer of one's own life**—that is, a moral relativist who tries to live life without the guidance of divine wisdom.

20:30–32

Reflection and Application (20:1–32)

The art of listening is a lost skill. All too often, a conversation between two individuals, rather than being an authentic dialogue, turns out to be little more than two monologues. This tendency is exacerbated on social media, where everyone seems eager to express their opinions (and attack those who don't share them) but is slow to listen and try to understand opposing viewpoints. The advice of Ben Sira and other biblical authors is particularly relevant in such situations. While it is often necessary to reprove sin and rebut falsehood, it is also a sign of wisdom to be "quick to hear, slow to speak, slow to anger" (James 1:19) and be patient enough to be "silent until the right moment" (Sir 20:7)—seeking to genuinely understand an opponent's point of view before launching into a potentially fruitless argument. Even in friendly interactions, who has never emerged out of a conversation with an uneasy sense that one's interlocutor was not really listening? Or, conversely, how often has a friend tried to share something personal with us, but we were "slow to hear and quick to speak"? While wisdom is expressed through *speaking*, it is primarily gained through *listening*—an art that is well worth developing through intentional practice (Sir 6:33).

IV.G. (i) The Wise and the Foolish: Sin's Deceptive Path (21:1–28)

> [1]**Have you sinned, my son? Do so no more,**
> > **but pray about your former sins.**
> [2]**Flee from sin as from a snake;**
> > **for if you approach sin, it will bite you.**
> **Its teeth are lion's teeth,**
> > **and destroy the souls of men.**

---

34. **Unwearied patience in seeking the Lord is better than a masterless charioteer of one's own life** (Sir 20:32, RSV-2CE, ESV-CE footnotes; compare NRSV footnote).

³All lawlessness is like a two-edged sword;
  there is no healing for its wound.

⁴Terror and violence will lay waste riches;
  thus the house of the proud will be laid waste.
⁵The prayer of a poor man goes from his lips to the ears of God,
  and his judgment comes speedily.
⁶Whoever hates reproof walks in the steps of the sinner,
  but he that fears the Lord will repent in his heart.
⁷He who is mighty in speech is known from afar;
  but the sensible man, when he slips, is aware of it.

⁸A man who builds his house with other people's money
  is like one who gathers stones for his burial mound.
⁹An assembly of the wicked is like tow gathered together,
  and their end is a flame of fire.
¹⁰The way of sinners is smoothly paved with stones,
  but at its end is the pit of Hades.

¹¹Whoever keeps the law controls his thoughts,
  and wisdom is the fulfilment of the fear of the Lord.
¹²He who is not clever cannot be taught,
  but there is a cleverness which increases bitterness.
¹³The knowledge of a wise man will increase like a flood,
  and his counsel like a flowing spring.
¹⁴The mind of a fool is like a broken jar;
  it will hold no knowledge.

¹⁵When a man of understanding hears a wise saying,
  he will praise it and add to it;
when a reveler hears it, he dislikes it
  and casts it behind his back.
¹⁶A fool's narration is like a burden on a journey,
  but delight will be found in the speech of the intelligent.
¹⁷The utterance of a sensible man will be sought in the assembly,
  and they will ponder his words in their minds.

¹⁸Like a house that has vanished, so is wisdom to a fool;
  and the knowledge of the ignorant is unexamined talk.
¹⁹To a senseless man education is chains on his feet,
  and like manacles on his right hand.
²⁰A fool raises his voice when he laughs,
  but a clever man smiles quietly.
²¹To a sensible man education is like a golden ornament,
  and like a bracelet on the right arm.

²²The foot of a fool rushes into a house,
  but a man of experience stands respectfully before it.

²³A boor peers into the house from the door,
　　but a cultivated man remains outside.
²⁴It is ill-mannered for a man to listen at a door,
　　and a discreet man is grieved by the disgrace.
²⁵The lips of strangers will speak of these things,
　　but the words of the prudent will be weighed in the balance.
²⁶The mind of fools is in their mouth,
　　but the mouth of wise men is in their mind.
²⁷When an ungodly man curses his adversary,
　　he curses his own soul.
²⁸A whisperer defiles his own soul
　　and is hated in his neighborhood.

OT: Gen 4:7; Prov 22:11; 23:32; Eccles 10:12
NT: Matt 7:13–14; 18:6–9; John 8:11
Catechism: interior penance, 1430–33; consequences of sin, 1472–73, 1487–88; sin, 1849–69

In this section, Ben Sira warns against various forms of sin (21:1–10), beginning **21:1–2** with a rhetorical question and forceful exhortation: **Have you sinned, my son? Do so no more**, for sin, which means to "miss the mark" in both Hebrew and Greek, is a failure to achieve the deepest purpose for which you were created. Thus, **pray about your former sins**, that God may forgive you and give you the moral strength not to sin again. **Flee from sin** and stay far from it as if it were **a snake**—like the serpent who tempted Eve in the garden (Gen 3:1–5); **for if you approach sin** by yielding to temptation, **it will bite you** and cause you great harm (Prov 23:32; Matt 18:6–9). Ben Sira illustrates the deadliness of sin by personifying it as a venomous snake and a dangerous lion whose **teeth destroy the souls of men** (Sir 27:10; Gen 4:7; 1 Pet 5:8).

All lawlessness, the proud refusal to abide by God's life-giving law, **is like** **21:3–5** **a two-edged sword**—a long, pointed sword, sharp on both edges, that is particularly deadly (Judg 3:16; Ps 149:6). Like a wound inflicted by this sword, the **wound** caused by lawlessness to the sinner's soul and the societal order can scarcely be healed (Prov 5:4)—even if one later seeks God's forgiveness. Lawless people engage in acts of **terror and violence** (or "insolence") against others that waste away **riches**—including their own—so that **the house of the proud** will eventually be uprooted, and they will lose everything they have (Prov 15:25). In contrast to the lawless, who proudly oppose God, **the prayer** of a humble, **poor man goes from his lips to the ears of God**, who hears him readily and responds promptly, so that justice is quickly granted him (Pss 18:6; 34:15; 86:1).

Whoever hates reproof and resents being corrected for wrongdoing (32:17) **21:6–7** follows **the steps of the sinner** and exposes his soul to mortal danger. In contrast, one who **fears the Lord** with respect and reverence—the mark of true wisdom—readily acknowledges his sins, repents quickly, and strives to avoid them in the future. While one who is **mighty in speech**—an eloquent or perhaps boastful person—**is known from afar** for his forceful speaking, the thought-ful, **sensible man, when he slips** and makes mistakes, is humble enough to be **aware** of his shortcomings (or perhaps recognizes the errors in the assertions of the mighty in speech).

21:8–10   A person **who builds his house**—that is, increases his own fortune—**with other people's money**, perhaps by excessive borrowing or by dishonest means, **is like one who gathers stones for his burial mound**: he constructs his own tomb and condemns himself to a premature death. **An assembly of the wicked** (or "lawless") **is like tow**—highly flammable fibers from the flax plant used for spinning into linen thread—**gathered together** and destined for **a flame of fire**. This does not necessarily refer to punishment in hell (a doctrine that was not fully developed in Ben Sira's day) but refers to a quick and decisive end for the wicked in this life. **The way of sinners** may seem secure and inviting, as if **smoothly paved with stones** (see Prov 14:12; 16:25; Matt 7:13), but it leads only to **the pit of** †**Hades**, the gloomy abode of the dead (Sir 14:16; 17:27).

21:11–12   Ben Sira now contrasts the wise and the foolish in both their words and ac-tions (21:11–28). In stark contrast to the lawless, **whoever keeps the law controls his thoughts** or "impulses." Jewish tradition confirms this idea: "Keep yourselves occupied with teachings of the †Torah, and [sin] will not control you."[35] Thus, **wisdom is the fulfillment** and perfection of **the fear of the Lord**, evident in the devout and wise observance of the law. By contrast, one **who is not clever cannot be taught** or disciplined. Cleverness (Greek *panourgia*) is a good that ought to be pursued (34:10). However, **cleverness** in the sense of craftiness can also involve a harmful cunning that **increases bitterness** because it is misused to deceive or hurt others (19:23–25; 2 Cor 11:3).

21:13–14   Ben Sira portrays the **knowledge** of the wise as increasing **like a flood**—not in a destructive way, but like a source of life-giving water. Their **counsel**, simi-larly, is refreshing **like a flowing spring** (literally, "a fountain of life") (24:30–31; Ps 36:9; Prov 10:11; 18:4). According to an ancient Jewish tradition, one who occupies himself with the Torah "becomes an ever-flowing fountain, a stream that never runs dry."[36] The **mind** (literally, "inward parts" or "heart") **of a fool**, on the other hand, **is like a broken jar** that cannot contain anything (Jer 2:13): it holds **no knowledge** or wisdom, for he soon forgets whatever he learns.

21:15–17   An intelligent person welcomes and cherishes words of wisdom. When he **hears a wise saying**, he readily praises it and adds his own wise insights to the conversation. By contrast, a self-indulgent **reveler** who lives luxuriously **dislikes** and dismisses words of wisdom, quickly changing the subject. While **a fool's** chatter is tiresome and tedious, **like a burden on a journey, the speech of**

---

35. Babylonian Talmud, *Qiddushin* 30b (Neusner, *Babylonian Talmud*, 12:136). St. Paul says some-thing analogous: "I say, then: live by the Spirit and you will certainly not gratify the desire of the flesh" (Gal 5:16 NABRE).

36. Mishnah, *Avot* 6:1, in Berkson, *Pirke Avot*, 213. Compare Ezek 47:1–12.

the intelligent and sensible person is gracious, pleasant, and refreshing (Prov 22:11; Eccles 10:12). Such speech is even **sought in the assembly** or public forum, and people are eager to **ponder his words in their minds** (literally, "in their heart") (Sir 15:5).

Like a house in ruins, **so is wisdom to a fool**: he is unable to dwell in wisdom's **21:18–21** "house," where she feasts with her followers (Prov 9:1–6); for **the knowledge of the ignorant** is futile, consisting of **unexamined**, incoherent **talk**. A **senseless** person views **education** or discipline as **chains on his feet** and **manacles on his right hand** that restrict his movement and hamper his freedom. The **fool** is shallow and boisterous: he **raises his voice when he laughs** (Sir 19:30; Eccles 7:6), in contrast to the **clever** person, who **smiles quietly** with self-restraint. The fool fails to see that wisdom's **education** does not enslave her disciples; it is a costly gift, **like a golden ornament** or a **bracelet**, that makes one beautiful and leads to true freedom (Sir 6:23–31; 21:21). Submitting to her discipline is a source of rest, joy, and protection.

With three antithetic †parallelisms, the bad social manners of the **fool, boor, 21:22–24** and **ill-mannered** person are contrasted with the good manners of the person **of experience**, who is **cultivated** and **discreet**. While the former is rude, shamelessly eavesdropping and violating people's privacy in their own homes, the latter is considerate and scrupulous in respecting these social boundaries and is **grieved by the disgrace** caused by the fool's indiscretions.

The lips of strangers will speak of these things. The meaning of this phrase **21:25–26** is unclear. One manuscript reads: "The lips of babblers speak things that are not their own"—in other words, they speak of what is not their concern (NRSV). By contrast, **the prudent** carefully consider their thoughts and weigh their words before speaking. Thus, **the mind** (literally, "heart"; compare Douay) **of fools is in their mouth**—that is, they speak before they think—while **the mouth of wise men is in their mind** ("heart")—they think before they speak.

The Speech of the Fool and of the Wise

LIVING TRADITION

St. Hilary of Poitiers (ca. 315–67) comments on the stark contrast between the speech of the fool and the speech of the wise:

> If a fool's heart is in his mouth, it is because he does not say what he has thought but thinks afterwards about what he has said. This refers to the tongue of the fool. . . . [But] the tongue of the wise is born of meditation on wisdom, and therefore of itself, like the pen of a scribe, it does nothing disordered or uncertain. It submits itself, rather, to what has been thought and read, which make it flow nimbly according to the judgment of reason.[a]

a. Hilary of Poitiers, *Homilies on the Psalms* 51.7 (Voicu, *Apocrypha*, 282).

21:27–28   When an ungodly man curses his adversary (literally, "curses Satan"; compare Job 1:6–12), he curses his own soul. Perhaps this means that the wicked shirk responsibility for their own sins by "cursing Satan" instead of confessing their guilt. Yet by failing to repent of their wrongdoings, they ultimately curse themselves. A whisperer who gossips or discloses another's faults for no valid reason commits *detraction* (Catechism 2477). In doing so, he harms his own reputation more than that of the one he is gossiping about and defiles his own soul, so that he is disrespected and hated in his own neighborhood (Sir 5:14; 19:4–17; 28:13).

IV.G. (ii) The Wise and the Foolish: The Fool's Wayward Path (22:1–18)

¹The indolent may be compared to a filthy stone,
    and every one hisses at his disgrace.
²The indolent may be compared to the filth of dunghills;
    any one that picks it up will shake it off his hand.

³It is a disgrace to be the father of an undisciplined son,
    and the birth of a daughter is a loss.
⁴A sensible daughter obtains her husband,
    but one who acts shamefully brings grief to her father.
⁵An impudent daughter disgraces father and husband,
    and will be despised by both.
⁶Like music in mourning is a tale told at the wrong time,
    but chastising and discipline are wisdom at all times.

⁷He who teaches a fool is like one who glues potsherds together,
    or who rouses a sleeper from deep slumber.
⁸He who tells a story to a fool tells it to a drowsy man;
    and at the end he will say, "What is it?"
¹¹Weep for the dead, for he lacks the light;
    and weep for the fool, for he lacks intelligence;
weep less bitterly for the dead, for he has attained rest;
    but the life of the fool is worse than death.
¹²Mourning for the dead lasts seven days,
    but for a fool or an ungodly man it lasts all his life.

¹³Do not talk much with a foolish man,
    and do not visit an unintelligent man;
guard yourself from him to escape trouble,
    and you will not be soiled when he shakes himself off;
avoid him and you will find rest,
    and you will never be wearied by his madness.
¹⁴What is heavier than lead?

And what is its name except "Fool"?
[15]Sand, salt, and a piece of iron
are easier to bear than a stupid man.

[16]A wooden beam firmly bonded into a building
will not be torn loose by an earthquake;
so the mind firmly fixed on a reasonable counsel
will not be afraid in a crisis.
[17]A mind settled on an intelligent thought
is like the stucco decoration on the wall of a colonnade.
[18]Fences set on a high place
will not stand firm against the wind;
so a timid heart with a fool's purpose
will not stand firm against any fear.

OT: Prov 1:22; 6:9–11; 24:30–34; 26:13–16
NT: Matt 25:24–27; 2 Thess 3:10–11
Catechism: sloth, 1866

While the wise are diligent, fools are lazy and—in Ben Sira's view—repugnant   22:1–2
(compare Prov 6:9–11; 24:30–34; 26:13–16). He compares **the indolent** (lazy
people) to **a filthy stone**, presumably soiled by animal or human feces, from
which people recoil in disgust, and to **the filth of dunghills** that soils **any one
that picks it up**.

Undisciplined children are a source of distress to their parents (22:3–6). **It**   22:3
is a disgrace and embarrassment **to be the father of an undisciplined son**[37]—
particularly in the Middle East, where the honor of the family is more highly
valued than individual honor, and the unruly child's actions reflect unfavorably
on the parents. The second half of the verse, which the RSV-2CE renders as
the birth of a daughter is a loss, seems to say that the birth of *any* daughter
is a loss.[38] Yet this translation is misleading. It is more likely that the adjective
"undisciplined" carries over to the daughter as well, so that a more accurate
rendering would be: "It is a disgrace to be the father of an undisciplined child;
if [this undisciplined child is] a daughter, she is born to his loss" (see NABRE).
Women in the ancient world were financially dependent upon men—first their
fathers, then their husbands. Thus, an undisciplined daughter would have not
only humiliated her parents; she would have caused them financial loss as well due
to marriage expenses or other costs if she remained unmarried or got divorced.

A sensible and prudent **daughter** is more likely to find a **husband**.[39] A well-   22:4–5
raised daughter will make a good wife; her virtues will attract a good husband

37. Although the RSV-2CE and other translations render the phrase as **undisciplined son**, there
is no word for "son" in the Greek text. It is more likely that Ben Sira means a "child" of either sex here.
38. The NRSV, ESV-CE, and NJB also follow this reading.
39. The Latin reads: *is an inheritance to her husband* (compare Douay).

179

who will cherish her as a treasure. But **an impudent** or insolent **daughter** who **acts shamefully** will bring **grief** to both her **father** and her **husband**; she will cause them heartache to the point that both will eventually despise her.

22:6   The next few verses describe challenges in teaching. Just as joyous **music** is inappropriate during seasons of **mourning**, so **a tale**—perhaps to instruct one's children—can be **told at the wrong time**. If they are not disposed to listen, exhorting them will be ineffective. Yet **chastising**—here in the sense of corporal punishment, which was more prevalent in Ben Sira's day than in today's context—**and discipline** are useful tools to train children in **wisdom at all times.**

22:7–8   **He who teaches a fool** engages in a futile task and only wastes his time; he is **like one who glues potsherds together.** Just as a broken pot, even when repaired, no longer holds its content reliably, so a fool does not retain anything that he is taught (Prov 1:22; 23:9; 24:7). The effort is as pointless as trying to rouse **a sleeper from deep slumber.** Likewise, telling **a story to a fool** is like telling it **to a drowsy man** who, being barely awake, does not pay attention to what he is told; **at the end**, when you are done speaking, he will ask, "**What is it** that you just said?"

22:9–10   GII adds verses 9–10, which are thematically related to verses 3–6.[40] **Children who are brought up in a good life,** with a clear sense of propriety, **conceal the lowly birth of their parents** if they come from lower social classes. In contrast, spoiled, arrogant **children stain the nobility** and reputation **of their kindred,** even if they come from higher social classes.

22:11–12   While it is natural to **weep for the dead, for he lacks the light** and can no longer see, one should **weep for the fool** even more because **he lacks intelligence** and is unable to "see" reality as it truly is. Indeed, one should shed tears **less bitterly for the dead,** who has found **rest** from this life, than for **the fool,** whose impoverished life **is worse than death.** In the Bible and Jewish tradition, **mourning for the dead lasts seven days** (see Gen 50:10; Jdt 16:24; Job 2:13); yet **for a fool or an ungodly man it lasts all his life** because his conduct continually brings grief to those around him.

22:13–15   **Do not talk much with a foolish man** who has nothing valuable to say, **and do not visit an unintelligent man,** for it is a waste of time. The longer Greek text adds: "for being without sense he will despise everything about you."[41] Fools cannot endure the presence of the wise because they hold diametrically opposed values. Therefore, **guard yourself from him** and avoid his company **to escape trouble** and avoid being **soiled when he shakes himself off** like a pig after wallowing in the mud, dirtying everything and irritating everyone with **his**

---

40. ⁹**Children who are brought up in a good life, conceal the lowly birth of their parents.** ¹⁰**Children who are disdainfully and boorishly haughty stain the nobility of their kindred** (Sir 22:9–10, RSV-2CE footnote). These are numbered 22:7–8 in the Greek text and in other English translations (NRSV, ESV-CE, NABRE footnotes).

41. NRSV footnote; compare ESV-CE footnote.

The Fool

Ben Sira derives his concept of "the fool" from earlier biblical books, especially Proverbs and Ecclesiastes. For these authors, a fool is not simply one who lacks intelligence but the opposite of one who is prudent and wise. The fool is not only uneducated; he despises wisdom and instruction (Prov 1:7; 15:5) and does not fear the Lord (Ps 14:1). He is undisciplined (Prov 5:23), lazy (24:30–31), perverse (19:1), reckless in speech (10:14), quick-tempered (29:11), contentious (20:3), angry (29:9), unrestrained (14:16), and spiritually blind (Eccles 2:14). The fool shamelessly flaunts his folly (Prov 13:16), refuses to take advice from others (18:2), and is always convinced of being right (12:15). Ultimately, folly is self-destructive (Prov 1:32), for it misleads (14:8) and punishes the fool (16:22), "tears down" a house (14:1), and leads to ruin (5:23; 19:3; see Matt 7:24–27). Accordingly, Proverbs personifies Lady Wisdom's counterpart and nemesis, "Dame Folly," as a promiscuous woman who leads young men to their destruction and death (Prov 7:6–27; 9:13–18).

madness. What is heavier than lead if not a **fool**, whose company is likened to carrying a burdensome load? **Sand, salt, and a piece of iron**—other heavy items that are difficult to carry (Job 6:3; Prov 27:3)—are still **easier to bear than a stupid man.** This refers not to someone with a low IQ but rather to a person who consistently refuses to pursue wisdom. The †Vulgate clarifies this by translating "stupid man" as *imprudent, foolish, and wicked* (compare Douay, 22:18).

Unlike the fool, who is fickle and burdensome, the wise person is stable and strong. Just as **a wooden beam** fastened **into a building** is held firmly enough to withstand the tremors of **an earthquake,** so a well-formed **mind firmly fixed on a reasonable counsel** is steadfast and unafraid of any **crisis.** The mind does not rely on its own cleverness but is **settled** and supported by **an intelligent thought** guided by wisdom, just as an elegant but fragile **stucco decoration** is supported by the solid **wall of a colonnade.** In contrast to these sturdy structures, **fences set on a high place will not stand firm against the wind.** Instead of "fences," some manuscripts read "small stones" (NABRE) or "pebbles" (NJB), which were placed on the top of garden and vineyard walls to alert watchers of predators such as jackals that might try to invade the property. Just as the pebbles would be easily blown off by the wind, so a cowardly, **timid heart with a fool's** fickle resolve **will not stand firm against any fear** caused by difficult situations.

22:16–18

Reflection and Application (22:1–18)

Compared to the more notable vices of pride, anger, and lust, laziness is often considered a relatively "harmless" sin. The wisdom authors do not share this view: neither Proverbs (6:9–11; 24:30–34) nor Sirach (22:1–2) conceals their contempt for the "indolent," "sluggard," or "slothful" person. In fact, spiritual apathy, traditionally known as "acedia" or "sloth," is one of the seven deadly sins—also referred to as "capital sins" because they are vices, bad habits that dispose us toward sinful acts and "engender other sins" (Catechism 1866).

In Dante's *Divine Comedy*, the souls that are saved but not yet purified must ascend Mount Purgatory and purge themselves of the seven capital sins before they can reach the earthly paradise and be taken up to heaven. These vices are all portrayed as failures to love God and neighbor. First, the penitents must rid themselves of the perverted love of self that aims at harming one's neighbor— the vices of *pride, envy, and wrath*. Second, they must overcome their deficient love for God, who is the highest good—this is the vice of *sloth*. Third, they must tame their excessive love for the lower goods of wealth, food, and sex—these are the vices of *avarice, gluttony, and lust.*[42]

Sloth, then—an oppressive sorrow or sluggishness of mind that neglects to do good[43]—acts as a type of "hinge" between the spiritual sins of pride, envy, and wrath and the material or carnal sins of avarice, gluttony, and lust. A slothful person who fails to love the highest good will struggle to resist temptations associated with perverted self-love or excessive love of lower goods. Accordingly, St. Gregory the Great assigns six "daughters" of sloth, or sins that arise from it: malice, spite, faintheartedness, despair, sluggishness in regard to the commandments, and wandering of the mind after unlawful things.[44] These clearly demonstrate that sloth is anything but a "harmless" vice. How, then, shall we overcome sloth? St. John Climacus recommends singing psalms, performing manual labor, thinking about death, and engaging in "prayer backed by a firm hope in the blessings of the future."[45]

IV.H. Preserving Friendship (22:19–26)

---

[19]**A man who pricks an eye will make tears fall,**
   and one who pricks the heart makes it show feeling.
[20]**One who throws a stone at birds scares them away,**
   and one who reviles a friend will break off the friendship.
[21]**Even if you have drawn your sword against a friend,**
   do not despair, for a renewal of friendship is possible.
[22]**If you have opened your mouth against your friend,**
   do not worry, for reconciliation is possible;

---

42. Dante, *Purgatorio* 17.112–38.
43. Thomas Aquinas, *Summa Theologiae* II-II q. 35 a. 1.
44. Gregory the Great, *Moralia on Job* 31.45; Thomas Aquinas, *Summa Theologiae* II-II q. 35 a. 4.
45. John Climacus, *The Ladder of Divine Ascent*, ed. Richard J. Payne, Classics of Western Spirituality (Mahwah, NJ: Paulist Press, 1982), 164.

but as for reviling, arrogance, disclosure of secrets, or a
    treacherous blow—
in these cases any friend will flee.

²³Gain the trust of your neighbor in his poverty,
    that you may rejoice with him in his prosperity;
stand by him in time of affliction,
    that you may share with him in his inheritance.
²⁴The vapor and smoke of the furnace precede the fire;
    so insults precede bloodshed.
²⁵I will not be ashamed to protect a friend,
    and I will not hide from him;
²⁶but if some harm should happen to me because of him,
    whoever hears of it will beware of him.

OT: Prov 20:19; 25:9–10; Sir 6:5–17; 12:8–18; 27:16–21
NT: Matt 18:21–22; John 13:13–15; Eph 4:32
Catechism: friendship, fruit of charity, 1829; forgiving enemies, 2842–45

This brief section on preserving and repairing friendships builds upon previous   **22:19–20** discussions of the same topic (6:5–17; 12:8–18). The **eye** and **heart** are two of the most sensitive and vulnerable parts of the human body—the eye, physically, and the heart, metaphorically, as the seat of human emotions and affections. Both are easily wounded but difficult to heal. Likewise, it is easy to throw **a stone at birds** to scare them and scatter them, but not as easy to gather them again. These metaphors illustrate the principle that it is easy to revile and damage a **friendship**, but much more difficult to mend it after it has been broken.

    Even if you have drawn your sword and engaged in a violent argument with   **22:21–22** **a friend**, or **opened your mouth** and exchanged sharp words with him or her, there is no need to **despair**, for **a renewal of friendship** through forgiveness and **reconciliation** is still **possible** (Matt 18:21–22; Eph 4:32). Yet some actions, such as **reviling** with contemptuous insults, **arrogance** or pride, breaching confidence through the **disclosure of secrets** (Prov 20:19; 25:9–10), **or a treacherous blow** or "stab in the back" (NJB) constitute such a breach of trust that they often irreversibly damage friendships. One can expect **any friend** to **flee** from such betrayals, to the point that reconciliation is very difficult if not impossible (Sir 27:16–21).

    Difficult times present opportunities to strengthen friendships. If you **gain**   **22:23–24** **the trust of your neighbor in his poverty** and help him (or her) **in time of affliction**, you will have proven that you are not a fair-weather companion of convenience but a true friend. Your friend will remember your loyalty and invite you to **rejoice with him in his prosperity**, and he may even share **his inheritance** with you (compare John 15:13–15).[46] Yet trust in friendship must also be

---

46. GII adds: **For one should not always despise restricted circumstances** [i.e., poverty], **nor admire a rich man who is stupid** (RSV-2CE footnote).

Five Vices That Dissolve Friendship

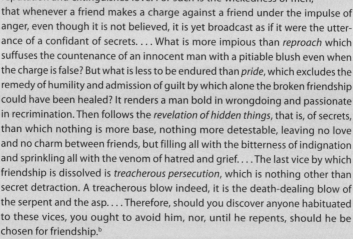

LIVING TRADITION

In his twelfth-century classic *Spiritual Friendship*, the Cistercian monk Aelred of Rievaulx comments on the five vices that dissolve friendship according to Sir 22:22: reviling (or slander), insulting reproach (a false accusation or taunt), arrogance (or pride), the disclosure of secrets, and a treacherous blow.[a]

Let us carefully consider these five vices, that we may not bind ourselves by the ties of friendship to persons whom either the fury of anger or some other passion tends to incite to these vices. *Slander*, indeed, injures reputation and extinguishes love. For such is the wickedness of men, that whenever a friend makes a charge against a friend under the impulse of anger, even though it is not believed, it is yet broadcast as if it were the utterance of a confidant of secrets. . . . What is more impious than *reproach* which suffuses the countenance of an innocent man with a pitiable blush even when the charge is false? But what is less to be endured than *pride*, which excludes the remedy of humility and admission of guilt by which alone the broken friendship could have been healed? It renders a man bold in wrongdoing and passionate in recrimination. Then follows the *revelation of hidden things*, that is, of secrets, than which nothing is more base, nothing more detestable, leaving no love and no charm between friends, but filling all with the bitterness of indignation and sprinkling all with the venom of hatred and grief. . . . The last vice by which friendship is dissolved is *treacherous persecution*, which is nothing other than secret detraction. A treacherous blow indeed, it is the death-dealing blow of the serpent and the asp. . . . Therefore, should you discover anyone habituated to these vices, you ought to avoid him, nor, until he repents, should he be chosen for friendship.[b]

a. Aelred follows the Vulgate of Sir 22:22 (22:27 in the Vulgate), which lists five vices rather than the Greek's four.
b. *Spiritual Friendship* 3.24–26. Aelred of Rievaulx, *Spiritual Friendship*, trans. Mary Eugenia Laker (Washington, DC: Cistercian Publications, 1974), 96–97. Adapted, with emphasis added.

fostered with mutual respect and kind words. Just as **vapor and smoke** appear before a fire bursts into flames, **so insults precede bloodshed** or murder. As the saying goes, familiarity breeds contempt: friends must guard their tongues and avoid insults lest they escalate into violence.

22:25–26   Ben Sira switches to the first person and asserts his own loyalty in friendship: **I will not be ashamed to protect a friend**, he says. Nor will he shirk responsibility and **hide from** his friend in his hour of need. However, if a friend is disloyal and causes him **harm**, the untrustworthy friend will damage his own reputation, for **whoever hears** of his treachery **will beware of him.**

IV.I. (i) Self-Control over Thoughts, Words, and Deeds: Prayer for Self-Control; Sinful Speech (22:27–23:15)

[27]O that a guard were set over my mouth,
    and a seal of prudence upon my lips,
that it may keep me from falling,
    so that my tongue may not destroy me!
[23:1]O Lord, Father and Ruler of my life,
    do not abandon me to their counsel,
    and let me not fall because of them!
[2]O that whips were set over my thoughts,
    and the discipline of wisdom over my mind!
That they may not spare me in my errors,
    and that it may not pass by my sins;
[3]in order that my mistakes may not be multiplied,
    and my sins may not abound;
then I will not fall before my adversaries,
    and my enemy will not rejoice over me.
[4]O Lord, Father and God of my life,
    do not give me haughty eyes,
    [5]and remove from me evil desire.
[6]Let neither gluttony nor lust overcome me,
    and do not surrender me to a shameless soul.

[7]Listen, my children, to instruction concerning speech;
    the one who observes it will never be caught.
[8]The sinner is overtaken through his lips,
    the reviler and the arrogant are tripped by them.
[9]Do not accustom your mouth to oaths,
    and do not habitually utter the name of the Holy One;
[10]for as a servant who is continually examined under torture
    will not lack bruises,
so also the man who always swears and utters the Name
    will not be cleansed from sin.
[11]A man who swears many oaths will be filled with iniquity,
    and the scourge will not leave his house;
if he offends, his sin remains on him,
    and if he disregards it, he sins doubly;
if he has sworn needlessly, he will not be justified,
    for his house will be filled with calamities.

[12]There is an utterance which is comparable to death;
    may it never be found in the inheritance of Jacob!
For all these errors will be far from the godly,
    and they will not wallow in sins.

> [13]Do not accustom your mouth to lewd vulgarity,
>   for it involves sinful speech.
> [14]Remember your father and mother
>   when you sit among great men;
> lest you be forgetful in their presence,
>   and be deemed a fool on account of your habits;
> then you will wish that you had never been born,
>   and you will curse the day of your birth.
> [15]A man accustomed to using insulting words
>   will never become disciplined all his days.

OT: Exod 20:7; Lev 19:12; 24:15–16; Prov 6:2
NT: Matt 5:34–37; Eph 5:4; Col 3:8; James 1:21; 5:12
Catechism: temperance, 1809; lust and gluttony, 1866; taking the name of the Lord in vain, 2150–55; purity of heart, 2517–27

22:27   Aware that imprudent words can cause him untold harm (20:7–8, 18–20; 22:22; 28:24–26), Ben Sira longs for better self-control over what he says, wishing he had **a guard** watching over his **mouth, and a seal of prudence** preventing his **lips** from speaking rashly, lest they lead to his downfall. This transitional verse links the previous discussion on preserving friendships and the following prayer for help against sin.

23:1   Next Ben Sira prays for divine protection over his thoughts (which rule speech, 23:1–3) and his desires (23:4–6), which he addresses in the rest of the chapter with advice on speech (23:7–15) and sex (23:16–28). Addressing God as **Lord, Father and Ruler of** his **life**—terms that express God's loving care and sovereign authority—he prays not to be abandoned to the **counsel** of his mouth, lips, and tongue. By personifying his organs of speech, as if they had a will of their own, Ben Sira emphasizes how easily they can lead to a person's downfall if not guarded by prudence. The fact that Ben Sira prays to God as "Father" indicates that this was a known practice for Jews of his day (2 Sam 7:12–14; Ps 103:13; Isa 63:16; Jer 3:4, 19) and that Jesus was not the first to do so (Matt 6:9; Mark 14:36; John 20:17; Gal 4:6).

23:2–3   Ben Sira wishes that **whips were set over** his **thoughts** to restrain and tame them, and **the discipline of wisdom over** his **mind** to rule it, for control of one's actions and words begins with controlling one's thoughts. This self-discipline consists in submitting to God's fatherly discipline—an expression of his love (Prov 3:11–12). Ben Sira wishes that the whips of chastisement would correct his **errors** of ignorance and **sins** so that these **may not abound**. Uninhibited thoughts open the door to a multitude of transgressions that ultimately lead to one's downfall and the triumph of one's enemies.

23:4–6   Repeating the address of verse 1 in nearly identical terms, Ben Sira implores the **Lord, Father and God of** his **life** to keep him from **haughty eyes** (an arrogant attitude) and **evil desire** (covetousness or lust). He prays that **neither**

186

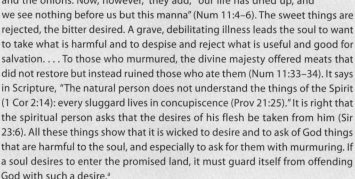

"Do Not Surrender Me to a Shameless Soul"   LIVING TRADITION

The fifth-century bishop of Carthage Quodvultdeus explains how the temptation of the Israelites to return to Egypt during the exodus prefigures the Christian's temptation to avoid what is good but difficult, and to choose what is harmful but pleasant:

> Forgetful of freedom and grace and desiring the Egyptian foods, the people were found guilty of murmuring against God and against Moses. They say, "Who will give us meat to eat? We remember the fish that we ate freely in Egypt, the cucumbers, the leeks, the garlic and the onions. Now, however," they add, "our life has dried up, and we see nothing before us but this manna" (Num 11:4–6). The sweet things are rejected, the bitter desired. A grave, debilitating illness leads the soul to want to take what is harmful and to despise and reject what is useful and good for salvation. . . . To those who murmured, the divine majesty offered meats that did not restore but instead ruined those who ate them (Num 11:33–34). It says in Scripture, "The natural person does not understand the things of the Spirit (1 Cor 2:14): every sluggard lives in concupiscence (Prov 21:25)." It is right that the spiritual person asks that the desires of his flesh be taken from him (Sir 23:6). All these things show that it is wicked to desire and to ask of God things that are harmful to the soul, and especially to ask for them with murmuring. If a soul desires to enter the promised land, it must guard itself from offending God with such a desire.[a]

a. *The Book of Promises and Predictions of God* 2.8.14 (Voicu, *Apocrypha*, 288).

gluttony nor lust—the two cardinal sins that are most closely associated with the body (Catechism 1866)—will **overcome** him, acknowledging that the desires of the flesh are particularly difficult to master. His plea that the Lord would not **surrender** him **to a shameless soul** is a prayer for protection from his *own* soul should it fall prey to these shameless passions.

As a spiritual father, Ben Sira addresses his readers as his **children**, offering them **instruction concerning speech**. Those who follow his advice **will never be caught** or ensnared by their own words (20:18; Prov 6:2), unlike **the sinner**, who **is overtaken** by his own reckless speech, or **the reviler and the arrogant**, who by insulting others are **tripped by** their own ill-considered words.   23:7–8

The wise should not become accustomed to swearing **oaths**. Solemn pledges that invoke God's name should be sworn only in the gravest of circumstances (Matt 5:34–37; James 5:12). One should also **not habitually utter the name of the Holy One** (Sir 4:14; 43:10; 47:8), for just as a disobedient servant is **examined** and beaten by his master, so one **who always swears and utters the Name** of God in vain will be punished for violating the second commandment of the †Decalogue (Exod 20:7; Deut 5:11).   23:9–10

23:11   Many afflictions await a person who **swears many oaths** and thereby profanes the name of God through his inability to keep all the oaths he swears (27:14; Lev 19:12). This causes him to be **filled with iniquity**, so that **the scourge** of divine punishment **will not leave his house**—for the family of a sinner often suffers the consequences of his transgressions. One whose word cannot be trusted incurs the wrath of God. **If he offends** by rashly swearing an oath, he sins, **and if he disregards it** by failing to fulfill what he has sworn to do, he is **doubly** guilty. If he swears casually or **needlessly, he will not be justified** or pardoned, and **his house** will be plagued **with calamities**.

23:12–13   **There is an utterance** or blasphemous way of speaking evil against God that is **comparable to death**—that is, punishable by death according to the †Torah (Lev 24:15–16). Ben Sira desires that such speech **never be found in the inheritance of Jacob**, among the Jewish people. Such conduct must remain **far from the godly**, who would not dare to **wallow in sins** like pigs roll in the mud. The wise must also stay clear of **lewd vulgarity** or indecent language, for it is also **sinful speech** before God (Eph 5:4; Col 3:8; James 1:21).

23:14–15   A good way to control one's speech is to **remember your father and mother** when among prominent people, lest you forget and speak carelessly or coarsely in the **presence** of people of importance and bring dishonor to your parents. Especially in a culture where honor and shame are paramount, one who disgraces himself may well regret having **been born** and **curse the day of** his **birth** (see Job 3:3; Jer 20:14). People are creatures of habit. Those who habitually use **insulting words** or abusive language rarely **become disciplined**. It is all the more vital to train one's speech from a young age and to pray to God for self-control over one's thoughts and words (Sir 23:1–3).

IV.I. (ii) Self-Control over Thoughts, Words, and Deeds: Sexual Sins; Adultery and Its Consequences (23:16–28)

> [16]**Two sorts of men multiply sins,**
> **and a third incurs wrath.**
> **The soul heated like a burning fire**
> **will not be quenched until it is consumed;**
> **a man who commits fornication with his near of kin**
> **will never cease until the fire burns him up.**
> [17]**To a fornicator all bread tastes sweet;**
> **he will never cease until he dies.**
> [18]**A man who breaks his marriage vows**
> **says to himself, "Who sees me?**
> **Darkness surrounds me, and the walls hide me,**
> **and no one sees me. Why should I fear?**

The Most High will not take notice of my sins."
¹⁹His fear is confined to the eyes of men,
   and he does not realize that the eyes of the Lord
   are ten thousand times brighter than the sun;
they look upon all the ways of men,
   and perceive even the hidden places.
²⁰Before the universe was created, it was known to him;
   so it was also after it was finished.
²¹This man will be punished in the streets of the city,
   and where he least suspects it, he will be seized.
²²So it is with a woman who leaves her husband
   and provides an heir by a stranger.
²³For first of all, she has disobeyed the law of the Most High;
   second, she has committed an offense against her husband;
and third, she has committed adultery through harlotry
   and brought forth children by another man.
²⁴She herself will be brought before the assembly,
   and punishment will fall on her children.
²⁵Her children will not take root,
   and her branches will not bear fruit.
²⁶She will leave her memory for a curse,
   and her disgrace will not be blotted out.
²⁷Those who survive her will recognize
   that nothing is better than the fear of the Lord,
   and nothing sweeter than to heed the commandments of the Lord.

OT: Exod 20:14; Lev 20:10; Deut 22:22–24; Prov 9:17; Wis 3:16–4:6
NT: John 8:4–5
Catechism: adultery, 2380–81

Ben Sira prayed for self-control over bodily urges and especially sexual desires   23:16–17
(23:4–6). He addresses those temptations here (23:16–28), beginning with a
numerical proverb: **Two sorts of men multiply sins, and a third incurs wrath**—
referring to the three sexual sins that follow. First, **the soul** that burns with sexual
passion is not **quenched until it is consumed**: an unrestrained sexual drive
ultimately burns itself out along with the person who gives in to it. Second, one
who commits fornication with his near of kin (literally, "a fornicator in the
body of his flesh")—perhaps referring to incest (Lev 18:6–18), masturbation,
or sexual licentiousness in general—will become enslaved by his compulsion
until the fire burns him up. Third, **to a fornicator all bread tastes sweet**: a
habitually immoral person will pursue sexual relations indiscriminately (Prov
9:17) and is unable to stop until the day of his death.
   A man who breaks his marriage vows (literally, "who wanders from his bed")   23:18
foolishly believes that his sin is hidden and **says to himself, "Who sees me?"**
Because he sins surrounded by **darkness**, enclosed by four **walls**, he imagines

that he has no reason to **fear**, thinking that even God **the Most High will not notice** his **sins** (16:17–23; Job 24:15). Such rationalization is typical of sinners, who convince themselves that their deeds remain hidden (Isa 29:15; Ezek 8:12).

23:19–21   The adulterer fears only **the eyes of men**: his sole concern is to escape the punishment and public disgrace that he would suffer if caught. He is oblivious to the all-seeing **eyes of the Lord**, which **are ten thousand times brighter than the sun** and shine upon his most **hidden** thoughts and actions (17:19–20; Ps 33:13–15; Prov 15:3, 11). **Before the universe was created**, every deed **was known** to the omniscient God; so he knows all things now and always (Sir 42:18; Ps 139:1–16). God will render to each one according to their works: despite the adulterer's secrecy, he will eventually be exposed and publicly **punished**—death by stoning, as prescribed by the law (Lev 20:10; Deut 22:22–24; John 8:4–5). In the meantime, the adulterer must live with the daily fear of being caught, a fate that will occur when and **where he least suspects it**.

23:22–23   Likewise, the adulteress, the **woman who leaves her husband** (i.e., she is unfaithful to him; women in the ancient world could rarely abandon or divorce their husbands) will be punished, especially if she **provides an heir**—that is, if she conceives a child—**by a stranger**, another man. Her wrongdoing is threefold: **first**, she has sinned against God by disobeying his **law** that prohibits adultery (Exod 20:14; Deut 5:18); **second,** she has sinned **against her husband** by her infidelity; **third**, she has sinned against herself by committing **adultery** through illicit sexual encounters. Moreover, by bringing forth illegitimate **children by another man**, she has disgraced them as well.

23:24–25   Like the adulterer, the adulteress will be caught and **brought before the assembly** for a public trial. **Punishment will fall** not only on her but also indirectly **on her children**. Illegitimate Jewish children were not considered part of the congregation of Israel and were unable to marry into the Jewish community and have children of their own (Deut 23:2; Wis 3:16–4:6). Because her children could **not take root** or find a respectable place in society, the adulteress's own **branches** could **not bear fruit**. Ancient Israel, like other traditional societies, held strong legal and social norms upholding marital fidelity so that childbearing and rearing would take place, whenever possible, in a family with a father and a mother. While this value remains of paramount importance in the Church, forgiveness is available to adulterers (John 8:1–11) and inclusion in the Christian community to those born out of wedlock.

23:26–28   The consequences of adultery are bitter and long-lasting for the adulteress and her posterity. **She will leave her memory for a curse**—possibly uttered against her by the tribunal or the assembly (Num 5:11–31)—**and her disgrace** will outlive her. **Those who survive her** and live after her death **will recognize** the value of fearing the Lord (and the consequences of not doing so) and of heeding his **commandments** (Pss 19:10; 119:103)—the fullest expression of the fear of the Lord that leads to the attainment of wisdom.[47]

Reflection and Application (22:27–23:28)

Although Ben Sira asks for prudence (22:27), his prayer (23:1–6) is primarily a petition for *temperance* or self-control, which is defined as "the moral virtue that moderates the attraction of pleasures and provides balance in the use of created goods" (Catechism 1809). This prayer is fitting in a day and age when so many people desperately seek to satisfy their desires but end up enslaved to their passions and ultimately unhappy. As Ben Sira says elsewhere, "Do not follow your base desires, but restrain your appetites" (18:30). There are many aspects of temperance. These include *shamefacedness* or a natural sense of shame (Ben Sira's "good shame," 4:21; 41:17–23)—that is, the modest recoiling from what is immoral or disgraceful; a sense of *honor* or *respectability* by which one loves the beauty of temperance; *moderation* in food and *sobriety* in drink; *chastity*, or "the successful integration of sexuality within the person" (Catechism 2337); and her sister *purity*, the right ordering of the thoughts, imagination, words, and desires. Also closely related to temperance are *continence*, which restrains the will from pursuing sexual pleasures; *meekness*, which moderates anger within one's soul; *modesty*, which moderates outward dress and movements; and *humility*, which moderates the mind's pursuit of excellence.[48]

---

47. GII adds verse 28: **It is a great honor to follow God, and to be received by him is long life** (RSV-2CE, NRSV footnotes; compare ESV-CE footnote).
48. Thomas Aquinas, *Summa Theologiae* II-II q. 143 a. 1.

Book Two

Sirach 24:1–43:33

Part V

Sirach 24:1–33:17

Lady Wisdom's hymn of praise, describing her journey from heaven to Israel's sanctuary on earth (24:1–34), marks the beginning of Book Two and Part V (see outline of Sirach). Ben Sira's practical wisdom teachings resume in chapter 25, where he gives advice on interpersonal relations and on gaining wisdom from youth to old age (25:1–12), followed by controversial reflections on wicked and virtuous women (25:13–26:27). He continues with more relational advice on dealing with others with honesty and integrity (26:28–27:15) and on avoiding offenses that harm friendships, such as betrayal, anger, strife, and slander (27:16–28:26). Ben Sira also provides financial advice on helping those in need by means of loans, alms, and surety (29:1–20), along with practical tips on living frugally and rearing children (29:21–30:13). While everyone seeks a happy life, not all succeed in attaining it, as many mistakenly believe it depends on their financial well-being. Ben Sira insists that health and gladness of heart, rather than wealth, are the key to happiness (30:14–31:11). Banquets are joyful occasions, and to fully enjoy them it is important to respect the proper etiquette in regard to eating, drinking, and speaking (31:12–32:13). Finally, Ben Sira concludes this part with general advice on fearing the Lord and trusting divine providence, along with a reflection on the diversity of people in the world (32:14–33:17).

V.A. (i) Lady Wisdom's Hymn of Praise: From Heaven to Earth (24:1–18)

[1]Wisdom will praise herself *and is honored in God*,
and will glory in the midst of her people.
[2]In the assembly of the Most High she will open her mouth,
and in the presence of his host she will glory.

In the midst of her people she is exalted;
   in holy fulness she is admired.
In the multitude of the chosen she finds praise,
   and among the blessed she is blessed, saying:
³"I came forth from the mouth of the Most High,
   the first-born before all creatures.
I ordained that an unfailing light
   should arise in the heavens,
   and I covered the earth like a mist.
⁴I dwelt in high places,
   and my throne was in a pillar of cloud.
⁵Alone I have made the circuit of the vault of heaven
   and have walked in the depths of the abyss.
⁶In the waves of the sea, in the whole earth,
   and in every people and nation I have gotten a possession.
⁷Among all these I sought a resting place;
   I sought in whose territory I might lodge.

⁸"Then the Creator of all things gave me a commandment,
   and the one who created me assigned a place for my tent.
And he said, 'Make your dwelling in Jacob,
   and in Israel receive your inheritance,
   and among my chosen put down your roots.'
⁹From eternity, in the beginning, he created me,
   and for eternity I shall not cease to exist.
¹⁰In the holy tabernacle I ministered before him,
   and so I was established in Zion.
¹¹In the beloved city likewise he gave me a resting place,
   and in Jerusalem was my dominion.
¹²So I took root in an honored people,
   in the portion of the Lord, who is their inheritance,
   and my abode was in the full assembly of the saints.

¹³"I grew tall like a cedar in Lebanon,
   and like a cypress on the heights of Hermon.
¹⁴I grew tall like a palm tree in En-gedi,
   and like rose plants in Jericho;
like a beautiful olive tree in the field,
   and like a plane tree I grew tall.
¹⁵Like cassia and camel's thorn I gave forth the aroma of spices,
   and like choice myrrh I spread a pleasant odor,
like galbanum, onycha, and stacte,
   and like the fragrance of frankincense in the tabernacle.
¹⁶Like a terebinth I spread out my branches,
   and my branches are glorious and graceful.

> [17]Like a vine I caused loveliness to bud,
>   and my blossoms became glorious and abundant fruit.

OT: Gen 1–2; Exod 25:8–9; Prov 8:22–31; Song 4:12–5:5; Hosea 14:5–7
NT: John 1:14; Col 1:15
Catechism: God creates by wisdom and love, 295
Lectionary: 24:1–2, 8–12: Second Sunday after Christmas; Common of the Blessed Virgin Mary

This chapter—Lady Wisdom's hymn of praise—is the central passage of the   24:1–2
book.[1] In the first part of the hymn, personified Wisdom reveals her divine
origin and cosmic universality: she is present everywhere, in heaven and on
earth (24:1–7). Ben Sira announces that **Wisdom will praise herself** and declare
her excellence in her own words. Being already *honored in God* ([†]Vulgate) in
the heavenly realms, she will also **glory** on earth among **her people**, Israel,
with whom she desires to dwell. In the heavenly **assembly of the Most High**—
presumably the angels (Ps 82:1)—Wisdom **will open her mouth** to speak God's
word (Prov 8:6–8), **and in the presence of his** angelic **host she will** declare her
glory. The Vulgate adds that she is *exalted, admired*, praised, and *blessed* in
the midst of her **chosen** people, Israel.

Lady Wisdom begins her hymn, speaking in the first person (see also Prov   24:3
8:22–9:12). Her origin **from the mouth of the Most High** identifies her with
God's word spoken at creation (Prov 2:6; Wis 7:25; Isa 48:3). The Vulgate adds that
she is *the first-born before all creatures* (Col 1:15): although she preexisted the
world, she is still a created being (Sir 24:8–9; Prov 8:22–31).[2] By ordaining *that
an unfailing light should arise in the heavens*, she echoes God's first words at
creation: "Let there be light" (Gen 1:3). She also **covered the earth like a mist**—
possibly alluding to the Spirit of God, who hovered over the waters at creation
(Gen 1:2; Wis 1:6–7; 9:17), or the "mist" that went up from the earth (Gen 2:6).

Wisdom **dwelt in high places**—in heaven—yet her **throne was in a pillar of**   24:4–5
cloud—the visible presence of God that led the Israelites through the wilderness (Exod 13:21–22). Wisdom's association with the pillar of cloud (Wis 10:17)
establishes not only a spatial connection between heaven and earth but also a
temporal one between creation and the time of the exodus. Like a rainbow she
encircled **the vault of heaven** above—the firmament made on the second day
of creation (Sir 43:12; Gen 1:6–8; Job 22:14)—and **walked in the depths of the**
abyss below (Gen 1:2). Thus, Wisdom is present and active in every realm of
creation—in heaven, on earth, and below the earth (Prov 8:27–28).

Lady Wisdom is active **in the waves of the sea, in the whole earth**—recalling   24:6–7
the separation of the waters from the dry land on the third day of creation (Gen

---

1. The RSV-2CE largely follows the text of the Vulgate throughout this chapter, including several
additions that are omitted from other English translations.
2. On the distinction between created and uncreated wisdom, see the commentary on Sir 1:4, 9, and
the sidebar "Created and Uncreated Wisdom," p. 51.

1:9–10); **and in every people** of the earth she acquired **a possession**—alluding to the creation of the human race on the sixth day of creation (Gen 1:26–31). Yet, although Wisdom is found **among all** nations at every moment of human history, she still sought a more intimate home and **resting place** among a particular people, **in whose territory** she **might lodge**.

24:8 This section (24:8–12) describes how Wisdom leaves her heavenly abode, "contracting" herself, as it were, to make her home in Israel's tabernacle. Though she is God's word, she remains distinct from him and acts in accordance with his will: for **the Creator of all things gave** her **a commandment** to leave heaven, as it were, and **assigned** a specific **place** for her **tent** or "tabernacle" (Greek *skēnē*), saying to her, **"Make your dwelling"** or "pitch your tabernacle" (John 1:14) **in Jacob**—that is, **in Israel**—so that you can **receive your inheritance**. The Vulgate further emphasizes Israel's status as God's elect people: *and among my chosen put down your roots*.

24:9 Wisdom continues to underscore her ancient origins: **from eternity** or "before the ages" (NRSV), **in the beginning**, before the world came into being, God **created** her. Since Wisdom was created, she is not eternal as God is. Yet **for eternity** (literally, "for all the ages") she will **not cease to exist**: although she has a beginning, she will have no end (Prov 8:23).

24:10–11 Wisdom now provides more details about her earthly home: **In the holy tabernacle** (Greek *skēnē*)—the sanctuary and seat of God's presence that accompanied Israel through the wilderness during the exodus (Exod 25:8–9; 40:34)—she **ministered** or "performed a liturgical ministry" before the Lord. Given that the tabernacle was an earthly representation of the heavenly sanctuary (Wis 9:8), Wisdom's liturgical ministry in the earthly tent mirrors her service before God in the heavenly sanctuary. Later she was also **established in Zion**—Jerusalem, which was conquered by King David (2 Sam 5:7)—where David's son Solomon built the temple that replaced the tabernacle as the new seat of God's presence (1 Kings 8:1–11). Wisdom was thus present with Israel both in the tabernacle during the exodus and in the temple at the time of the Davidic Kingdom. Jerusalem is God's **beloved city** (see Pss 87:2; 132:14), which he gave to Wisdom as **a resting place** (Ps 132:8, 14) and as her **dominion**, where she could exercise her power and authority.

24:12 By saying that she **took root in an honored people**—the people of Israel, who are **the portion of the Lord** (17:17; Deut 32:9)—Wisdom reasserts that she is establishing her residence in Jerusalem. Additionally, she introduces a new metaphor that will be developed in the following verses: Wisdom is also a firmly planted, life-giving tree. The Vulgate adds: *and my abode was in the full assembly of the saints*—as God's praise is found in the assembly of the faithful (Ps 149:1).

24:13 From her "root" in Israel, Lady Wisdom grows like a majestic tree. Ben Sira depicts her using imagery of lush vegetation and spices that evokes the garden

Figure 7. Model of the Jerusalem temple in the Second Temple period

of Eden, the temple liturgy, the Song of Songs, and the prophetic vision of the future restoration of Israel (24:13–18). Read in light of other passages where she is depicted as a loving mother or wife calling her followers to "love her" (4:11–12; 15:2–3) and in light of the banquet invitation that follows (24:19–22), this imagery, brimming with echoes of the Song of Songs, implies that Lady Wisdom is calling Israel to a nuptial encounter with her, restoring her people to the lost paradise by means of the temple liturgy, which in turn anticipates the future messianic age. She **grew tall like a cedar**, a beautiful evergreen tree that grows predominantly **in Lebanon** and provides strong, durable wood (Ps 92:12), **and like a cypress**, a tall evergreen tree, **on the heights of Hermon**, a mountain northwest of Israel at the border of Lebanon and Syria. Both cedars and cypresses are mentioned in the Song of Songs (Song 1:17),[3] as are Lebanon and Hermon (3:9; 4:8; 5:15). According to Ezekiel, both trees were found in the garden of Eden (Ezek 31:8), and both types of wood were used in the construction of the temple (1 Kings 5:6–10; 6:15–36). The two trees are also characteristic of the time of redemption, also known as the messianic age, as described by the prophets (Isa 41:19; 60:13; Hosea 14:5–8).

Wisdom also **grew tall like a palm tree**—a symbol of peace and prosperity. 24:14
In the Song of Songs, the beloved's stature is likened to a palm tree (Song 7:8–9). Palm trees decorate the doors and walls of both Solomon's temple (1 Kings 6:29–35) and the future temple in Ezekiel's vision (Ezek 40:16; 41:18–20, 25–26). **En-gedi**, an oasis on the western shore of the Dead Sea, appears in the Song

---

3. The Hebrew word for "cypress" is sometimes translated as "fir tree" (Ezek 31:8) or "pine" (Song 1:17).

of Solomon (Song 1:14). Flowers such as **rose plants** or lilies also characterize the Canticle (Song 2:1–2, 12, 16; 6:2–3), the tabernacle and temple furnishings (Exod 25:31–34; 1 Kings 7:19, 22, 26), and the future messianic age (Isa 61:11; Hosea 14:5). **Jericho**, a famous city in the southern Jordan Valley west of the Jordan River, was destroyed by Joshua and the Israelites at the time of the conquest (Josh 6) and is known as "the city of palm trees" (2 Chron 28:15). Wisdom is also likened to **a beautiful olive tree**, which is widely grown in Israel and symbolizes peace and security. Its oil was used both for the lamp (Exod 27:20) and anointing oil (30:24) of the sanctuary and was offered with sacrifices (29:2, 40; Lev 2:1–7). The cherubim and doors of the temple were made of olive wood (1 Kings 6:23, 31–33), and olive trees are also prophesied to characterize the messianic age (Isa 41:19; Hosea 14:6). The **plane tree** is a tall, fast-growing tree with large leaves that is rarely mentioned in the Old Testament but is present in Ezekiel's vision of the garden of Eden (Ezek 31:8).

24:15   Lady Wisdom is also likened to fragrant spices: **cassia** (or cinnamon) **and camel's thorn** (perhaps calamus or aromatic cane), together with other **spices** and **choice myrrh**, were used to make the anointing oil of the tabernacle (Exod 30:23–25). These fragrances are frequently mentioned in nuptial contexts (Ps 45:8; Song 4:13–14; 5:1). **Galbanum, onycha, and stacte** were used to make the incense offered in the **tabernacle**, together with **frankincense** (Exod 30:34–35), which is also featured in the Canticle (Song 3:6; 4:6). Wisdom's association with the anointing oil and incense as she ministers in the tabernacle (Sir 24:10) confirms her liturgical and priestly role in Israel's sacred worship, mediating between God and his people.

24:16–18 Wisdom returns to the analogy of trees: **Like a terebinth**—a far-spreading tree possibly related to the pistachio (sometimes translated as "oak")—she **spread out** her **branches**, which become **glorious and graceful**. The imagery continues to suggest that she invites her followers to return to the garden of Eden by joining her in a nuptial union enacted in Israel's temple worship. **Like a vine**—often mentioned in nuptial settings (Song 6:11; 7:8, 12; 8:11–12)—Wisdom **caused loveliness** or grace **to bud**. Wine was offered with the sacrifices in the tabernacle and temple (Exod 29:40), and it will flow abundantly in the messianic age (Isa 25:6; Hosea 14:7; Joel 2:24; Amos 9:13–14). Wisdom's **blossoms became glorious and abundant fruit**—other texts identify this as symbolizing long life, riches, and honor (Prov 3:16; 8:18–21). Wisdom's life-giving "fruit" (especially when read together with v. 22) suggests a contrast with the fruit of the tree of knowledge, which was deceivingly "a delight to the eyes" and "to be desired to make one wise" (Gen 3:6) but ultimately brought death. GII adds verse 18,[4] in which Lady Wisdom describes herself as **the mother of beautiful love, of fear,**

4. **I am the mother of beautiful love, of fear, of knowledge, and of holy hope; being eternal, I therefore am given to all my children, to those who are named by him** (Sir 24:18, RSV-2CE footnote; compare NRSV, ESV-CE, NABRE footnotes).

of knowledge, and of holy hope. She offers these rich gifts along with herself, who is **eternal**, to her **children, who are** chosen and **named by** God.

V.A. (ii) Lady Wisdom's Hymn of Praise: Wisdom's Feast (24:19–34)

[19]"Come to me, you who desire me,
  and eat your fill of my produce.
[20]For my teaching is sweeter than honey,
  and my inheritance sweeter than the honeycomb,
  and my remembrance lasts throughout all generations.
[21]Those who eat me will hunger for more,
  and those who drink me will thirst for more.
[22]Whoever obeys me will not be put to shame,
  and those who work with my help will not sin."

[23]All this is the book of the covenant of the Most High God,
  the law which Moses commanded us
  as an inheritance for the congregations of Jacob.
[25]It fills men with wisdom, like the Pishon,
  and like the Tigris at the time of the first fruits.
[26]It makes them full of understanding, like the Euphrates,
  and like the Jordan at harvest time.
[27]It makes instruction shine forth like light,
  like the Gihon at the time of vintage.
[28]Just as the first man did not know her perfectly,
  the last one has not fathomed her;
[29]for her thought is more abundant than the sea,
  and her counsel deeper than the great abyss.

[30]I went forth like a canal from a river
  and like a water channel into a garden.
[31]I said, "I will water my orchard
  and drench my garden plot";
  and behold, my canal became a river,
  and my river became a sea.
[32]I will again make instruction shine forth like the dawn,
  and I will make it shine afar;
[33]I will again pour out teaching like prophecy,
  and leave it to all future generations.
[34]Observe that I have not labored for myself alone,
  but for all who seek instruction.

OT: Prov 9:1–6; Bar 4:1; Ezek 47:1–12
NT: Matt 11:28–30; John 4:14; Rev 22:1
Catechism: Mary, Seat of Wisdom, 721

24:19-20 **Come to me:** Lady Wisdom invites those **who desire** her (1:26; Wis 6:13) to dine with her at her banquet (Sir 24:19–22; Prov 9:1–6; Matt 11:28–30), so they may **eat** their **fill of** her **produce**—her "fruits" of life, riches, and honors (Sir 6:19; Prov 3:16; 8:18–19). Eating Wisdom's fruit is likened to eating from the tree of life (Prov 3:18), in contrast to eating from the tree of knowledge, which brought alienation and death (Gen 2:9, 16–17; 3:19). Wisdom's **teaching is sweeter than honey**—as are God's words and commandments (Pss 19:10; 119:103; Prov 16:24; 24:13–14) and the delights of married love (Song 4:11; 5:1). The **inheritance** she grants her disciples is **sweeter than the honeycomb.** The †Vulgate adds that Wisdom's *remembrance lasts throughout all generations.*

24:21-22   Lady Wisdom not only invites her followers to eat at her table. At this feast, *she* is the one who is consumed: **Those who eat** and **drink** her **will hunger** and **thirst for more** of her (John 4:14; 6:35, 53–56). The surprising metaphor of "eating" and "drinking" Wisdom points to the familiar exhortation to *obey* her; those who do so **will not be put to shame, and those who work** with her **will not sin.** The themes of life-giving obedience and work, shielding one from shame and sin, again echo the Eden narrative, offering a contrast to eating the fruit of the tree of the knowledge of good and evil, an act of disobedience that sought wisdom but instead brought sin, shame, and death (Sir 51:18; Gen 3:6–7, 19; Prov 8:35–36).

In the Light of Christ (24:19–22)

Lady Wisdom's invitation to "eat" and "drink" her recalls Jesus's words in the Gospel of John, where he promises that whoever comes to him "shall not hunger," and whoever believes in him "shall never thirst" (John 4:14; 6:35). Jesus, as Wisdom incarnate, may have Sir 24:21 in mind when he invites us to eat his flesh and drink his blood (John 6:53–56). Lady Wisdom's invitation to obedience here parallels Jesus's invitation to abide in him and in his word. Wisdom's remembrance, like the sacramental presence of Jesus's body and blood, is both sweet and enduring to all generations.

    The figure of Lady Wisdom in Sir 24 has also been traditionally associated with Mary, who is known and acclaimed in Christian tradition as the "Seat of Wisdom" (Catechism 721).

24:23-24   Lady Wisdom has concluded her speech. Ben Sira now explains that **all this**—Wisdom's self-revelation in verses 3–22—is **the book of the covenant of the Most High God,** which he gave to Israel at Mount Sinai. Wisdom is thus identified with the †Torah, **the law which Moses commanded** to Israel **as an inheritance** (17:11; Exod 24:7–8; Bar 4:1), a divinely given heritage **for the congregations of Jacob,** the people of Israel (Deut 33:4). The Torah, therefore,

Wisdom as Preexistent Torah

BIBLICAL BACKGROUND

Like Ben Sira, the ancient rabbis identified divine wisdom with the †Torah. Drawing from Prov 8:30, where Wisdom describes herself as a "master workman" working alongside God at creation, they held that the divine wisdom revealed in the Torah existed before the creation of the world and functioned like an architect, disclosing the "blueprint" of the world. The †Midrash on Genesis depicts the creation of the cosmos as a collaboration between God and his wisdom—the Torah—personifying it through a parable: God creates the world through the Torah (his wisdom), just as a king builds a palace through the skills of an architect:

> The Torah declares: "I was the working tool of the Holy One, blessed be He" (Prov 8:30). In human practice, when a mortal king builds a palace, he builds it not with his own skill but with the skill of an architect. The architect moreover does not build it out of his head, but employs plans and diagrams to know how to arrange the chambers and the doorways. Thus God consulted the Torah when he created the world. So the Torah declared, *"In the beginning God created"* (Gen 1:1); *beginning* referring to the Torah, as in the verse, *"The Lord made me as the beginning of His way"* (Prov 8:22).[a]

> a. Midrash Genesis Rabbah 1:1, in Harry Freedman and Maurice Simon, eds., *Midrash Rabbah* (London: Soncino, 1939), 1:1. The last point is based on a pun on the Hebrew word for "in the beginning" (*bereshit*), which could also mean "by means of the beginning." Since Wisdom is both the "beginning of the Lord's way" (Prov 8:22) and the Torah, the authors of the Midrash reinterpret "In the beginning God created . . ." as "By means of 'the beginning' [i.e., by means of the Torah] God created . . ."

bestows wisdom, and "in the Law wisdom is expressed in the language of men."[5] Since Wisdom predates the world (Sir 1:4; 24:9), this suggests that the Torah also existed before creation. GII adds verse 24.[6] Since God gave the law to Israel as their guide, they are empowered to be **strong in the Lord** (see Eph 6:10) and have the means to **cleave to him so that he may strengthen** them (Deut 10:20; 13:4). All other pursuits are futile, for **the Lord Almighty alone is God, and besides him there is no savior** (see Isa 43:11).

The Torah, as the source of wisdom, is now closely associated with the four rivers that flowed from the garden of Eden (Gen 2:10–14) and with the Jordan River. **It fills** those who observe its commandments **with wisdom, like the Pishon** (of unknown location) and **the Tigris** (which flows the length of modern   24:25–27

---

5. J. Gavigan, B. McCarthy, and T. McGovern, eds., *The Navarre Bible: Wisdom Books* (New York: Scepter, 2004), 464.

6. **Do not cease to be strong in the Lord, cleave to him so that he may strengthen you; the Lord Almighty alone is God, and besides him there is no savior** (Sir 24:24, RSV-2CE footnote; compare NRSV, ESV-CE, NABRE footnotes).

Iraq into the Persian Gulf) **at the time of the first fruits** in springtime, when the water reaches its highest levels. The law also brims with **understanding, like the Euphrates** (which rises in Turkey and flows across Syria and Iraq, until it joins with the Tigris) **and like the Jordan** (which flows through the Jordan Valley in the east of Israel) **at harvest time,** also in the spring. The Torah **makes instruction shine forth like light,**[7] **like the Gihon**—another river of paradise of unknown location, and also a spring on the eastern slope of Mount Zion in Jerusalem (1 Kings 1:33; 2 Chron 32:30)—**at the time of vintage,** in autumn, when grapes were picked. This identification with the four rivers of Eden implies that the wisdom of the Torah—elsewhere described as a life-giving fountain (Prov 16:22; 18:4; Bar 3:12)—originally flowed in Eden and was intended for all humankind in the primeval paradise, long before she made her abode in Israel. The association of Wisdom with the Jordan River here, in addition to the four rivers of Eden, points to her presence in Israel.

24:28–29   No one can fully plumb the depths of Wisdom. **Just as the first man,** Adam, **did not know her perfectly,** despite her presence in Eden, even a hypothetical **last** man **has not fathomed her,** nor will he ever be able to do so, because **her thought is more abundant than the** vast **sea, and her counsel deeper than the great abyss** (24:5; Ps 36:6). The scope and depth of Wisdom's insights are unsearchable.

24:30–31   Ben Sira now speaks in the first person, describing his own vocation as a teacher of wisdom. He began as a modest **canal,** drawing a small quantity of water from the great **river** of wisdom, **and like a water channel** irrigating **a garden,** he transmitted wisdom to others, becoming a source of life and fruitfulness for them (Isa 58:11). Though initially he intended only to **water** his **orchard and drench** his **garden plot,** seeking wisdom for himself and those closest to him, eventually his **canal** grew wider, **became a river,** and then expanded into a vast **sea** of wisdom (Isa 11:9)—so that he is now writing a wisdom book that will benefit many. This ever-widening current alludes to the waters flowing out of Ezekiel's end-time temple, which become a source of life in the wilderness and produce trees bearing miraculous fruit (Ezek 47:1–12; Joel 3:18; Zech 14:8; Rev 22:1).

24:32–34   Ben Sira's task of communicating wisdom to others is not yet complete. He still intends to **make instruction shine forth like the dawn**—as the Torah is a shining light to Israel and the nations (Ps 119:105; Wis 18:4; Isa 2:5)—and to **pour out teaching like prophecy**: he considers his mission of teaching wisdom a prophetic one that will reach even **future generations,** as indeed it has. In this sense, his own labor and quest for wisdom were not solely for his own benefit but for **all who seek instruction.**[8]

---

7. Or perhaps "pours forth instruction like the Nile" (NRSV; compare Syriac, NABRE, NJB).
8. Sir 24:34 is nearly identical to 33:17.

Courting Lady Wisdom through Salvation History

BIBLICAL BACKGROUND

Wisdom's hymn of praise evokes many familiar Old Testament themes. Lady Wisdom's followers are frequently invited to love her and sometimes even "marry" her.[a] This nuptial symbolism is evident in the many echoes of the Song of Songs in Sir 24: the trees, plants, flowers, spices, frankincense, honey, and springs of water suggest that communion with Lady Wisdom is akin to the joyful, ecstatic union of lover and beloved described in the Song. At the same time, the imagery in Sir 24 hints that she was present at key moments in salvation history.

Wisdom's presence at creation and in the garden of Eden is reflected in the setting of lush vegetation, rivers, spices, and fragrances that evokes the ancient paradise (Gen 2:8–14; Ezek 31:8).[b] Eden was Wisdom's primary sanctuary; she dwelt with Adam and Eve and was intended to be "married" to the entire human race. But she was lost when they ate of the forbidden tree of knowledge, which offered them a false wisdom but brought alienation and death (Gen 3:5–7, 17–22).

Wisdom was restored when God gave the Torah to Israel at Mount Sinai (Exod 19–24; Bar 4:1)—which Jewish tradition views as God's betrothal of Israel.[c] Loving Wisdom is thus best expressed by keeping the commandments, for both Wisdom and the commandments heal sin and restore life (Deut 30:19–20; Prov 3:1–2, 16–18; Sir 1:20).

Wisdom also continued to dwell with God's people in the liturgy of the tabernacle and temple—which perpetuated God's presence in Israel's history, commemorating the Sinai covenant in every generation. This is evident in Sir 24's imagery of cedars, cypress, palm trees, and flowers, which were all prominent in the building, spices, and fragrances of both the tabernacle (Exod 30:23, 34) and the temple (1 Kings 5–7). Rabbinic literature also depicts the temple as a bridal chamber where God was nuptially joined to Israel, symbolized by the cherubim in the holy of holies that embraced each other as a sign of the love between them.[d]

Finally, Sir 24's imagery of trees, vines, flowers, and streams of water echoes the prophets' eschatological vision of the messianic age, when the Lord will turn the desert into a new Eden.[e] This suggests that Wisdom will be present at the end of human history, as the marriage between God and his people is consummated and humanity returns to the tree of life (Rev 19:7–9; 21:2–3; 22:1–2).

a. Prov 4:6; 8:17; Wis 7:10; 8:2; Sir 4:12; 15:2.
b. The book of *Jubilees*, written around the same time as Sirach, confirms these literary parallels. In an expansion on Adam's expulsion from Eden, Adam takes from paradise some of the spices mentioned in Sir 24 ("frankincense, galbanum, stacte, and spices") to bring them to God as an offering (*Jubilees* 3.27). See also *Apocalypse of Moses* 29.6.
c. Mekhilta de-Rabbi Ishmael, *Bahodesh* 3. See André Villeneuve, *Divine Marriage from Eden to the End of Days: Communion with God as Nuptial Mystery in the Story of Salvation* (Eugene, OR: Wipf & Stock, 2021), 58–64.
d. Babylonian Talmud, *Yoma* 54a.
e. Isa 14:8; 35:1–2; 41:18–19; 51:3; 60:13; Ezek 47:1–12; Hosea 14:5–9; Joel 3:18.

V.B. Wisdom in Interpersonal Relations (25:1–12)

¹My soul takes pleasure in three things,
    and they are beautiful in the sight of the Lord and of men:
agreement between brothers, friendship between neighbors,
    and a wife and husband who live in harmony.
²My soul hates three kinds of men,
    and I am greatly offended at their life:
a beggar who is proud, a rich man who is a liar,
    and an adulterous old man who lacks good sense.

³You have gathered nothing in your youth;
    how then can you find anything in your old age?
⁴What an attractive thing is judgment in gray-haired men,
    and for the aged to possess good counsel!
⁵How attractive is wisdom in the aged,
    and understanding and counsel in honorable men!
⁶Rich experience is the crown of the aged,
    and their boast is the fear of the Lord.

⁷With nine thoughts I have gladdened my heart,
    and a tenth I shall tell with my tongue:
a man rejoicing in his children;
    a man who lives to see the downfall of his foes;
⁸happy is he who lives with an intelligent wife,
    and he who has not made a slip with his tongue,
    and he who has not served a man inferior to himself;
⁹happy is he who has gained good sense,
    and he who speaks to attentive listeners.
¹⁰How great is he who has gained wisdom!
    But there is no one superior to him who fears the Lord.
¹¹The fear of the Lord surpasses everything;
    to whom shall be likened the one who holds it fast?

OT: Ps 133:1; Prov 18:22; 31:10–31; Wis 4:9
NT: Matt 5:3–11; 1 Tim 2:2; 5:17
Catechism: the person and society, 1878–85

25:1–2   Ben Sira now considers people who deserve either praise or blame especially in how they relate to others. In two numerical proverbs, he contrasts three praiseworthy behaviors with three blameworthy ones. He delights **in three things**, which are **beautiful** and pleasing both to **the Lord** and to **men** because they create peace and concord within society (1 Tim 2:2): **agreement between brothers** (Sir 7:12; Ps 133:1) emphasizes the importance of unity within the family; **friendship between neighbors** extends goodwill beyond the household;

and **a wife and husband who live in harmony** testify to the role of marriage as the most fundamental unit of society. By contrast, Ben Sira **hates three kinds of men** because of their conduct. While pride is always unpleasant (Sir 10:7–18), **a beggar who is proud** is particularly objectionable, as he seeks support while maintaining an arrogant attitude. Similarly, while lying is always wrong (20:24–26), **a rich man who is a liar** is especially disgraceful, as the wealthy have no material need and no reason to be deceitful. Lastly, while adultery is always morally reprehensible (Exod 20:14), **an adulterous old man who lacks good sense** is especially repugnant, since a person with such life experience should exemplify wisdom and virtue.

Addressing a hypothetical foolish old man, Ben Sira blames him for hav-   25:3–6
ing **gathered nothing** of wisdom in his **youth**, presumably due to pursuing frivolous things. If such a man failed to seek wisdom when he was young, how should he expect to **find** it in his **old age**? In contrast to the foolish old man, Ben Sira praises the **judgment** of **gray-haired men** who have lived well and sought wisdom throughout their lives, so that they now **possess good counsel** in their old age (Wis 4:9; 1 Tim 5:17). He considers highly **attractive** and beautiful the **wisdom, understanding and counsel** that these **honorable men** have acquired. They can now draw from their **rich experience**—their **crown**—to help and guide others. Their wisdom is most evident in that they **boast** not in power or wealth but in **the fear of the Lord**—the beginning and crown of wisdom (Sir 1:14, 18).

Ben Sira begins a †numerical proverb that extends to verse 11, listing ten   25:7–8
praiseworthy **thoughts**, which some have referred to as Ben Sira's "ten beatitudes" (compare Matt 5:3–11). These bring him such joy that he wishes to **tell** others about them. The first is **a man rejoicing in his children** who have grown to adulthood and turned out well (Ps 127:3–5). The second is **a man who lives to see the downfall of his foes**—wicked men who prospered for too long and seemed to cast a shadow on God's justice (Pss 54:7; 92:11). The third is the **happy** man **who lives with an intelligent**—that is, wise and discerning—**wife** (Sir 26:1–4); according to wisdom literature, she is a gift of surpassing value (Prov 31:10–31).[9] The fourth is missing from the Greek text but appears in the Hebrew and Syriac, declaring happy "the one who does not plow with ox and ass together"[10] (compare Deut 22:10)—implying that a man is blessed if he is well-matched with a compatible wife. The fifth is the man who has avoided an embarrassing or foolish **slip with his tongue** that would have brought him trouble or shame (Sir 14:1; 20:18; James 3:2). The sixth is the man who **has not served a man inferior to himself**, either unworthy in intelligence or character, or perhaps from a lower social class. Serving such a person would have been considered an embarrassment in the ancient world (Eccles 10:5–7).

---

9. Proverbs describes finding a wife in almost the exact same terms as finding wisdom (Prov 8:35; 18:22).
10. NRSV; compare NABRE, NJB.

25:9–12   The seventh praiseworthy thing is the **happy** man **who has gained good sense**. The Latin, following the Syriac, reads perhaps more plausibly, *gained a (true) friend* (see NRSV, NABRE). The eighth is someone **who speaks to attentive listeners** and commands their respect. The ninth **great** achievement is for one to have **gained wisdom**. Although this appears to be the ultimate goal of every disciple, it is surpassed by the tenth, for **no one** is **superior to him who fears the Lord**. While the fear of the Lord is the beginning of wisdom (1:14), it is also its crown and full measure (1:16, 18), so that the fear of the Lord by which one gives him honor, reverence, and obedience is, in some sense, even better than possessing wisdom. Thus, **the fear of the Lord surpasses everything**: nothing is more important than maintaining this humble disposition of awe before him. The answer to Ben Sira's rhetorical question, **To whom shall be likened the one who holds it fast?** is clearly "no one." The longer Greek text adds verse 12: **The fear of the Lord is the beginning of love for him, and faith is the beginning of clinging to him.**[11] This thought mirrors the connection Ben Sira previously established between loving wisdom and having faith in her (4:11–16).

V.C. (i) On Good and Evil Women: The Wicked Wife (25:13–26)

> [13]Any wound, but not a wound of the heart!
> Any wickedness, but not the wickedness of a wife!
> [14]Any attack, but not an attack from those who hate!
> And any vengeance, but not the vengeance of enemies!
> [15]There is no venom worse than a snake's venom,
> and no wrath worse than an enemy's wrath.
> [16]I would rather dwell with a lion and a dragon,
> than dwell with an evil wife.
> [17]The wickedness of a wife changes her appearance,
> and darkens her face like that of a bear.
> [18]Her husband takes his meals among the neighbors,
> and he cannot help sighing bitterly.
> [19]Any iniquity is insignificant compared to a wife's iniquity;
> may a sinner's lot befall her!
> [20]A sandy ascent for the feet of the aged—
> such is a garrulous wife for a quiet husband.
> [21]Do not be ensnared by a woman's beauty,
> and do not desire a woman for her possessions.
> [22]There is wrath and impudence and great disgrace
> when a wife supports her husband.
> [23]A dejected mind, a gloomy face,

11. RSV-2CE, NRSV, ESV-CE footnotes; compare NABRE footnote.

and a wounded heart are caused by an evil wife.
Drooping hands and weak knees
   are caused by the wife who does not make her husband happy.
²⁴From a woman sin had its beginning,
   and because of her we all die.
²⁵Allow no outlet to water,
   and no boldness of speech in an evil wife.
²⁶If she does not go as you direct,
   separate her from yourself.

OT: Prov 6:25; 12:4; 21:19; 25:24; 27:15
NT: 2 Cor 11:3; Eph 5:22–24; Col 3:18; 1 Tim 2:8–15
Catechism: original sin and death, 397–400

Beginning with 25:13 and continuing to 26:27, Ben Sira offers counsel about
marriage, good and evil wives, and raising daughters. His treatment of women
is often seen as harsh, to the point that some have considered his views misogynistic. But it is important to keep a few points in mind to understand what Ben
Sira is saying (see the section "Sirach as Sacred Scripture" in the introduction,
pp. 32–34). First, the author addresses a particular culture very different from
our own—one in which women did not have the rights that they enjoy today.
Ben Sira's counsel on women and his severe critique of "evil wives" must be
viewed as the product of the patriarchal society of his time, where leadership
within the family and society was predominantly assigned to fathers, and men
and husbands held near total power over their wives. Thus, considerable adapta-
tion would be required to apply his counsel in contemporary Western culture.
Second, these teachings, like most of the wisdom literature, are written by a
man speaking to younger men and therefore offer a male perspective. Imagining how similar and dissimilar wise counsel from a mature woman to younger
women about the flaws of men and the challenges of marriage might be can
provide balance. Third, the words of praise Ben Sira extends to the "wise," "good,"
"intelligent," and "modest" wife (7:19; 25:8; 26:1–4, 13–18; 40:23) indicate that
his harshness is directed not at all women indiscriminately but specifically at
wicked ones—the female equivalent of the male fool he criticizes with similar vehemence throughout his book (e.g., 20:13–20; 22:7–15). Ben Sira warns
against the miseries of associating with *both* foolish men and wicked women;
both should be avoided at all costs. Finally, this Old Testament teaching lacks
the fuller revelation of Christ, his teaching and that of the apostles regarding
marriage and divorce, along with the grace of the New Covenant through Christ's
death and resurrection. As such, it is incomplete, and Christians must apply it
in the light of the fuller revelation brought by Christ.

   Any physical **wound** is better than a painful, emotional **wound of the heart**   25:13–15
caused by marital conflict. For a man, **any wickedness** is preferable to **the**

wickedness done by **a wife** (or "woman," NRSV, NABRE), given the closeness of the relationship and the pain that she can cause through injurious words or actions. More generally, **any attack** is more bearable than one from hateful foes, and **any vengeance** preferable to that **of enemies** who seek to inflict maximum harm, for their wrath (Syriac and Latin: "a woman's wrath") is as deadly as **a snake's venom.**

25:16–19   Using a bold hyperbole for rhetorical effect, Ben Sira states that he would **rather dwell with a lion and a dragon** than **with an evil wife** or hateful woman, who should be avoided at all costs (Prov 21:19; 25:24; 27:15). The notion that her **wickedness** affects **her appearance** underscores the power of evil, which can distort even a person's external countenance so that it **darkens her face like that of a** ferocious **bear** (see 1 Sam 17:34–37; 2 Sam 17:8; 2 Kings 2:24). The unhappy **husband** who cannot bear his wife's presence is so distressed that he **takes his meals** (Hebrew: "sits") **among the neighbors, sighing bitterly** from the grief she has caused him. Given that **a wife's iniquity** is the greatest torment for her husband, Ben Sira wishes that **a sinner's lot befall her**—that is, that God would punish her in a manner appropriate for sinners.

25:20–22   As a **sandy ascent** is difficult to climb for **the aged,** so an overly talkative, **garrulous wife** is difficult to endure **for a quiet husband.** The warning not to **be ensnared by** (literally, "do not fall for") **a woman's beauty** appears frequently in Scripture; ignoring it has led to the downfall of many men (9:8; Jdt 10:19; 16:7–9; Prov 6:25). Less common is the advice not to **desire** or marry **a woman for her possessions** (Hebrew: "for what she has"), allowing the man to live off her wealth. Ben Sira views this as shameful, and it was indeed a source of **great disgrace** in the ancient world for **a wife** to financially support **her husband:** societal norms dictated that a man should be the primary provider for his family. A man should choose a wife not for her appearance or wealth but for her strength of character and godliness (Prov 31:30). In a modern context, while it may be preferable for a husband to provide for his family, especially if the wife is involved at home in the care of small children, financial reasons, the job market, or other practical circumstances may not allow this today. If so, there is no shame in being a stay-at-home father.

25:23–24   A husband's marriage can affect his mental and physical state: **a dejected mind, a gloomy face, a wounded heart, drooping hands and weak knees** are the signs of discouragement and depression caused by **an evil wife** who **does not make her husband happy** (just as an evil husband can make his wife's life equally miserable). These warnings lead Ben Sira to make a sweeping theological statement: **From a woman**—Eve, when she was deceived by the serpent and ate the forbidden fruit (Gen 3:6)—**sin had its beginning,** for her disobedience led to Adam's fall (2 Cor 11:3; 1 Tim 2:14); **and because of her we all die.** While

Death through Eve; Life through Mary

LIVING TRADITION

In his classic second-century work *Against Heresies*, St. Irenaeus of Lyons illustrates how the "knot" of Eve's disobedience and unbelief was untied by Mary's obedience and faith—an image that later gave rise to the popular devotion to "Mary, Undoer of Knots."

[Eve] was disobedient, and became the cause of death for herself and for the entire human race. In the same way, Mary, though she had a man destined for her beforehand, yet nevertheless a virgin, was obedient and was made the cause of salvation for herself and the entire human race.... In like manner, the knot of Eve's disobedience was untied by Mary's obedience. For what the virgin Eve tied by her unbelief, this Mary untied by her belief.[a]

a. Irenaeus, *Against Heresies* 3.22.4, in *St. Irenaeus of Lyons: Against the Heresies, Book 3*, ed. M. C. Steenberg, trans. Dominic J. Unger, Ancient Christian Writers 64 (New York: Newman, 2012), 104.

Ben Sira places the blame on Eve for the entrance of death in human history, St. Paul emphasizes Adam's culpability (Rom 5:12, 17–19; 1 Cor 15:22).

A wise man should not remain passive if his wife is unruly. Just as one must **25:25–26** **allow no outlet to water** by preventing a jar or cistern from leaking, so too must the wise man, as head of the household (1 Cor 11:3; Eph 5:22–24), allow **no boldness of speech in an evil wife**: he should not allow her to speak unchecked, particularly if she engages in gossip or slander, is insulting or verbally abusive, or blasphemes God. If she continues to be belligerent, the man is advised to **separate her from** himself (literally, "cut her away from your flesh"). This likely refers to divorce, as it was permitted by the Mosaic law (Deut 24:1–4). In the Gospels, however, Jesus explains that the permission to divorce was a concession to human sinfulness, and he calls his followers to a higher standard of lifelong fidelity, as God intended from the beginning (Gen 2:24; Mark 10:2–12). Nevertheless, certain circumstances may arise in marriages that make separation necessary (1 Cor 7:10–15).

V.C. (ii) On Good and Evil Women: The Virtuous Wife; the Wicked Wife; the Headstrong Daughter (26:1–18)

¹Happy is the husband of a good wife;
  the number of his days will be doubled.
²A loyal wife rejoices her husband,
  and he will complete his years in peace.
³A good wife is a great blessing;
  she will be granted among the blessings of the man who fears
  the Lord.

⁴Whether rich or poor, his heart is glad,
   and at all times his face is cheerful.

⁵Of three things my heart is afraid,
   and of a fourth I am frightened:
The slander of a city, the gathering of a mob,
   and false accusation—all these are worse than death.
⁶There is grief of heart and sorrow when a wife is envious of a
   rival,
   and a tongue-lashing makes it known to all.
⁷An evil wife is an ox yoke which chafes;
   taking hold of her is like grasping a scorpion.
⁸There is great anger when a wife is drunken;
   she will not hide her shame.
⁹A wife's harlotry shows in her lustful eyes,
   and she is known by her eyelids.
¹⁰Keep strict watch over a headstrong daughter,
   lest, when she finds liberty, she use it to her hurt.
¹¹Be on guard against her impudent eye,
   and do not wonder if she sins against you.
¹²As a thirsty wayfarer opens his mouth
   and drinks from any water near him,
so will she sit in front of every post
   and open her quiver to the arrow.

¹³A wife's charm delights her husband,
   and her skill puts fat on his bones.
¹⁴A sensible and silent wife is a gift of the Lord,
   and there is nothing so precious as a disciplined soul.
¹⁵A modest wife adds charm to charm,
   and no balance can weigh the value of a chaste soul.
¹⁶Like the sun rising in the heights of the Lord,
   so is the beauty of a good wife in her well-ordered home.
¹⁷Like the shining lamp on the holy lampstand,
   so is a beautiful face on a stately figure.
¹⁸Like pillars of gold on a base of silver,
   so are beautiful feet with a steadfast heart.

OT: Prov 31:10–31; Sir 36:21–26; 40:23
NT: Titus 2:4–5; 1 Pet 3:1–8
Catechism: male and female, 369–73, 2331–36; marriage in God's plan, 1601–17, 1643–51
Lectionary: 26:1–4, 13–16: St. Monica; St. Hedwig, Religious; Common of Holy Men and Women; Sacrament of
   Marriage

26:1-2   This section partially offsets the negative comments regarding evil wives in
   the previous verses. In contrast to the miserable husband of an evil wife, Ben
   Sira calls **happy** or blessed **the husband of a good** and godly **wife** (40:23; Prov

Figure 8. An ancient Jewish wedding

12:4; 31:10–12). Because she is faithful to the law, she embodies wisdom and becomes a source of long life (Prov 3:1–2, 13–18), even to the point that her husband's lifespan **will be doubled**. A **loyal**, virtuous, or excellent **wife** (Prov 31:10) brings joy to **her husband**, allowing him to live out **his years in peace** (see Ps 128). The benefits, of course, are mutual, for a good marriage brings happiness to both spouses. While the focus here is on the happiness a good wife brings to her husband, it is equally true that a virtuous husband brings great happiness to his wife. Similarly, an evil, drunken, or unfaithful husband causes great sorrow to his wife.

A good wife is a great blessing—literally, "a good portion" or good gift— that **the man who fears the Lord** is fortunate to have. The man seeking a good wife, therefore, is well advised to grow in the fear of the Lord (26:23; Prov 18:22; 19:14). In contrast to the wretched man who pursued an ungodly woman for her wealth (Sir 25:21–23), the man married to a good wife—whether he is **rich or poor**—**is glad** and consistently **cheerful**, for a happy marriage is more important than material prosperity. 26:3–4

With a †numerical proverb, Ben Sira resumes his critique of the evil wife. He returns to the subject by expressing dread of **three things** that cause great harm: **the slander** and malicious reports that spread in **a city, the gathering of a** frenzied **mob** dominated by emotion rather than reason, and a **false accusation** that leads to unjust charges, corrupts judicial proceedings, and undermines justice. Although Ben Sira considers these to be **worse than death**, he names a **fourth** that also frightens him: the **grief of heart and sorrow** that arises **when a wife is envious of a rival**. This may refer to polygamy, which may still have 26:5–6 been practiced in Ben Sira's day,[12] or to a situation in which a wife is suspicious and jealous of other women (37:11). Malicious **tongue-lashing** and slander not only has devastating effects within the home; it also reaches beyond it, making the feud **known to all** and bringing shame upon the family. Ben Sira may be implicitly warning his disciples of the dangers of bigamous or polygamous marriages, which cause great harm to all parties involved. All four situations illustrate the destructiveness of vicious talk.

26:7–9   **An evil wife** is like a loose-fitting **ox yoke** that **chafes** and hurts the ox by moving back and forth; attempting to restrain her can be as dangerous as **grasping a scorpion**. **Great anger** also arises **when a wife is drunken**, making her more prone to act offensively and shamelessly. **A wife's harlotry**—or perhaps more accurately, a "woman's fornication"—**shows in her lustful eyes** or "haughty glance"; **she is known by her eyelids**, flirtatiously fluttering and winking, and possibly enhanced with makeup (Prov 6:25; Jer 4:30; Ezek 23:40).

26:10–12   Ben Sira advises fathers to **keep strict watch** over a stubborn, **headstrong daughter** who insists on having her own way (7:24–25; 42:9–14). If she is not well supervised, **when she finds liberty**, she will abuse it and take advantage of any opportunity, often **to her** own **hurt**. A protective father in Ben Sira's traditional society would have had to be **on guard against** the **impudent** (shameless) **eye** of such a daughter and remain vigilant for any actions that might bring shame upon her family through sexual immorality. A graphic euphemism describes the promiscuous daughter as being as eager for a sexual encounter as a **thirsty wayfarer** willing to drink **from any water near him**, and as a **quiver** ready to receive any **arrow**. Since wisdom writings primarily address men, Ben Sira warns the fathers of young women; other passages in Proverbs (5:1–10, 15–20; 6:23–25; 7:4–27) and Sirach (26:19–21) directly warn young men against sexual temptation.

26:13–14   Ben Sira returns to praising the good wife (26:1–4), whose **charm delights her husband**, and whose **skill** in managing the household (including animal care, farming, trading, and cooking) **puts fat on his bones**—a sign of health and prosperity in the ancient world (Deut 31:20; Neh 9:25) that would have made her husband happy and content. **A sensible and silent wife** who speaks discreetly and with restraint—in contrast to the garrulous wife (Sir 25:20)—**is a gift from the Lord**; her self-discipline makes her particularly commendable and a model of wisdom, for **nothing** is **so precious as a disciplined soul** (6:18–22).

26:15–16   A holy and **modest wife adds charm to charm** (or "grace upon grace"), and **a chaste**, self-controlled, and disciplined **soul** is of such value that it cannot be weighed. As bright and radiant as **the sun rising in the heights of the Lord**—either at sunrise or perhaps the noonday sun at its zenith (43:9)—**so is the beauty**

---

12. Instances of polygamy among the Jews well into the Christian era are attested by Josephus (*Antiquities* 17.1.2) and Justin Martyr (*Dialogue with Trypho* 134). It is still sanctioned in the Talmud (*Yebamot* 44a, 65a), though the sages advise against it.

of a good wife in her well-ordered home. The Greek phrase for "well-ordered home" is "*kosmos* of her home." The term *kosmos* means "world" or "universe," so the verse could be rendered as "Like the radiance of the noonday sun in the Lord's heaven is the beauty of a good wife in the world of her home." The good wife's home is a beautiful, well-ordered microcosm of the world. The similarity of language between 26:16 and 50:5–7 suggests that she rules over her home as the high priest symbolically rules over the cosmos.

The beauty of the good wife is now compared to the splendor of the holy light   26:17–18 shining in the sanctuary: **Like the shining lamp on the holy lampstand**—the seven-branched menorah in the temple (Exod 25:31–39; 1 Macc 4:49–50)— **so is** the **beautiful face** and **stately figure** of a godly wife. **Like** the **pillars of gold on a base of silver** upon which hung the veil at the entrance of the holy of holies (Exod 26:32; compare Song 3:10; 5:15) are her **beautiful feet** and her **steadfast heart**. These cosmological allusions imply that the good wife, through her faithful obedience to the word of God, her liturgical role in the home, and her acts of kindness, in some sense "holds the world together," as expressed in Jewish tradition: "Upon three things the world stands: upon the †Torah, upon [temple] worship, and upon acts of kindness."[13]

V.C. (iii) On Good and Evil Women: Calling Men to Sexual Integrity (26:19–27)

The longer Greek version, followed by the Syriac, adds verses 19–27:[14]

> [19]My son, keep sound the bloom of your youth,
>   and do not give your strength to strangers.
> [20]Seek a fertile field within the whole plain,
>   and sow it with your own seed, trusting in your fine stock.
> [21]So your offspring will survive
>   and, having confidence in their good descent, will grow great.
> [22]A harlot is regarded as spittle,
>   and a married woman as a tower of death to her lovers.
> [23]A godless wife is given as a portion to a lawless man,
>   but a pious wife is given to the man who fears the Lord.
> [24]A shameless woman constantly acts disgracefully,
>   but a modest daughter will even be embarrassed before her
>   husband.
> [25]A headstrong wife is regarded as a dog,
>   but one who has a sense of shame will fear the Lord.

13. Mishnah, *Avot* 1:2, in William Berkson, *Pirke Avot: Timeless Wisdom for Modern Life*, trans. Menachem Fisch (Philadelphia: The Jewish Publication Society, 2010), 185.
14. RSV-2CE, ESV-CE, NABRE footnotes, NRSV.

> ²⁶A wife honoring her husband will seem wise to all,
>   but if she dishonors him in her pride she will be known to all
>   as ungodly.
> Happy is the husband of a good wife;
>   for the number of his years will be doubled.
> ²⁷A loud-voiced and garrulous wife is regarded as a war trumpet
>   for putting the enemy to flight,
>   and every person like this lives in the anarchy of war.

26:19–21   **My son** indicates the beginning of a new section, where Ben Sira exhorts his male readers to sexual propriety and warns them against fornication and adultery: **keep sound the bloom of your youth** or "the peak of your age," **and do not give your strength**—your potential children—**to strangers** by engaging in sexual relations with women other than your wife. Any children born of adultery would grow up as if they were the children of the woman's husband (Prov 5:7–17; 31:3). Instead, **seek a fertile field within the whole plain**—a euphemism for finding a good wife from among all available women—**and sow it with your own seed,** begetting children and establishing a family with her, **trusting in your fine stock** or excellent descent (Tob 4:12–13). Unlike children conceived in adultery, the **offspring** of a sound marriage **will survive**—perhaps an allusion to the prosperity and fruitfulness promised as rewards for faithfulness to the covenant (Deut 28:11). **Having confidence in their good descent** and certainty about their parentage, these children raised in a stable home **will grow great** and prosper.

26:22–23   The prostitute and adulteress are to be avoided at all costs: **A harlot is** scorned **as spittle,** and an adulterous **married woman** is even more dangerous, for she is **a tower of death to her lovers** (literally, "to those who use her"). Ben Sira views the quality of a wife as either a reward or punishment for a man, depending on his fear of the Lord or lack thereof (26:3). Every man gets the wife he deserves, according to the Lord's favor (Prov 12:4; 18:22; 19:14; 31:10): **A godless wife ... to a lawless man, but a pious wife ... to the man who fears the Lord.**

26:24–25   **A shameless woman constantly acts disgracefully** and embarrasses her husband, **but a modest daughter is embarrassed** (or "acts modestly") even **before her husband.** While a stubborn, **headstrong wife** is considered as unclean as **a dog** (26:10), one with **a sense of shame** (decency or modesty) **will fear the Lord**—a great virtue for both women and men.

26:26–27   The wisdom or foolishness of a woman is revealed in how she treats her husband (compare 1 Cor 11:7): one who honors and respects **her husband** seems **wise to all,** but one who pridefully **dishonors him** becomes **known to all as ungodly** and brings shame upon herself. Thus (repeating 26:1), **happy is the husband of a good wife,** for she will prolong his life. By contrast, a boisterous, overly talkative wife is like **a war trumpet** sounding the charge to put **the enemy to flight**, and a man who submits to such an overbearing woman **lives** in a constant state of **anarchy**, as in **war** (25:20).

Reflection and Application (25:13–26:27)

Although Ben Sira discusses both the "evil wife" and the "good wife," one must admit that his portrait of women comes across as predominantly negative—even considering that most of his criticisms throughout his book are directed at *men*. Much of his critique reflects on the interpersonal consequences of sin, which affect the people closest to us—especially spouses. If Ben Sira views women in light of the fall—by which relationships between husbands and wives have become "marked by lust and domination" (Catechism 400; see Gen 3:16)—and through the lens of the patriarchal culture in which he lived, we must keep in mind woman's original vocation as "a helper fit for [her husband]" (Gen 2:18, 20–24), yet sharing with him perfect equality and the same inalienable dignity: both are human persons created in the image of God, reflecting his wisdom and goodness (Catechism 369). It is therefore also true that man and woman are called to *exist mutually "one for the other,"* helping each other in an exchange of interpersonal communion.[15] Although wives are still instructed to defer to their husbands under the New Covenant (Eph 5:22–24; Col 3:18), both husbands and wives must also be "subject to one another out of reverence for Christ" (Eph 5:21), and husbands are called to love their wives "as Christ loved the Church and gave himself up for her" (Eph 5:25; see also Col 3:19). As every person—and particularly every woman—seeks to discover the fullness of their dignity and vocation in union with God, the best model and "most complete expression of this dignity and vocation"[16] remains Mary, the mother of the Incarnate Word, who fully and perfectly lived out her dignity and vocation as a woman.

V.D. Honesty and Integrity in Dealing with Others (26:28–27:15)

> [28]At two things my heart is grieved,
>   and because of a third anger comes over me:
> a warrior in want through poverty,
>   and intelligent men who are treated contemptuously;
> a man who turns back from righteousness to sin—
>   the Lord will prepare him for the sword!

15. John Paul II, *Mulieris Dignitatem* 7.
16. John Paul II, *Mulieris Dignitatem* 5.

²⁹A merchant can hardly keep from wrongdoing,
and a tradesman will not be declared innocent of sin.
²⁷:¹Many have committed sin for a trifle,
and whoever seeks to get rich will avert his eyes.
²As a stake is driven firmly into a fissure between stones,
so sin is wedged in between selling and buying.
³If a man is not steadfast and zealous in the fear of the Lord,
his house will be quickly overthrown.

⁴When a sieve is shaken, the refuse remains;
so a man's filth remains in his thoughts.
⁵The kiln tests the potter's vessels;
so the test of just men *is in tribulation*.
⁶The fruit discloses the cultivation of a tree;
so the expression of a thought discloses the cultivation of a
man's mind.
⁷Do not praise a man before you hear him speak,
for this is the test of men.

⁸If you pursue justice, you will attain it
and wear it as a glorious robe.
⁹Birds flock with their kind;
so truth returns to those who practice it.
¹⁰A lion lies in wait for prey;
so does sin for the workers of iniquity.

¹¹The talk of the godly man is always wise,
but the fool changes like the moon.
¹²Among stupid people watch for a chance to leave,
but among thoughtful people stay on.
¹³The talk of fools is offensive,
and their laughter is wantonly sinful.
¹⁴The talk of men given to swearing makes one's hair stand on end,
and their quarrels make a man stop his ears.
¹⁵The strife of the proud leads to bloodshed,
and their abuse is grievous to hear.

OT: Prov 12:7; 14:11; 15:9; 21:21
NT: Matt 6:33; 7:16–19; 12:33–37
Catechism: living in the truth, 2465–70
Lectionary: 27:4–7: 8th Sunday in Ordinary Time (Year C)

26:28   Ben Sira now addresses certain sins against honesty and integrity that harm interpersonal relationships, beginning with a †numerical proverb describing three reversals of fortune. He is **grieved** at the first two because they are injustices: **a warrior** who, instead of being honored for his courage, is afflicted by **poverty, and intelligent men** who, instead of being respected for their wisdom,

are treated contemptuously (compare Job 30:1–10). Yet while their misfortune lies outside their control, the third situation—**a man who turns back from righteousness to sin**—angers Ben Sira because this man is responsible for his own undoing. Because he has freely chosen evil over good, **the Lord will prepare him for the sword**—signifying the judgment of a violent death.

Because people who engage in commercial activities are constantly trying to make a profit, **a merchant** will find it difficult to resist greed and **wrongdoing.** The temptation toward greed and avarice is so great that many have sinned **for a trifle** (or "for gain")—even to make the smallest profit. **Whoever seeks to get rich** at all costs will ignore the voice of conscience, **avert his eyes**, and overlook shady dealings for the sake of expediency (Prov 28:27). **As a stake** or tent peg **is driven firmly into a fissure between stones** to hold it tightly, **so sin is wedged in** almost inevitably in business transactions that involve **selling and buying.** Thus, **if a man** who conducts business **is not steadfast and zealous in the fear of the Lord** by frequently examining his conscience on the integrity of his dealings with others, **his house will be quickly overthrown**, and his wealth gained dishonestly will be lost (Prov 12:7; 14:11). Thankfully, experience shows that there are honest businesspeople who fear the Lord and conduct fair trade. `26:29–27:3`

With three comparisons, Ben Sira illustrates that reasoning and conversation reveal a person's true worth. **When a sieve is shaken** to sift grain or corn, the flour passes through the mesh, while **the refuse**—the straw and dung left by the oxen that threshed the grain—**remains** in the sieve; **so a man's filth**—his faults and sinful habits—**remains in his thoughts** and is revealed when he talks. As **the kiln** or furnace **tests the potter's vessels** by baking them in intense heat, so the quality of the **just** person is tested and revealed in the furnace of *tribulation.*[17] As **the fruit discloses** how well **a tree** has been cultivated, so the verbal **expression** of a person's **thought discloses** how well this person has cultivated his **mind** (literally, "a man's heart") and what he truly cares for. These three analogies lead to a practical conclusion: **Do not praise a man before you hear him speak,** for what people like to talk about reveals their true character. Jesus may have had this text from Sirach in mind in formulating some of his teachings on speech (see Matt 7:16–19; 12:33–37). `27:4–7`

Every person must choose to pursue either justice or iniquity and will reap the rewards or punishments fitting that choice. Righteousness is its own reward; thus, those who **pursue justice will attain it** (see Prov 21:21; Matt 6:33; Rom 9:30–32) **and wear it as a glorious robe** (Job 29:14; Isa 59:17; Eph 6:14)—as the wisdom seeker "wears" wisdom like a splendid garment (Sir 6:31) and like the "glorious robe" of the high priest (45:7–13; Wis 18:24). Just as **birds flock** with other birds of **their kind, so truth returns to those who** strive to live by it and **practice it** (Sir 13:15). By contrast, as a fierce **lion lies in wait for prey**, so the `27:8–10`

---

17. Vulgate. The Greek reads "in his conversation" (NRSV) or "reasoning" (ESV-CE). See the fuller treatment of this topic in the commentary on Sir 2:4–6.

Testing the Potter's Vessels

LIVING TRADITION

In the third century AD, St. Cyprian, bishop of Carthage, comments on the formative role of tribulation and suffering in the Christian life:

> When weakness and inefficiency and any destruction seize us, then our strength is made perfect. Then, if our faith is put to the test, it will stand fast and receive a crown, as it is written: "The furnace tries the vessels of the potter, and the trial of tribulation tests just people" (Sir 27:5). This, in short, is the difference between us and others who do not know God, that in misfortune they complain and murmur, while adversity does not call us away from the truth of virtue and faith but strengthens us by its suffering.[a]

a. Cyprian of Carthage, *On Mortality* 13, in Sever J. Voicu, ed., *Apocrypha*, ACCS:OT 15 (Downers Grove, IL: InterVarsity, 2010), 307–8.

sin of those who work **iniquity** will hunt them down and ultimately devour them (21:2; Gen 4:7; 1 Pet 5:8).

27:11–12   **The talk of the godly man is always wise.** To emphasize the steadfastness and brilliance of the godly, the Latin reads instead, *A holy man continues in wisdom as the sun* (see Douay, 27:12). In contrast, **the fool** is inconsistent and unreliable and **changes like the moon** from night to night. Keeping company with such a person is a waste of time. If you find yourself **among stupid people**, therefore, **watch for a chance to leave** (literally, "watch the time"), **but among thoughtful people stay on**, for time in their company is a well-spent opportunity to learn from their wisdom (6:36).

27:13–15   **The talk of fools is offensive**, lacking propriety and good taste, **and their laughter is wantonly sinful** (literally, "an extravagance of sin"), filled with crude jokes and vulgarities. By contrast, a wise person speaks and acts with dignity (Prov 10:23; Eph 4:29; 5:4, 15–17). The speech of those **given to swearing** and cursing (literally, "a man of many oaths") **makes one's hair stand on end** in embarrassment due to its abundance of profanities, and the violent **quarrels** that inevitably follow **make a man stop his ears** in disgust. **The strife of the proud leads to** violence and **bloodshed**, and their abusive curses and insults are **grievous to hear** (23:11). It is best to avoid the company of fools altogether before their conversation degenerates into such a brawl.

V.E. (i) Offenses against Friendship: Betrayal, Deceit, and Anger (27:16–28:7)

> [16]Whoever betrays secrets destroys confidence,
> and he will never find a congenial friend.

¹⁷Love your friend and keep faith with him;
  but if you betray his secrets, do not run after him.
¹⁸For as a man destroys his enemy,
  so you have destroyed the friendship of your neighbor.
¹⁹And as you allow a bird to escape from your hand,
  so you have let your neighbor go, and will not catch him
    again.
²⁰Do not go after him, for he is too far off,
  and has escaped like a gazelle from a snare.
²¹For a wound may be bandaged,
  and there is reconciliation after abuse,
but whoever has betrayed secrets is without hope.

²²Whoever winks his eye plans evil deeds,
  and no one can keep him from them.
²³In your presence his mouth is all sweetness,
  and he admires your words;
but later he will twist his speech
  and with your own words he will give offense.
²⁴I have hated many things, but none to be compared to him;
  even the Lord will hate him.
²⁵Whoever throws a stone straight up throws it on his own head;
  and a treacherous blow opens up wounds.
²⁶He who digs a pit will fall into it,
  and he who sets a snare will be caught in it.
²⁷If a man does evil, it will roll back upon him,
  and he will not know where it came from.
²⁸Mockery and abuse issue from the proud man,
  but vengeance lies in wait for him like a lion.
²⁹Those who rejoice in the fall of the godly will be caught in a
    snare,
  and pain will consume them before their death.
³⁰Anger and wrath, these also are abominations,
  and the sinful man will possess them.
²⁸:¹He that takes vengeance will suffer vengeance from the Lord,
  and he will firmly establish his sins.
²Forgive your neighbor the wrong he has done,
  and then your sins will be pardoned when you pray.
³Does a man harbor anger against another,
  and yet seek for healing from the Lord?
⁴Does he have no mercy toward a man like himself,
  and yet pray for his own sins?
⁵If he himself, being flesh, maintains wrath,
  will he then seek forgiveness from God?
  Who will make expiation for his sins?

⁶Remember the end of your life, and cease from enmity,
remember destruction and death, and be true to the
commandments.
⁷Remember the commandments, and do not be angry with your
neighbor;
remember the covenant of the Most High, and overlook
ignorance.

OT: Deut 32:35; Prov 6:16–19; Sir 22:19–22
NT: Matt 5:21–26; 6:12–15; 18:23–35; Mark 11:25; James 2:13
Catechism: forgiving others, 1425, 2842–45; anger and vengeance, 2259–62, 2302; respect for the truth, 2489
Lectionary: 27:30–28:7: 24th Sunday in Ordinary Time (Year A)

27:16–18 Ben Sira now addresses offenses that harm friendship. The first is betraying a confidence (27:16–21). Friends who trust each other typically confide in each other, and this calls for discretion (Catechism 2489). **Whoever betrays secrets** breaches a friend's trust and **destroys confidence** between them; having undermined his own trustworthiness, **he will never find a congenial friend** (literally, "a friend to his soul") willing to confide in him again (22:22). Thus, **love** and respect **your friend and keep faith** by being loyal to him; if you reveal to someone else what he has confided in you, **do not run after him** to try to repair the friendship **you have destroyed**. Avoid such a breach of trust in the first place rather than trying to fix it after irreparable damage has been done.

27:19–21 As **a bird** that escapes **from your hand** will never come back, so **you have let your neighbor go** and forfeited his friendship by betraying his trust. You should not expect to **catch him again** among your circle of friends. **Do not go after him** to seek reconciliation, **for he is too far off** from you in heart and soul, having **escaped like a** swift **gazelle** running away **from a snare**. While **a wound** can still heal after it is **bandaged**, and **reconciliation** can still be attained after exchanging words of reproach, **whoever has betrayed secrets is without hope** of seeing the friendship restored (22:19–22).

27:22–24 Another offense that undermines trust is insincerity and deceit (27:22–29). Those who mislead others will reap the consequences of their own actions. **Whoever winks his eye** as a sign of duplicity (Prov 6:12–13; 10:10; 16:30) **plans evil deeds**. His mind is so set on wrongdoing that **no one can** dissuade him or convince him to change his course of action. **In your presence** the deceptive person's **mouth is all sweetness**—he appears friendly and kind to you (Sir 12:16), **and he admires your words**, pretending to agree with you. Yet **later**, when you are no longer present, **he will twist his speech** and speak very differently behind your back, **and with your own words he will give offense** (literally, "he makes a stumbling block with your words") and use them against you. Of all hateful things, **none** is comparable to the duplicitous and hypocritical person, so that **even the Lord will hate him**. When the Bible speaks of God hating evil or evildoers (Ps 5:5; Prov 6:16–19; 8:13), it refers not to personal animosity but to a decisive rejection of what is incompatible with God's nature, which is holiness and love (1 John 4:8). In the same way, we are to love good and hate evil (Ps 97:10; Amos 5:15; Rom 12:9).

Evil eventually returns to its perpetrators, just as **a stone** thrown **straight up** falls back on the **head** of the one who has thrown it. Similarly, **a treacherous blow opens up wounds** (the Latin adds *in the deceiver*)—that is, the one who strikes treacherously harms himself. Likewise, one who **digs a pit will fall into it**, and one **who sets a snare will be caught in it**—common images in the Old Testament (Ps 9:15–16; Prov 26:27; Eccles 10:8). These metaphors illustrate that one who **does evil** will see that same evil **roll back upon him** and hurt him; yet **he will not know** its origin. When evil strikes him, he will not realize that it is the fruit of his own doing. 27:25–27

As **mockery and abuse issue from the proud man** (literally, "are of the proud man"), so they will also befall him (compare NABRE). The **vengeance** of the people he has offended **lies in wait**, personified as **a lion** ready to devour him. **Those who rejoice in the fall of the godly** are particularly malicious and **will be caught in a snare**—often one that they have set, as was the case with Haman (Esther 5:14; 7:9–10; 9:24–25). Not only will they die prematurely, but **pain will consume them before their death** (compare Job 21:19–20). 27:28–29

Anger and wrath also are abominations, destroying relationships just as the betrayal of secrets, treachery, and mockery do. **The sinful** person holds onto anger, refusing to let it go until it controls him. Anger often arises from a misplaced sense of justice that seeks to punish others for the wrongs they have done. Yet vengeance belongs not to man but to God, who alone enacts perfect justice (Deut 32:35; Rom 12:19; Heb 10:30). The one who tries to assume this role and **takes vengeance** on others—which the †Torah strictly prohibits (Lev 19:18)—**will suffer vengeance from the Lord**, who **will firmly establish** (or "keep a strict account of," NRSV) **his sins**. 27:30–28:1

The concept of forgiving others as a condition for obtaining God's forgiveness is often thought of as a Christian idea (Matt 6:12–15; 18:23–35; James 2:13). Yet Ben Sira anticipates it here as he exhorts his readers: **Forgive your neighbor the wrong he has done, and then your sins will be pardoned** by God **when you pray.** The idea is also preserved in postbiblical Jewish tradition: "For whom does [God] pardon iniquity? For the one who pardons transgression [in others]."[18] 28:2

With four rhetorical questions Ben Sira underlines the importance of avoiding resentment and granting forgiveness to others. **A man** cannot **harbor anger** or hold a grudge **against another**, refusing to forgive, **and yet seek for healing**—from illness, interior wounds, or his own sin—**from the Lord** (Exod 15:26; 28:3–5

18. Babylonian Talmud, *Rosh Hashanah* 17a, in Jacob Neusner, *The Babylonian Talmud: A Translation and Commentary* (Peabody, MA: Hendrickson, 2011), 6b:86–87.

Hosea 6:1). It would be hypocritical to **have no mercy toward** others **and yet pray** to obtain forgiveness for one's **own sins**. If one who is **flesh**—a mortal human prone to sin (Sir 17:31; 1 Cor 15:50; Gal 5:19)—**maintains wrath** against others, he should not expect to obtain **forgiveness from God**. How can anyone **make expiation** or atonement **for his sins**, as was done in Old Testament times through the offering of sacrifices (Lev 4:27–35), now that he has forfeited God's forgiveness? Jesus confirms that only the merciful shall obtain mercy (Matt 5:7) and only those who forgive others will be forgiven (6:12, 14–15)—a teaching that he dramatizes in the parable of the unforgiving servant (18:23–35).

28:6–7   A key to living well is to **remember**, first, **the end of your life** (literally, "the last things"); since life is short, do not remain angry but **cease from enmity** today. Second, **remember** the **destruction and death** that will inevitably come when the Lord renders to each according to their works (7:36; 11:26–28; 38:20), **and be true to** his **commandments**, for observing them is the only thing of lasting value (Eccles 12:13; Matt 19:17). Third, Ben Sira repeats: **Remember the commandments**, especially the one that enjoins you to "**not** hate **your neighbor**," take vengeance, or **be angry**, but "love your neighbor as yourself" (Lev 19:17–18). Fourth, **remember the covenant** that God **the Most High** made with Israel at Mount Sinai (Sir 17:12; 24:23; 39:8; Exod 24:7–8), **and overlook** the faults that others commit involuntarily through **ignorance**.

V.E. (ii) Offenses against Friendship: Strife and Slander (28:8–26)

> [8]Refrain from strife, and you will lessen sins;
>   for a man given to anger will kindle strife,
> [9]and a sinful man will disturb friends
>   and inject enmity among those who are at peace.
> [10]In proportion to the fuel for the fire, so will be the burning,
>   and in proportion to the obstinacy of strife will be the
>   burning;
> in proportion to the strength of the man will be his anger,
>   and in proportion to his wealth he will heighten his wrath.
> [11]A hasty quarrel kindles fire,
>   and urgent strife sheds blood.
> [12]If you blow on a spark, it will glow;
>   if you spit on it, it will be put out;
>   and both come out of your mouth.
>
> [13]Curse the whisperer and deceiver,
>   for he has destroyed many who were at peace.
> [14]Slander has shaken many,
>   and scattered them from nation to nation,

and destroyed strong cities,
> and overturned the houses of great men.
[15]Slander has driven away courageous women,
> and deprived them of the fruit of their toil.
[16]Whoever pays heed to slander will not find rest,
> nor will he settle down in peace.
[17]The blow of a whip raises a welt,
> but a blow of the tongue crushes the bones.
[18]Many have fallen by the edge of the sword,
> but not so many as have fallen because of the tongue.
[19]Happy is the man who is protected from it,
> who has not been exposed to its anger,
who has not borne its yoke,
> and has not been bound with its chains;
[20]for its yoke is a yoke of iron,
> and its chains are chains of bronze;
[21]its death is an evil death,
> and Hades is preferable to it.
[22]It will not be master over the godly,
> and they will not be burned in its flame.
[23]Those who forsake the Lord will fall into its power;
> it will burn among them and will not be put out.
It will be sent out against them like a lion;
> like a leopard it will mangle them.
[24]See that you fence in your property with thorns,
> lock up your silver and gold,
[25]make balances and scales for your words,
> and make a door and a bolt for your mouth.
[26]Beware lest you err with your tongue,
> lest you fall before him who lies in wait.

OT: Ps 101:5; Prov 15:18; 26:20–21; 29:22; Sir 19:4–17; 22:19–22
NT: Matt 5:21–26; 7:1–5; 2 Cor 12:20; James 3:1–10; 4:11–12
Catechism: slander, 2475–79

Ben Sira now warns against quarreling (28:8–12). **Refrain from strife**—that   28:8–10
is, arguments and quarrels—because these increase occasions of sin. A hot-
tempered man **will kindle strife** like a fire by starting pointless arguments
(Prov 15:18; 26:21; 29:22). Whether intentional or not, **a sinful man** disrupts
friendships and causes strife simply by his presence, sowing discord **among
those who are at peace**. Just as a **fire** burns more intensely when **fuel** is added
to it, so too does the intensity of a quarrel increase when the belligerents persist
in **obstinacy** and stubbornness. Likewise, the more a man increases in **strength**
and **wealth**—and becomes accustomed to getting his way—the more his position of power makes him prone to **anger** and **wrath**.

28:11-12   A sudden **quarrel kindles fire** that may start out small but can quickly rage out of control and cause devastating damage (James 3:5–6). Similarly, a hasty **strife** can rapidly escalate from a verbal argument to physical violence and bloodshed. Conflicts are better managed early on, before they grow out of control. Just as one who blows **on a spark** makes it **glow** and turn into a flame, so provocative words can turn a minor conflict into a major one. There is a better course of action: just as one who spits on the spark puts it out, so gentle, patient words can diffuse a conflict (Prov 15:1; James 3:9–10). **Your mouth** is a source of either conflict or peace, death or life (Prov 18:21).

28:13   Ben Sira again addresses the evils of slander and vicious talk (28:13–26; compare 5:14; 22:19–22; James 3:1–12). Because **the whisperer and deceiver** (or "gossiper and double-tongued") sows strife through slander, Ben Sira urges his readers to **curse** such a person (Sir 5:14–6:1; 19:4–17), **for he has destroyed many who were at peace**. Ben Sira accepts the biblical principle that evil must be purged from the community because it spreads like a cancer (Deut 19:16–19; 27:26). Such excommunications, however, are often intended to prompt the sinner toward repentance and reconciliation (1 Cor 5:5–7).

28:14-16   **Slander** is literally "a third tongue" in Greek, meaning the tongue of a meddlesome person who interferes in the affairs of two others. With hyperbolic language, Ben Sira emphasizes the destructive power of gossip and slander, describing how these sins of speech have **shaken many** individuals, societies, and even nations, scattering people **from nation to nation**, destroying **strong cities**, and overturning **the houses of great men**. **Slander has** even **driven away courageous** or virtuous **women** who were **deprived of the fruit of their toil**, possibly when their husbands divorced them after their reputations were ruined by false accusations (7:26). **Whoever pays heed to** gossip or **slander**, therefore, is not innocent, as engaging in such speech involves a degree of participation in the sin. For this reason, one who listens to gossip or slander cannot expect to **find rest** or **peace** of mind.

28:17-18   The painful **blow of a whip raises a welt**—a visible mark on the body from a lash. Yet even this wound is minor compared to **a blow of the tongue**, as malicious words figuratively **crush the bones**, causing deeper wounds to the soul than a whip can inflict on the body (Prov 15:4; 25:15). While **many** have **fallen** in battle **by the edge of the sword**, even more have met their downfall **because of the tongue** that engaged in vicious talk.

28:19-21   **Happy is the man** whom God has **protected** from slander, from the inevitable **anger** at its evil effects, and from engaging in it. Slander enslaves not only the slanderer but also the slandered and those who believe the slander. It is compared to a heavy **yoke** and constraining **chains**—in stark contrast to the liberating "yoke" and "chains" of Wisdom (6:24–25, 29–30; 21:19). Slander brings **an evil death**—not only the "death" of one's reputation but also the shame and social stigma that follow, which seem even worse than †**Hades**, the realm of the dead (14:16).

The "Evil Tongue"

LIVING TRADITION

Jewish tradition views gossip and slander—known in Hebrew as *lashon hara'* (the "evil tongue")—as grievous sins. This view is based on two commandments of the †Torah: "You shall not go up and down as a slanderer among your people" (Lev 19:16), and "You shall not wrong one another" (25:17), which both Jewish and Catholic tradition understand as forbidding harm through speech—*even if it is true.* Some have compared harmful speech to an arrow: once released, words, like arrows, cannot be recalled; the harm they cause can be neither stopped nor predicted—for words, like arrows, often go astray. According to the †Talmud, one who engages in *lashon hara'* is considered as though he has denied the fundamental belief in God. The †sages even consider slander to be as serious as the three cardinal sins in Judaism: idolatry, forbidden sexual relations, and bloodshed. This is because *lashon hara'* kills three: the person who speaks it, the person who hears it, and the person about whom it is told.[a]

Christian tradition also emphasizes the gravity of sins of speech. Jesus warns against insulting (Matt 5:22) or wrongly judging one's brother (7:1–2), and the apostles often condemn gossip and slander (Rom 1:29–31; 2 Cor 12:20; 1 Pet 2:1). These injunctions are based on the eighth commandment, "You shall not bear false witness against your neighbor" (Exod 20:16), which requires respect for the reputation of persons and forbids "every attitude or word likely to cause unjust injury," such as *rash judgment* (assuming without foundation the moral fault of a neighbor), *detraction* (disclosing a person's faults to others), and *calumny* or slander (harming the reputation of others and giving occasion for false judgments concerning them).[b]

a. Babylonian Talmud, *Arakhin* 15b.
b. Catechism 2477–79.

Although hardly anyone escapes being the target of slander (28:13–15), it will **28:22–23** not rule **over the godly**—either because they will be delivered from its harmful effects, or because they refuse to engage in it, as Ben Sira forcefully exhorts (28:24–26)—so that they are not **burned in its** devastating **flame**. **Those who forsake the Lord**, however, **will fall into its power** and suffer its consequences. Because they have abandoned virtue and engaged in malicious talk, harming others and themselves, like an uncontrollable fire their gossip **will burn among them**, and like a ferocious **lion** or **leopard**, the anger unleashed by their calumnies **will mangle them** and tear them to pieces.

Some manuscripts (followed by the Syriac and Latin) order verses 24–25 **28:24–26** as follows: 24a, 25b, 24b, 25a (NRSV, ESV-CE, NABRE), resulting in a clearer meaning: just as you **fence in your property with thorns** (v. 24a) to protect it

Wounds of the Tongue

LIVING
TRADITION

In his *Homilies on Numbers,* Origen emphasizes the profound harm that sins of speech inflict on the soul, underscoring the importance for believers to resist them:

> If a wound is inflicted on the body . . . wounds of this sort . . . are barely healed with great pain and suffering over a long period of time. . . . Pass now from the example of the body to the wounds of the soul. However often the soul sins, just that often it is wounded. . . . O, if we could only see how with each sin our inner person is wounded, how bad words inflict a wound! Have you not read, they say, that "swords inflict wounds, but not as much as the tongue." The soul is wounded, then, even by the tongue; it is also wounded by evil thoughts and desires; but it is fractured and shattered by the works of sin. If we could see all this and feel the scars of a soul that has been wounded, we would certainly resist sin to death.[a]

a. Origen, *Homilies on Numbers* 8.1.6–8 (Voicu, *Apocrypha,* 316–17).

from intruders, you should **make a door and a bolt for your mouth** (v. 25b) to guard it from speaking words of slander (22:27; Ps 141:3). And just as you **lock up your silver and gold** (v. 24b) to prevent them from being stolen, you should **make balances and scales for your words** (v. 25a) to weigh them carefully before they fly out of your mouth (16:25; 21:25). In summary, be careful not to **err with your tongue, lest you** say something imprudent and **fall before him who lies in wait**, ready to use your own words against you (14:1; 21:7; James 3:2; 4:11).

Reflection and Application (27:16–28:26)

What is the remedy against malicious speech? According to Jewish tradition, the disciple of a †sage should keep occupied with †Torah, while an ordinary person should humble himself, for one who is humble will not speak wrongly about another (Prov 15:4).[19] Christians can learn much from these principles: indeed, studying Scripture and cultivating humility are both effective ways to become more self-aware of one's speech concerning others.

Controlling one's tongue, moreover, requires practicing at least three cardinal virtues: *prudence*, which guides us to discern and choose intelligently when, what, and how to speak; *justice*, which focuses on what we owe to God and neighbor, such as respect for the reputation of others; and *temperance*, which is the will's mastery over instincts, restraining the impulse to speak impulsively or carelessly.

19. Babylonian Talmud, *Arakhin* 15b.

Growing in these virtues is vital, for, according to the psalmist, the one who shall sojourn in the Lord's tent and dwell in his presence is "he who walks blamelessly, and does what is right, and speaks truth from his heart; who does not slander with his tongue, and does no evil to his friend, nor takes up a reproach against his neighbor" (Ps 15:1–3).

V.F. Lending and Borrowing; Almsgiving and Guaranteeing Loans (29:1–20)

¹He that shows mercy will lend to his neighbor,
     and he that strengthens him with his hand keeps the
        commandments.
²Lend to your neighbor in the time of his need;
     and in turn, repay your neighbor promptly.
³Confirm your word and keep faith with him,
     and on every occasion you will find what you need.
⁴Many persons regard a loan as a windfall,
     and cause trouble to those who help them.
⁵A man will kiss another's hands until he gets a loan,
     and will lower his voice in speaking of his neighbor's money;
but at the time for repayment he will delay,
     and will pay in words of unconcern,
     and will find fault with the time.
⁶If the lender exerts pressure, he will hardly get back half,
     and will regard that as a windfall.
If he does not, the borrower has robbed him of his money,
     and he has needlessly made him his enemy;
he will repay him with curses and reproaches,
     and instead of glory will repay him with dishonor.
⁷Because of such wickedness, therefore, many have refused to lend;
     they have been afraid of being defrauded needlessly.

⁸Nevertheless, be patient with a man in humble circumstances,
     and do not make him wait for your alms.
⁹Help a poor man for the commandment's sake,
     and because of his need do not send him away empty.
¹⁰Lose your silver for the sake of a brother or a friend,
     and do not let it rust under a stone and be lost.
¹¹Lay up your treasure according to the commandments of the
        Most High,
     and it will profit you more than gold.
¹²Store up almsgiving in your treasury,
     and it will rescue you from all affliction;

¹³more than a mighty shield and more than a heavy spear,
   it will fight on your behalf against your enemy.

¹⁴A good man will be surety for his neighbor,
   but a man who has lost his sense of shame will fail him.
¹⁵Do not forget all the kindness of your surety,
   for he has given his life for you.
¹⁶A sinner will overthrow the prosperity of his surety,
   ¹⁷and one who does not feel grateful will abandon his
   rescuer.
¹⁸Being surety has ruined many men who were prosperous,
   and has shaken them like a wave of the sea;
   it has driven men of power into exile,
   and they have wandered among foreign nations.
¹⁹The sinner who has fallen into suretyship
   and pursues gain will fall into lawsuits.
²⁰Assist your neighbor according to your ability,
   but take heed to yourself lest you fall.

OT: Exod 22:25–27; Lev 25:35–37; Deut 15:7–11; Prov 6:1–5; 11:15; 14:21; 17:18
NT: Matt 6:19–20; 19:21; 25:18, 29; James 5:3
Catechism: almsgiving and love for the poor, 2443–49

29:1–2   Ben Sira turns to the topic of household economics or personal finances, focusing on lending and borrowing, which were common practices in ancient
Israelite society. **He that shows mercy** or kindness will willingly **lend** money to a
neighbor—in this context, his Jewish neighbor (Lev 19:18). **He that strengthens**
and supports a neighbor by lending him a **hand keeps the commandments**, for
the †Torah instructs Israelites to lend money without charging interest to fellow Israelites (Exod 22:25; Lev 25:35–37; Deut 15:7–11). Ben Sira echoes these
commandments: **Lend to your neighbor** when he is in **need**, for it is an act of
charity, and when you are the one who has taken out a loan, **repay your neighbor promptly** (literally, "on time"), when the loan falls due (Sir 4:31; Ps 37:21).
29:3–4   **Confirm your word** by keeping your promise to repay the loan on time, **and
keep faith**—that is, be honest **with him** (27:17). If you repay your loans faithfully, you will establish good credit and **on every occasion** you will secure the
loans **you need** in the future. Yet **many** irresponsible **persons regard a loan as
a windfall** that is theirs to keep (20:9)—like fruit blown off a tree by the wind
that requires no effort to pick. Such people **cause trouble to those who help
them** by failing to pay back their loans.
29:5   A dishonest person in financial need will hypocritically **kiss another's hands**,
feigning love and respect toward the potential lender **until he gets a loan**.
Perhaps he will disingenuously **lower his voice**, appearing respectful while
speaking of his neighbor's money that he hopes to borrow. **But at the time**

for repayment he will delay, offering only **words of unconcern**—excuses and empty promises—**and will find fault with the time**, claiming that the due date for repayment is too soon.

If the lender exerts pressure on such a borrower, demanding repayment, he   29:6–7 will be fortunate to **get back** even **half, and will regard** any amount repaid **as a windfall. If he does not** insist on getting repaid, he will not be repaid at all: **the borrower has robbed him of his money** and **needlessly made** the lender **his enemy.** Perhaps repressing a sense of shame and guilt, the borrower may even **repay** the lender **with curses and reproaches, and instead of glory** or gratitude will **repay him with dishonor. Because of such wickedness** on the part of bad borrowers who abuse the generosity of their lenders, **many have refused to lend** their money to others for fear of **being defrauded needlessly** and losing their possessions altogether.

Giving alms is another way of helping the needy (29:8–13). **Be patient** and   29:8–9 merciful toward a person **in humble circumstances**; be quick to assist him, and **do not** delay or **make him wait for your alms.** Give to **a poor** person **for the commandment's sake**—as prescribed by the Torah (Deut 15:7–11). Helping the needy is a duty of God's people (Sir 3:30–4:6; Prov 14:21, 31; 19:17); thus, one must **not send** a poor person **away empty**-handed (compare James 2:14–15; 1 John 3:16–18).

Lose your silver means to generously give your money to **a brother** or **friend**   29:10–13 in need; **do not let it rust** or tarnish **under a stone**, for if you hoard your money it will be wasted and **lost** (Matt 6:19; 25:18; Luke 12:16–21; James 5:3). Instead, **lay up your treasure** by distributing your wealth **according to** God's **commandments, and it will profit you more than gold.** This creates a paradox: the person who hoards ends up losing, while the person who gives liberally provides for the future. Therefore, **store up almsgiving in your treasury**, for giving alms is an investment in the "bank" of God's mercy. This concept is echoed in Jesus's teaching on almsgiving (Matt 6:19–20; 19:21; see 1 Tim 6:18–19).

"Lending" to the Lord secures divine favor (Prov 19:17; Matt 6:20; 19:21), ensuring that he will remember your generosity and **rescue you from all affliction** in your time of need (Sir 3:14–15, 30–31; 12:2; Tob 4:7–11). To shift from an economic to a military metaphor, almsgiving is so powerful that it protects **more than a mighty shield** and serves as a weapon **more** potent **than a heavy spear**, for **it will fight** on behalf of generous givers against their enemies.

Another way of assisting a neighbor is by "acting as surety"—that is, guar-   29:14–15 anteeing to repay a loan if a borrower defaults on his obligation (29:4–6). While Proverbs warns against this practice, seeing it as risky and unwise (Prov 6:1–5; 11:15; 22:26–27), Ben Sira acknowledges the risk but appreciates the potential benefit to a poor neighbor and commends the person who is willing to do so (Sir 8:13). Ultimately, choosing whether or not to guarantee a loan is a matter of prudence. **A good man** is willing to **be surety for his neighbor** by

Rescued through Almsgiving

LIVING TRADITION

Drawing from Sirach and other scriptural texts, St. Augustine argues that it is not enough merely to avoid sins to inherit the kingdom of God. One must also actively do good, including giving generously to the poor. These charitable deeds have atoning power and store up merit for the day of judgment—not by their intrinsic value, but as the overflow of God's grace manifest in the life of a believer (Eph 2:8–10).

> Those who will receive the kingdom have given aid to the poor. . . . If they had not, their lives otherwise suited to holiness would have remained sterile, limiting themselves to abstaining from sins, not violating chastity or abandoning themselves to drunkenness, not stealing or doing anything bad. If they had not added charitable actions, they would remain sterile, only observing the first part of the commandment, "Stay far away from evil," and not the other part, "and do good" (Ps 37:27). Thus, when it says, "Come, receive your kingdom," this call is not motivated by the fact that they have lived in chastity, refrained from stealing, or that they have not taken advantage of the poor, or robbed other people's possessions or perjured themselves. Rather, it says, "Enter into the kingdom because I was hungry and you gave me something to eat" (Matt 25:35). . . . It is written, "As water extinguishes a blazing fire, so aid given to the poor cancels one's sins" (Sir 3:30). [This demonstrates] the importance of mercy in order to extinguish and to cancel sins. . . . Therefore, they will be saved, not because they have not sinned but because they have redeemed their sins with their good works.[a]

a. Augustine, *Sermon* 389.5 (Voicu, *Apocrypha*, 320).

cosigning on a loan, but one who is without **shame**, lacking honor, decency, and compassion, **will fail** his neighbor and refuse to provide surety. However, Ben Sira reminds the borrower: **Do not forget all the kindnesses** of the person who has acted as **your surety, for he has given his life** by risking his financial stability **for you.**

29:16–18   An unscrupulous and ungrateful **sinner** will squander **the prosperity** of the benefactor who acted as **surety**. Neglecting or abandoning one's obligations to the guarantor and **rescuer** could lead him to financial ruin. For this reason, cosigning on loans should be done only with prudent consideration, as **being surety has ruined many** wealthy and powerful people. The loss they incurred shook them **like a wave of the sea**; they not only lost their homes and possessions but were **driven into exile** and **wandered among foreign nations**, being forced to seek work abroad.

29:19–20   Conversely, another kind of **sinner** guarantees the loans of others not out of benevolence but with the intent to take advantage of borrowers by extorting money from them. The dishonest guarantor who **pursues gain**—perhaps by charging interest from borrowers, a practice prohibited by the Torah (Exod

22:25)—**will fall into lawsuits** and suffer consequences for his extortion. In sum, despite the risks of providing surety, **assist your neighbor** generously and **according to your ability**, but remain cautious and be wary of dishonest people **lest you fall** and incur significant loss.

Reflection and Application (29:1–20)

Ben Sira's advice on lending, giving alms, and guaranteeing loans points to the virtue of *liberality* or generosity, which involves the proper use of wealth for good purposes—especially when it comes to *giving* to others.[20] As indicated by the only known saying of Jesus not recorded in the Gospels—"It is more blessed to give than to receive" (Acts 20:35)—the virtue of liberality contributes to human happiness. A liberal person "liberates" money from his or her own possession, thus demonstrating detachment from material wealth.[21] Because it is directed toward others and promotes harmonious human fellowship, liberality is closely related to the cardinal virtue of *justice*, which concerns rendering to each their due.[22] However, liberality is even more pleasing than justice, because the liberal or generous person willingly gives *more* than what is owed, imitating God's generosity (James 1:5).

Liberality is the "golden mean" between the excesses of covetousness (or avarice)—the excessive love of possessing wealth or material things (see the Reflection and Application section for 14:3–19, pp. 134–35)—and prodigality, the careless and foolish squandering of riches.[23] A wise and prudent person will avoid both covetousness and prodigality, being willing to help others generously without recklessly endangering his own possessions.

V.G. On Living Independently and Raising Children (29:21–30:13)

> [21]The essentials for life are water and bread
>   and clothing and a house to cover one's nakedness.
> [22]Better is the life of a poor man under the shelter of his roof
>   than sumptuous food in another man's house.
> [23]Be content with little or much.
> [24]It is a miserable life to go from house to house,
>   and where you are a stranger you may not open your mouth;
> [25]you will play the host and provide drink without being thanked,
>   and besides this you will hear bitter words:

---

20. Aristotle, *Nicomachean Ethics* 4.1.
21. Thomas Aquinas, *Summa Theologiae* II-II q. 80 a. 1–4.
22. Thomas Aquinas, *Summa Theologiae* II-II q. 80 a. 5.
23. Aristotle, *Nicomachean Ethics* 4.1; Thomas Aquinas, *Summa Theologiae* II-II qq. 118–19.

²⁶"Come here, stranger, prepare the table,
  and if you have anything at hand, let me have it to eat."
²⁷"Give place, stranger, to an honored person;
  my brother has come to stay with me; I need my house."
²⁸These things are hard to bear for a man who has feeling:
  scolding about lodging and the reproach of the moneylender.
³⁰:¹He who loves his son will whip him often,
  in order that he may rejoice at the way he turns out.
²He who disciplines his son will profit by him,
  and will boast of him among acquaintances.
³He who teaches his son will make his enemies envious,
  and will glory in him in the presence of friends.
⁴The father may die, and yet he is not dead,
  for he has left behind him one like himself;
⁵while alive he saw and rejoiced,
  and when he died he was not grieved;
⁶he has left behind him an avenger against his enemies,
  and one to repay the kindness of his friends.

⁷He who spoils his son will bind up his wounds,
  and his feelings will be troubled at every cry.
⁸A horse that is untamed turns out to be stubborn,
  and a son unrestrained turns out to be willful.
⁹Pamper a child, and he will frighten you;
  play with him, and he will give you grief.
¹⁰Do not laugh with him, lest you have sorrow with him,
  and in the end you will gnash your teeth.
¹¹Give him no authority in his youth,
  and do not ignore his errors.
¹²Bow down his neck in his youth,
  and beat his sides while he is young,
lest he become stubborn and disobey you,
  and you have sorrow of soul from him.
¹³Discipline your son and take pains with him,
  that you may not be offended by his shamelessness.

OT: Prov 13:24; 22:6; 23:13–14; 29:15, 17
NT: Phil 4:11–12; 1 Tim 6:6–8; Heb 13:5
Catechism: education of children, 1652–58, 2201–6, 2214–31; poverty of heart, 2544–47

29:21–23 In the ancient Greco-Roman world, a man could improve his life by living in the household of a wealthy benefactor, enjoying better food and a more comfortable home, but at the cost of his independence and self-respect since he placed himself at the service of the benefactor. Ben Sira advises against this kind of dependency, recommending instead a more frugal life and contentment with the necessities—**water, bread, clothing**, and a modest **house** that provides privacy and shelter. **Better is the** frugal **life of a poor man** living independently under his own **roof than sumptuous food in another man's house** while being dependent and obligated to him. True happiness lies in being **content** with what you have, whether **little or much** (see Phil 4:11–12; 1 Tim 6:6–8; Heb 13:5). GII adds: **and you will not hear reproach for your sojourning**—meaning that if you live in your own home, no one will accuse you of being a permanent guest dependent on others' hospitality.[24]

One who relies on others for sustenance leads **a miserable life**, going **from house to house** as a visitor in other people's homes. As **a stranger**, he will not dare to speak freely in a place where he does not belong. Acting as a servant of the housemaster, he will **play the host**, welcoming guests and providing them **drink without being thanked** for his service. Worse yet, the guests will humiliate him with rude and **bitter words**. **29:24–25**

"Come here, stranger," the guests will say condescendingly to the sojourner as if he were a servant, **"prepare the table** for a meal, and give me whatever you have **to eat."** Equally rudely, the host will order him to **give** up his **place** to an **honored person,** such as his **brother** or some other important guest (see Luke 14:7–11). If the host needs space in his **house,** there may be no more room for the sojourner, making him unwelcome. **29:26–27**

These things discussed in verses 1–27 **are hard to bear** for a sensible, self-respecting person, because being scolded **about lodging** at someone else's expense and being reproached by a **moneylender** for defaulting on debts would shame him. For this reason, a wise, sensible person should take care to live independently and pay off his debts. **29:28**

Ben Sira now turns to the education and training of children (30:1–13). Reflecting the cultural context of his time, he assumes that a good father should be rigorous in disciplining his children, with corporal punishment as a normal part of a child's education. This portrait of a strict, disciplinarian father (in contrast to the indulgent father who spoils his son in v. 7) mirrors Wisdom's own approach: she disciplines her children for their own good because she loves them (4:17–18; 6:18–31). Nevertheless, not all of Ben Sira's advice should be observed literally in a modern context; it should be understood in light of the teachings of the New Testament and the Church. For Ben Sira, a father **who loves his son** should **whip him often,**[25] correcting his misbehavior with appropriate corporal punishment (Prov 13:24; 23:13–14; 29:15) so that the father **may rejoice** in how the child **turns out** when he grows into a mature and responsible adult. While children need firm correction to grow into people of good character, physical abuse is never acceptable. The point of this passage is not to inflict harm but to avoid spoiling children. As St. Paul writes, parents **30:1**

---

24. Sir 29:23, RSV-2CE footnote; compare NRSV, ESV-CE, NABRE.

25. It is likely that Ben Sira exaggerates and is *not* speaking literally when he says "whip him often"; modern parents also sometimes use hyperbole when they speak about punishing children.

should "not provoke [their] children to anger, but bring them up in the discipline and instruction of the Lord" (Eph 6:4; see also Col 3:21; Catechism 2223).

30:2–3   A father **who disciplines his son** through education and training (Prov 22:6; 29:17), teaching him to behave virtuously, **will profit by him**—for such a son will be a blessing to the household. His father **will boast of him among acquaintances** and **friends** and will even **make his enemies envious** of his well-behaved son and harmonious household.

30:4–6   Even if the **father** dies, it is as though **he is not dead, for he has left behind** a legacy: his son, raised to be **like himself**. While he was **alive** the father **rejoiced** over his beloved son, **and when he died**—that is, while on his deathbed—**he was not grieved** because he knew that his son had learned his ways and would continue where he left off. In dying, the father **left behind him an avenger** who would defend the security and honor of his family **against his enemies**—sons were expected to stand by their father and their family in ancient Israel (Ps 127:5)—and who could **repay the kindness of his friends** even after his death.

30:7–8   By contrast, a father **who spoils his son** and allows him to misbehave without punishment encourages his evil conduct. Through his own reckless behavior, the son incurs **wounds** that the father will need to **bind up**. If the father is too soft or sentimental, **his feelings will be troubled** every time his wayward son cries. Just as an **untamed horse** remains **stubborn** and wild, so does **a son unrestrained** by discipline become **willful** and reckless.

30:9–10   **Pamper a child, and he will frighten you** (literally, "astonish you"—in a bad way); **play with him** or indulge him, **and he will give you grief**. Ben Sira warns that a father who is overly familiar with his child may lose the child's respect. He exhorts the father not to **laugh with him**, perhaps to avoid encouraging frivolous behavior, but (in line with ancient customs) to exercise a measure of emotional self-restraint to avoid future **sorrow** because of **him**. If the child remains undisciplined and reckless, the father **will gnash** his **teeth** in mental distress and turmoil (Ezek 18:2; Matt 8:12; 13:42). This advice, however, should not be taken literally; fathers can play with their children while still maintaining appropriate respect and healthy emotional boundaries (see the Reflection and Application section below).

30:11–13   To train a son well, a father should **give him no authority**, meaning he should not allow the child to do whatever he wants. The father should also **not ignore his errors** but correct them patiently and steadfastly. Returning to the metaphor of training a horse (30:8), the father should **bow down his neck** (i.e., train him to be obedient) **in his youth, and beat his sides** as a rider whips his horse **while he is young, lest he become stubborn** and rebellious—like the wayward son of Deut 21:18–21, whom the †Torah condemns to death—and

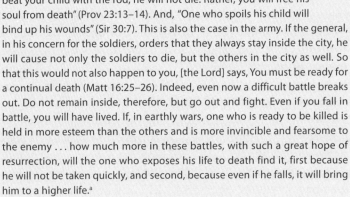

Training One's Children

LIVING TRADITION

St. John Chrysostom, drawing inspiration from the words of Proverbs and Sirach, advises parents not to spoil their children but to discipline them for their own good. Just as a general trains his troops to prepare them for battle against enemy armies, so parents must train their children for the spiritual battle against sin and worldly temptations.

One who is always helping his child ruins him, while the one who does not always help saves him. A wise man said the same thing: "If you beat your child with the rod, he will not die. Rather, you will free his soul from death" (Prov 23:13–14). And, "One who spoils his child will bind up his wounds" (Sir 30:7). This is also the case in the army. If the general, in his concern for the soldiers, orders that they always stay inside the city, he will cause not only the soldiers to die, but the others in the city as well. So that this would not also happen to you, [the Lord] says, You must be ready for a continual death (Matt 16:25–26). Indeed, even now a difficult battle breaks out. Do not remain inside, therefore, but go out and fight. Even if you fall in battle, you will have lived. If, in earthly wars, one who is ready to be killed is held in more esteem than the others and is more invincible and fearsome to the enemy . . . how much more in these battles, with such a great hope of resurrection, will the one who exposes his life to death find it, first because he will not be taken quickly, and second, because even if he falls, it will bring him to a higher life.[a]

a. John Chrysostom, *Homilies on the Gospel of Matthew* 55.2 (Voicu, *Apocrypha*, 324–25).

cause the father **sorrow of soul**.[26] While this advice seems excessively harsh, the modern reader should remember that the author speaks metaphorically and hyperbolically within the context of horse training: just as a rider trains his horse by beating its sides, so a father should discipline his son with appropriate firmness. Jesus also used striking hyperboles to emphasize the importance of self-discipline, without expecting his words to be taken literally (Matt 5:29–30). In sum, a father should **discipline** his **son and take pains with him** (Hebrew: "and make his yoke heavy" by keeping him engaged with responsibilities), that he may grow to be a God-fearing man, so that the father will **not be offended by his shamelessness** if he remains stubborn and disobedient. Fathers then, as now, loved their sons and were often inclined to indulge them. Ben Sira underscores that fatherly discipline is essential for a son to grow into a well-rounded individual.

26. The fact that there is no record of the death penalty ever being carried out on a "stubborn and rebellious son" as described in Deut 21:18–21 indicates that this law may have been given primarily as a deterrent against youthful disobedience and to encourage parental discipline rather than to actually enforce the execution of wayward sons. On the injunction to beat the son, see note 25 above.

Reflection and Application (29:21–30:13)

Though Ben Sira's view of parental education seems harsh by today's standards, he still offers valuable lessons for modern parents. While the ancients tended to err on the side of excessive discipline, many parents today fall into the opposite error by failing to correct their children and adopting a lax, laissez-faire attitude, often reflected in expressions such as "I don't want to impose my values on them," "Let them grow up and make their own decisions," "They will learn from their own mistakes," or "It's the school's job to educate them." Such attitudes are diametrically opposed to the biblical and Catholic view of education, which holds that parents are the *primary educators* of their children, responsible for their moral education and spiritual formation. Because family life is "an initiation into life in society," the educational role of parents is "primordial and inalienable" and "of such importance that it is almost impossible to provide an adequate substitute" (Catechism 2207, 2221). This role includes creating a home "where tenderness, forgiveness, respect, fidelity, and disinterested service are the rule"; educating children in the virtues, which requires "an apprenticeship in self-denial, sound judgment, and self-mastery"; and guiding and correcting them by example (Catechism 2223). Parents are responsible for evangelizing and catechizing their children from their earliest years (Catechism 2225–26). Although this is a challenging task, it is a noble and crucial one in an age when the culture continues to drift further from a Christian worldview. Today's parents are blessed to have access to an abundance of good Catholic books, websites, podcasts, and other resources to assist them in their role as primary educators of their children.

V.H. Health and Gladness of Heart, Not Wealth, Lead to a Happy Life (30:14–31:11)

[14]Better off is a poor man who is well and strong in constitution
    than a rich man who is severely afflicted in body.
[15]Health and soundness are better than all gold,
    and a robust body than countless riches.
[16]There is no wealth better than health of body,
    and there is no gladness above joy of heart.
[17]Death is better than a miserable life,
    and eternal rest than chronic sickness.

[18]Good things poured out upon a mouth that is closed
    are like offerings of food placed upon a grave.
[19]Of what use to an idol is an offering of fruit?
    For it can neither eat nor smell.

So is he who is afflicted by the Lord;
²⁰he sees with his eyes and groans,
like a eunuch who embraces a maiden and groans.

²¹Do not give yourself over to sorrow,
and do not afflict yourself deliberately.
²²Gladness of heart is the life of man,
and the rejoicing of a man is length of days.
²³Delight your soul and comfort your heart,
and remove sorrow far from you,
for sorrow has destroyed many,
and there is no profit in it.
²⁴Jealousy and anger shorten life,
and anxiety brings on old age too soon.
²⁵A man of cheerful and good heart
will give heed to the food he eats.

³¹:¹Wakefulness over wealth wastes away one's flesh,
and anxiety about it removes sleep.
²Wakeful anxiety prevents slumber,
and a severe illness carries off sleep.
³The rich man toils as his wealth accumulates,
and when he rests he fills himself with his dainties.
⁴The poor man toils as his livelihood diminishes,
and when he rests he becomes needy.

⁵He who loves gold will not be justified,
and he who pursues money will be led astray by it.
⁶Many have come to ruin because of gold,
and their destruction has met them face to face.
⁷It is a stumbling block to those who are devoted to it,
and every fool will be taken captive by it.

⁸Blessed is the rich man who is found blameless,
and who does not go after gold.
⁹Who is he? And we will call him blessed,
for he has done wonderful things among his people.
¹⁰Who has been tested by it and been found perfect?
Let it be for him a ground for boasting.
Who has had the power to transgress and did not transgress,
and to do evil and did not do it?
¹¹His prosperity will be established,
and the assembly will relate his acts of charity.

OT: Tob 3:6, 10, 13; Prov 15:15; 17:22; Eccles 5:10–11; 11:9–10
NT: Matt 5:3; 6:19–21, 24; Mark 10:23; Luke 12:16–20; 16:9–13; 1 Tim 6:9–10
Catechism: our vocation to beatitude, 1716–24; the passions, 1762–70; avarice, 2536

30:14–16   In this section, Ben Sira argues that health contributes more to happiness than wealth does (30:14–25). A person is **better off poor** yet healthy and fit **than rich** but **afflicted in body** (see Matt 5:3). **Health and soundness** of body **are better** and of greater value **than all gold, and a robust body than countless riches** (Hebrew: "and a good spirit than pearls"; compare NABRE). The Hebrew of verse 15 supports the notion conveyed in verse 16 that not just the **health of body** but also a sound mind or **joy of heart** is far superior to all material possessions.

30:17   For those who suffer, **death** may seem **better** than a bitter, **miserable life,** and **eternal rest**—the sleep of death, which offers reprieve from life's hardships—may seem preferable to **chronic sickness**. However, this is no argument for euthanasia. While righteous people sometimes express a desire to die when suffering acutely, they ultimately entrust their lives to God (Tob 3:6, 10–13; Job 3:11; Eccles 4:1–2). They recognize that their lives are a gift from God and that God remains the sovereign Master of life. They understand they are stewards, not owners, of their lives, and that life is not theirs to dispose of (Catechism 2280).

30:18–20   The sick person is compared to three things that cannot enjoy life: a grave (v. 18), an idol (v. 19), and a eunuch (v. 20). **Good things** (i.e., food) given to **a mouth that is closed** due to illness **are like offerings of food placed upon a grave** for the dead (prohibited in Deut 26:14) or offered to an idol (Hebrew). A person too sick to eat cannot enjoy good food any more than a dead person or an idol. Offering **fruit** to **an idol**—a common practice in Near Eastern religions but ridiculed in Israel (Deut 4:28; Ps 115:4–7; Dan 14:1–22)—is useless to the idol that **can neither eat nor smell**. Similarly, food is useless to one **who is afflicted by the Lord** with a serious illness. **He sees** the food **and groans** in frustration, like a **eunuch who embraces a maiden and groans** because he is unable to enjoy sexual intimacy.

30:21–22   The following verses (30:21–31:2) propose attitudes that foster physical, mental, and emotional health. By exhorting his reader, **Do not give yourself over to sorrow** by yielding to chronic unhappiness, Ben Sira implies that sorrow is not an uncontrollable feeling but often the result of a choice and act of the will. **Do not afflict yourself** encourages the reader not to **deliberately** distress themselves, as one can choose, to some extent, not to dwell on negative emotions such as sorrow, anxiety, and depression (Eccles 11:9–10). Cheerfulness brings health benefits: **gladness of heart** gives **life** meaning and makes it worth living, and **rejoicing is length of days**—that is, it prolongs one's life expectancy (Prov 17:22).

30:23   **Delight your soul** (literally, "deceive your soul"; compare 14:16) **and comfort your heart** (†Vulgate: *have mercy on your soul, pleasing God*; see Douay, 30:24). As the saying goes, happiness is a state of mind. Just as you can choose to resist negative emotions, you can "trick yourself" and choose to embrace joy regardless of your circumstances by removing **sorrow** and its chief cause—worry—**far from you** (compare Matt 6:34). **For sorrow has destroyed many,** leading them

The Anxiety of Riches

St. John Chrysostom highlights the paradox that, while pursuing riches leads to bondage, embracing poverty leads to freedom:

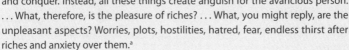

> Why, O mortal, do you pile up gold? Why acquire for yourself a more bitter slavery? A harsher imprisonment? Why create for yourself a more piercing anxiety? . . . If you want to be formidable, eliminate the occasions by which [others] might take advantage of and harm you. Have you never heard the proverb that says that not even a hundred people together could ever despoil a poor, naked person? In fact, he has the greatest defender, poverty, one that not even the king could subjugate and conquer. Instead, all these things create anguish for the avaricious person. . . . What, therefore, is the pleasure of riches? . . . What, you might reply, are the unpleasant aspects? Worries, plots, hostilities, hatred, fear, endless thirst after riches and anxiety over them.[a]

a. John Chrysostom, *Homilies on the Gospel of Matthew* 83.2–3 (Voicu, *Apocrypha*, 326).

into depression and despair—**and there is no profit in it**. Jewish tradition also highlights the futility of worry: "Do not worry about tomorrow's sorrow, 'For you do not know what a day may bring forth' (Prov 27:1). Perhaps tomorrow you will no longer exist and it will turn out that you will worry about a world that is not yours."[27]

Jealousy and anger shorten life—a fact supported by modern medicine and   30:24–25
psychology—and **anxiety** not only proves futile but also accelerates aging. A **cheerful** person, unburdened by worries, can gratefully enjoy **the food he eats** as long as his health enables him to do so (Prov 15:15).

Although wealth is a blessing, worrying about it can be hazardous to one's   31:1–2
health (31:1–11). **Wakefulness** due to worry **over wealth**—perhaps stemming from a guilty conscience over dishonest gain (40:5–8; Prov 13:11, 22; Eccles 5:11–14) or from fear of loss—**wastes away one's flesh**, causing fatigue and impacting one's health. Moreover, **anxiety** about possessions disrupts **sleep**. **Wakeful anxiety** (Hebrew: "anxiety about sustenance")—potentially rooted in worries about making a living—**prevents slumber**, much like **severe illness** leads to insomnia.

In these verses, Ben Sira reflects on a common situation of social inequality   31:3–4
in which the rich become richer and the poor become poorer. Although both labor and toil, the **rich** person's **wealth accumulates, and when he rests** he enjoys life's luxuries, indulging in delicacies (see Luke 12:16–20). By contrast, the **poor** man's **livelihood diminishes** no matter how hard he works. If he does get a chance to rest **he becomes needy** and cannot make ends meet.

27. Babylonian Talmud, *Yebamot* 63b (Neusner, *Babylonian Talmud*, 8:329).

31:5–7   In verses 5–7, however, Ben Sira warns that wealth also has its downside. **He who loves gold will not be justified** before God, for he is driven by greed; **he who pursues money** is **led astray** by his own covetousness, inevitably falling into sin (Prov 28:20; Eccles 5:10). **Many have come to ruin because of gold,** since avarice leads not only to financial loss but also to moral and spiritual **destruction** (1 Tim 6:9–10). Though wealth is morally neutral, it often becomes **a stumbling block,** causing those **devoted to it** (as to an idol) to trip and fall. **Every fool will be taken captive** and enslaved by their own greed (Matt 6:24; Luke 16:9–13), for covetousness is nothing less than idolatry (Col 3:5).

31:8–9   A better outcome for the rich is possible: **Blessed is the rich man** who has preserved his integrity and remains **blameless, who does not** succumb to greed or **go after gold** (Hebrew: "mammon"). **Who is he?** Such a righteous rich person is rare (Mark 10:23–25). He is called **blessed, for he has done wonderful things** by acquiring wealth without committing sin.

31:10–11   **Who has been tested by** wealth **and been found perfect?** The implied answer to this rhetorical question is "very few people." The righteous rich person has all the more **a ground for boasting,** because very few people with **the power to transgress** have resisted the temptation to **do evil.** By safeguarding his integrity, this person's **prosperity will be established,** for wealth is ultimately a blessing from God (Deut 30:5, 9). Such a man will likely be generous as well, and the whole community will recognize **his acts of charity.**

Reflection and Application (30:14–31:11)

Everyone desires to be happy (Catechism 1718). Yet we often perceive happiness as something that largely depends on our circumstances or emotional states (also known as "passions"). When life does not go according to our plans, hopes, or desires, we experience disappointment, sadness, or discouragement. While these emotions are normal, they need not dominate our soul; if we allow them to do so, our happiness will remain constantly at the mercy of external circumstances, which we can never fully control.

In the Beatitudes, Jesus proposes a radically different path to human happiness (Matt 5:3–12). This path—marked by poverty of spirit, mourning, meekness, hunger and thirst for righteousness, mercy, purity of heart, and peace—reflects Jesus's own journey to the cross. God calls every person to this counterintuitive path to happiness, which is nothing less than a sharing in Christ's own joy and divine life (Catechism 1720–21; Matt 25:21).

Because this happiness surpasses natural human understanding, it must be received by faith as a free gift of God (Catechism 1722). It requires us to make decisive choices, choosing joy in God's love rather than seeking it in the goods of this world: "True happiness is not found in riches or well-being, seeking it in human fame or power, or in any human achievement—however beneficial it may be—such as science, technology, and art, or indeed in any creature, but in God alone, the source of every good and of all love" (Catechism 1723).

V.I. Proper Etiquette with Food and Wine at Banquets (31:12–32:13)

¹²Are you seated at the table of a great man?
Do not be greedy at it,
and do not say, "There is certainly much upon it!"
¹³Remember that a greedy eye is a bad thing.
What has been created more greedy than the eye?
Therefore it sheds tears from every face.
¹⁴Do not reach out your hand for everything you see,
and do not crowd your neighbor at the dish.
¹⁵Judge your neighbor's feelings by your own,
and in every matter be thoughtful.
¹⁶Eat like a human being what is set before you,
and do not chew greedily, lest you be hated.
¹⁷Be the first to stop eating, for the sake of good manners,
and do not be insatiable, lest you give offense.
¹⁸If you are seated among many persons,
do not reach out your hand before they do.

¹⁹How ample a little is for a well-disciplined man!
He does not breathe heavily upon his bed.
²⁰Healthy sleep depends on moderate eating;
he rises early, and feels fit.
The distress of sleeplessness and of nausea
and colic are with the glutton.
²¹If you are overstuffed with food,
get up in the middle of the meal, and you will have relief.
²²Listen to me, my son, and do not disregard me,
and in the end you will appreciate my words.
In all your work be industrious,
and no sickness will overtake you.
²³Men will praise the one who is liberal with food,
and their testimony to his excellence is trustworthy.
²⁴The city will complain of the one who is miserly with food,
and their testimony to his miserliness is accurate.

²⁵Do not aim to be valiant over wine,
for wine has destroyed many.

²⁶Fire and water prove the temper of steel,
   so wine tests hearts in the strife of the proud.
²⁷Wine is like life to men,
   if you drink it in moderation.
What is life to a man who is without wine?
   It has been created to make men glad.
²⁸Wine drunk in season and temperately
   is rejoicing of heart and gladness of soul.
²⁹Wine drunk to excess is bitterness of soul,
   with provocation and stumbling.
³⁰Drunkenness increases the anger of a fool to his injury,
   reducing his strength and adding wounds.

³¹Do not reprove your neighbor at a banquet of wine,
   and do not despise him in his merrymaking;
speak no word of reproach to him,
   and do not afflict him by making demands of him.
³²˸¹If they make you master of the feast, do not exalt yourself;
   be among them as one of them;
take good care of them and then be seated;
   ²when you have fulfilled your duties, take your place,
that you may be merry on their account
   and receive a wreath for your excellent leadership.

³Speak, you who are older, for it is fitting that you should,
   but with accurate knowledge, and do not interrupt the music.
⁴Where there is entertainment, do not pour out talk;
   do not display your cleverness out of season.
⁵A ruby seal in a setting of gold
   is a concert of music at a banquet of wine.
⁶A seal of emerald in a rich setting of gold
   is the melody of music with good wine.

⁷Speak, young man, if there is need of you,
   but no more than twice, and only if asked.
⁸Speak concisely, say much in few words;
   be as one who knows and yet holds his tongue.
⁹Among the great do not act as their equal;
   and when another is speaking, do not babble.

¹⁰Lightning speeds before the thunder,
   and approval precedes a modest man.
¹¹Leave in good time and do not be the last;
   go home quickly and do not linger.
¹²Amuse yourself there, and do what you have in mind,
   but do not sin through proud speech.

> ¹³**And for these things bless him who made you
> and satisfies you with his good gifts.**

OT: Ps 104:15; Prov 20:1; 23:1–8, 29–35; 31:4–5; Sir 37:29–31
NT: Luke 21:34; Gal 5:19–21; Eph 5:18; 1 Pet 4:3; 1 John 2:16
Catechism: gluttony as capital sin, 1866; drunkenness, 1852; temperance in food and drink, 2290

Turning to guidelines on etiquette at banquets, Ben Sira advises moderation   **31:12–13**
in eating (31:12–24), drinking (31:25–31), and conversation (32:1–13). If you
are **seated at the table of a great man** for some banquet or festive occasion, **do
not be greedy** (literally, "do not open your throat at it"), displaying a gluttonous
impatience to eat, and do not comment on the quantity of food on the table—as
praising a host's food was considered rude in ancient Eastern cultures (Prov
23:1–3). A **greedy eye** (literally, "evil eye") **is a bad thing**, for it expresses both
envy and gluttony, two of the capital sins. The eye is particularly **greedy** because
it covets many things (14:9; 1 John 2:16), and it easily **sheds tears** because it
cannot have everything it wants.

A polite guest should not **reach out** ravenously to grasp **everything** on the   **31:14–15**
dinner table, nor should he **crowd** his **neighbor** to reach **the dish** and take the
best portions. **Judge your neighbor's feelings by your own** (Hebrew: "know
that your neighbor is like you"), **and in every matter** be considerate of others
and not just of yourself (Matt 7:12).

Eat like a civilized **human being** rather than like an animal. **Do not chew**   **31:16–18**
greedily—for example, by taking huge bites or overfilling your mouth—lest
you be seen as someone with poor manners. Show moderation and **be the first
to stop eating**; do not, like some young men, be a ravenous, **insatiable** eater,
but restrain your appetite **lest you give offense.** Similarly, at the beginning of
the meal, **do not reach out your hand** to fill your plate before the other guests.

Figure 9. Fresco of a *symposion* (banquet)

31:19–21   Just **a little** food is sufficient **for a well-disciplined** person who eats in moderation. Unlike the glutton, **he does not breathe heavily upon his bed** after overeating but sleeps soundly and feels better. It is well known that **healthy sleep depends on moderate eating.** The temperate and disciplined person **rises early, and feels fit** (literally, "and his soul with him"), while the glutton suffers from **sleeplessness, nausea** (indigestion), **and colic** (pain or cramps in the gut). To someone who ignores this advice and suffers stomach pain from overeating, Ben Sira suggests they **get up in the middle of the meal** to vomit—a practice that may have been common in the ancient Greco-Roman world—hopefully, to find **relief** from the overeating rather than to continue eating. This time-conditioned practice is obviously ill-advised today.

31:22–24   Ben Sira again exhorts his disciple to **listen** to his advice, for while it requires discipline and self-denial, **in the end** he will **appreciate** its value. He counsels his disciple to be **industrious** (or "moderate") in all things so that **no sickness** or misfortune **will overtake** him. From criticizing gluttony and praising moderation, Ben Sira turns to generosity and stinginess regarding food. In ancient as in modern times, hospitality was highly regarded in the Middle East. People readily **praise the one who is liberal with food** and **complain** about a **miserly** host; **their testimony** to the generous host's **excellence** and to the stingy host's **miserliness** is considered **trustworthy** and **accurate.** When a person hosts a banquet, they leave an honorable or shameful impression that will precede them wherever they go (Prov 23:6–8).

31:25–27   Turning to the pleasures and hazards of drinking wine (31:25–31), Ben Sira warns his readers not to try **to be valiant over wine**, proving their manhood and strength by excessive drinking (Isa 5:22), **for wine has destroyed many**, as often attested in Scripture (Jdt 13:2; Prov 20:1; 23:29–35). As a furnace tests **the temper of steel** and the work of the metalsmith, **so wine tests** the **hearts** of the **proud** when they quarrel, revealing their true character. Nevertheless, **wine is like life to men**—a blessing when drunk **in moderation.** The rhetorical question, **What is life to a man who is without wine?** implies, hyperbolically, that life is not worth much without it, for God **created** wine **to make men glad** (see Judg 9:13; Ps 104:15).

31:28–30   Ben Sira contrasts **wine drunk** at the right time in the right amount, which brings **rejoicing of heart and gladness of soul**, and **wine drunk to excess**, which brings only **bitterness of soul**, along with **provocation and stumbling** (Hebrew: "headache, derision, and disgrace"). Rabbinic tradition teaches a similar lesson: "If one has merit, wine makes him glad, if not, it makes him sad."[28] **Drunkenness** not only leads to unhappiness; by inhibiting self-control, it can cause a drunken **fool** to lose his temper and hurt himself—whether through self-inflicted injury or by quarreling with others—**reducing his strength and**

---

28. Babylonian Talmud, *Yoma* 76b (Neusner, *Babylonian Talmud*, 5a:297).

Banquets in the Ancient World

BIBLICAL BACKGROUND

The modern reader may find Ben Sira's interest in banquet etiquette intriguing. Does such a topic really belong in the Bible? Does God truly care about etiquette at meals?

Banquets in the ancient world were not just meals but significant social events and public occasions that defined social boundaries and created social obligations between participants. In Greco-Roman culture, a formal banquet—known as a *symposion*—typically consisted of a festive evening meal followed by a drinking party that included entertainment and philosophical conversation. It was an occasion for both festive joy and instruction. Dinner guests reclined around a U-shaped table while eating and conversing, and a guest's position at the table was an indication of relative honor (see Luke 14:7–11).

Social etiquette at a *symposion* demanded that participants appear humble and even deferential to their host and to other guests. Thus, etiquette mattered at such events, where many people would be watching. Anyone seeking to be well thought of and to succeed in life would welcome advice about conducting himself honorably and wisely at a banquet. Then as now, a festive meal provides a concrete opportunity to put others before oneself and to show charity and respect.

adding wounds, perhaps by making him "an easy target for angry blows" (GNT). Drunkenness is a "work of the flesh" that excludes one from the kingdom of God (Luke 21:34; Gal 5:19–21; 1 Pet 4:3).

Despite the risks of drunkenness, one should **not reprove** a **neighbor at a**   31:31
banquet of wine, for it is a joyful occasion; nor should one look down on a person or spoil **his merrymaking** with words of **reproach**. In Ben Sira's day as in ours, a banquet is not the proper time or place to offer fraternal correction or to make **demands** of people who are enjoying themselves (20:1).

Ben Sira turns to the etiquette of conversation at banquets (32:1–13). One   32:1–2
who is chosen to be **master of the feast**—the master of ceremonies who organizes and presides over the banquet (2 Macc 2:27; John 2:8)—should **not exalt** himself or act as if he is more important than others. Instead, he should modestly mingle with the guests **as one of them**. He should **take good care of them** and ensure their comfort; only after having **fulfilled** his **duties** of hospitality is he free to sit down and **be merry** with them. In this way he will have earned a ceremonial **wreath** or garland of flowers on the head (Isa 28:1; Wis 2:8), a token of appreciation and honor for his **excellent leadership**.

It is **fitting** that **older** men, being wiser, be expected to **speak** at banquets,   32:3–6
but they should do so **with accurate knowledge**, without pompous words, and without interrupting **the music** or **entertainment** provided at the dinner party.

The Pleasures and Dangers of Wine

St. Ambrose explains that wine can be used for evil or for good. When abused without restraint it leads to drunkenness and disgrace; when consumed in moderation it not only promotes health and relaxation but also becomes a source of salvation in the Eucharist.

> God gave us wine, knowing well that when drunk in moderation it contributes to health and increases discernment, whereas gulped without measure, it gives birth to vices. He left to human freedom the choice between frugal sobriety and the damage of abuse and guilt of drunkenness. Noah became drunk and, groggy from wine, fell into a deep sleep. In this way he who gained glory through the flood was disgraced by wine. But the Lord also preserved in wine the good qualities of his creature, even making its fruit contribute to our salvation, making the forgiveness of our sins derive from it.[a]

a. Ambrose, *Hexameron* 5.17.72 (Voicu, *Apocrypha*, 331–32).

They should **not pour out talk**—for the guests may prefer to enjoy the music rather than listen to long speeches—or make an untimely show of their **cleverness** by attempting to impress others with wit or wisdom. A music **concert at a banquet of wine** is highly valued, being likened to **a ruby seal** or **a seal of emerald in a rich setting of gold**, as it greatly enhances the enjoyment of the banquet (Eccles 2:8; Isa 5:12).

32:7–9   On the other hand, a **young man** should be modest and not overly self-assertive or talkative at a banquet. He should be aware of his junior position and speak **only if asked**. His words should be brief and **few**, showing that he is knowledgeable yet self-restrained by holding **his tongue. Among the great**—whether eminent or elderly people—he should not **act as their equal** but should defer to them; **and when another is speaking**, he should **not babble** or make frivolous remarks, which would make him a nuisance.

32:10–11   As **lightning speeds before the thunder**, so **approval precedes a modest man**. Once he has established a good reputation, he is welcome wherever he goes. Another mark of good manners is not to overstay one's welcome but to **leave in good time**, without delay, and **not be the last** at the dinner party. When the time comes to go home, do so **quickly** without lingering at the door.

32:12–13   Once at home after the banquet, it is fine to relax and **amuse yourself**, being now freed from the restraints of etiquette. However, one should beware not to **sin through proud speech**; the pleasant atmosphere at banquets may lead people to speak carelessly, but restraint in speech is still necessary after the party is over. For all **these things**—good food, wine, music, and conversation—it is fitting to **bless** God, **who made you and satisfies you** (literally, "intoxicates you") **with his good gifts**.

Reflection and Application (31:12–32:13)

Gluttony—the immoderate consumption of food—is a vice often overlooked, perhaps because it is considered more "harmless" than other sins. Yet gluttony is one of the seven deadly sins or vices from which all other sins derive. Along with lust, it is the most carnal of the deadly sins (committed with our bodies), in contrast to purely spiritual sins such as pride and envy. While gluttony may sometimes be a relatively minor or venial sin, it becomes more serious when it endangers one's health. If an inordinate desire for food leads one to abandon virtue and God altogether, gluttony can even become a mortal sin.[29]

Gluttony is not limited to simply eating too much; it can also involve eating too hastily or impatiently (being unable to wait for the next meal), too greedily (voraciously gulping down food), too sumptuously (seeking only fine foods), or too daintily (being overly particular about food preparation).[30] St. Gregory the Great identifies five "daughters" of gluttony, or sins that derive from it: unseemly joy (inappropriate laughter), scurrility (untimely or offensive humor), uncleanness (loss of sexual self-control), loquaciousness (excessive talkativeness), and dullness of mind.[31]

Closely related to gluttony is the sin of drunkenness—the immoderate desire for and consumption of alcohol. Like gluttony, drunkenness can be a mortal sin when a person "willingly and knowingly deprives himself of the use of reason, whereby he performs virtuous deeds and avoids sin."[32] By impairing their reason, people who indulge in drunkenness greatly increase their risk of falling into other sins.

Since gluttony and drunkenness are principally sins against *temperance*, they are best combated by exercising self-control and self-denial, especially through acts of abstinence, fasting, and prayer—for which the season of Lent is particularly fitting. However, since ascetic practices alone have limited effectiveness in restraining bodily cravings (Col 2:23), St. Paul reminds Christians: "Live by the Spirit and you will certainly not gratify the desire of the flesh" (Gal 5:16 NABRE). Paul urges us to set our minds not on the things of the flesh but on the things of the Spirit (Rom 8:5–13; Eph 5:18–20). Sometimes the support of a counselor or a twelve-step group can be essential in helping a person overcome addiction to food or drink.

V.J. Fearing the Lord, Keeping the Law, and Trusting in Divine Providence (32:14–33:17)

> [14]He who fears the Lord will accept his discipline,
> and those who rise early to seek him will find favor.

---

29. Thomas Aquinas, *Summa Theologiae* II-II q. 148 a. 2.
30. Thomas Aquinas, *Summa Theologiae* II-II q. 148 a. 4.
31. Gregory the Great, *Moralia on Job* 31.45; Thomas Aquinas, *Summa Theologiae* II-II q. 148 a. 6.
32. Thomas Aquinas, *Summa Theologiae* II-II q. 150 a. 2 (trans. Fathers of the English Dominican Province [New York: Benziger Bros., 1948]).

¹⁵He who seeks the law will be filled with it,
  but the hypocrite will stumble at it.
¹⁶Those who fear the Lord will form true judgments,
  and like a light they will kindle righteous deeds.
¹⁷A sinful man will shun reproof,
  and will find a decision according to his liking.

¹⁸A man of judgment will not overlook an idea,
  and an insolent and proud man will not cower in fear.
¹⁹Do nothing without deliberation;
  and when you have acted, do not regret it.
²⁰Do not go on a path full of hazards,
  and do not stumble over stony ground.
²¹Do not be overconfident on a smooth way,
  ²²and give good heed to your paths.
²³Guard yourself in every act,
  for this is the keeping of the commandments.

²⁴He who believes the law gives heed to the commandments,
  and he who trusts the Lord will not suffer loss.
³³:¹No evil will befall the man who fears the Lord,
  but in trial he will deliver him again and again.
²A wise man will not hate the law,
  but he who is hypocritical about it is like a boat in a storm.
³A man of understanding will trust in the law;
  for him the law is as dependable as an inquiry by means of Urim.

⁴Prepare what to say, and thus you will be heard;
  bind together your instruction, and make your answer.
⁵The heart of a fool is like a cart wheel,
  and his thoughts like a turning axle.
⁶A stallion is like a mocking friend;
  he neighs under every one who sits on him.

⁷Why is any day better than another,
  when all the daylight in the year is from the sun?
⁸By the Lord's decision they were distinguished,
  and he appointed the different seasons and feasts;
⁹some of them he exalted and hallowed,
  and some of them he made ordinary days.
¹⁰All men are from the ground,
  and Adam was created of the dust.
¹¹In the fulness of his knowledge the Lord distinguished them
  and appointed their different ways;
¹²some of them he blessed and exalted,
  and some of them he made holy and brought near to himself;

but some of them he cursed and brought low,
   and he turned them out of their place.
¹³As clay in the hand of the potter—
   for all his ways are as he pleases—
so men are in the hand of him who made them,
   to give them as he decides.

¹⁴Good is the opposite of evil,
   and life the opposite of death;
so the sinner is the opposite of the godly.
¹⁵Look upon all the works of the Most High;
   they likewise are in pairs, one the opposite of the other.
¹⁶I was the last on watch;
   I was like one who gleans after the grape-gatherers;
by the blessing of the Lord I excelled,
   and like a grape-gatherer I filled my wine press.
¹⁷Consider that I have not labored for myself alone,
   but for all who seek instruction.

OT: Deut 30:15–20; Ps 119:105; Prov 6:23; Wis 1:12–14; Sir 2:16; 15:1
NT: Matt 7:13–14; 23:23–28; James 1:23–24
Catechism: the two ways, 1696; the law as way to life, 2052–74

Ben Sira now reflects on the fear of the Lord and the †Torah as guide to right   **32:14–15**
living. Life is best lived by honoring God and keeping his commandments
(32:14–33:17; Eccles 12:13). **He who fears the Lord** demonstrates true honor and
reverence by accepting the Lord's **discipline** (Hebrew *musar*; Greek *paideia*)—his
training, correction, or chastening (Sir 4:17; 18:14; Prov 3:11–12; Heb 12:5–6).³³
Those who earnestly **rise early to seek him**, therefore, **will find favor** with God
(Sir 4:12; 6:36; 39:5). **He who seeks the law** by studying it and searching out its
meaning (Eccles 1:13; Ezra 7:10) **will be filled with** its wisdom and nourished by
it as he learns to master it and put it into practice. In contrast, **the hypocrite**—
who may study the Torah but has no intention of observing it, or does so only to
gain human approval—**will stumble** and be ensnared by it (Hebrew, NABRE).
Anyone who does not genuinely value God's law cannot truly grow in character
and will ultimately suffer loss (Matt 23:23–28; James 1:23–24).

   Those who fear the Lord and observe the law **will form true judgments**   **32:16–17**
and know what is right and just (Prov 28:5). Since the Torah is a guiding **light**
(Ps 119:105; Prov 6:23), those who follow it **will kindle righteous deeds**—that
is, they will produce good works that shine as light (Hebrew: "will bring forth
much wisdom from their heart") (Matt 5:14–16). **A sinful man**, however, shuns
reproof—despising criticism and correction—and prefers to make decisions

33. For more on the Hebrew word *musar*, see the commentary on the prologue and on 6:20–22.

according to his liking (Hebrew: "and forces the law to suit his purpose"). Rather than obeying the Torah, he reinterprets it to justify his own lifestyle.

32:18   While a wise person with **judgment** is humble enough to consider someone else's **idea**, suggestion, or warning—coming, for example, from one's spouse, children, or subordinate—**an insolent and proud man** is not deterred by a healthy **fear** of negative outcomes (Hebrew: "a scorner will not receive instruction") and does whatever seems right to him (Prov 12:15).

32:19–20 It is a mark of wisdom to **do nothing without deliberation** and to think carefully before acting (37:16), then not to **regret** the action by looking back and changing one's mind. By contrast, it is foolish to **go on a path full of hazards** by choosing a dangerous course of action that may lead to stumbling **over stony ground** (Hebrew: "do not stumble over an obstacle twice," i.e., by repeating the same mistake).

32:21–24 The wise person should **not be overconfident** on an apparently safe but unfamiliar road; instead, he should consider carefully his **paths**, for they may hide unexpected dangers. **Guard yourself in every act** by being cautious in all that you do; **the commandments** call for such prudence (Deut 4:9; Prov 16:17; 19:16). Conversely, one **who believes the law gives heed to the commandments** (Hebrew: "He who keeps the Torah guards his soul"), and one who **trusts the Lord will not suffer loss** (Hebrew: "will not be put to shame"). In other words, accepting the authority of the divine law, observing the commandments, and trusting the Lord forms a hedge of protection that enables the just person to flourish (2:16; 15:1; 19:20).

In the Light of Christ (32:14–24)

Like most authors of the Old Testament, Ben Sira is unaware of rewards and punishments after death. Following Deuteronomy's law of retribution (Deut 28) and like Proverbs (Prov 24:12), he therefore expects God's justice, which rewards the righteous and punishes the wicked, to be fulfilled in this life. While often this works out in practice, sometimes it does not. God's perfect justice, which often remains shrouded in mystery in this life, is more fully revealed in the later Old Testament understanding of life after death (Wis 3:1–10; Dan 12:2–3), and even more so with the New Testament promise that rewards and punishments will be meted out at the final judgment. The fuller revelation in Christ teaches that God's perfect justice ultimately prevails, partly in this life and fully in the next (Matt 16:27; Rom 2:6–11; Rev 20:12).

33:1–3   Ben Sira develops the thought of the previous verse: **no evil will befall** or hurt the one **who fears the Lord**. Although such a person will not always be shielded from **trial** or temptation, God will keep him safe and **deliver him**, especially against moral evil (Job 5:19; Prov 12:21). Thus **a wise man will not hate** but love **the law**, because he understands that it is the key to a flourishing, secure life in communion with God. Those who are **hypocritical about** the law, however, giving it lip service but not observing it, are **like a boat in a storm**, tossed around by life and unstable in all that they do. A sensible person relies on **the law** because it is **as dependable as an inquiry by means of Urim**. The Urim and the Thummim were sacred objects worn in the high priest's breastplate and used to determine God's will (Sir 45:10; Exod 28:30; 1 Sam 14:41).[34] The Torah is thus the sure way to discern the Lord's will.

When you are asked to speak, **prepare** and think in advance what you plan to say so that you may **be heard** and respected; draw from **your instruction**, training, and experience to **answer** those who question you. Do not be like **a fool**, whose **heart** is **like a cart wheel** with **thoughts** going round and round **like a turning axle** because he has not prepared what he wants to say, constantly changing his mind. A **mocking friend** is just as unreliable: like **a stallion** that **neighs under every one who sits on him**, he either praises or objects to whomever is speaking, lacking clear convictions. **33:4–6**

While Ben Sira generally emphasizes human free will by reminding his readers that they can *choose* to pursue wisdom, in the next section he explains that the world consists of many contrasting things and people because of divine predestination (33:7–15). **33:7–9**

Why is any day better or holier (i.e., the Sabbath and religious holidays) **than another,** when all **daylight** comes **from the sun** and all days appear to be the same? **By the Lord's decision** (Greek: "knowledge"; Hebrew: "wisdom") he **distinguished** various days and **appointed different seasons** and Jewish **feasts** such as Passover, Pentecost, and Tabernacles, which **he exalted and hallowed** to reveal his purposes to Israel and the world (Gen 2:3; Lev 23; Deut 16:1–17).

Just as all days seem the same, so **all** human beings are also created equal **from the ground**, like **Adam**, who was **created of the dust** of the earth and returned to it when he died (Gen 2:7; 3:19; Job 10:9; Eccles 3:20). Yet in his infinite **knowledge the Lord distinguished** people from one another and **appointed their different ways**, granting them distinct roles, functions, and destinies. **33:10–11**

Some, such as the people of Israel, **he blessed and exalted** (Gen 12:2; Exod 19:5–6; 32:13); **some**, such as the Aaronic priests (Exod 28:1), **he made holy and brought near to himself**. Others, such as the Canaanites, **he cursed and brought low** by expelling them from **their place** because of their wickedness (Gen 9:25; Lev 18:24–30; Deut 18:9–12). Although the Lord chooses some people to receive **33:12–13**

---

34. It is unclear whether the Urim and Thummim were still in use in Ben Sira's time. There is no clear evidence of their use after the time of King David, though Ezra 2:63 and Neh 7:65 attest to their continued significance in the †postexilic period.

a unique calling, those who are cursed have brought this upon themselves by freely choosing to do evil. Nevertheless, God is sovereign over all his creatures: **As clay** is **in the hand of the potter**—to be molded **as he pleases**—**so** people and their destinies **are in the hand of** God, **who made them**; they will receive whatever **he decides** according to his just judgment (Isa 29:16; 45:9; Jer 18:4; Rom 9:21). The Catechism explains the interplay between human freedom and God's sovereignty: "To God, all moments of time are present in their immediacy. When therefore he establishes his eternal plan of 'predestination,' he includes in it each person's free response to his grace" (Catechism 600).

33:14–15   **Good is the opposite of evil, and life the opposite of death; so the sinner is the opposite of the godly.** These three pairs of opposites are not metaphysical necessities in the world (as some forms of Gnosticism hold), since God declared his creation to be "very good" (Gen 1:31; Catechism 339). While the material world reflects God's goodness, life, and excellence, the presence of evil, death, and sin in creation is the result of humanity's tragic ethical choices (Gen 3:1–7; Wis 1:12–14). In other words, while Christianity rejects *metaphysical dualism* (the notion that good and evil, life and death are necessary aspects of existence), it acknowledges the reality of *ethical dualism*—that every person faces a decisive moral choice between two ways, **one the opposite of the other**—as stated in the ancient *Didache*: "There are two ways, the one of life, the other of death; but between the two, there is a great difference."[35]

33:16–17   Ben Sira briefly reflects on his own calling and on how he acquired his wisdom. He considers himself **the last on watch** in a succession of wisdom teachers, gleaning knowledge from the wisdom of his predecessors **like one who gleans after the grape-gatherers**. Yet he does not give himself credit for his own excellence but attributes it to **the blessing of the Lord**, for **like a grape-gatherer** he **filled** his **wine press** of wisdom (Prov 9:1–5) from the study of Scripture and Israel's tradition. Moreover, he labored not for himself **alone**, merely to satisfy his curiosity or to win fame, but for the benefit of **all who seek instruction** (Sir 24:34).[36] Ben Sira's earnest desire to educate and edify others through his work offers a praiseworthy model for parents, teachers, and evangelists to emulate.

---

35. *Didache* 1.1; see also Deut 30:15–20; Matt 7:13–14; Catechism 1696.
36. Sir 33:17 (RSV-2CE) is numbered 33:17–18 in most other versions (NRSV, ESV-CE, NABRE, NJB).

Part VI

Sirach 33:18–38:23

In Part VI, Ben Sira addresses some topics that are unique to him and not discussed elsewhere in the Bible. The first is his concern for maintaining financial and material autonomy to avoid becoming dependent on others (33:18–23), along with his rather harsh view on disciplining slaves (33:24–31). His skepticism toward dreams (34:1–8) and his praise of travel as a means of growing in the fear of the Lord (34:9–17) are also topics unique to him. Ben Sira further expresses concern for true worship, achieved by offering worthy sacrifices (34:18–35:11) and humble prayers that prompt the Lord to act (35:12–20). An example of a rich prayer follows, in which Ben Sira pleads with God that he would deliver Israel from her foreign oppressors (36:1–17). He also offers unique advice on wisely choosing a wife, friends, and counselors in a world where not everyone can be trusted (36:18–37:15); discerning between true and false wisdom (37:16–26); exercising temperance in eating (37:27–31); honoring physicians (38:1–8); and dealing with sickness (38:9–15) and death (38:16–23).

VI.A. Maintaining Independence and Disciplining Slaves (33:18–31)[1]

> [18]Hear me, you who are great among the people,
>   and you leaders of the congregation, listen.
>
> [19]To son or wife, to brother or friend,
>   do not give power over yourself, as long as you live;
>   and do not give your property to another,
>   lest you change your mind and must ask for it.

---

1. Most other translations use different verse numbers for the remainder of this chapter: Sir 33:18–31 (RSV-2CE) is 33:19–33 in other versions (NRSV, ESV-CE, NABRE, NJB).

²⁰While you are still alive and have breath in you,
   do not let any one take your place.
²¹For it is better that your children should ask from you
   than that you should look to the hand of your sons.
²²Excel in all that you do;
   bring no stain upon your honor.
²³At the time when you end the days of your life,
   in the hour of death, distribute your inheritance.

²⁴Fodder and a stick and burdens for a donkey;
   bread and discipline and work for a servant.
²⁵Set your slave to work, and you will find rest;
   leave his hands idle, and he will seek liberty.
²⁶Yoke and thong will bow the neck,
   and for a wicked servant there are racks and tortures.
²⁷Put him to work, that he may not be idle,
   for idleness teaches much evil.
²⁸Set him to work, as is fitting for him,
   and if he does not obey, make his chains heavy.
²⁹Do not act immoderately toward anybody,
   and do nothing without discretion.

³⁰If you have a servant, let him be as yourself,
   because you have bought him with blood.
³¹If you have a servant, treat him as a brother,
   for as your own soul you will need him.
If you ill-treat him, and he leaves and runs away,
   which way will you go to seek him?

OT: Exod 21:1–11; 23:12; Lev 25:39–51; Deut 15:12–18; 23:15–16
NT: 1 Cor 7:20–24; Eph 6:5–9; Col 3:22–4:1; Philem 10–18; 1 Pet 2:18–21
Catechism: slavery, 2414

33:18–19 Ben Sira advises people of prominence and **leaders of the congregation**—perhaps the religious or secular leaders of the Jewish community—to preserve their property and personal independence (33:18–23). It is unwise to hand over control prematurely, even to those closest to you, such as **son or wife**, **brother or friend**, giving them the **power** to administer your affairs or make decisions for you while you are still alive. Nor should you **give your property** or personal belongings **to another, lest you** later **change your mind** and need to reclaim them. Ben Sira is not advising against generosity but against prematurely bestowing assets in a way that would make one needlessly dependent on others.

33:20–21 The more prudent course of action **while you are still alive** is to **not let any one take your place**—that is, not let others control your life by allowing them to acquire your possessions. It is **better that your children should ask** for your assistance than that you become needy and reliant on **your sons** to provide for your needs, becoming financially dependent on them (2 Cor 12:14).

Excel in all that you do: the Hebrew and Syriac versions read, "Keep control over all your affairs" (NABRE), which better fits the context. **Bring no stain upon your honor** by becoming dependent on your children in your old age. Instead, wait until the **end** of **the days of your life**—that is, **the hour of death**—to **distribute your inheritance** to your heirs. This advice implies that written wills were not common in Israel in Ben Sira's day, and that fathers typically distributed their inheritance orally when they were close to death. **33:22–23**

Ben Sira's instructions on the treatment of domestic servants[2] reflect the harshness of a culture in which slavery was common. He advocates severity toward the lazy or wicked slave (33:24–28) and kindness toward the good slave (33:29–31). The comparison of **a servant** to **a donkey** illustrates the demeaning nature of human slavery, which the Old Testament regulated but still tolerated (see the Reflection and Application section below). Just as the donkey is fed with **fodder**, chastised with **a stick**, and given **burdens** to carry, the domestic servant is fed with **bread**, chastised with **discipline**, and given **work** to do (Prov 26:3). **33:24**

Ben Sira advises a master to set his **slave to work** to avoid trouble and **find rest**, for if the servant remains **idle**, he will have the time and opportunity to **seek liberty** and escape. Just as a **yoke and thong** (or "harness") **will bow the neck** of a beast of burden and keep it under control, a rebellious and **wicked servant** is disciplined through **racks and tortures** (or "stocks and chastisements") (Luke 12:46). Although such practices are harsh and shocking by modern standards, Israelite law placed limits on the punishment of servants, prohibited their mistreatment, and protected their rights. A master who struck and killed his slave was to be punished; if he seriously injured the slave, the slave was to be freed (Exod 21:20, 26–27). Nevertheless, it was in the master's best interest to put his domestic servant **to work, that he may not be idle**, as from the master's perspective **idleness teaches much evil**—in other words, it gives the servant an opportunity to cause trouble. If the servant **does not obey**, the master is advised to **make his chains heavy** to prevent rebellion or escape. **33:25–28**

However, a householder should avoid being excessively harsh toward his slaves. He must **not act immoderately toward anybody**—including his servants—and should exercise **discretion** and good judgment in all things. He should view **a servant** as himself, for he has **bought him with blood**—that is, with his own livelihood. Indeed, a master should treat his servant **as a brother**, for as his **own soul** he **will need him** and his faithful service (7:20–21). If the master were to **ill-treat him**, the domestic might escape, making it difficult to **seek him** and get him back. Although no master desired his slaves to escape, the **33:29–31**

---

2. Although the RSV-2CE translates the Greek word *oiketēs* as (domestic) "servant," the term refers not to a paid household worker, as in modern English, but to an unpaid and owned slave.

†Torah forbids Israelites from returning runaway slaves to their former masters or oppressing them (Deut 23:15-16; Philem 10-18). This was unprecedented in the ancient world, where law codes often imposed harsh penalties—even death—on those who aided a slave's escape.[3]

Reflection and Application (33:18-31)

The modern reader might find it ironic that Ben Sira advocates for both the financial independence of congregational leaders and the harsh treatment of slaves within the same context. Ancient societies were not egalitarian, and most relied on slavery to function. Most slaves were prisoners of war, though some sold themselves into slavery to settle debts, became slaves as punishment for crimes, or were born into slavery. The Bible accepts slavery as part of the social order; yet it is also the primary human condition from which God delivers his people. Indeed, God's liberation of the Israelites from Egyptian slavery became the paradigmatic model of his salvation (Exod 20:2). Paradoxically, the Lord refers to the Israelites whom he redeemed as "my slaves" (Lev 25:55), emphasizing that true freedom comes from serving him.

The institution of slavery, like other societal ills such as divorce, poverty, and war, has no place in God's plan of salvation for humanity. Yet because of the hardness of the human heart (Matt 19:8), God tolerated some evils in Old Testament times, regulating them to reduce and ultimately eliminate them. This is why the Old Testament contains "matters imperfect and provisional" (Catechism 122) that would be later perfected in the fullness of God's revelation in Christ.

Although the Old Testament does not condemn slavery, it provides regulations for the fair treatment of both Israelite and non-Israelite slaves (Exod 21:1-11; Lev 25:39-51). Slaves were permitted to share in the Passover meal (Exod 12:44) and participate in the religious life of their household (Deut 12:12, 18; 16:11, 14), and they were required to rest on the Sabbath (Exod 20:10; 23:12; Deut 5:14). Hebrew slaves were to be released after six years of service (Exod 21:2) and during the Year of Jubilee (Lev 25:40). These regulations for the just treatment of slaves—extraordinary for their time—represent the early recognition of slavery as an evil, a truth that the Church (and most modern societies) fully recognized much later, after centuries of reflection on biblical teaching.

---

3. See Muhammad A. Dandamayev, "Slavery (Ancient Near East)," in *Anchor Bible Dictionary*, ed. David Noel Freedman (New York: Doubleday, 1992), 6:58–62. Code of Hammurabi, 15–16, in William W. Hallo and K. Lawson Younger, *The Context of Scripture*, vol. 2, *Monumental Inscriptions from the Biblical World* (Leiden: Brill, 2000), 338.

The New Testament also takes the institution of slavery for granted. However, the trajectory of deliverance from slavery is evident in the ministry of Jesus, who came to "proclaim release to the captives" (Luke 4:18–19). While slaves are still instructed to obey their masters (1 Cor 7:20–24; Eph 6:5–9; Col 3:22–4:1; 1 Pet 2:18–21), Paul urges Philemon to treat his fugitive slave Onesimus "no longer as a slave" but as "a beloved brother" (Philem 16). Thus, the gospel foreshadows a more egalitarian and just society in which slavery has no place. In Christ Jesus, there is "neither slave nor free" (Gal 3:28; Col 3:11), and the experience of Christian discipleship as a form of servitude to Christ becomes a privilege and honor (Matt 10:24–25; Mark 10:42–44; Luke 17:7–10; Rom 1:1).

On the basis of the seventh commandment, which prohibits stealing—including the "stealing" of humans (Exod 20:15)—the Church today categorically denounces the enslavement of human beings as a grave sin against their dignity and fundamental rights:

> The seventh commandment forbids acts or enterprises that for any reason—selfish or ideological, commercial, or totalitarian—lead to the *enslavement of human beings*, to their being bought, sold and exchanged like merchandise, in disregard for their personal dignity. It is a sin against the dignity of persons and their fundamental rights to reduce them by violence to their productive value or to a source of profit. (Catechism 2414)

VI.B. Do Not Trust in Dreams; Travel and Fear of the Lord (34:1–17)

¹A man of no understanding has vain and false hopes,
　　and dreams give wings to fools.
²As one who catches at a shadow and pursues the wind,
　　so is he who gives heed to dreams.
³The vision of dreams is this against that,
　　the likeness of a face confronting a face.
⁴From an unclean thing what will be made clean?
　　And from something false what will be true?
⁵Divinations and omens and dreams are folly,
　　and like a woman with labor pains the mind has fancies.
⁶Unless they are sent from the Most High as a visitation,
　　do not give your mind to them.
⁷For dreams have deceived many,
　　and those who put their hope in them have failed.
⁸Without such deceptions the law will be fulfilled,
　　and wisdom is made perfect in truthful lips.

⁹An educated man knows many things,
　　and one with much experience will speak with understanding.

¹⁰He that is inexperienced knows few things,
    but he that has traveled acquires much cleverness.
¹¹I have seen many things in my travels,
    and I understand more than I can express.
¹²I have often been in danger of death,
    but have escaped because of these experiences.

¹³The spirit of those who fear the Lord will live,
    for their hope is in him who saves them.
¹⁴He who fears the Lord will not be timid,
    nor play the coward, for he is his hope.
¹⁵Blessed is the soul of the man who fears the Lord!
    To whom does he look? And who is his support?
¹⁶The eyes of the Lord are upon those who love him,
    a mighty protection and strong support,
a shelter from the hot wind and a shade from noonday sun,
    a guard against stumbling and a defense against falling.
¹⁷He lifts up the soul and gives light to the eyes;
    he grants healing, life, and blessing.

OT: Lev 19:26; Deut 18:10–14; Ps 112:1–9; Jer 23:25–27; 29:8–9
NT: Matt 1:20–24; 2:12–13, 19–22; Acts 16:16–18
Catechism: fallen angels, 391–95; divination, 2116

34:1–3   Although the Bible recounts several instances of God speaking through dreams, Ben Sira warns against trusting in dreams, divinations, and omens to determine the future or the will of God (34:1–8). **A man of no understanding** harbors **vain and false hopes** that are not grounded in reality and have no chance of coming to pass; **dreams give wings to fools**, as they are often the subconscious product of one's own imagination. Trusting in dreams is as foolish as trying to grasp at **a shadow** or pursue **the wind** (Eccles 1:14; 2:17): such actions are the most futile of endeavors and amount to nothing more than chasing fantasies. **The vision of dreams is this against that**—the reflection of the dreamer's own wishful thinking—as is **the likeness of a face confronting a face** in a mirror (Prov 27:19).

34:4–5   Just as **an unclean thing** can never make something else **clean**, and just as **something false** can never produce something **true**, a vivid dream does not create reality. Trusting in dreams is as foolish as trusting in **divinations** (attempts to gain supernatural knowledge or predict the future by occult means) **and omens** (which involve interpreting natural signs or events as predictors of future outcomes, such as finding meaning in the flight of birds). The †Torah strictly prohibits such occult practices (Lev 19:26; Deut 18:10–14; Jer 29:8; Acts 16:16–18). Like a feverish **woman** in labor who suffers from illusions while giving birth, **the mind has fancies** that have nothing to do with reality and thus should not be trusted.

On Discerning Dreams

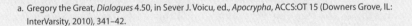

LIVING TRADITION

St. Gregory the Great identifies six sources of dreams. Drawing from Sirach's warning, he advises exercising prudence and careful discernment before placing trust in them.

Know that the images that occur in dreams can be impressed on the soul in six different ways. Sometimes dreams are caused by bad digestion or by fasting, at times they are the fruit of an illusion, at other times of reflection and illusion together, at still other times of revelation, and, finally, at times of reflection and revelation together. Everyone experiences the first two types. The other four we find in the pages of sacred Scripture. If, in fact, dreams were not for the most part provoked by the hidden enemy through an illusion, the wise man would not have put us on guard, saying, "Dreams have led many into error, and those who put their hope in them have gone astray" (Sir 34:7).... Clearly, precisely because dreams have such different characteristics and origins, the more difficult it is to discern what their source is, the less should one be inclined to put faith in them. The saints, however, by a special sensibility they possess, are able to distinguish between illusions and revelations and to penetrate the meaning of the words and images in visions. Thus they know either what they have received from the good spirit or what illusion they have been victimized by. But if a soul is not prudent regarding dreams, it will find itself lost in a forest of vanity through the work of the deceiving spirit, whose art it is at times to predict many true things, so as to then imprison the soul in the snare of a single lie.[a]

a. Gregory the Great, *Dialogues* 4.50, in Sever J. Voicu, ed., *Apocrypha*, ACCS:OT 15 (Downers Grove, IL: InterVarsity, 2010), 341–42.

Ben Sira recognizes that some dreams may be **sent from the Most High as a** **34:6–7** **visitation**—as seen throughout the Bible.[4] Yet he does not provide any guidelines for discerning whether or not a dream comes from God, and his general rule of thumb remains: **do not give your mind** or pay attention to a dream unless there is compelling evidence that it was sent by God. **For dreams have deceived many**—as attested elsewhere in Scripture (Jer 23:25–27; 29:8–9)—**and those who put their hope in them** were bitterly disappointed when they realized they had been led astray by their own wishful thinking.

Without the **deceptions** of fleeting dreams that arise from the subconscious, **34:8** **the law will be fulfilled** through conscious and intentional obedience to the Lord's commandments, for **wisdom is made perfect in truthful lips** that speak honestly. Wisdom is attained not by relying on dreams but by faithfully adhering to the Torah and speaking truthfully.

Another way of gaining experience and wisdom is through travel (34:9–12). **34:9–10** Unlike the dreamer, **an educated** or well-traveled person **knows many things,**

4. Gen 28:10–17; 31:10–13; 37:5–10; 41:1–32; Dan 2:1–19, 27–45; Matt 1:20–24; 2:12–13, 19–22.

and one with much experience, having acquired broad insights from many people on his journeys, **will speak with understanding** and wisdom. While an **inexperienced** person, being untried or untested, **knows few things,** one who **has traveled,** having had many opportunities to develop skill and resourcefulness, **acquires much cleverness** by putting that wisdom into practice.

34:11–12   Switching to the first person, Ben Sira includes a brief autobiographical note, explaining that the **many things** he has seen in his **travels** have broadened his perspective and given him a wealth of understanding, for which he is grateful. Though he often has found himself **in danger of death,** he believes he **escaped** partly due to the **experiences** he gained throughout his travels (51:13).

34:13–15   Ben Sira ultimately attributes his deliverance from danger not to his own cleverness but to the Lord, whom he fears. He describes the blessings of those who fear the Lord and trust in him (34:13–17). **The spirit of those who fear the Lord will live,** even when faced with life-threatening dangers, **for their hope is** firmly rooted not in elusive dreams (34:1) but in God, **who saves them.** One **who fears the Lord** is neither **timid** nor a **coward** but finds great courage in God and thus does not fear life's perils, for the Lord **is his hope** (see the commentary on 2:15–18). For this reason, **blessed is the soul** of one **who fears the Lord:** this person steadfastly looks to God and relies on him as his only **support.** The fear of the Lord is not a servile fear but a deep reverence that elicits God's blessings (Ps 112:1–9).

34:16–17   Ben Sira employs familiar biblical metaphors to describe the Lord's providence over those who fear him: his **eyes are upon those who love him** (15:19; Pss 33:18; 34:15); he is **a mighty protection and strong support** for his people (Pss 18:2–3; 61:3–4; 91:1–4; Prov 30:5). He is a **shelter from the hot wind and a shade from noonday sun,** which can quickly induce dehydration and sunstroke (Ps 121:5–6; Isa 4:6; 25:4–5). He is also **a guard against stumbling and a defense against falling** (Pss 91:11–12; 121:3). The Lord, moreover, **lifts up the soul** (Sir 40:26) **and gives light to the eyes** (Pss 13:3, 36:9; Prov 15:30), bestowing cheerfulness and happiness upon those who love and fear him, along with **healing** (Ps 30:2), **life, and blessing** (Pss 21:4; 36:9; 133:3)—the fullness of his gifts to humankind.

Reflection and Application (34:1–17)

The modern decline of Christianity in Western nations has been accompanied by a resurgence of pagan and occult practices, which remain common throughout the world. Yet those who pride themselves on being "spiritual but not religious" often overlook the fact that Satan and his demons are also "spiritual but not religious" (Catechism 391–95). The Church continues to forbid occult practices for the same reasons that the †Torah does: these practices not only constitute an attempt at "playing God" by seeking supernatural knowledge of the future, but also they open the door to deceptive and dangerous demonic activity that leads the soul away from God and his salvation:

> All forms of *divination* are to be rejected: recourse to Satan or demons, conjuring up the dead or other practices falsely supposed to "unveil" the future (Deut 18:10; Jer 29:8). Consulting horoscopes, astrology, palm reading, interpretation of omens and lots, the phenomena of clairvoyance, and recourse to mediums all conceal a desire for power over time, history, and, in the last analysis, other human beings, as well as a wish to conciliate hidden powers. They contradict the honor, respect, and loving fear that we owe to God alone. (Catechism 2116)

VI.C. True Worship: Worthy Sacrifices, Virtuous Life, and Humble Prayer (34:18–35:20)

¹⁸If one sacrifices from what has been wrongfully obtained, the
offering is blemished;
the gifts of the lawless are not acceptable.
¹⁹The Most High is not pleased with the offerings of the ungodly;
and he is not propitiated for sins by a multitude of sacrifices.
²⁰Like one who kills a son before his father's eyes
is the man who offers a sacrifice from the property of the poor.
²¹The bread of the needy is the life of the poor;
whoever deprives them of it is a man of blood.
²²To take away a neighbor's living is to murder him;
to deprive an employee of his wages is to shed blood.

²³When one builds and another tears down,
what do they gain but toil?
²⁴When one prays and another curses,
to whose voice will the Lord listen?
²⁵If a man washes after touching a dead body, and touches it again,
what has he gained by his washing?
²⁶So if a man fasts for his sins,
and goes again and does the same things,
who will listen to his prayer?
And what has he gained by humbling himself?

^{35:1}He who keeps the law makes many offerings;
he who heeds the commandments sacrifices a peace offering.
²He who returns a kindness offers fine flour,
and he who gives alms sacrifices a thank offering.
³To keep from wickedness is pleasing to the Lord,
and to forsake unrighteousness is atonement.
⁴Do not appear before the Lord empty-handed,
⁵for all these things are to be done because of the commandment.

⁶The offering of a righteous man anoints the altar,
  and its pleasing odor rises before the Most High.
⁷The sacrifice of a righteous man is acceptable,
  and the memory of it will not be forgotten.
⁸Glorify the Lord generously,
  and do not stint the first fruits of your hands.
⁹With every gift show a cheerful face,
  and dedicate your tithe with gladness.
¹⁰Give to the Most High as he has given,
  and as generously as your hand has found.
¹¹For the Lord is the one who repays,
  and he will repay you sevenfold.

¹²Do not offer him a bribe, for he will not accept it;
  and do not trust to an unrighteous sacrifice;
for the Lord is the judge,
  and with him is no partiality.
¹³He will not show partiality in the case of a poor man;
  and he will listen to the prayer of one who is wronged.
¹⁴He will not ignore the supplication of the fatherless,
  nor the widow when she pours out her story.
¹⁵Do not the tears of the widow run down her cheek
  as she cries out against him who has caused them to fall?
¹⁶He whose service is pleasing to the Lord will be accepted,
  and his prayer will reach to the clouds.
¹⁷The prayer of the humble pierces the clouds,
  and he will not be consoled until it reaches the Lord;
he will not desist until the Most High visits him,
  and the just judge executes judgment.
¹⁸And the Lord will not delay,
  neither will he be patient with them,
till he crushes the loins of the unmerciful
  and repays vengeance on the nations;
till he takes away the multitude of the insolent,
  and breaks the scepters of the unrighteous;
¹⁹till he repays man according to his deeds,
  and the works of men according to their devices;
till he judges the case of his people
  and makes them rejoice in his mercy.
²⁰Mercy is as welcome when he afflicts them
  as clouds of rain in the time of drought.

OT: 1 Sam 15:22; Pss 34:6; 50:8–15; Isa 1:11–13; Jer 14:12; Amos 5:21–24
NT: Luke 1:71–75; Acts 10:34; Rom 2:11
Catechism: true worship and the virtue of religion, 2095–105
Lectionary: 35:12–14, 16–17: 30th Sunday in Ordinary Time (Year C)

In Ben Sira's day, Jewish worship was centered on the offering of sacrifices in　34:18–19
the Jerusalem temple. Like the prophets who preceded him, he criticizes those
who offer sacrifices with an improper inner disposition or a disregard for social justice (34:18–26). Such offerings are empty rituals that the Lord does not
accept (1 Sam 15:22; Isa 1:11–13; Hosea 6:6; Amos 5:21–24). **If one sacrifices**
an animal that was stolen or otherwise **wrongfully obtained, the offering is**
blemished—rendered as if it were physically defective—and thus unfit for sacrifice (Lev 22:18–25; Deut 15:21; Mal 1:8). **The gifts of the lawless**—those who
disregard either the ritual or moral precepts of the †Torah—**are not acceptable**
to God **the Most High** (Prov 15:8; 21:27). He is **not propitiated for sins** (i.e., he
does not forgive sins) simply by receiving **a multitude of sacrifices**. The proper
disposition of the offerer is more important than the number of sacrifices offered
(Sir 5:6; 7:9; Ps 50:8–15; Catechism 2100).

Like one who kills a son before his father's eyes**—a shocking comparison　34:20–22
alluding to the fate of King Zedekiah in 2 Kings 25:6–7—is the individual **who**
offers a sacrifice stolen from **the poor**. Such an offering is an abomination to
the Lord because it deprives the poor of their livelihood—and God is, after
all, the Father of the poor and needy (Ps 68:5). **The bread of the needy** is not
a luxury but the very **life of the poor**, essential for their survival. Therefore,
whoever deprives them of their sustenance by stealing from them is **a man**
of blood—that is, a murderer. The same applies to taking away **a neighbor's**
livelihood or depriving **an employee of his wages** (Sir 4:1–6; Lev 19:13; Deut
24:14–15; James 5:4).

Three pairs of opposite actions underline the principle that a good act is　34:23–26
canceled out by its opposite: **When one builds and another tears down**, the
one who builds has labored in vain and accomplished nothing. **When one prays**
and another curses, two contradictory petitions rise to the Lord. If someone
washes after touching a dead body (a source of ritual impurity, Num 19:11–12)
but then **touches it again**, he becomes ritually unclean again. Similarly, **if a**
man fasts for his sins but then repeats the same offenses, the penitential act
becomes worthless, and God will not **listen to his prayer**. He has **gained** nothing **by humbling himself**, for God does not listen to the prayers of those who
fail to repent and turn from their sins (Isa 58:3–7; Jer 14:12).

In contrast to the hypocritical behavior depicted above, Ben Sira now de-　35:1
scribes the kind of worship that is acceptable to God (35:1–11). **He who keeps**
the law makes many offerings—which can be interpreted in two ways: (1) One
who keeps the law and **heeds the commandments** will offer the many sacrifices
that the law prescribes, including the **peace offering** that expresses fellowship
with God (Lev 3:1–17). (2) Keeping the ethical commandments of the law is
the spiritual equivalent of offering many sacrifices, including the peace offering.
The concept of spiritual sacrifice gained importance during the exile, when the
temple was temporarily absent, and later when many were too distant to worship

there. This concept becomes central in the New Testament (Rom 12:1–2; Heb 13:16; 1 Pet 2:5). Verses 2–3 seem to favor the second interpretation, while verses 4–11 appear to support the first.

35:2–3 One **who returns a kindness** to others acts as though he **offers fine flour**— that is, a cereal or grain offering—to the Lord (Lev 2:1–16), and one **who gives alms** is like one who **sacrifices a thank offering**—a type of peace offering presented in gratitude to God (Lev 7:12–15). Thus, acts of kindness and almsgiving are equivalent to bringing freewill offerings to God in the temple. The opportunity to offer such spiritual sacrifices would have been significant for Jews living in Alexandria in Ben Sira's time, for whom travel to the temple in Jerusalem was either difficult or impossible. Likewise, refraining **from wickedness** by avoiding sins in the first place is as **pleasing to the Lord** as sacrifices, and forsaking **unrighteousness** altogether is better than seeking **atonement** and forgiveness later by presenting sin offerings to God (5:5; 17:29).

35:4–5 Although Ben Sira emphasizes the spiritual significance of the temple sacrifices, he does not lessen the obligation of his fellow Jews to perform the rites of worship prescribed in the Torah. They should not **appear before the Lord** in the temple **empty-handed**, without any sacrifice to offer (7:31; Exod 23:15; 34:20; Deut 16:16), **for all these things**—the sacrifices—are to be offered in obedience to **the commandment**—that is, the whole body of legislation concerning the private sacrifices that Israelites were to offer in the temple (Lev 1–7).

35:6–7 **The offering** of a just person **anoints** (literally, "greases") **the altar** with the fat dripping from the burning animals, **and its pleasing odor rises before the Most High**—a common expression describing sacrifices **acceptable** to the Lord (Lev 1:9, 13). The **memory** of such a sacrifice—referring to the memorial portion of the cereal offering that was mixed with oil and frankincense and burned on the altar (Lev 2:1–2)—is lasting, for **it will not be forgotten** by God.

35:8–11 Ben Sira exhorts the righteous to **glorify the Lord generously** (literally, "with a good eye"; compare Prov 22:9) with sacrifices and not to withhold **the first fruits** or freewill offerings that they are to bring to the Lord (Deut 26:2; Prov 3:9). A gift is most pleasing to God when offered with **a cheerful face** (2 Cor 9:7), and a **tithe**—10 percent of one's harvest or income (Deut 12:6; 14:23; Tob 1:6–7)—when given **with gladness**. Each person is to **give** back to God **as he has given, and as generously** as he is able, as a token of appreciation for God's bountiful blessings. Indeed, **the Lord** can **repay sevenfold** or more those who generously and joyfully offer him worthy gifts (Prov 19:17).

35:12–13 God is perfectly just to all, and especially the humble (35:12–20). He cannot be "bought off" with **a bribe**, nor is his justice compromised by **an unrighteous sacrifice**, as a corrupt judge is swayed by dishonest gifts; **the Lord** is a righteous **judge** who shows **no partiality**. He does not show favoritism when rendering judgment (Deut 10:17; 2 Chron 19:7; Acts 10:34; Rom 2:11), not even by favoring or discriminating against **a poor man** (Lev 19:15). Yet he listens attentively **to the prayer of one who is wronged** or oppressed (Ps 34:6).

God does **not ignore the supplication of the fatherless** or the complaint of   35:14–15
the widow: this divine concern for orphans and widows is often emphasized in the Torah (Exod 22:22–23; Deut 10:17–18; 24:17). Presumably, the two mourn the loss of the same man—their father and husband. The Lord sees the widow's **tears** and hears her cries **against him who has caused** them—perhaps the man who killed her husband, or possibly even God himself.

He whose service is pleasing to the Lord—likely a faithful Jew represent-   35:16–17
ing the people of Israel, oppressed by their enemies (35:18–19)—is **accepted** with favor by God, **and his prayer** (36:1–17), because it is offered in humility, **pierces the clouds** and **reaches the Lord** in heaven. The just Israelite steadfastly perseveres in prayer: he does not rest **until the Most High** answers, **visits him**, and **executes judgment** by punishing Israel's foes and oppressors. While Ben Sira may be referring specifically to the ⁺Seleucids in the early second century BC, the principle of persevering in prayer applies to all generations (Luke 18:1–8).

Ben Sira assures his readers that **the Lord will not delay** in answering the just   35:18–20
person's prayer: he will show no forbearance to the nations that oppress Israel (Luke 1:71–75; 18:7–8) but will crush **the loins of the unmerciful** (compare Deut 33:11), enact **vengeance on the** wicked **nations**, annihilate **the multitude of the insolent** who persecuted his people, and shatter **the scepters of the un-righteous**, thereby ending their domination over others. In the end, God **repays** all nations according to their words and **deeds**; he will judge **the case of his people** Israel with favor, so that they will **rejoice in his mercy** (Hebrew: "in his salvation"; Isa 25:9). The revelation of the Lord's just judgment and **mercy** will be **as welcome** in times of affliction as **clouds of rain** in a devastating **drought** (Ps 72:6; Prov 16:15; Isa 45:8).

Reflection and Application (34:18–35:20)

Today, one hears constant clamors for justice coming from various social movements advocating for equality between groups on the basis of race, gender, or socioeconomic classes. Yet most social justice activists overlook a central aspect of justice: the *virtue of religion*. If justice "consists in the constant and firm will to give their due to God and neighbor," then the virtue of religion focuses on the first part of this definition—justice toward God (Catechism 1807). Modern social justice activists might be surprised to learn that it is impossible to be a truly just person without giving God his due through the virtue of religion.

The word "religion" derives from the Latin *religare* ("to bind together") and points to the relational bond between man and God established through proper divine worship.[5] This bond is grounded in the first commandment of the †Decalogue—"You shall worship the Lord your God and him only shall you serve" (Matt 4:10; Exod 20:2–5; Deut 6:4–5, 13–14)—and in the theological virtues of faith, hope, and love (Catechism 2083–94). The virtue of religion includes acts of devotion (giving oneself steadily to the service of God), adoration (acknowledging and worshiping God alone), prayer (lifting up the mind to God with praise, thanksgiving, intercession, and petition), sacrifice, oblations, and tithes (offering one's possessions to God and his Church), and promises and vows (dedicating oneself or some good work to God).[6]

Perhaps most counterintuitive for people living in a postmodern, pluralistic world is the fact that the virtue of religion cannot be properly practiced in all religions without distinction. In the Old Testament, the prophets viewed the worship of Baal not as a valid "alternative spirituality" but as a grave apostasy from the true worship owed to the God of Israel (1 Kings 18:20–40). Today, offering God genuine worship can occur only within the bounds of the truth that he revealed to humanity through Christ and the Church he founded. Thus, Christians are to "awaken in each man the love of the true and the good" by making known "the worship of the one true religion which subsists in the Catholic and apostolic Church" (Catechism 2105).

VI.D. Prayer for National Deliverance (36:1-17)

[1]Have mercy upon us, O Lord, the God of all, and look upon us,
  and show us the light of your mercy;
[2]send fear of you upon the nations.
[3]Lift up your hand against foreign nations
  and let them see your might.
[4]As in us you have been sanctified before them,
  so in them may you be magnified before us;
[5]and let them know you, as we have known
  that there is no God but you, O Lord.
[6]Show signs anew, and work further wonders;
  make your hand and your right arm glorious.
[7]Rouse your anger and pour out your wrath;
  destroy the adversary and wipe out the enemy.
[8]Hasten the day, and remember the appointed time,
  and let people recount your mighty deeds.
[9]Let him who survives be consumed in the fiery wrath,
  and may those who harm your people meet destruction.

5. Thomas Aquinas, *Summa Theologiae* II-II q. 81 a. 1.
6. Thomas Aquinas, *Summa Theologiae* II-II q. 82–91; Catechism 2095–103.

¹⁰Crush the heads of the rulers of the enemy,
  who say, "There is no one but ourselves."
¹¹Gather all the tribes of Jacob,
  and give them their inheritance, as at the beginning.
¹²Have mercy, O Lord, upon the people called by your name,
  upon Israel, whom you have likened to a first-born son.
¹³Have pity on the city of your sanctuary,
  Jerusalem, the place of your rest.
¹⁴Fill Zion with the celebration of your wondrous deeds,
  and your temple with your glory.
¹⁵Bear witness to those whom you created in the beginning,
  and fulfil the prophecies spoken in your name.
¹⁶Reward those who wait for you,
  and let your prophets be found trustworthy.
¹⁷Listen, O Lord, to the prayer of your servants,
  according to the blessing of Aaron for your people,
and direct us in the way of righteousness,
and all who are on the earth will know
  that you are the Lord, the God of the ages.

OT: 1 Kings 8:60; Isa 2:12–17; 11:11–12; Ezek 36:8–11; 39:27–29; Zech 14:9
NT: Luke 1:46–55, 68–79
Catechism: Christ will come again as judge, 668–82; deliver us from evil, 2850–54

Having expressed confidence that God will answer the just person's petition,   36:1–3
Ben Sira now prays in the first-person plural (we, us, our) on Israel's behalf. He
implores: **Have mercy upon us** (Hebrew: "Save us"), **O Lord, the God of all**
creation, **and look upon us**—your people Israel, whom you love—and reveal
the light of your mercy by delivering us from our enemies and sending the
fear of you upon hostile **nations** (the Latin adds: "that have not sought you")
(compare 1 Chron 14:17). In the Old Testament, while the expression "the nations" (Hebrew *goyim*; Greek *ethnē*) can be a neutral term describing the peoples
of the earth (Pss 67:4; 117:1), it can also carry a pejorative sense, denoting the
pagan rivals and enemies of Israel (2 Kings 16:3; Ps 2:1). Ben Sira petitions the
Lord to **lift up** his **hand** in judgment and strike these wicked **foreign nations**—
likely the Greek †Seleucids, who occupied the land of Israel at that time—so
that they might **see** God's power and **might**.

Just as the Lord was **sanctified** in Israel before the nations, revealing his jus-   36:4–5
tice and mercy by punishing his people for their sins, sending them into exile,
subjecting them to foreign domination, and then returning them to the land
(Ezek 20:41; 28:25; 39:27), so Ben Sira prays that God **be magnified** by judging
the nations **before** Israel (Ezek 38:21–23). This is so that the nations may come
to **know** the Lord as the one true God, just as Israel has come to know **that there
is no God** but him (Exod 6:7; 1 Kings 8:60; Isa 45:14; Zech 14:9).

36:6–7   Ben Sira asks the Lord to perform new **signs** and **wonders** like those he manifested when he delivered Israel from Egypt (Exod 7:3), and to **make** his **hand** and **right arm glorious** by displaying his power to the nations that do not know him (Exod 15:6; Ps 98:1; Isa 63:12). One senses that Ben Sira has specific enemies in mind when he petitions God to **pour out** his **wrath** (Isa 42:13) and **destroy the adversary** and **enemy** of Israel—presumably referring again to the reigning and increasingly hostile Seleucids.

36:8–10   Ben Sira continues to pray: **Hasten the day** of the Lord (Hebrew: "Hasten the end" of the present age), **the appointed time** when God will execute his final judgment on the heathen nations and usher in the messianic age (Isa 2:12–17; Obad 15; Zeph 1:7–18), so that **people** may **recount** his **mighty deeds** throughout the world (Pss 75:1–2; 145:12). Ben Sira desires that any evildoer **who survives** the natural catastrophes, famines, or wars likely to accompany the day of judgment **be consumed** supernaturally in God's **fiery wrath**, and that **those who harm** God's **people**, Israel, be utterly destroyed. His request that God would **crush the heads of the rulers of the enemy** likely refers again to the Seleucids (with a possible allusion to Gen 3:15 or Num 24:17), who arrogantly say, **"There is no one but ourselves"** ruling in power over others (Isa 47:8–10; Dan 11:18; Zeph 2:15). Significantly, less than two centuries after these words were written, God did in fact usher in the messianic age with the birth of Jesus. New signs and wonders marked his first coming, although the definitive judgment of evildoers awaits Jesus's second coming.

36:11   Even though many Jews had returned to Judea from the Babylonian exile, many more remained scattered in foreign lands in Ben Sira's time. In light of this, he prays: **Gather all the tribes of Jacob**—that is, the whole people of Israel—**and give them their inheritance**, the land of Israel, as it was **at the beginning**, when the twelve tribes conquered the land under Joshua and later subdued it under King David (2 Sam 7:1). God's promise to gather the tribes of Israel back to their land is one of the most frequently mentioned prophecies in the Bible.[7] Ben Sira's prayer also shows that Jews of the †Second Temple period did not consider the prophetic promises to be fulfilled by the partial return of exiles from Babylon.

36:12–13   Ben Sira then asks that the **Lord** show **mercy upon the people called by** his **name**, for it is God himself (Hebrew: "El") who renamed Jacob as **Israel** (Gen 32:28; 35:10; Jer 14:9). By calling his people by his name, the Lord adopted Israel as his **first-born son** (Exod 4:22; Wis 18:13; Hosea 11:1), establishing a uniquely intimate relationship with them (Catechism 441). Acknowledging Israel's special status, Ben Sira also pleads with the Lord to **have pity on the city** of his **sanctuary** (or "holy city"), **Jerusalem**, the dwelling **place** of God's **rest** and presence (Deut 12:10–11; 1 Kings 8:13; Ps 132:8).

---

7. E.g., Isa 11:11–12; 27:13; Jer 3:18; 30:3; 31:8–10; Ezek 36:8–11; 39:25–27; Amos 9:14.

Ben Sira not only asks God to spare Jerusalem but also requests that the Lord   36:14–16
fill Zion with the celebration of his **wondrous deeds** (Hebrew: "with your
majesty"), and the **temple** with his **glory**—as he did at the earlier dedications
of the tabernacle and temple (Exod 40:34–35; 1 Kings 8:11; Hag 2:7). Ben Sira
further prays that God would **bear witness** to Israel, his firstborn, whom he
created in the beginning of his redemptive work (Hebrew: "the first of your
works"), **and fulfil the prophecies** (Hebrew: "establish the vision") foretelling
God's future victory over Israel's enemies. He expresses that it would be just for
God to **reward those who** patiently **wait** for him to fulfill his promises, so that
his **prophets** may **be found trustworthy** as their words come to pass.

Ben Sira concludes his prayer with a final appeal: **Listen, O Lord, to the**   36:17
prayer of your servants, the faithful remnant of Israel (compare 1 Kings 8:30;
Dan 9:17), **according to the blessing of Aaron** that bestowed God's grace and
peace upon the nation (Num 6:22–27). By guiding Israel **in the way of righteousness**, the Lord will reveal his glory and power, so that all peoples of **the
earth will know** that he is **the Lord, the God of the ages** or "eternal God" (Gen
21:33; Isa 40:28).

Reflection and Application (36:1–17)

Although Ben Sira's prayer reflects a specific historical context—Israel's call
for God's deliverance from the increasing oppression of the Seleucids in the early
second century BC—it can also be read and prayed †typologically by Christians
today as a call for God's deliverance from evil. In fact, the Church includes this
prayer as part of Morning Prayer (Mondays, Week II). The oppression of God's
people is not limited to Ben Sira's time. Christians must continually struggle
against spiritual, social, cultural, and political forces hostile to the gospel and to
Christ's reign. In the midst of this battle, Christians can pray Ben Sira's words as
a call for the day of the Lord, when Christ's reign will be "fulfilled 'with power
and great glory' by the king's return to earth" (*Catechism* 671; see Luke 21:27;
compare Matt 25:31). In the present time, still marked by distress and the trial
of evil, Ben Sira's prayer remains a fitting precursor to the ancient Christian
prayer *Marana tha*—"Our Lord, come!" (1 Cor 16:22; see *Catechism* 672–73).

VI.E. On Choosing a Wife, Friends, and Counselors (36:18–37:15)

> ¹⁸The stomach will take any food,
>   yet one food is better than another.
> ¹⁹As the palate tastes the kinds of game,
>   so an intelligent mind detects false words.

²⁰A perverse mind will cause grief,
   but a man of experience will pay him back.
²¹A woman will accept any man,
   but one daughter is better than another.
²²A woman's beauty gladdens the countenance,
   and surpasses every human desire.
²³If kindness and humility mark her speech,
   her husband is not like other men.
²⁴He who acquires a wife gets his best possession,
   a helper fit for him and a pillar of support.
²⁵Where there is no fence, the property will be plundered;
   and where there is no wife, a man will wander about and sigh.
²⁶For who will trust a nimble robber
   that skips from city to city?
So who will trust a man that has no home,
   and lodges wherever night finds him?

³⁷:¹Every friend will say, "I too am a friend";
   but some friends are friends only in name.
²Is it not a grief to the death
   when a companion and friend turns to enmity?
³O evil imagination, why were you formed
   to cover the land with deceit?
⁴Some companions rejoice in the happiness of a friend,
   but in time of trouble are against him.
⁵Some companions help a friend for their stomachs' sake,
   and in the face of battle take up the shield.
⁶Do not forget a friend in your heart,
   and be not unmindful of him in your wealth.

⁷Every counselor praises counsel,
   but some give counsel in their own interest.
⁸Be wary of a counselor,
   and learn first what is his interest—
   for he will take thought for himself—
lest he cast the lot against you
   ⁹and tell you, "Your way is good,"
   and then stand aloof to see what will happen to you.
¹⁰Do not consult with one who looks at you suspiciously;
   hide your counsel from those who are jealous of you.
¹¹Do not consult with a woman about her rival
   or with a coward about war,
with a merchant about barter
   or with a buyer about selling,
with a grudging man about gratitude
   or with a merciless man about kindness,

with an idler about any work
  or with a man hired for a year about completing his work,
  with a lazy servant about a big task—
  pay no attention to these in any matter of counsel.
¹²But stay constantly with a godly man
  whom you know to be a keeper of the commandments,
  whose soul is in accord with your soul,
  and who will sorrow with you if you fail.
¹³And establish the counsel of your own heart,
  for no one is more faithful to you than it is.
¹⁴For a man's soul sometimes keeps him better informed
  than seven watchmen sitting high on a watchtower.
¹⁵And besides all this pray to the Most High
  that he may direct your way in truth.

OT: Gen 2:18, 20; Prov 18:22; Sir 6:5–17; 12:8–18; 26:1–4
NT: Rom 12:2; 16:1–19; Phil 1:9–10; 2:3–4; 3:17–19
Catechism: choosing wisely in accord with conscience, 1786–89, 1954

Some things—and people—are better than others; wisdom lies in discerning **36:18–20**
between them and choosing what is good. There is a parallel between the discernment of the senses and that of the intellect: just as **one food is better than
another**, and **the palate tastes** the difference between good and bad **game, so
an intelligent mind detects** falsehood from truth in speech. While a **perverse
mind** (or "deceitful heart") causes **grief** and trouble to others through lies, a
person **of experience** knows how to counter and repay such mischief. This
counsel on wise discernment is next applied to choosing a wife (36:21–26),
friends (37:1–6), and advisers (37:7–15).

Returning to the topic of women (25:13–26:18), Ben Sira emphasizes the bless- **36:21**
ing of finding a good wife (Prov 18:22). In Ben Sira's time, a **woman** typically had
little or no say in choosing a husband, and so would **accept any man**. In contrast,
a man who could choose whom to marry was advised to select his wife wisely,
as **one daughter** could differ greatly from **another**, not only in beauty but, more
importantly, in character and virtues.

A **woman's beauty gladdens** a man's face and brings him delight, for it **sur- 36:22–24
passes every human desire**. Yet, while men typically seek women of exceptional
beauty (26:16), a man who marries a woman known for her **kindness and humility** is more fortunate than others (compare Prov 15:4). Indeed, a man who
finds a good wife obtains **his best possession** and a great blessing (Sir 26:1–4),
for she will be **a helper fit for him**—echoing the language of Eve's creation
(Gen 2:18, 20)—**and a pillar of support** through both the joys and trials of life.

Without a protective **fence** to guard it from intruders, a **property will be 36:25–26
plundered** (Hebrew: "the vineyard is laid waste"; Prov 24:30–31; Isa 5:5). Likewise, **where there is no wife**—who serves as a protective presence around her

husband—**a man will wander** aimlessly **and sigh** in despair. The Hebrew text describes the man without a wife as "a fugitive and a wanderer" (NRSV)—reflecting the sad state of Cain after he murdered Abel (Gen 4:12, 14). Within this Old Testament context, Ben Sira implies that the unmarried man, like Cain, lives in a type of exile, as vulnerable as an unfenced vineyard. Just as no one trusts **a nimble robber** who moves **from city to city**, so people do not trust an unmarried **man** who **has no home** (literally, "no nest") and, wandering restlessly from place to place, **lodges wherever night finds him** (see Prov 27:8).

37:1–3   Ben Sira returns to one of his favorite topics—friendship—and the need to discern true from false friends (37:1–6; see 6:5–17; 12:8–18; 22:19–26). Though every companion may claim, **"I too am a friend,"** not all are sincere: some are **friends only in name** and seek their own gain (Prov 20:6). It is particularly painful—**a grief to the death**—when a former **companion and friend turns** into an enemy (Sir 22:19–26; 27:16–21). Ben Sira personifies and rhetorically addresses the evil inclination present in every human heart that leads to such betrayals: **O evil imagination, why were you formed to cover the land with deceit** and harm so many friendships (Pss 41:9; 55:12–14)?[8]

37:4–6   **Some companions rejoice in the happiness of a friend** only to benefit themselves (Hebrew: "A harmful friend will look to your table"), eager to share in good times and enjoy hospitality, **but in time of trouble** they turn **against him** or stand aloof, indifferent to the friend's plight (6:8–12). These fair-weather companions only **help a friend for their stomachs' sake**, hoping to get invited to good meals. The Hebrew reads instead: "A good friend will fight against the foe" (NABRE). **In the face of battle** the true friend will **take up the shield** to defend his companions from attacks (Ps 35:2). Thus, the wise person is advised to **not forget** a true **friend in** his **heart** (Hebrew: "in battle"), and to remember him in **wealth** by rewarding him generously for his loyalty.

37:7–9   It is also a mark of wisdom to avoid bad advisers (37:7–11) and to choose good ones (37:12–15). While **every counselor praises** his *own* **counsel**, some have only **their own interest** and advantage in mind. Thus, **be wary of a counselor**, and before listening to him, first consider his motives and what he stands to gain from his own advice—for an unscrupulous counselor will think of **himself** first and may even plot **against you**, acting in his favor rather than yours. He may even recommend a bad course of action, saying, **"Your way is good,"** only to **stand aloof** as misfortunes befall you to his own advantage.

37:10–11   It is also unwise to seek advice from **one who looks at you suspiciously** and does not trust you; **hide your counsel** and plans **from those who are jealous of you**, lest they give you harmful advice. Ben Sira lists nine types of people from whom one should not seek **counsel**, either because they have a vested interest

---

8. On the evil inclination, see the commentary on 15:14 and the sidebar "The Good and Evil Inclinations" (p. 141).

in their own advice or because they are of dubious character and would likely give harmful guidance regarding the matter at hand.

One should seek advice from **a godly man** (10:19–20), one who conscien-   37:12
tiously keeps **the commandments**, for if he is faithful to the law, he will likely be faithful to you as well. If this person's **soul is in accord with your soul**—that is, he is like-minded with you—he will rejoice with you in your success and **sorrow with you if you fail**.

Nevertheless, before accepting the advice of others, it is best to **establish the**   37:13–15
counsel of your own heart—in other words, rely on your own judgment—for if you fear the Lord, **no one is more faithful to you than** your own heart's counsel. No one looks after your own interests more than you do, and your own delib-erations may often provide the best guidance (1:11–13; 6:32–37). Your own **soul** and conscience are often more reliable **than seven watchmen sitting high on a watchtower**, counselors observing all around them but not having your best inter-est in mind. Above all, whether you seek the advice of others or rely on your own judgment, **pray to the Most High** for his guidance, **that he may direct your way in truth** and keep you on the right path (Prov 16:9).

Reflection and Application (36:18–37:15)

Like Ben Sira, traditional Judaism holds marriage in high regard. On the basis of God's order of creation, in which he created woman as man's helper because it is "not good that the man should be alone" (Gen 2:18), and so the two could be joined as "one flesh" to "be fruitful and multiply" (1:27–28; 2:24), the †Talmud considers marriage so essential to a man's well-being that it asserts hyperbolically: "Any man who has no wife lives without joy, blessing, goodness," and "Any man who has no wife is no man."[9]

Christian tradition likewise asserts the goodness of marriage as established by God for "the well-being of the individual person and of both human and Christian society" (Catechism 1603). Yet Christ, by choosing to remain celibate, gave a new meaning to celibacy: those who freely forsake the good of marriage "for the sake of the kingdom of heaven," dedicating their lives entirely to the Lord and to the service of the Church, become a radiant sign of Christ's reign on earth (Matt 19:12; 1 Cor 7:8, 25–38; Catechism 1579, 1618–20, 2231).

VI.F. On Wisdom and Restraining One's Appetites (37:16–31)

> [16]**Reason is the beginning of every work,**
> **and counsel precedes every undertaking.**

9. Babylonian Talmud, *Yebamot* 62b, in Jacob Neusner, *The Babylonian Talmud: A Translation and Commentary* (Peabody, MA: Hendrickson, 2011), 8:324–25.

> [17]As a clue to changes of heart
>   [18]four turns of fortune appear,
> good and evil, life and death;
>   and it is the tongue that continually rules them.
> [19]A man may be shrewd and the teacher of many,
>   and yet be unprofitable to himself.
> [20]A man skilled in words may be hated;
>   he will be destitute of all food,
> [21]for grace was not given him by the Lord,
>   since he is lacking in all wisdom.
> [22]A man may be wise to his own advantage,
>   and the fruits of his understanding may be trustworthy
>   on his lips.
> [23]A wise man will instruct his own people,
>   and the fruits of his understanding will be trustworthy.
> [24]A wise man will have praise heaped upon him,
>   and all who see him will call him happy.
> [25]The life of a man is numbered by days,
>   but the days of Israel are without number.
> [26]He who is wise among his people will inherit confidence,
>   and his name will live for ever.
>
> [27]My son, test your soul while you live;
>   see what is bad for it and do not give it that.
> [28]For not everything is good for every one,
>   and not every person enjoys everything.
> [29]Do not have an insatiable appetite for any luxury,
>   and do not give yourself up to food;
> [30]for overeating brings sickness,
>   and gluttony leads to nausea.
> [31]Many have died of gluttony,
>   but he who is careful to avoid it prolongs his life.

OT: Deut 30:19; Prov 3:1–2, 16–18; 4:10, 22; 9:11; 18:21
NT: 1 Cor 6:12; 10:23
Catechism: natural law as God's wisdom, 1954; temperance, 1809; gluttony, 1866

37:16–18 This section contrasts true and false wisdom (37:16–26). **Reason** (Greek *logos*) **is the beginning of every work** and successful human endeavor, **and counsel** obtained from good advisers (37:7–15) should precede **every undertaking**. The next statement, unclear in Greek ("**As a clue to changes of heart four turns of fortune appear**"), makes more sense in the Hebrew: "The root of all conduct is the heart; it sprouts four branches" (see also NRSV, NABRE). All human conduct originates in the heart or mind; it is a ground where conflicting ideas can diverge into four directions, which are really just two distinct paths: **good,**

which leads to **life**, or **evil**, which leads to **death** (33:14; Deut 30:19). Yet it is ultimately not one's thoughts but what **the tongue** utters **that continually rules** and directs the course of one's existence toward either life or death (Prov 18:21).

Some teachers are more effective than others. One **may be shrewd** and clever   37:19–21
at teaching others, yet **unprofitable to himself** and unable to manage his own affairs wisely because he does not practice what he teaches. A skillful and eloquent speaker may even **be hated** if he causes offense; struggling to make a living, he will find it difficult to even put **food** on his table. God withheld from him the winning **grace** to speak with tact and sensitivity to an audience because he failed to pursue and attain **wisdom** (1 Cor 1:17–2:5).

By contrast, one who is **wise to his own advantage** not only instructs **his own**   37:22–24
people but also knows how to benefit from his own wisdom (Prov 12:14). Since he practices what he preaches, others consider **the fruits of his understanding** to be **trustworthy** (or "praiseworthy") and reliable. A **wise** person who manages well his own affairs draws respect and **praise** from others, who, impressed by his accomplishments, **call him happy** or blessed (Greek *makarizō*). Ben Sira is speaking from a natural perspective, according to which living wisely and virtuously leads to a relatively peaceful and happy life. In the Gospels, Jesus points to a deeper and more lasting happiness, calling "happy" or "blessed" (Greek *makarios*) those who follow him on the path of the Beatitudes (Matt 5:3–12).

In contrast to the limited **life of a man**, which is **numbered by days**, the   37:25–26
lifespan of **Israel** is beyond counting because God has promised the nation a long and enduring history (Jer 31:35–37). Still, even a **wise** individual, though mortal, can **inherit confidence** or "honor." One who has established a lasting reputation will not be soon forgotten: **his name will live** and be remembered **for ever** (Sir 39:9; 41:13; 44:13–14).

Ben Sira now exhorts the reader to exercise temperance when eating (see   37:27–28
Catechism 1809; the Reflection and Application section for 22:27–23:28 [p. 191]): **My son, test your soul** (or, more fittingly, "govern your appetite," NABRE) **while you live**, learning from your own experience to stay healthy. Consider **what is bad** for you, **and do not** allow yourself to eat unhealthy foods or to overeat (31:12–24). Not every kind of food **is good for every one**, just as **not every person enjoys** the same food (36:18; 1 Cor 6:12; 10:23).

Temperance calls for restraining one's appetites concerning both the quality   37:29–31
and quantity of food. One should refrain from having **an insatiable appetite** for fine delicacies, and from indulging in **food** without moderation (31:17). Gluttonous **overeating** can lead to obesity and **sickness** such as high blood pressure, diabetes, and other chronic diseases. Indeed, it can even lead to an early death (Prov 5:23). That **many have died of gluttony** should serve as a warning to the reader: **he who is careful to avoid it** and eats with moderation **prolongs his life**. This counsel demonstrates how applied practical wisdom is truly a source of health and longevity (Sir 1:18; Prov 3:1–2, 16–18; 4:10, 22).

VI.G. On Physicians, Sickness, and Death (38:1-23)

¹Honor the physician with the honor due him, according to your
    need of him,
    for the Lord created him;
²for healing comes from the Most High,
    and he will receive a gift from the king.
³The skill of the physician lifts up his head,
    and in the presence of great men he is admired.
⁴The Lord created medicines from the earth,
    and a sensible man will not despise them.
⁵Was not water made sweet with a tree
    in order that his power might be known?
⁶And he gave skill to men
    that he might be glorified in his marvelous works.
⁷By them he heals and takes away pain;
    ⁸the pharmacist makes of them a compound.
His works will never be finished;
    and from him health is upon the face of the earth.

⁹My son, when you are sick do not be negligent,
    but pray to the Lord, and he will heal you.
¹⁰Give up your faults and direct your hands aright,
    and cleanse your heart from all sin.
¹¹Offer a sweet-smelling sacrifice, and a memorial portion of fine flour,
    and pour oil on your offering, as much as you can afford.
¹²And give the physician his place, for the Lord created him;
    let him not leave you, for there is need of him.
¹³There is a time when success lies in the hands of physicians,
    ¹⁴for they too will pray to the Lord
that he should grant them success in diagnosis
    and in healing, for the sake of preserving life.
¹⁵He who sins before his Maker,
    may he fall into the care of a physician.

¹⁶My son, let your tears fall for the dead,
    and as one who is suffering grievously begin the lament.
Lay out his body with the honor due him,
    and do not neglect his burial.
¹⁷Let your weeping be bitter and your wailing fervent;
    observe the mourning according to his merit,
for one day, or two, to avoid criticism;
    then be comforted for your sorrow.
¹⁸For sorrow results in death,
    and sorrow of heart saps one's strength.

> [19]In calamity sorrow continues,
>   and the life of the poor man weighs down his heart.
> [20]Do not give your heart to sorrow;
>   drive it away, remembering the end of life.
> [21]Do not forget, there is no coming back;
>   you do the dead no good, and you injure yourself.
> [22]"Remember my doom, for yours is like it:
>   yesterday it was mine, and today it is yours."
> [23]When the dead is at rest, let his remembrance cease,
>   and be comforted for him when his spirit has departed.

OT: Exod 15:26; 2 Chron 16:12; Ps 24:3–4; Prov 3:7–8; Isa 38:1–5; Hosea 6:1
NT: Matt 4:24; 5:4; 24:50; 25:13; Mark 5:38; James 5:14–15
Catechism: no more mourning, 1044; Anointing of the Sick, 1499–532; the Beatitudes, 1716; the passions, 1762–70

From the health hazards of gluttony, Ben Sira turns to the topics of physicians **38:1–3** and illness (38:1–15). His respect for doctors is ahead of his time. The Old Testament sees sickness as a consequence of the fall and sometimes as a punishment for sin (Deut 28:21–22), suggesting that one should turn not to doctors but to God to find healing (2 Chron 16:12; Prov 3:7–8; 4:20–22; Isa 38:1–5). Ben Sira's view is consistent with his approach to practical wisdom, holding that God normally works for the good of man through human agency. Thus, the wise person should **honor the physician** with due **honor** (or "for his service," NRSV), because everyone occasionally gets sick and has **need of him**. Going to a doctor does not slight God's providence, **for the Lord created** physicians and gave them the skill to heal. This **healing** is not of their own doing but **comes from the Most High** (compare Exod 15:26). A doctor is even appreciated by the ruling powers, and he may well **receive a gift from the king** as a reward for his work. The God-given **skill of the physician lifts up his head**—that is, his expertise makes him distinguished and earns him respect from the community—so that **he is admired** even by powerful people (Prov 22:29).

The Lord created medicines from the earth—plants and herbs with heal- **38:4–6** ing properties—as part of his wise design of creation, **and a sensible**, prudent person **will not despise them** but will honor God by making good use of them. Ben Sira recalls the incident during the exodus when God made bitter **water sweet** after Moses threw **a tree** into it, demonstrating **his power** in the created things of the world so that it **might be known** in Israel (Exod 15:23–25). Likewise, **he gave** medical **skill** to human beings so they might recognize him and glorify him **in his marvelous works** of healing (Sir 17:9) through the agency of physicians and medicine (2 Kings 20:7).

By those medicines, the physician **heals and takes away pain**, in collabora- **38:7–8** tion with **the pharmacist**, who **makes of them a compound**. Thus God's **works** of healing—here naturally through the agency of doctors and supernaturally through miracles—continue in every generation and will not end as long as this world endures. Since God is the author of life, he also bestows **health** (Greek: "peace") **upon the face of the earth**.

38:9–10   And yet, one who is **sick** should not rely exclusively on the skill of the physician (compare 2 Chron 16:12) nor **be negligent** in relation to God, who gives life and health. His first recourse should be to **pray to the Lord** with faith that **he will heal** him (Sir 38:2; Exod 15:26; Hosea 6:1). The exhortation to renounce one's **faults** implies a correlation between physical and spiritual health, even though both the Old and New Testaments recognize that sickness is not always a consequence of personal sin (Job 2:7; Isa 38; John 9:1–3). Nevertheless, since illness can be a chastisement that God sometimes inflicts on people for wrongdoing (Deut 29:21–29; Ps 32), the sick person should examine his conscience, **direct** his **hands aright** toward good deeds, **and cleanse** his **heart from all sin** by repentance (Ps 24:3–4; Prov 3:7–8).

38:11–12   To emphasize his prayer for healing, Ben Sira advises his Jewish reader to **offer a sweet-smelling sacrifice**—the grain offering that included **a memorial portion of fine flour** offered with oil and frankincense as a gift to God (Lev 2:1–3). Pouring abundant **oil** on the **offering** (literally, "make your offering fat") is a sign of devotion. Ben Sira's advice implies that prayer, repentance, and devotion to God have an impact on one's health. This view is confirmed in the New Testament, although there it is the sick person, not a sacrifice, that is anointed (James 5:14–16; Catechism 1499, 1508). Seeking healing from God does not mean neglecting natural means of healing. Rather, it is appropriate to seek out **the physician, for the Lord created him** (see Sir 38:1), and the sick have **need of him.**

38:13–15   Sometimes, **success** in one's recovery and continued good health **lies in the hands of physicians**, not only because of their skills but because **they too**, being aware that they have received these skills from God, the author of life (38:2), **will pray** that he grants them **success in diagnosis and in healing** the sick, thus preserving **life**. Ben Sira assumes that the physicians of his day are theists who humbly turn to God for help—an assumption we can no longer always make today. Nevertheless, whether or not they are aware of it, physicians are agents of God's healing, appointed for the good of humanity. As for the person **who sins before his Maker**, Ben Sira agrees with the divine decree (Deut 28:58–61): such a person may fall ill and require **the care of a physician**, perhaps so that his affliction might lead him to repentance and conversion (compare 1 Cor 5:5).

38:16   Ben Sira turns to the topic of mourning the dead (38:16–23). One who has suffered loss should let **tears fall for the dead**, for it is proper to mourn the deceased. **One who is suffering grievously** over the loss of a loved one should **begin the lament**—the traditional Jewish lamentation for the dead, which was sometimes accompanied by the loud wailing of professional mourning men and women (2 Sam 1:17; Jer 7:29; 9:17–18; Mark 5:38). Relatives of the deceased should **lay out** and prepare **his body** for burial with due **honor** and proper ceremony. Honorably burying the dead is a sacred duty in both Judaism and Christianity (Tob 1:17–18; 4:3–4).

In Middle Eastern cultures, both ancient and modern, people do not sup- **38:17** press their emotions at the death of a loved one. In this context, it is appropriate for mourners to express their pain freely and loudly with **bitter weeping** and **fervent wailing** while also beating their chests (Isa 22:4; Jer 16:7; Zech 12:10). They are expected to **observe the mourning** period according to the deceased person's **merit** for an appropriate length of time—typically at least **one** or **two** days of weeping and wailing **to avoid criticism**, lest they appear insensitive. But then the mourners are to **be comforted for** their **sorrow** by pulling themselves together and controlling their emotions. Though the formal period of mourning in Judaism lasts seven days (Sir 22:12; Job 2:13), mourners should regain their composure after the initial days of mourning. According to the †Talmud, "Three days are for weeping, seven for lamenting, thirty for not getting a haircut and not wearing meticulously groomed clothing."[10]

Excessive **sorrow** can afflict the soul to such an extent that it can result in **38:18–19** the mourner's **death**, for **sorrow of heart saps one's** physical and emotional **strength**. The Talmud concurs, stating that "whoever grieves excessively for his deceased will weep for yet another death"—that is, potentially his own.[11] **In calamity sorrow continues**: the Greek is unclear; some manuscripts read instead, "When a [deceased] person is carried away [for burial], sorrow is over" (NABRE; compare NRSV). Yet **the life of the poor**, afflicted **man** who remains trapped in prolonged grief needlessly **weighs down his heart** (also obscure in the Greek).

Because mourning can be so harmful to the soul, mourners should not wholly **38:20–21** give their **heart to sorrow**. Even when there are good reasons to express sorrow, at some point mourners must **drive it away**, as it is pointless and harmful to waste all of one's energy mourning. The mourner must remember **the end of life**: life is short, and we must make the best of it while we can. There is obviously **no coming back** from death to this life here on earth (Wis 2:1). Those who mourn excessively do **no good** to **the dead** and will only **injure** themselves.

In the Greek text, Ben Sira imagines the dead man speaking to the mourner **38:22–23** in the first person, reminding him that they share a common fate: **"Remember my doom, for yours is like it**—you too will die; **yesterday** this fate **was mine, and today it is yours."**[12] Remain alert and sober, therefore, because you do not know when it will be your turn. Once the deceased **is at rest**, the mourners should "let him go" and allow **his remembrance** to fade after a reasonable pe-riod of mourning. One should not sink into depression or isolate oneself but **be**

---

10. Babylonian Talmud, *Moed Qatan* 27b (Neusner, *Babylonian Talmud*, 7c:149).
11. Babylonian Talmud, *Moed Qatan* 27b (Neusner, *Babylonian Talmud*, 7c:149).
12. The Hebrew text is in the third person, continuing the thought of the narrator ("Remember his doom . . .") (see also ESV-CE, NABRE).

On Sorrow and Grief

LIVING TRADITION

Although Ben Sira warns against excessive display of sorrow, he in no way disparages grief when shown in the right context and appropriate measure. Church Father St. Paulinus of Nola (355–431) recalls the heroes of Scripture who shed tears over the dead: Abraham wept over Sarah's passing (Gen 23:2) and showed care by purchasing a burial site for her (23:9). Jacob honored his beloved Rachel by setting up a pillar on her grave (35:19–20). Joseph shed pious tears for his deceased father, Jacob (50:1). David lamented and drenched his bed with tears almost every night (Ps 6:6–7). Tobit was praised for burying a poor man instead of attending to his own needs (Tob 12:12–13). Even Jesus wept for his friend Lazarus (John 11:35), assuming our human condition "to the point of shedding tears for the dead and acting like a weak human person toward him whom he was going to raise by divine power." In his humanity, "the merciful and compassionate Lord also grieved over the condition of the human race, and in those tears with which he grieved our sins, he also cleansed them."[a]

a. Paulinus of Nola, *Letter 13 to Pammachius* (Voicu, *Apocrypha*, 359–60).

comforted by others when the deceased's **spirit has departed**. In the Gospel of Matthew, Jesus promises that those who mourn shall be comforted (Matt 5:4).

Reflection and Application (38:1–23)

Sorrow is a passion, a natural emotional reaction to a present hardship (such as the death of a loved one); in itself, it is neither morally good nor evil. Yet like the other passions, it takes on a moral quality insofar as it engages the reason and the will (Catechism 1762–70; see the Reflection and Application section for 30:14–31:11 [pp. 242–43]). If guided by the reason and will (e.g., by moderating the intensity and duration of one's sorrow in proportion to its cause), sorrow can become virtuous. Sorrow can, for instance, make a person more compassionate, patient, and kind. Yet if not governed by reason and will, sorrow can give rise to vices, making a person bitter, apathetic, or self-centered. Though Christians should not suppress their emotions, they should remain aware that in our fallen world, our emotions are often wounded, disordered, and prone to mislead. It is the disciple's task and responsibility to wisely govern their emotions, always directing them toward the good (Catechism 1768).

Part VII

Sirach 38:24–43:33

Ben Sira begins Part VII by comparing the professions of skilled workers with the superior vocation of the scribe, who is free to dedicate himself wholeheartedly to the pursuit of wisdom (38:24–39:11). This leads to a hymn of praise to God the Creator, reflecting on his good providence over the universe (39:12–35). Ben Sira also addresses the age-old problem of human suffering and offers guidance on how to live joyfully in a world full of sorrow (40:1–30) and how to prepare well for death (41:1–13). His distinction between "good" and "bad" shame (41:14–42:8) is unique in biblical literature, as is his advice regarding fathers and daughters (42:9–14). Finally, having concluded the didactic part of his book, Ben Sira's hymn on God's wondrous works of creation (42:15–43:33) provides a fitting transition from his wisdom teachings to the praise of Israel's forefathers that follows.

VII.A. Manual Trades and the Wisdom of the Scribe (38:24–39:11)

24The wisdom of the scribe depends on the opportunity of leisure;
and he who has little business may become wise.
25How can he become wise who handles the plow,
and who glories in the shaft of a goad,
who drives oxen and is occupied with their work,
and whose talk is about bulls?
26He sets his heart on plowing furrows,
and he is careful about fodder for the heifers.
27So too is every craftsman and master workman
who labors by night as well as by day;
those who cut the signets of seals,
each is diligent in making a great variety;

he sets his heart on painting a lifelike image,
and he is careful to finish his work.
²⁸So too is the smith sitting by the anvil,
intent upon his handiwork in iron;
the breath of the fire melts his flesh,
and he wastes away in the heat of the furnace;
he inclines his ear to the sound of the hammer,
and his eyes are on the pattern of the object.
He sets his heart on finishing his handiwork,
and he is careful to complete its decoration.
²⁹So too is the potter sitting at his work
and turning the wheel with his feet;
he is always deeply concerned over his work,
and all his output is by number.
³⁰He moulds the clay with his arm
and makes it pliable with his feet;
he sets his heart to finish the glazing,
and he is careful to clean the furnace.

³¹All these rely upon their hands,
and each is skilful in his own work.
³²Without them a city cannot be established,
and men can neither sojourn nor live there.
³³Yet they are not sought out for the council of the people,
nor do they attain eminence in the public assembly.
They do not sit in the judge's seat,
nor do they understand the sentence of judgment;
they cannot expound discipline or judgment,
and they are not found using proverbs.
³⁴But they keep stable the fabric of the world,
and their prayer is in the practice of their trade.
³⁹:¹On the other hand he who devotes himself
to the study of the law of the Most High
will seek out the wisdom of all the ancients,
and will be concerned with prophecies;
²he will preserve the discourse of notable men
and penetrate the subtleties of parables;
³he will seek out the hidden meanings of proverbs
and be at home with the obscurities of parables.
⁴He will serve among great men
and appear before rulers;
he will travel through the lands of foreign nations,
for he tests the good and the evil among men.
⁵He will set his heart to rise early
to seek the Lord who made him,
and will make supplication before the Most High;

he will open his mouth in prayer
and make supplication for his sins.

⁶If the great Lord is willing,
he will be filled with the spirit of understanding;
he will pour forth words of wisdom
and give thanks to the Lord in prayer.
⁷He will direct his counsel and knowledge rightly,
and meditate on his secrets.
⁸He will reveal instruction in his teaching,
and will glory in the law of the Lord's covenant.
⁹Many will praise his understanding,
and it will never be blotted out;
his memory will not disappear,
and his name will live through all generations.
¹⁰Nations will declare his wisdom,
and the congregation will proclaim his praise;
¹¹if he lives long, he will leave a name greater than a thousand,
and if he goes to rest, it is enough for him.

OT: Prov 1:2, 6; 10:7; Wis 1:4–6; 8:8; Sir 41:12–13
NT: Acts 17:11; 18:24; 1 Tim 4:13; 2 Tim 3:14–15
Catechism: study of Sacred Scripture, 131–33
Lectionary: 39:6–10: St. Leo the Great, Pope and Doctor; Common of Doctors of the Church

Ben Sira now compares skilled workers (38:24–34) with the scribe (39:1–11).   38:24
The wisdom of the scribe—a professional religious scholar who specializes
in the study and teaching of the †Torah and other sacred texts—**depends on
the opportunity of leisure**. The Greek term for "leisure" is *scholē*, from which
we get the English words "school" and "scholar." The etymology underscores
Ben Sira's point that the scribe or scholar must have **little business** and ample
leisure, unburdened by manual labor, to engage in intellectual pursuits and
become wise.

In contrast to the scribe or scholar, it is much more difficult for a farmer   38:25–26
to **become wise**, as he **handles the plow**, takes pride **in the shaft of a goad** (a
sharp stick used to lead cattle), **drives oxen**, and talks **about bulls**. Preoccupied
with **plowing furrows** and constantly concerned about providing **fodder for
the heifers**, he has no time to acquire wisdom through study.

Similarly, **every craftsman and master workman** devotes himself to engrav-   38:27
ing **signets of seals** in jewelry and precious stones, which can be pressed into
soft wax as the owner's unique signature. Though valuable, this **diligent** and
attentive labor (45:11; Exod 28:11) limits his ability to dedicate himself to the
pursuit of wisdom.

As a third example, **the smith** or metalworker performs strenuous work at   38:28
the anvil, a block of iron or steel upon which he hammers **his handiwork** after

heating the **iron** to extremely high temperatures. In addition to enduring the intense **heat of the furnace,** he is deafened by **the sound of the hammer, his eyes** are focused on his task, and **finishing his handiwork** demands intense concentration under extremely harsh conditions, leaving him no time or energy for the study of wisdom.

38:29–30   Similarly, **the potter** must produce many everyday items, such as cups, dishes, pots, and so on (Jer 18:3–4). While **turning the wheel with his feet,** he **moulds the clay** and fashions the pottery **with his arm,** bakes it in the kiln, adds decorative **glazing,** then heats it again before cleaning **the furnace.** Like the others, the potter is too busy with his trade to dedicate himself to the pursuit of wisdom.

38:31–32   These four types of laborers—the farmer, the craftsman, the smith, and the potter—**rely upon their hands** and are **skilful** in their **work.** They perform vital tasks essential to the functioning of society, for **without them a city cannot be established, and men can neither sojourn nor live** in places lacking their services.

38:33–34   Yet, in Ben Sira's time, manual laborers were not considered qualified to serve on the town **council** or hold judicial or other positions of civil leadership **in the public assembly,** as they lacked the necessary intellectual formation and schooling in wisdom. Still, their work is indispensable: through it, they uphold **the fabric of the world** and provide a vital foundation for every society. Although they have little time for study and prayer, their labor is not without spiritual value; indeed, **the practice of their trade** can be seen as its own form of **prayer.**

39:1   **On the other hand,** the profession of the scribe or †sage surpasses all other occupations, because he alone **devotes himself** to the study of the Hebrew Scriptures in their traditional tripartite division: **the law of the Most High** (the Torah), **the wisdom of all the ancients** (the Writings), and the **prophecies** (the Prophets).[1] The Torah—the main focus of the scribe's attention—is the foundation of all wisdom. Ben Sira idealizes the scribe as a person who lives out perfectly the wisdom expounded in the rest of his book (39:1–11).

39:2–4   In addition to being a Scripture scholar, the scribe is also an expert in Israel's oral traditions. He memorizes, interprets, and expounds upon a wealth of wisdom sayings passed down in various forms, including **the discourse of notable men, the subtleties of parables,** and **the hidden meanings of proverbs** (see Prov 1:2, 6; Wis 8:8). Because of his wisdom, the scholar is influential among **great men** and **rulers** of society and often holds governmental roles such as that of ambassador. He is typically well traveled, having visited many **foreign nations** and seen much of the world (Sir 34:9–12), and has learned to discern **good** from **evil** through his life experiences and travel.

---

1. On the tripartite division of the Hebrew Bible, see the commentary on the prologue.

Figure 10. A Jewish scribe at work

Unlike the farmer, craftsman, smith, and potter, who set their hearts on their 39:5–6
manual labors (38:26–30), the scribe diligently rises **early to seek the Lord**,
not only through intellectual study but especially by offering **supplication** and
prayer before **the Most High**. Aware that sin is a major obstacle to attaining
wisdom (Ps 51:6–7; Wis 1:4–6), the scribe makes daily **supplication for his
sins** and asks God for forgiveness. He understands that despite his own efforts,
wisdom remains a gift from God. Only if the Lord wills it can he **be filled with
the spirit of understanding** (Isa 11:2), enabling him to speak **words of wisdom**
for the instruction and edification of others **and give thanks to the Lord** for
the gifts he has received.

Guided by divine wisdom, the scribe **will direct his counsel and knowledge** 39:7–8
rightly toward good purposes; he will **meditate** on the Lord's mysteries and
secrets (1:2–4, 6, 8–10), **reveal instruction** as he teaches others what he has
learned, and **glory** (rejoice) **in the law** that the Lord gave to Israel when he
formed his **covenant** with them on Mount Sinai (17:12; 24:23; 28:7).

The sage will acquire a lasting and honored reputation. **Many will praise his** 39:9–11
understanding, and on account of his wisdom **his memory** will not be forgotten. Like the great men of Israel, he will be remembered long after his death,
and his name will live through many **generations** to come (37:26; 41:12–13;
Prov 10:7). Even Gentile **nations will declare his wisdom** (see Sir 44:15), and
the Jewish **congregation will proclaim his praise**. Whether he **lives** a **long**
life and his **name** is respected more **than a thousand** others, or **he goes to rest**
and dies young, it will still be **enough**, for he will have left an enduring legacy
to his people.

Reflection and Application (38:24–39:11)

It is indeed a wonderful privilege to devote oneself to the study of Scripture. However, not everyone can be a professional scholar or †sage. Just as in Ben Sira's time, most people must work in secular professions to earn a living and provide for their families while contributing to the orderly functioning of society. Nevertheless, acquiring some level of proficiency in the Sacred Scriptures should not be left only to experts. Scripture is not only the "support and vigor" of biblical scholars; it serves the Christian faithful as "strength for their faith, food for the soul, and a pure and lasting font of spiritual life."[2] If we want our life of faith to thrive, we must regularly nourish it with the word of God. For this reason, the Church "forcefully . . . exhorts all the Christian faithful . . . to learn 'the surpassing knowledge of Jesus Christ' [Phil 3:8], by frequent reading of the divine Scriptures."[3] As St. Jerome famously said, "Ignorance of the Scriptures is ignorance of Christ."[4] Ben Sira's sage remains an inspiration to Christians, reminding them that no task is more noble than to spend time studying the word of God: "Blessed rather are those who hear the word of God and keep it!" (Luke 11:28).

VII.B. Praise of God, Creator of All (39:12–35)

> [12]I have yet more to say, which I have thought upon,
>   and I am filled, like the moon at the full.
> [13]Listen to me, O you holy sons,
>   and bud like a rose growing by a stream of water;
> [14]send forth fragrance like frankincense,
>   and put forth blossoms like a lily.
> Scatter the fragrance, and sing a hymn of praise;
>   bless the Lord for all his works;
> [15]ascribe majesty to his name
>   and give thanks to him with praise,
> with songs on your lips, and with lyres;
>   and this you shall say in thanksgiving:
> [16]"All things are the works of the Lord, for they are very good,
>   and whatever he commands will be done in his time."
>
> [17]No one can say, "What is this?" "Why is that?"
>   for in God's time all things will be sought after.
> At his word the waters stood in a heap,
>   and the reservoirs of water at the word of his mouth.

2. *Dei Verbum* 21; see also Catechism 131.
3. *Dei Verbum* 25; see also Catechism 133.
4. Jerome, *Commentary on Isaiah*, prologue.

[18]At his command whatever pleases him is done,
and none can limit his saving power.
[19]The works of all flesh are before him,
and nothing can be hid from his eyes.
[20]From everlasting to everlasting he beholds them,
and nothing is marvelous to him.
[21]No one can say, "What is this?" "Why is that?"
for everything has been created for its use.

[22]His blessing covers the dry land like a river,
and drenches it like a flood.
[23]The nations will incur his wrath,
just as he turns fresh water into salt.
[24]To the holy his ways are straight,
just as they are obstacles to the wicked.
[25]From the beginning good things were created for good people,
just as evil things for sinners.
[26]Basic to all the needs of man's life
are water and fire and iron and salt
and wheat flour and milk and honey,
the blood of the grape, and oil and clothing.
[27]All these are for good to the godly,
just as they turn into evils for sinners.

[28]There are winds that have been created for vengeance,
and in their anger they scourge heavily;
in the time of consummation they will pour out their strength
and calm the anger of their Maker.
[29]Fire and hail and famine and pestilence,
all these have been created for vengeance;
[30]the teeth of wild beasts, and scorpions and vipers,
and the sword that punishes the ungodly with destruction;
[31]they will rejoice in his commands,
and be made ready on earth for their service,
and when their times come they will not transgress his word.

[32]Therefore from the beginning I have been convinced,
and have thought this out and left it in writing:
[33]The works of the Lord are all good,
and he will supply every need in its hour.
[34]And no one can say, "This is worse than that,"
for all things will prove good in their season.
[35]So now sing praise with all your heart and voice,
and bless the name of the Lord.

OT: Gen 1:31; Wis 11:5; Sir 24:13–31
NT: Rom 8:28; Eph 5:18–19; Col 3:16; Heb 13:15
Catechism: God is truth and love, 214–21; divine providence, 302–14; thanksgiving and praise, 2637–43

39:12   **I have yet more to say**: with this transition, Ben Sira begins a hymn of praise, celebrating the role of divine providence in creation, which also serves as a theodicy—an attempt to explain the presence of evil in the world. An invitation to praise God (39:12–15) is followed by the hymn itself (39:16–35). By stating that he is **filled, like the moon at the full**, Ben Sira indicates that with this hymn he sees himself at the height of his literary inspiration (50:6).

39:13–15   **Listen to me**: Ben Sira urges his readers, whom he views as his **holy sons**, to praise God with terms reminiscent of the Song of Songs, used elsewhere to describe wisdom (chap. 24) and the ministry of the high priest (chap. 50). They are to **bud like a rose** (24:14) **growing by a stream of water** (24:30–31; 50:8; Song 4:15), **send forth fragrance like frankincense** (Sir 24:15; 50:9; Song 4:14), and **put forth blossoms like a lily** (Sir 24:17; Song 2:1–2). These parallels suggest that as people **sing a hymn of praise** and **bless the Lord for all his works**, ascribing **majesty to his name** and giving **thanks to him**, they are imitating wisdom, performing a liturgical service while being joined to her in a spousal relationship.

39:16–17   The hymn focuses on **the works of the Lord**, which he established at creation and declared to be **very good** (39:33; Gen 1:31). His work of creation is not yet complete but continues throughout human history, for **whatever he commands will be done in his time**—including blessing the righteous and punishing sinners through the created world (Sir 39:22–31; Eccles 3:11). People should not question the wisdom of God's creation by asking **"What is this?"** or **"Why is that?"** for all questions will be answered **in God's time**. For now, his dealings with creation remain a mystery, as when **the waters stood in a heap, and the reservoirs of water** were made at the command of his **word**—a reference to either the gathering of the seas at creation (Gen 1:6–10; Pss 33:7; 104:5–9) or the parting of the sea during the exodus (Exod 15:8; Ps 78:13), or both.

39:18–20   All creation obeys the Lord's **command** and fulfills his purposes, so that **whatever pleases him is done** (39:31). No one can **limit his saving power**, implying a close correlation between God's work of creation and salvation. All human deeds are **before him**, and in his omniscience **nothing can be hid from his eyes** (15:19; 17:15–19; 42:18–25): from the beginning to the end of time, he sees all human actions. The Hebrew adds: "Is there any limit to his saving action? To him, nothing is small or insignificant" (NABRE), and **nothing** is too **marvelous** for him to accomplish.

39:21–23   To the questions of the skeptics (39:17), Ben Sira asserts that **everything has been created** for a purpose. Although God's **blessing covers the dry land like a river** (Hebrew: "the Nile"—the primary river in Egypt) **and drenches it like a flood** (Hebrew: "the Euphrates"—the chief river of Mesopotamia), he will pour out **his wrath** upon **the nations** that have not sought after him, **just as he turns fresh water into salt**—an allusion to the judgment of Sodom and Gomorrah (Gen 13:10; 19:24–28; Deut 29:22–23).

To those who are **holy**, God's **ways are straight** and good, leading to blessed-　39:24–25
ness; yet the same ways are **obstacles** that frustrate the designs of **the wicked**.
From the beginning, God has used every aspect of creation to establish his
justice: he created **good things** to reward **good people**, and **evil things** to punish **sinners** (Wis 11:5; Rom 8:28). Ben Sira proceeds to give examples of each.

Ten things are **basic to all the needs of man's life**—water, fire, iron, salt,　39:26–31
flour, milk, honey, wine, oil, and **clothing**. These essential items are **good** for
the godly but **evils for sinners**, perhaps because sinners misuse these good
things to commit evil deeds. In contrast, God **created** nine destructive forces—
natural (such as violent **winds, fire, hail, famine**, and **pestilence**), animal (**wild
beasts, scorpions**, and **vipers**), and man-made (the **sword** of war)—to punish
the ungodly and unleash **destruction** upon them. Many of these destructive
agents appear in prophecies of judgment throughout Scripture. These instruments of punishment are personified as God's servants who willingly obey **his
commands** and unfailingly accomplish his will **on earth**, punishing sinners
according to the Deuteronomic law of retribution, which states that the righteous will be blessed and the wicked cursed (Deut 28). Ironically, while the
wicked persistently disobey God's commandments, these forces of destruction
never **transgress his word**.

In the epilogue of the poem, Ben Sira reiterates his thesis (39:16). **From**　39:32–35
the beginning of his reflections, he has been **convinced** that all of the Lord's
works are **good** and that everything in life has a purpose that will be revealed
in due time, when God **will supply every need**. Thus, **no one** should raise the
skeptics' questions (39:17, 21) or doubt God's justice by claiming that some
aspect of creation—even its most destructive forces (39:28–30)—**is worse** than
another or lacking a purpose, **for all things will prove good in their season**.
Accordingly, Ben Sira ends his hymn as he started it—with an invitation to
sing praise and **bless the name of the Lord** (39:14–15; Eph 5:18–19; Col 3:16;
Heb 13:15).

Reflection and Application (39:12–35)

Ben Sira's hymn of praise explores the mystery of divine providence and the
problem of theodicy—the effort to explain why there is evil in a world created
by an omnipotent and good God. As the skeptics express it (39:17, 21, 34), the
existence of destructive forces in the world appears to contradict the notion of
God's goodness or justice: How could a good God allow things like hurricanes
and tornadoes, famines and pandemics, predatory animals, or devastating wars
to inflict such suffering upon the human race? Ben Sira anticipates the Church's
response that the universe was created "in a state of journeying" toward its "ultimate perfection" and that divine providence "protects and governs all things

which he has made" toward this final perfection (Catechism 302). God guides his creation through "secondary causes"—meaning through the cooperation of his creatures, whether this occurs through human decisions, life's circumstances, or the forces of nature. Through these causes "God is at work in you, both to will and to work for his good pleasure" (Phil 2:13; see Catechism 308).

Indeed, the presence of evil, suffering, and death in the world remains a stumbling block that causes people to doubt God's goodness or power (or both). At the deepest level, these forces were introduced by human sin (Wis 2:23–24; Rom 5:12; Catechism 400–409). In a fallen world, God allows *physical evil* to endure as long as creation has not reached perfection, along with *moral evil*, which is entirely the result of man's free choice. Yet the Lord in his almighty providence "permits evil in order to draw forth some greater good" (Catechism 412; see also 312) so that "in everything God works for good for those who love him" (Rom 8:28).

VII.C. (i) Human Sorrow and Joy (40:1–30)

¹Much labor was created for every man,
    and a heavy yoke is upon the sons of Adam,
from the day they come forth from their mother's womb
    till the day they return to the mother of all.
²Their perplexities and fear of heart—
    their anxious thought is the day of death,
³from the man who sits on a splendid throne
    to the one who is humbled in dust and ashes,
⁴from the man who wears purple and a crown
    to the one who is clothed in burlap;
⁵there is anger and envy and trouble and unrest,
    and fear of death, and fury and strife.
And when one rests upon his bed,
    his sleep at night confuses his mind.
⁶He gets little or no rest,
    and afterward in his sleep, as though he were on watch,
he is troubled by the visions of his mind
    like one who has escaped from the battlefront;
⁷at the moment of his rescue he wakes up,
    and wonders that his fear came to nothing.
⁸With all flesh, both man and beast,
    and upon sinners seven times more,
⁹are death and bloodshed and strife and sword,
    calamities, famine and affliction and plague.
¹⁰All these were created for the wicked,
    and on their account the flood came.

[11]All things that are from the earth turn back to the earth,
  and what is from the waters returns to the sea.

[12]All bribery and injustice will be blotted out,
  but good faith will stand for ever.
[13]The wealth of the unjust will dry up like a torrent,
  and crash like a loud clap of thunder in a rain.
[14]A generous man will be made glad;
  likewise transgressors will utterly fail.
[15]The children of the ungodly will not put forth many branches;
  they are unhealthy roots upon sheer rock.
[16]The reeds by any water or river bank
  will be plucked up before any grass.
[17]Kindness is like a garden of blessings,
  and almsgiving endures for ever.

[18]Life is sweet for the self-reliant and the worker,
  but he who finds treasure is better off than both.
[19]Children and the building of a city establish a man's name,
  but a blameless wife is accounted better than both.
[20]Wine and music gladden the heart,
  but the love of wisdom is better than both.
[21]The flute and the harp make pleasant melody,
  but a pleasant voice is better than both.
[22]The eye desires grace and beauty,
  but the green shoots of grain more than both.
[23]A friend or a companion never meets one amiss,
  but a wife with her husband is better than both.
[24]Brothers and help are for a time of trouble,
  but almsgiving rescues better than both.
[25]Gold and silver make the foot stand sure,
  but good counsel is esteemed more than both.
[26]Riches and strength lift up the heart,
  but the fear of the Lord is better than both.
There is no loss in the fear of the Lord,
  and with it there is no need to seek for help.
[27]The fear of the Lord is like a garden of blessing,
  and covers a man better than any glory.

[28]My son, do not lead the life of a beggar;
  it is better to die than to beg.
[29]When a man looks to the table of another,
  his existence cannot be considered as life.
He pollutes himself with another man's food,
  but a man who is intelligent and well instructed guards
    against that.

[30]In the mouth of the shameless begging is sweet,
   but in his stomach a fire is kindled.

OT: Gen 3:19; Job 7:1–4; 14:1–2; Ps 90:9–10; Eccles 2:22–23; Wis 4:3–5
NT: Rom 5:12
Catechism: human suffering, 272, 385, 1500–1505; divine justice, 1021–22

Ben Sira now reflects on the sufferings of life (40:1–11), divine retribution (40:12–17), the joys of life (40:18–27), and the shame of begging (40:28–30).

40:1   Despite the goodness of creation, **much labor** is the lot of **every** common **man**—not just ordinary work but the **heavy yoke** of relentless toil, lack of leisure, and anxiety (Job 7:1–3; 14:1–2; Ps 90:9–10; Eccles 2:22–23) that weighs **upon the sons of Adam**—that is, all humans—**from the day** they are born until **the day they return to the mother of all**—the earth, where they are buried when they die (Sir 16:30–17:2; Gen 3:19; Rom 5:12).

40:2–4   All humans share universal **perplexities and fear of heart** because they dread the specter of **death** that looms over everyone, from the rich and powerful king sitting **on a splendid throne**, wearing **purple** (his royal robes) **and a crown**, to the poorest of the poor **who is humbled in dust and ashes** (Job 30:19) and **clothed in burlap**—a coarse cloth typically worn by the destitute.

40:5–7   Seven unsettling emotions or passions afflict everyone's soul: **anger, envy, trouble, unrest, fear of death, fury,** and **strife.** Even at night there is **no rest** or relief from this anguish, as **sleep** is restless and **troubled by visions** of haunting nightmares (Job 7:4). For instance, a man might dream of trying to escape an enemy pursuing him **from the battlefront**, only to wake up just before reaching safety and realize that **his fear** was entirely imaginary and **came to nothing.**

40:8–9   In addition to psychological turmoil, all living beings, **both man and beast**, face mortal threats to their existence. God, in his providence, uses these perils to establish his justice on earth, and they impact **sinners seven times more.** These woes include violent **death** through **bloodshed, strife and sword** in war, **calamities** or natural disasters, **famine and affliction** (perhaps through accidents or illness), **and plague** (Isa 51:19; Ezek 5:17; 28:23).

40:10–11   The fact that these threats to life were **created for the wicked** underscores the doctrine of divine retribution found in both the Old and New Testaments, which holds that God rewards all people according to their works (Deut 28; Prov 17:13; John 5:29; Rom 2:6). For example, **the flood** enacted God's judgment by destroying sinful humanity (Gen 6–8). The flood illustrates the principle that **all** living **things** originating **from the earth**—plants, animals, and humans—**turn back to the earth** when they die, just as water creatures return **to the sea.** The Hebrew and Syriac versions read: "and what is from above returns above" (NABRE)—referring to the human spirit that returns to God at death (Eccles 12:7).

40:12–14   Ben Sira elaborates on the principle of retribution upon the righteous and the wicked (40:12–17). **All bribery**—roundly condemned in the Old Testament

(Exod 23:8; Deut 16:19; Ps 15:5)—**and injustice**—gains obtained through dishonest means—**will be blotted out**. In contrast, **good faith**—characterized by loyalty and integrity in dealing with others—will leave a lasting legacy and endure **for ever**. **The wealth of the unjust will dry up** like the wadis in the Judean desert that carry torrential streams of water in the winter but become completely dry riverbeds in the summer (Job 6:15–18). Similarly, just as **a loud clap of thunder** fades into silence, unjust wealth will vanish. **A generous man** (literally, "one who opens his hand" to give to others) will rejoice as surely as **transgressors will utterly fail** and come to ruin. The law of retribution foreshadows Jesus's saying: "Give, and it will be given to you" (Luke 6:38).

Although children cannot choose the family in which they are born, they **40:15–17** often learn to imitate the virtues or vices of their parents. For this reason, the **children of the ungodly** (Hebrew: "The offshoot of violence," NABRE) **will not put forth many branches**; in other words, they will leave no lasting legacy (23:25; Job 8:11–12; Wis 4:3–5) because they are like **unhealthy roots upon sheer rock** that can never grow deep (Ps 1:4; Matt 13:5). Like **reeds** by a **river bank**, they are promptly **plucked up**—either uprooted by high waters or eaten by grazing animals (Gen 41:2, 18). While wickedness is destined to fail, **kindness** flourishes **like a garden of blessings** (literally, "a paradise in blessings"), **and almsgiving** leaves a lasting legacy, enduring **for ever**. The Hebrew of verse 17 reads: "But goodness, like eternity, will never be cut off, and righteousness endures forever" (NABRE).

In contrast to the afflictions discussed in 40:1–11, Ben Sira turns to the joys **40:18** of life (40:18–27). He lists ten pairs of blessings, each followed by something that is "better than both," culminating in the greatest good to be sought—the fear of the Lord. **Life is sweet for the self-reliant**, financially independent person **and the worker** who can live in comfort (Hebrew: "Wealth and wages make life sweet," NRSV; compare NABRE); yet one who **finds treasure**—possibly referring to wisdom (1:25)—**is better off than both.**

Children and the building of a city establish a man's name, for he will **40:19** be remembered through the legacy of his children who bear his name (Deut 25:5–6) or through a city named after him (2 Sam 5:9). The Hebrew adds: "but better than either is the one who finds wisdom. Cattle and orchards make one prosperous" (NRSV; compare NABRE); but **a blameless** or devoted **wife is accounted better than both** (see Sir 7:19; 25:8; 26:1–4, 13–18).

Close relationships that cultivate wisdom are more valuable than the plea- **40:20–22** sures of the senses: **Wine and music** are enjoyable and **gladden the heart, but the love of wisdom** (Hebrew: "the love of friends" or "of lovers," 6:14–17; 7:18; 9:10) **is better than both**. The sounds of musical instruments such as the **flute** and **harp** produce a **pleasant melody**, yet **a pleasant voice** that speaks with wisdom is **better than both** (20:5–8, 13, 27). Similarly, **the eye** delights in **grace and beauty**, appreciating what is aesthetically pleasing; however, the sight of

green shoots of grain in a bountiful harvest, providing a plentiful food supply, is valued **more than both**.

40:23–24   **A friend** or **companion** is always valued, yet a sensible **wife** loyal to **her husband is better than both** (compare Prov 19:14), for together they will establish a family and she will remain with him for a lifetime. **Brothers** and relatives who can **help** are invaluable **for a time of trouble**, yet **almsgiving rescues better than both**, for the Lord rewards richly one who is generous with the poor (Sir 3:30–4:6; 17:22; 29:8–13).

40:25–27   **Gold and silver** help one **stand** firm by providing financial security, yet **good counsel is esteemed more than both** because it helps one achieve wisdom and success (22:16; 25:4–5; 37:13, 16). By offering security, **riches and strength** also **lift up the heart** or "build up confidence" (NRSV). Yet all these are surpassed by **the fear of the Lord**—the ultimate good that Ben Sira likens to **a garden** or paradise **of blessing** (Hebrew: "Eden of blessing") (40:17). The fear of the Lord as the "beginning of wisdom" thus leads back to the communion with God that Adam and Eve enjoyed in Eden (1:11–30; 15:1; 24:13–31). It also shelters a person **better than any glory**, akin to the divine presence that rested over the sanctuary (Exod 40:34–35; 1 Kings 8:10–11).

40:28–30   If wealth is desirable because of the security it provides, begging must be avoided at all costs. Ben Sira considers begging so humiliating that it is **better to die than to beg** (29:24–28; 30:17)—an exaggeration for rhetorical effect. One who **looks to the table of another** to covet his food leads a wretched **existence** that can scarcely **be considered as life**. For Ben Sira, one who relies on the food of others **pollutes himself** and loses his self-respect. By contrast, an **intelligent and well instructed** person avoids such humiliation by earning a living, achieving financial independence, and providing for his own needs. Even if a **shameless** person convinces himself that **begging is sweet** as he depends on others to survive, still **a fire is kindled** within him, burning him with shame at the thought of enjoying another's food.

Reflection and Application (40:1–30)

Ben Sira's view of poverty aligns with the Old Testament's perspective on the topic: those who are so deprived of economic resources that they are unable to make ends meet lead a miserable life. According to the †Torah, economic prosperity is a sign of divine favor (Deut 6:10–11; 8:7–10; 15:4–6; 28:1–14), and poverty can be the result of divine punishment (28:15–19). At the same time, the Torah demonstrates God's compassion for the poor and prescribes measures to support the most vulnerable members of society (Lev 19:9–10; Deut 15:7–11; 24:19–22).

Proverbs emphasizes that poverty often results from an individual's actions. A person can become poor due to laziness (Prov 6:6–11), the pursuit of pleasure

(21:17), greed (28:22), or the failure to heed counsel (13:18). Yet Proverbs also admonishes the wealthy and powerful not to oppress the poor (14:21), because they are under the Lord's special care (14:31).

A poor person who must beg to survive adds humiliation and shame to material poverty. It is no wonder that Ben Sira urges his readers to avoid poverty and begging at all costs. Rabbinic tradition concurs, considering begging to be among the most undesirable situations in life: "There are three [individuals] whose lives are no lives, and they are: 1) one who depends upon his companion's table, 2) one whose wife controls him, and 3) one whose body is subject to sufferings."[5]

Paradoxically, poverty also mirrors the universal human condition in a fallen world. Every person can make the words of Job his own: "Naked I came from my mother's womb, and naked shall I return; the LORD gave, and the LORD has taken away; blessed be the name of the LORD" (Job 1:21).

Jesus himself embraced human poverty. Born into a modest family, he chose a life of simplicity and poverty (Catechism 517, 525). As St. Paul writes, "Though he was rich, yet for your sake he became poor, so that by his poverty, you might become rich" (2 Cor 8:9). In the Beatitudes, Jesus calls his followers to embrace a new attitude toward poverty: "Blessed are you poor, for yours is the kingdom of God" (Luke 6:20). By his example of poverty, Christ "calls us to accept freely the privation and persecutions that may come our way" (Catechism 520).

The paradox extends into Christian life. While the Church considers aiding the poor an essential part of her mission (Catechism 2443–49), Christ's followers are also called to a deeper renunciation: to "renounce all that [they] have]" for his sake (Luke 14:33) and embrace the poverty of spirit he exemplified (Catechism 2544–47). Thus, the Church, "urged on by the Spirit of Christ, must walk the road Christ himself walked, a way of poverty and obedience, of service and self-sacrifice even to death" (Catechism 852). Christ transformed the meaning of poverty so that, with chastity and obedience, it has become one of the three evangelical counsels that most fully reflect his perfect charity (Catechism 915).

VII.C. (ii) Death (41:1–13)

¹O death, how bitter is the reminder of you
to one who lives at peace among his possessions,
to a man without distractions, who is prosperous in everything,
and who still has the vigor to enjoy his food!

5. Babylonian Talmud, *Betsah* 32b, in Jacob Neusner, *The Babylonian Talmud: A Translation and Commentary* (Peabody, MA: Hendrickson, 2011), 6a:192.

²O death, how welcome is your sentence
  to one who is in need and is failing in strength,
very old and distracted over everything;
  to one who is contrary, and has lost his patience!
³Do not fear the sentence of death;
  remember your former days and the end of life;
this is the decree from the Lord for all flesh,
  ⁴and how can you reject the good pleasure of the Most High?
Whether life is for ten or a hundred or a thousand years,
  there is no inquiry about it in Hades.

⁵The children of sinners are abominable children,
  and they frequent the haunts of the ungodly.
⁶The inheritance of the children of sinners will perish,
  and on their posterity will be a perpetual reproach.
⁷Children will blame an ungodly father,
  for they suffer reproach because of him.
⁸Woe to you, ungodly men,
  who have forsaken the law of the Most High God!
⁹When you are born, you are born to a curse;
  and when you die, a curse is your lot.
¹⁰Whatever is from the dust returns to dust;
  so the ungodly go from curse to destruction.

¹¹The mourning of men is about their bodies,
  but the evil name of sinners will be blotted out.
¹²Have regard for your name, since it will remain for you
  longer than a thousand great stores of gold.
¹³The days of a good life are numbered,
  but a good name endures for ever.

OT: Gen 3:19; Ps 90:5–12; Eccles 12:7; Hosea 13:14
NT: Luke 16:19–23; 1 Cor 15:55
Catechism: original sin and death, 400–412; death in Christ, 1005–14

41:1 Death is inevitable (41:1–4). Yet there is a great difference between the death of the wicked (41:5–11) and that of the righteous (41:12–13). Ben Sira personifies death by addressing it in the second person (compare Hosea 13:14; 1 Cor 15:55): **O death, how bitter is the reminder of you to one who lives at peace.** For someone living comfortably, feeling secure in his material **possessions, without distractions** or worries, **prosperous in everything**, and still healthy enough to enjoy good **food** and drink, the thought of death threatens to end his pleasant existence and strip away everything he cherishes.

41:2 By contrast, Death—personified as a judge delivering a **sentence**—brings relief to the person who suffers intensely, **who is in need** and **failing in strength,**

The Bitterness of Death

In his commentary on Sirach, the ninth-century Frankish monk Rabanus Maurus explains that death is bitter especially for those who become attached to this present world instead of seeking the future life of the kingdom of God.

> The death of the flesh, which is the end of bodily life, is bitter for one who trusts in the prosperity of this world and the pursuit of riches, since he has not learned to love the joys of the future life. But since "the world and its disordered desires are passing away" [1 John 2:17], all those who love it will weep when it is no more.[a]

For the same reason, Thomas à Kempis, author of the fifteenth-century spiritual classic *The Imitation of Christ*, encourages Christians to prepare for death every day of their lives.

> Very soon your life here will end; consider, then, what may be in store for you elsewhere. Today we live; tomorrow we die and are quickly forgotten. Oh, the dullness and hardness of a heart which looks only to the present instead of preparing for that which is to come! Therefore, in every deed and every thought, act as though you were to die this very day. If you had a good conscience you would not fear death very much. It is better to avoid sin than to fear death. If you are not prepared today, how will you be prepared tomorrow? . . . Blessed is he who keeps the moment of death ever before his eyes and prepares for it every day.[b]

a. Rabanus Maurus, *On Ecclesiasticus* 9.2, in Sever J. Voicu, ed., *Apocrypha*, ACCS:OT 15 (Downers Grove, IL: InterVarsity, 2010), 372.
b. Thomas à Kempis, *The Imitation of Christ* 1.23 (trans. Aloysius Croft and Harold Bolton [London: Catholic Way Publishing, 2013], 36–37).

whether **very old** and burdened with worries, or weary of life's struggles and hardships (Job 21:23–26; Eccles 12:1–7; Luke 16:19–23). The Hebrew is even more vivid: the weak man is described as "stumbling and tripping on everything, with sight gone and hope lost" (NABRE).

Since death is the common lot of everyone (Wis 7:6), Ben Sira advises: **Do not fear the sentence of death**; instead, **remember your former days and the end of life**. While the RSV-2CE interprets this as a call to reflect on one's past life and future death, the Greek literally states, "Remember your former and latter (ones)" or, as the NRSV translates, "Remember those who went before you and those who will come after." In other words, death is also the fate of your ancestors and your descendants. Since this is the Lord's **decree** for all living beings, it is futile to **reject** his will or contest what he has determined about each person's death. Regardless of your lifespan, whether **ten or a hundred or**   41:3-4

a thousand years, there is no inquiry about it in †Hades: no one in the realm
of the dead will care how long you lived on earth (14:12, 16; 17:27).

41:5–7   Ben Sira considers the **children of sinners** to be **abominable**—not because
of their parents' sins, for which they are not responsible, but because they follow
the same evil paths and surround themselves with ungodly influences. **The inheritance of the children of sinners will perish**, as grave sin can unleash curses
passed on from parents to children (Exod 20:5), and their own offspring **will be
a perpetual reproach**, in contrast to the enduring and honorable memory of the
righteous (Sir 37:26; 39:9–11; 41:13). Such curses also appear in family strife, as
disgraced children **blame an ungodly father** for their condition, recognizing that
they suffer disgrace and **reproach because of him**. While Ben Sira's language
toward ungodly children is harsh, it remains true that God loves all children
in their innocence and that even children raised in difficult circumstances can
still choose to turn away from evil and toward the good (Ezek 18:14–31).

41:8–9   Ben Sira pronounces a **woe** upon **ungodly** people **who have forsaken the
law of the Most High God**—perhaps Jews of his time who abandoned †Torah
observance in favor of Greek practices and customs (1 Macc 3:5–8). These people
are **born to a curse,** which will remain with them until they **die**. The Hebrew of
verse 9 describes how children suffer due to their parents' godlessness: "If you
have children, calamity will be theirs; you will beget them only for groaning.
When you stumble, there is lasting joy; and when you die, a curse is your lot"
(NRSV; compare NABRE).

41:10–11   Although it is the lot of all human beings, made **from the dust**, to return **to
dust** (40:11; Gen 3:19), **the ungodly** face a more terrifying destiny, going **from
curse to destruction**. The Hebrew reads: "All that is from nothing returns to
nothing, so too the godless—from void to void" (NABRE; see also Isa 40:17).
While people may mourn the lifeless **bodies** of the deceased, there is a fate far
worse than physical death: **the evil name** or reputation **of sinners will be blotted out**, and they will be forgotten forever. In contrast, the Hebrew reads: "The
human body is a fleeting thing, but a virtuous name will never be annihilated"
(NABRE).

41:12–13   Therefore, it is wise to **have regard for your name** and protect your reputation in life, as it will outlast you and, in characteristic Jewish hyperbole, endure
longer than the greatest treasure **of gold**, long after your death. While **the days
of a good life** on earth **are numbered**, the lasting memory of **a good name** and
reputation **endures for ever** (15:6; 37:26; 39:9–11).

Reflection and Application (41:1–13)

Memento mori—"Remember that you must die." This timeless saying was
already known in antiquity, when ancient philosophers reflected on life's

ephemeral nature, and Plato wrote that "those who pursue philosophy aright study nothing but dying and being dead."[6] The Bible frequently attests to the brevity and fragility of life (Ps 90:5–12; Isa 40:6–7) and considers it shortsighted and utterly foolish to forget that in death, we will lose everything and appear naked before God (James 4:13–15; 1 John 2:17). The inevitability of death "lends urgency to our lives: remembering our mortality helps us realize that we have only a limited time in which to bring our lives to fulfillment" (Catechism 1007; see also Eccles 12:1–7). Thus, one who wishes to live well must constantly keep death in mind.

Though death entered the world through sin and was not part of God's original plan (Gen 3:3, 19; Wis 2:24), it was transformed by Christ's own death and resurrection; his obedience transformed the curse of death into a blessing (Catechism 1008–9). In baptism, the Christian is incorporated into Christ's death and "dies with Christ" in order to live a new life with him (2 Tim 2:11).

VII.D. Good and Bad Shame; Fathers and Daughters (41:14–42:14)

[14]My children, observe instruction and be at peace;
hidden wisdom and unseen treasure,
what advantage is there in either of them?
[15]Better is the man who hides his folly
than the man who hides his wisdom.
[16]Therefore show respect for my words:
For it is not good to retain every kind of shame,
and not everything is confidently esteemed by every one.

[17]Be ashamed of immorality, before your father or mother;
and of a lie, before a prince or a ruler;
[18]of a transgression, before a judge or magistrate;
and of iniquity, before a congregation or the people;
of unjust dealing, before your partner or friend;
[19]and of theft, in the place where you live.
Be ashamed before the truth of God and his covenant.
Be ashamed of selfish behavior at meals,
of surliness in receiving and giving,
[20]and of silence, before those who greet you;
of looking at a woman who is a harlot,
[21]and of rejecting the appeal of a kinsman;
of taking away some one's portion or gift,
and of gazing at another man's wife;

6. Plato, *Phaedo* 64a, in *Euthyphro; Apology; Crito; Phaedo; Phaedrus*, trans. Harold North Fowler, Loeb Classical Library 36 (Cambridge, MA: Harvard University Press, 1914), 223.

²²of meddling with his maidservant—
  and do not approach her bed;
of abusive words, before friends—
  and do not upbraid after making a gift;
²³of repeating and telling what you hear,
  and of revealing secrets.
Then you will show proper shame,
  and will find favor with every man.

⁴²:¹Of the following things do not be ashamed,
  and do not let partiality lead you to sin:
²of the law of the Most High and his covenant,
  and of rendering judgment to acquit the ungodly;
³of keeping accounts with a partner or with traveling companions,
  and of dividing the inheritance of friends;
⁴of accuracy with scales and weights,
  and of acquiring much or little;
⁵of profit from dealing with merchants,
  and of much discipline of children,
  and of whipping a wicked servant severely.
⁶Where there is an evil wife, a seal is a good thing;
  and where there are many hands, lock things up.
⁷Whatever you deal out, let it be by number and weight,
  and make a record of all that you give out or take in.
⁸Do not be ashamed to instruct the stupid or foolish
  or the aged man who quarrels with the young.
Then you will be truly instructed,
  and will be approved before all men.

⁹A daughter keeps her father secretly wakeful,
  and worry over her robs him of sleep;
when she is young, lest she not marry,
  or if married, lest she be hated;
¹⁰while a virgin, lest she be defiled
  or become pregnant in her father's house;
or having a husband, lest she prove unfaithful,
  or, though married, lest she be barren.
¹¹Keep strict watch over a headstrong daughter,
  lest she make you a laughingstock to your enemies,
a byword in the city and notorious among the people,
  and put you to shame before the great multitude.

¹²Do not look upon any one for beauty,
  and do not sit in the midst of women;
¹³for from garments comes the moth,
  and from a woman comes woman's wickedness.

¹⁴**Better is the wickedness of a man than a woman who does good;
and it is a woman who brings shame and disgrace.**

OT: Sir 4:20–21; 24:22; 51:18, 29
NT: Rom 9:33; 10:11; 1 Pet 2:6
Catechism: conscience, 1776–94; coveting and purity of heart, 2514–27

Ben Sira addresses his readers as his **children**, inviting them to **observe** his   41:14–15
teachings so they may live well and **be at peace**. He reiterates the advice given
in 20:30–31: **hidden wisdom**, like an **unseen treasure**, is of little use to anyone.
While it is good for a man to conceal **his folly**, one **who hides his wisdom**
squanders a gift that could benefit others.

The Hebrew text adds a title: "Instruction concerning Shame." For their   41:16
own good, Ben Sira's readers should **respect** his instructions. He distinguishes
between two types of shame: *proper shame*, which leads one away from sin
(41:17–23), and *improper shame*, which makes a person recoil from doing good
deeds (42:1–8; see 4:21). While not **every kind of shame** is beneficial, some
forms of shame are appropriate and fitting—the right reaction of a well-formed
conscience to certain evils. Yet not every situation **is confidently esteemed by
all**—that is, not everyone rightly approves of shame when it is warranted.

Ben Sira lists numerous behaviors that *should* elicit shame, especially when   41:17–23
done in the presence of others: sexual **immorality** (Greek *porneia*) (18:30–31;
23:16–21), especially before **father or mother** (i.e., if they find out about it); telling
a lie before an important official such as **a prince** or **ruler** (7:13; 20:24–25); committing **a transgression** or crime **before a judge**, an **iniquity** before a religious or
civil **congregation**, or some **unjust dealing** before a **friend**. One should also feel
shame over **theft**, especially at home among family and neighbors; breaking an
oath or promise **before the truth of God and his covenant**; and displaying **selfish
behavior at meals** (literally, "stretching the elbow over pieces of bread," 31:12–14).
Other shameful behaviors include **surliness** or bad manners when **receiving
and giving** gifts, responding with cold or indifferent **silence** to **those who greet
you**, and **looking** with lust at a prostitute. Additional actions warranting shame
include **rejecting** a relative's **appeal** for help; **taking away** a person's **portion or
gift**—such as portions of sacrifices reserved for priests (7:31; Exod 29:26–28) or
offerings intended for the poor; **gazing at another man's wife**, thus violating the
commandment against covetousness (Exod 20:17), which can lead to adultery
(Sir 9:8; Prov 6:25–29; Matt 5:28); **meddling with his maidservant**, also implying
sexual impropriety; using **abusive words, before friends**, such as reproving or
insulting them **after making a gift** (see Sir 18:15–18; 20:14–15); and engaging in
gossip or indiscreetly **revealing secrets** (19:7–8; 22:22; 27:16–21). Unlike those
today who advise against feeling any shame, Ben Sira insists that these behaviors
should provoke a healthy sense of **proper shame** and aversion in a well-formed
conscience, motivating the wise to avoid them (Catechism 1777). The person

endowed with this proper sense of shame will steer clear of these disgraceful sins and **find favor** with everyone. Although shame entered the human condition through the fall (Gen 2:25; 3:7), it should not always be repressed or dismissed, as it can rightly guide a person to avoid sin or, if committed, to repent and confess it.

42:1–5   Ben Sira now turns to *improper shame*. He encourages his reader: **do not be ashamed** of doing what is right, and **do not let partiality** or peer pressure **lead you to sin**—in other words, "do not sin to save face" (NRSV; compare NABRE), regardless of what others may think. One should *not* be ashamed of observing **the law of the Most High** and remaining faithful to **his covenant** (17:12; 45:5), even when many Jews were tempted by Hellenistic ways of life. Nor should one be ashamed **of rendering** a fair **judgment to acquit the ungodly** when accusations against them are unfounded (Deut 1:17; 16:18–20). One should also not be embarrassed about **keeping accounts** or sharing expenses **with a partner** or **traveling companions**, or about sharing an **inheritance** with other heirs. In business transactions, one should not be ashamed of ensuring **accuracy with scales and weights**, which enables honest dealings with others (Lev 19:35–36; Prov 11:1). Similarly, there is no shame in **acquiring** wealth—whether **much or little**—or in making an honest **profit** when **dealing with merchants**. At home, one should not be ashamed of rigorously disciplining one's **children**—a moral obligation for parents (Sir 30:1–13)—or **of whipping a wicked servant**—a harsh measure reflecting cultures where slavery was common but that is no longer applicable today (33:24–31). All these actions are concrete expressions of wisdom that demand moral integrity, courage, and strength. In other words, Ben Sira's improper shame is essentially the fear of being criticized or mocked for doing what is right. Those who pursue wisdom will grow in courage and strength of character so that they will diligently do good and avoid evil, and thus "will not be put to shame" (24:22; see also 51:18, 29).

42:6–8   Ben Sira continues to discuss actions that one should not be ashamed of. Reflecting the mentality of his day, he suggests that **where there is an evil**, untrustworthy **wife**, a husband should secure his valuables with **a seal** or keep her at home to prevent her from going astray. Likewise, **where there are many hands** prone to steal, one should **lock things up** to protect valuables. In business dealings and transactions, it is best to avoid disputes by accurately counting everything **by number and weight, and make a record of all** expenses and income. Above all, one should **not be ashamed to instruct the stupid or foolish**, or to reprimand an **aged man** who immaturely **quarrels with the young** (Hebrew: "an old man engaged in sexual immorality"; compare NRSV, ESV-CE), for wisdom's purpose is to guide sinners back to virtuous behavior. Far from being shameful, these actions are praiseworthy. One who has the courage to do what is right, however difficult or unpopular, **will be truly instructed**, proficient in wisdom, and **approved before all**.

In the Middle East, shame is a family affair, so that if a misdeed becomes   **42:9–10**
public, not only the perpetrator but also the entire family is shamed. This is
especially true for women, whose precarious situation in ancient society helps
explain Ben Sira's strict advice on how fathers should watch over their daughters
(42:9–14; compare 26:10–12). **A daughter keeps her father secretly wakeful**, as
he is concerned about her future; **worry over her robs him of sleep**, regardless
of her state in life. Ben Sira outlines five main sources of a father's worry: **when
she is young**, she may **not marry** if a suitable husband cannot be found. If she
does get **married**, she could **be hated** and divorced by her husband (Deut 24:1).
While she is still **a virgin**, she could **be defiled or become pregnant** due to rape
or fornication while still living in **her father's house**, which would disqualify
her for marriage since virginity was typically required of a new bride. If she
has **a husband**, she could **prove unfaithful** by committing adultery, an offense
punishable by death (Deut 22:22). Finally, even if **married**, she could **be barren**, which would bring disgrace and disappointment to the entire family (Gen
25:21; Judg 13:2; 1 Sam 1:2).

To avoid these distressing scenarios, Ben Sira advises the father to **keep strict**   **42:11**
watch over a headstrong daughter (26:10), lest she misbehave and make him
a laughingstock to his **enemies** and an object of gossip and derision **in the
city** and **among the people**. Such behavior could bring public **shame** not only
upon him but upon his entire family before the whole community. The Hebrew
adds further precautions: "See that there is no lattice in her room, no spot that
overlooks the approaches to the house" (NRSV; compare NABRE)—to prevent
her from becoming a temptation to passersby (Prov 7:6). Like his advice on
disciplining sons (Sir 30:1–13), Ben Sira's counsel on disciplining daughters is
strict. Though his severity may seem jarring to modern readers, it reflects his
concern for raising children in the fear of the Lord and in wisdom. His approach
mirrors that of Lady Wisdom herself, who rigorously disciplines her children
before embracing them in love (4:17–18; 6:18–31).

Do not look upon any one for beauty: The Greek is unclear, but the Hebrew   **42:12–13**
more aptly continues the thought of the preceding verses: "Do not let her parade
her beauty before any man, or spend her time among married women" (NRSV;
compare NABRE)—possibly because such company could lead to gossip. Just as
a **moth** feeds on clothing, a woman may learn **wickedness** from other women.
In a modern context, the principle that "bad company ruins good morals" still
holds true (1 Cor 15:33), although this advice does not imply avoiding fellowship with other godly women.

Ben Sira concludes this section with a statement that sounds extreme in   **42:14**
the RSV-2CE but is somewhat milder in the Greek. Does he truly consider **the
wickedness of a man** to be better than **a woman who does good**? It is possible that he means a woman who only *appears* to do good, or "does pleasing
things" with an intention to seduce. A closer reading of the second half of the

verse confirms this interpretation; while the RSV-2CE (**and it is a woman who brings shame and disgrace**) sounds resolutely misogynistic, the ESV-CE likely captures the author's intention and meaning in the Greek text more accurately: "and a shameful woman brings disgrace." In other words, "the harm a man can cause is preferable to a woman who feigns to do good and a woman who brings shame to the point of reproach."

Alternatively, the NABRE (following the Hebrew) may better convey the sense of this difficult verse as referring to the parents of a rebellious daughter: "Better a man's harshness than a woman's indulgence, a frightened daughter than any disgrace." In other words, it may be preferable for a rebellious daughter to be raised by a strict father rather than an overly indulgent mother, as the daughter needs strong guidance, clear boundaries, and firm discipline. It is better that she learns good behavior, even if motivated by fear of punishment, than to learn "the hard way" through behavior that could disgrace the whole family.

VII.E. (i) God's Wondrous Work of Creation: The Heavens (42:15–43:12)

> [15]I will now call to mind the works of the Lord,
> and will declare what I have seen.
> By the words of the Lord his works are done,
> and in his will, justice is carried out.
> [16]The sun looks down on everything with its light,
> and the work of the Lord is full of his glory.
> [17]The Lord has not enabled his holy ones
> to recount all his marvelous works,
> which the Lord the Almighty has established
> that the universe may stand firm in his glory.
> [18]He searches out the abyss, and the hearts of men,
> and considers their crafty devices.
> For the Most High knows all that may be known,
> and he looks into the signs of the age.
> [19]He declares what has been and what is to be,
> and he reveals the tracks of hidden things.
> [20]No thought escapes him,
> and not one word is hidden from him.
> [21]He has ordained the splendors of his wisdom,
> and he is from everlasting and to everlasting.
> Nothing can be added or taken away,
> and he needs no one to be his counselor.
> [22]How greatly to be desired are all his works,
> and how sparkling they are to see!

²³All these things live and remain for ever
    for every need, and are all obedient.
²⁴All things are twofold, one opposite the other,
    and he has made nothing incomplete.
²⁵One confirms the good things of the other,
    and who can have enough of beholding his glory?

⁴³:¹The pride of the heavenly heights is the clear firmament,
    the appearance of heaven in a spectacle of glory.
²The sun, when it appears, making proclamation as it goes forth,
    is a marvelous instrument, the work of the Most High.
³At noon it parches the land;
    and who can withstand its burning heat?
⁴A man tending a furnace works in burning heat,
    but the sun burns the mountains three times as much;
it breathes out fiery vapors,
    and with bright beams it blinds the eyes.
⁵Great is the Lord who made it;
    and at his command it hastens on its course.

⁶He made the moon also, to serve in its season
    to mark the times and to be an everlasting sign.
⁷From the moon comes the sign for feast days,
    a light that wanes when it has reached the full.
⁸The month is named for the moon,
    increasing marvelously in its phases,
an instrument of the hosts on high
    shining forth in the firmament of heaven.

⁹The glory of the stars is the beauty of heaven,
    a gleaming array in the heights of the Lord.
¹⁰At the command of the Holy One they stand as ordered,
    they never relax in their watches.
¹¹Look upon the rainbow, and praise him who made it,
    exceedingly beautiful in its brightness.
¹²It encircles the heaven with its glorious arc;
    the hands of the Most High have stretched it out.

OT: Gen 1; Pss 19:1–6; 33:6–9; 139:1–18; Wis 9:1; Jer 31:35–36
NT: John 1:1–3; Rom 1:20; Heb 4:13
Catechism: the mystery of creation, 295–301

Ben Sira has concluded his teachings on practical wisdom. He now launches   **42:15–17**
into a hymn praising **the works of the Lord** in the natural world (see Ps 77:12).
The hymn references the Genesis creation account and serves as a prelude
to the hymn on the ancestors of Israel that follows. The first part praises
God's omnipotence and omniscience as revealed in his work of creation (Sir

42:15–25). By the creative power of his **words** (Greek *logos*), **the Lord** fashioned the universe (Gen 1; Ps 33:6; Wis 9:1; John 1:1–3); **in his will, justice is carried out** in the world, revealing his own justice and goodness. As **the sun** illuminates **everything with its** radiant **light**, the Lord's **work** in creation reveals **his glory** to all living beings (Ps 19:1–6). His creation is so magnificent that even his **holy ones**—the angels (Job 15:15; Ps 89:7; Dan 8:13)—lack the power **to recount all his marvelous works**, which God made so that **the universe may stand firm in his glory** and continually reveal his greatness (Sir 18:4–7; 43:27–31).

42:18–19   While the universe remains impenetrable to the angelic or human mind, nothing escapes the mind of God, who **searches out the abyss** (the mysterious, subterranean "deep," 1:3; 24:5; Gen 1:2; Ps 33:7), as well as **the hearts of men** (their innermost thoughts, Ps 139:1–18; Prov 15:11; Heb 4:13), **and considers their crafty devices** or innermost secrets. **For the Most High** in his omniscience **knows** everything, **and he looks into the signs of the age**—or, following the Hebrew, "sees from of old the things that are to come" (NRSV, NABRE). He discloses **what has been and what is to be,** for both the past and the future are eternally present to him, and **reveals** the traces of **hidden things**, exposing the evidence of things unseen (Heb 11:1).

42:20–21   God's knowledge and understanding are limitless: no human **thought** or **word is hidden from him**. He perfectly arranged **the splendors of his wisdom** in the created world, and he is unchanging, remaining the same forever. **Nothing can be added or taken away** from his perfect nature or his works (18:6; Eccles 3:14), and in his infinite wisdom he does not need the assistance of any **counselor** to govern the universe (Isa 40:13–14; Rom 11:34).

42:22–23   The first part of the hymn concludes by praising the beauty and splendor of creation. The Lord's works are beautiful and **greatly to be desired** because they reflect his infinite goodness (Rom 1:20), as well as being **sparkling** and dazzling to the eye—a joy to behold. All elements of creation **live and remain for ever**—not that they are eternal, but that their laws are firmly established **for every need,** each fulfilling a specific role and remaining perfectly **obedient** to God's eternal purpose and design (Sir 39:21).

42:24–25   The harmony of creation is such that **all things are twofold** or exist in pairs, with **one opposite the other**, such as day and night, light and darkness, hot and cold (33:15). **He has made nothing incomplete**, lacking, or superfluous, for everything in creation serves a specific purpose. Every creature **confirms** and supplements the virtues and excellence **of the other**, and no one **can have enough of beholding his glory**, for it is infinitely beautiful.

43:1   The second part of the hymn, echoing Genesis, begins by praising the firmament and the sun (43:1–5), the moon (43:6–8), the stars, and the rainbow (43:9–12). The first witness to God's glory is **the clear firmament** (Gen 1:6–8; Ps 19:1), which reveals **heaven** in a glorious sight.

The personified **sun** announces each new day **as it goes forth** (Ps 19:4–6),   **43:2–5**
serving as **a marvelous instrument** made by **the Most High**. Its power is such
that **at noon it parches the land** (Hebrew: "it causes the world to boil") with a
burning heat that no human can **withstand**. Like a blazing **furnace** it scorches
the mountains, breathes out fiery vapors (Hebrew: "its fiery tongue consumes
the world"), and with its bright rays **it blinds the eyes** that dare to gaze at it.
Humanity's helplessness before the sun serves as a permanent reminder of the
infinite power of **the Lord who made it** and sends it **on its course** daily across
the sky (Ps 19:5–6).

In his infinite wisdom, God **made the moon also**: even more than the sun, it   **43:6–7**
plays an essential role in Judaism (which follows a hybrid solar/lunar calendar)
to mark the times and seasons (Gen 1:14; Ps 104:19) and to **be an everlasting
sign** of God's glory as long as the world endures (Pss 72:5; 89:37; Jer 31:35–36).
The **moon** determines the religious **feast days** of Israel's liturgical calendar (Lev
23; Num 28:11), for it is **a light that wanes** after it completes its course and
reaches **the full** moon. To this day the Jewish calendar is primarily lunar, with
each month beginning on the new moon.

The month is named after **the moon**: the Hebrew word *khodesh* means both   **43:8**
"month" and "new moon," deriving from the word *khadash* ("new"). This explains the pun in the Hebrew text: "month by month [*khodesh*] it renews itself
[*mitkhadash*]," **increasing marvelously in its phases** as it waxes fuller every
night until it becomes a full moon. It is **an instrument** or beacon leading **the
hosts on high**—the army of stars—to shine forth **in the firmament of heaven**.

The glory of the stars reveals **the beauty of heaven**, which itself reflects   **43:9–10**
God's own beauty. The stars are **a gleaming array** and shining ornament **in
the heights of the Lord** (the sky). Like all other created beings, they exist to

The Rainbow: Sign of Covenant and Judgment
LIVING TRADITION

Rabanus Maurus explains that the rainbow not only recalls the past
judgment of the flood but also announces a future judgment by fire
(2 Pet 3:3–12):

> God almighty set the rainbow as a sign between himself and humanity,
> indicating that he would never again destroy the world with a flood.
> And this is why the rainbow has the color of both water and fire—in part
> light blue and in part red—so that it might testify to both judgments,
> to the one that is to come and to the one that has already taken place,
> since the world will be burned by fire and was once destroyed by the
> waters of the flood.[a]

a. Rabanus Maurus, *On Ecclesiasticus* 9.7 (Voicu, *Apocrypha*, 381).

accomplish God's purpose (39:16–34; 42:23; Ps 119:91): at the Lord's **command**, the stars **stand** in their **ordered** positions; like soldiers standing guard at their post, **they never relax in their watches** (compare Bar 3:34), bearing witness to God's infinite power.

43:11–12 The extraordinary beauty of **the rainbow** calls all people to **praise** the Lord **who made it** (50:7; Ezek 1:28). As **it encircles the heaven with its glorious arc**, it reminds humankind that **the hands** of the Almighty **have stretched it out** like a bowstring, as it were, to be the sign of his covenant with humanity after the flood (Gen 9:12–17).

VII.E. (ii) God's Wondrous Work of Creation: The Earth (43:13–33)

> ¹³By his command he sends the driving snow
>   and speeds the lightning of his judgment.
> ¹⁴Therefore the storehouses are opened,
>   and the clouds fly forth like birds.
> ¹⁵In his majesty he amasses the clouds,
>   and the hailstones are broken in pieces.
> ¹⁶At his appearing the mountains are shaken;
>   at his will the south wind blows.
> ¹⁷The voice of his thunder rebukes the earth;
>   so do the tempest from the north and the whirlwind.
> He scatters the snow like birds flying down,
>   and its descent is like locusts alighting.
> ¹⁸The eye marvels at the beauty of its whiteness,
>   and the mind is amazed at its falling.
> ¹⁹He pours the hoarfrost upon the earth like salt,
>   and when it freezes, it becomes pointed thorns.
> ²⁰The cold north wind blows,
>   and ice freezes over the water;
> it rests upon every pool of water,
>   and the water puts it on like a breastplate.
> ²¹He consumes the mountains and burns up the wilderness,
>   and withers the tender grass like fire.
> ²²A mist quickly heals all things;
>   when the dew appears, it refreshes from the heat.
>
> ²³By his counsel he stilled the great deep
>   and planted islands in it.
> ²⁴Those who sail the sea tell of its dangers,
>   and we marvel at what we hear.
> ²⁵For in it are strange and marvelous works,
>   all kinds of living things, and huge creatures of the sea.

²⁶Because of him his messenger finds the way,
and by his word all things hold together.

²⁷Though we speak much we cannot reach the end,
and the sum of our words is: "He is the all."
²⁸Where shall we find strength to praise him?
For he is greater than all his works.
²⁹Terrible is the Lord and very great,
and marvelous is his power.
³⁰When you praise the Lord, exalt him as much as you can;
for he will surpass even that.
When you exalt him, put forth all your strength,
and do not grow weary, for you cannot praise him enough.
³¹Who has seen him and can describe him?
Or who can extol him as he is?
³²Many things greater than these lie hidden,
for we have seen but few of his works.
³³For the Lord has made all things,
and to the godly he has granted wisdom.

OT: Job 36:30–33; 41:1–34; Pss 29; 107:23–30; 147:15–18; 148:8
NT: Matt 24:27; Acts 17:28; Rom 1:20
Catechism: God's transcendence, 300, 2129; praise, 2639–43

Ben Sira turns from the astral bodies to meteorological phenomena that also   **43:13–15**
fulfill God's purposes (43:13–26). The terrifying image of the storm foreshadows
God's future judgment upon the world (Ps 29). **By his command he** speedily
sends forth **the driving snow**—rare but not unheard of in Israel (Pss 147:15–18;
148:8)—and **the lightning of his judgment**—a common biblical metaphor (Job
36:30–33; Matt 24:27; Rev 8:5). It is as if God had **storehouses** of weather systems
that he can open at will to release **the clouds**, which **fly forth like birds** (Deut
28:12; Job 38:22–23; Jer 10:13). **In his majesty** and power **he amasses** (literally,
"strengthens") **the clouds**, gathering them for a storm, **and the hailstones are
broken in pieces**, as if chipped from a massive piece of ice in the heavens.

When the Lord appears, **the mountains** tremble as if **shaken** by a mighty   **43:16–18**
earthquake (see Exod 19:18; Judg 5:5; Ps 68:8), and at his command the hot
and dry **south wind blows** (Ps 78:26) upon the land. When he speaks, **thunder
rebukes the earth** in yet another manifestation of his power (Ps 29:3; Isa 29:6),
and he unleashes the violent **tempest from the north and the whirlwind** of
divine judgment (Isa 40:24; Jer 23:19). Yet after his fury has passed, the Lord
serenely **scatters the snow like birds flying down** toward the ground, covering
it **like locusts alighting**. The image shifts to one of calm, as **the eye marvels at
the beauty** of the snow's **whiteness, and the mind is amazed at its** quiet **falling**.

The cold of winter is another manifestation of God's power (Ps 147:16–   **43:19–20**
18; Prov 25:13). **He pours the hoarfrost** (frozen dew) **upon the earth like** a

sprinkling of white **salt, and when it freezes, it becomes** icicles resembling sharp, **pointed thorns.** In some parts of Israel, **the cold north wind blows,** causing a layer of **ice** to form **over the water,** which Ben Sira personifies as a soldier donning this protective layer of ice **like a breastplate.**

43:21–22 Eventually, the cold of winter gives way to the heat of summer, which can cause devastating droughts across Israel: the Lord **consumes the mountains and burns up the wilderness** in the Negeb to the south, **and withers the tender grass like fire** even in the greener Galilee to the north, due to the intense heat and lack of rain from April to October. Thankfully, a soothing **mist** provides much-needed moisture and **quickly heals all things; when the dew appears,** like a doctor providing relief to a sick patient **it refreshes** the land **from the heat** (compare Deut 33:28; Ps 133:3; Prov 19:12).

43:23–25 By the Lord's **counsel he stilled the great deep** or "abyss" (Hebrew *tehom*), the unsearchable depths of the oceans unleashed during the flood and personified as a monster to be subdued (16:18; 42:18; Gen 1:2; 7:11; 8:2), and he **planted islands** in the sea. Although there are many tales about the **dangers** of sailing the sea that cause listeners to **marvel,** the Lord demonstrates his infinite power by ruling over it (Ps 107:23–30; Mark 4:39). The power of the sea gave it a mysterious aura among the ancients, who believed it contained **strange and marvelous** creatures, **all kinds of living things, and huge creatures** such as the mythical sea monster called Rahab or Leviathan, symbols of the forces of evil (Job 41; Isa 27:1; 51:9).

43:26 As he concludes his survey of God's great works in creation (43:1–25), Ben Sira asserts that every force of nature is God's **messenger,** an emissary that always **finds the way** of doing his will as commanded **by his word,** which holds **all** creation **together.**

43:27–28 The last part of the poem shifts the focus back to God, who is worthy of praise because of his power revealed in creation. While there is much to say about him—and there will always be more—**we cannot reach the end,** for our words can never fully capture his power and wisdom. Thus, **the sum of our words is: "He is the all"**—a saying reminiscent of Greek philosophy asserting that God is present in every aspect of the created world (see Acts 17:28). Confronted by God's infinite splendor, people can never summon the **strength to praise him** adequately, for while he is present within creation, he also transcends it, being infinitely **greater than all his works** (Ps 145:3; Catechism 300). God must not be mistaken for creation itself (the error of pantheism; see Wis 13:1–5; Rom 1:20); rather, he is the "absolutely transcendent God who revealed himself to Israel" (Catechism 2129).

43:29–30 Though aware of the limitations of human speech, Ben Sira breaks out in praise: **Terrible is the Lord**—that is, awe-inspiring and fearsome—**and very great** (Ps 96:4), **and marvelous is his power** manifested in creation. Despite the inadequacy of human words to **praise the Lord,** we are called to **exalt him** as much as is humanly possible, even though **he will surpass even that**. Every person can choose to **exalt him** with all their **strength** (Deut 6:5) and **not grow weary**. The contemplation of God's power in creation should remind every wise person that we **cannot praise him enough**. It is an invitation to break forth in an unending song of praise (Isa 40:28–31).

With rhetorical questions, Ben Sira further emphasizes the limited human **43:31–33** capacity to know God: no one **has seen him** or can adequately **describe him** or **extol him as he is** (compare Ps 106:2). **Many** more, **greater** mysteries of God's creation **lie hidden** from sight, for only a **few of his works** have been revealed to human beings (Sir 16:21; Job 26:14). Indeed, **the Lord has made all things** that exist; yet despite the limitations of the human intellect, **to the godly** who fear him **he has granted wisdom** to uncover some of these mysteries.

Reflection and Application (42:15–43:33)

Ben Sira's hymn is a powerful reminder that praise should be a normal part of the Christian life. Though prayer naturally includes offering petitions to God and interceding for others, it is lacking if it becomes merely a litany of requests. A rich life of prayer is filled with thanksgiving and praise. While thanksgiving acknowledges God for the good things he has done, praise "lauds God for his own sake and gives him glory, quite beyond what he does, but simply because HE IS" (Catechism 2639).

God created us for "the praise of his glory" (Eph 1:12, 14; see also 1:6). Of course, he does not *need* our praise, for he is the fullness of being and of every perfection (Catechism 213). Why, then, does the Lord call for praise? He delights in it because praise "shares in the blessed happiness of the pure of heart who love God in faith before seeing him in glory" (Catechism 2639). When we praise the Lord, we testify that in Christ, through the Holy Spirit, we are children of God. Thus, we are called to praise God not only to recognize our identity but also to experience true joy. Praise is vital because it embraces other forms of prayer and carries them toward God, who is both the source and goal of prayer. It is no surprise that St. Paul exhorts the early Christians to "[address] one another in psalms and hymns and spiritual songs, singing and making melody to the Lord with all your heart" (Eph 5:19; compare Col 3:16).

What words should we use to praise God? The book of Psalms is an excellent place to start. The Psalter is a treasury of prayers encompassing hymns, petitions, lamentations, and thanksgiving—yet it is always sustained by praise. It is fitting that the Hebrew title of the Psalter is *Tehillim*, meaning "the praises," and that one of the most well-known Hebrew words, *hallelujah*, means "praise the Lord" (Catechism 2588–89).

As seen in the book of Revelation, the great assembly of the redeemed in heaven will forever sing the praise and glory of him who sits on the throne, and of the Lamb (Rev 19:1–8; Catechism 2642). This eternal reality makes it all the more vital that we learn to offer God our praise in this life: "Through him then let us continually offer up a sacrifice of praise to God, that is, the fruit of lips that acknowledge his name" (Heb 13:15). Readers may wish to include in their sacrifice of praise this and other prayers of Ben Sira (Sir 22:27–23:6; 36:1–17; 51:1–12).

Book Three

Sirach 44:1–50:29

Part VIII

Sirach 44:1–50:29

Chapter 44 marks the beginning of Book Three and the final major part of Sirach. Divine wisdom is not only manifest in the natural world; it is most visible in the heroic figures of biblical history. Following an introduction (44:1–15), Ben Sira praises Israel's famous ancestors, beginning with an overview of the early patriarchs (44:16–23); then Moses, Aaron, and Phinehas (45:1–26); Joshua, Caleb, the Judges, and Samuel (46:1–20); Nathan and David (47:1–11); Solomon and the divided kingdom (47:12–25); the prophets Elijah and Elisha in the northern kingdom of Israel (48:1–16); Hezekiah and Isaiah in the southern kingdom of Judah (48:17–25); and finally King Josiah, the great prophets, and the †postexilic heroes of Israel (49:1–16). This section presents the most extensive survey of salvation history found in Scripture.[1] Ben Sira stresses the importance of remembering these pious men so that others may learn from their wisdom. He also highlights the significance of liturgical worship, as seen in Aaron's prominent role and the detailed description of the ministry of Simeon the high priest (50:1–24), before concluding with a brief mention of Judah's neighbors and an author's postscript (50:25–29).

VIII.A. Praise of Israel's Forefathers (44:1–15)

> [1]Let us now praise famous men,
>   and our fathers in their generations.
> [2]The Lord apportioned to them great glory,
>   his majesty from the beginning.
> [3]There were those who ruled in their kingdoms,
>   and were men renowned for their power,

1. See also Jdt 5:5–21; Pss 78; 105; 106; 135; 136; Wis 10; 1 Macc 2:51–60; Acts 7:2–53.

giving counsel by their understanding,
  and proclaiming prophecies;
⁴leaders of the people in their deliberations
  and in understanding of learning for the people,
  wise in their words of instruction;
⁵those who composed musical tunes,
  and set forth verses in writing;
⁶rich men furnished with resources,
  living peaceably in their habitations—
⁷all these were honored in their generations,
  and were the glory of their times.
⁸There are some of them who have left a name,
  so that men declare their praise.
⁹And there are some who have no memorial,
  who have perished as though they had not lived;
they have become as though they had not been born,
  and so have their children after them.
¹⁰But these were men of mercy,
  whose righteous deeds have not been forgotten;
¹¹their prosperity will remain with their descendants,
  and their inheritance to their children's children.
¹²Their descendants stand by the covenants;
  their children also, for their sake.
¹³Their posterity will continue for ever,
  and their glory will not be blotted out.
¹⁴Their bodies were buried in peace,
  and their name lives to all generations.
¹⁵Peoples will declare their wisdom,
  and the congregation proclaims their praise.

OT: Job 21:8; Ps 112:6; Prov 10:7; Wis 8:13; Sir 39:8–11; 41:6–13
NT: Matt 26:13; Heb 11:1–40
Catechism: communion of saints, 946–59; memory of the saints, 1090
Lectionary: 44:1, 10–15: Sts. Joachim and Anne, Parents of the Blessed Virgin Mary

44:1–2 The Greek text adds the title "Hymn of the Fathers," and the Hebrew, "Praise of the Fathers of Old." Ben Sira sets out to **praise famous men** (Hebrew: "men of mercy" or "devout men," compare 44:10)—that is, the heroes of the faith and **fathers** of **generations** past who left a lasting memory. As a reward for their faith and wisdom, the Lord **apportioned to them** his own **glory** and gave them a share in **his majesty from the beginning** of time.

44:3–6 Ben Sira lists twelve categories of heroes worthy of praise because they shared in God's glory. Some **ruled in their kingdoms**, like David and Solomon (47:1–22), or were **renowned for their power**, such as Joshua, Caleb, the Judges, and Samuel (46:1–20). Others were counselors who gave advice **by**

their understanding, like Nathan and Isaiah (47:1; 48:20–22), or seers who proclaimed **prophecies**, such as Elijah, Elisha, Isaiah, Jeremiah, Ezekiel, and the twelve minor prophets (48:1–16; 49:8–10). Still others were **leaders of the people** (Hebrew: "princes of nations"), like Joseph, Zerubbabel, and Nehemiah (49:11–15), or lawgivers who, **in their deliberations** and **understanding** of the people's **learning**, provided guiding rules, like Moses (44:23–45:5). Some were †sages, **wise in their words of instruction** or "skilled in composition" and "speakers of proverbs in keeping with their traditions" (Hebrew), like Solomon and Ben Sira himself. Others **composed musical tunes**, like David, or **set forth verses in writing**, such as Solomon and Hezekiah (Isa 38:9–20). Among these were **rich men furnished with resources**, such as Abraham, Isaac, and Jacob (Sir 44:19–23), and those who lived **peaceably in their habitations**, like Job before and after his trials (Job 1:1–5; 42:10–17).

    All these godly heroes **were honored** and given **glory** during their lifetimes.   **44:7–9**
Some **left a name** and were remembered long after their deaths: their good reputation outlived them, and people continued to praise them in Ben Sira's time and beyond (39:9–11; 41:12–13). Yet others **have no memorial** and were utterly forgotten, having **perished as though they had** neither **lived** nor **been born** (compare Job 10:19; Obad 16), along with **their children**. Ben Sira may be referring to holy men who, unfortunately, have remained unknown (Wis 3:1–3), or, perhaps more likely in light of Sir 41:6–13, to godless men who are rightly forgotten.

    In contrast to the many saints and sinners whose memory has faded into   **44:10–13**
oblivion, Ben Sira now recalls famous **men of mercy** (44:1), godly men **whose righteous deeds** were neither **forgotten** nor lost at their deaths but **remain with their descendants** as an **inheritance** for many generations to come

Sinners Are Forgotten

Rabanus Maurus reflects on how, in the end, the wicked will leave no lasting memory and will be entirely forgotten:

> The godless and sinners were not worthy of memory, because if the Scripture says something of them, it does so not to praise them but to blame. In the psalm it is written of them, "The fortresses of the enemy have been pulled down forever, the memory of the city you destroyed has disappeared. Their memory has disappeared with a roar" [Ps 9:6]. At the end of the world, in fact, to the devil's joy, those who it has been determined belong to his city will fall, and their memory will perish with a fantastic din when they go to eternal punishment.[a]

a. Rabanus Maurus, *On Ecclesiasticus* 10.1, in Sever J. Voicu, ed., *Apocrypha*, ACCS:OT 15 (Downers Grove, IL: InterVarsity, 2010), 385.

(45:25–26; Job 21:8). Their godly legacy is preserved because **their descendants** still faithfully uphold God's **covenants,**[2] honoring the memory of their ancestors. It is through this generational faithfulness that the **posterity** of these righteous heroes **will continue for ever**—in other words, they will always have living descendants—**and their glory** will never fade or **be blotted out.**

44:14–15   The **bodies** of these heroes in the faith were given an honorable burial, so they rest **in peace, and their name lives** on in the memory of future **generations,** who remember them for ages to come (41:11–13; Ps 112:6; Wis 8:13). **Peoples** continue to **declare their wisdom**—as Ben Sira does here—**and the congregation** (Greek *ekklēsia*) of God's people—first Israel and later the Church (*ekklēsia*)—**proclaims their praise,** just as it honors the scribe and sage (Sir 39:10).

VIII.B. The Early Patriarchs: Enoch, Noah, Abraham, Isaac, and Jacob (44:16–23)

[16]Enoch pleased the Lord, and was taken up;
    he was an example of repentance to all generations.

[17]Noah was found perfect and righteous;
    in the time of wrath he was taken in exchange;
therefore a remnant was left to the earth
    when the flood came.
[18]Everlasting covenants were made with him
    that all flesh should not be blotted out by a flood.

[19]Abraham was the great father of a multitude of nations,
    and no one has been found like him in glory;
[20]he kept the law of the Most High,
    and was taken into covenant with him;
he established the covenant in his flesh,
    and when he was tested he was found faithful.
[21]Therefore the Lord assured him by an oath
    that the nations would be blessed through his posterity;
that he would multiply him like the dust of the earth,
    and exalt his posterity like the stars,
and cause them to inherit from sea to sea
    and from the River to the ends of the earth.
[22]To Isaac also he gave the same assurance
    for the sake of Abraham his father.

2. See Sir 17:12; 24:23; 28:7; 39:8; 45:15, 24–25.

²³The blessing of all men and the covenant
  he made to rest upon the head of Jacob;
he acknowledged him with his blessings,
  and gave him his inheritance;
he determined his portions,
  and distributed them among twelve tribes.

OT: Gen 5:24; 6–9; 12–22; 26–28; 49
NT: Matt 1:1–2; Acts 7:1–8; Rom 4:1–25; Gal 3:6–18; Heb 11:5–22; 2 Pet 2:5
Catechism: the covenants with Noah and Abraham, 56–61

Ben Sira praises the early patriarchs of the book of Genesis. Interestingly, he **44:16** skips over Adam and begins his overview of salvation history with **Enoch**, who **pleased the Lord** (Hebrew: "walked with the Lord") **and was taken up** to heaven (Gen 5:24; see Sir 49:14). While Genesis does not specify why God "took" Enoch, Ben Sira asserts that he was **an example of repentance to all generations**. This interpretation is a theological development, as there is no record in earlier texts of Enoch sinning and repenting. The Hebrew text of Sirach instead states that he was "a sign of knowledge to all generations." According to other traditions, God took him to preserve him from evil (Wis 4:10–14; Heb 11:5).

Noah was the only one **found perfect and righteous** in his generation (Gen **44:17–18** 6:9; 7:1; 2 Pet 2:5); **in the time of wrath**, when God destroyed the world with the flood because of the sins of humankind (Gen 6:11–13), **he was taken in exchange** (literally, "he became an exchange") for the human race, or "renewed the race" (NABRE). Noah, his wife, their three sons, and their wives (Gen 7:13)

Enoch Walked with God

LIVING TRADITION

Drawing inspiration from the apocryphal *Apocalypse of Peter* (second century), Rabanus Maurus comments on the taking up of Enoch to heaven and anticipates his future return alongside Elijah at the end of the world. Rabanus is likely identifying Enoch and Elijah with the two witnesses who will be martyred by the antichrist according to the book of Revelation (Rev 11:3–11).

Enoch . . . walked with God and was taken up into paradise [Gen 5:24]. And in this way the splendor of the saints shines, because from the pains of this world they are taken up to the peace of the heavenly kingdom. It is believed that he will return together with Elijah at the end of the world, to counsel men and women so that they would turn from their sins to repentance. In this way, together with his companion, he will pay the debt of death in the persecution of the antichrist.[a]

a. Rabanus Maurus, *On Ecclesiasticus* 10.3 (Voicu, *Apocrypha*, 386).

constituted the surviving **remnant left** to repopulate **the earth** after **the flood** wiped out all living beings. The Lord made **everlasting covenants** with Noah (Hebrew: "by an eternal sign [God] sealed it with him"), promising that he would never again blot out **all flesh** by means of **a flood**. The sign of God's pledge not to flood the earth again was the rainbow (Gen 9:12–17).

44:19–20   **Abraham was the great father of a multitude of nations** (Gen 17:4–5), beginning with Israel; thus, he remains unsurpassed **in glory** (Hebrew: "he kept his glory without stain"). The assertion that **he kept the law of the Most High** seems anachronistic, since the †Torah was given to Israel centuries after Abraham. Yet God says of Abraham in Gen 26:5 that he "kept my charge, my commandments, my statutes, and my laws." On the basis of this verse, ancient Jewish commentaries hold that Abraham kept the law even before it had been revealed to Israel. Abraham also entered into a **covenant with** God, sealed **in his flesh** with the sign of circumcision (Gen 17:9–11). Yet it is **when he was tested** and proved himself willing to sacrifice his son Isaac that **he was found faithful** (Gen 22:1–19; 1 Macc 2:52; Heb 11:17).

44:21   Because of Abraham's faithfulness, **the Lord assured him** with a solemn, binding **oath** that he would bless all **nations** through his descendants (Gen 22:16–18). The Lord promised to **multiply him like the dust of the earth** (Gen 13:16), **exalt his posterity like the stars** (15:5), **and cause** his descendants, the children of Israel, **to inherit** the land of Canaan **from sea to sea** (perhaps the Red Sea to the Mediterranean), and from the **River to the ends of the earth**— a hyperbole possibly encompassing the area between the Euphrates and the Mediterranean coast (Exod 23:31; Deut 11:24; Josh 1:4).

44:22–23   To Abraham's son **Isaac also** the Lord **gave the same assurance** (Gen 26:3–6, 24), promising to establish his universal **blessing** and **covenant** with Isaac's son **Jacob**, whom God renamed "Israel" (32:28; 35:10)—even though Jacob deceived Isaac into giving him the blessing of the firstborn that belonged to his elder brother, Esau (27:1–29; 28:3–4, 13–15). Despite this, God **gave him his inheritance**, the land of Israel, which he divided into **portions** and **distributed** among his twelve sons, the fathers of the **twelve tribes** of Israel (Gen 35:22–26; 49:1–28).

VIII.C. (i) Heroes of the Exodus: Moses (45:1–5)

> [1]From his descendants the Lord brought forth a man of mercy,
>   who found favor in the sight of all flesh
> and was beloved by God and man,
>   Moses, whose memory is blessed.
> [2]He made him equal in glory to the holy ones,
>   and made him great in the fears of his enemies.

> [3]By his words he caused signs to cease;
>   the Lord glorified him in the presence of kings.
> He gave him commands for his people,
>   and showed him part of his glory.
> [4]He sanctified him through faithfulness and meekness;
>   he chose him out of all mankind.
> [5]He made him hear his voice,
>   and led him into the thick darkness,
> and gave him the commandments face to face,
>   the law of life and knowledge,
> to teach Jacob the covenant,
>   and Israel his judgments.

OT: Exod 2; 7–12; 20; 33–34; Num 12
NT: Heb 3:1–6
Catechism: the Mosaic covenant, 62–63

Somewhat surprisingly, Ben Sira omits Joseph (Gen 37–50) and goes directly from **45:1** Jacob to the book of Exodus, covering the figures of Moses (Sir 45:1–5), Aaron (45:6–22), and Phinehas (45:23–26). From Jacob's **descendants**, the twelve tribes of Israel, **the Lord brought forth a man of mercy** (44:10), **who found favor** before **all** people—including Pharaoh's daughter (Exod 2:5–10), Reuel and his daughters (2:16–22), and the Egyptians (11:3)—**and was beloved by God** (33:11; Num 12:7–8) **and man**. This man of mercy is, of course, **Moses,** who led the Israelites out of Egypt and **whose memory is blessed** in perpetuity (compare Sir 39:9; 44:10–15).

The Lord made Moses **equal in glory to the holy ones**—that is, the angels **45:2–3** (42:17; Exod 34:29–30)—and fearsome to **his enemies**. By Moses's **words** God swiftly unleashed the ten plagues upon the Egyptians (Exod 7–12; Deut 4:34; 26:8) and then **caused** the plagues **to cease**, thus glorifying Moses **in the presence of kings**—namely, Pharaoh (Exod 7:1–7). God **gave him commands for his people**—the †Decalogue and other precepts of the †Torah—**and showed him part of his glory** by allowing Moses to see his "back" (Exod 33:18–23; 34:5–8).

The Lord **sanctified** Moses and set him apart because of his **faithfulness and** **45:4–5** **meekness** (Num 12:3–8; Heb 3:2, 5), choosing him **out of all mankind** (literally, "from all flesh") to lead Israel out of Egypt and mediate God's covenant with them. God allowed Moses to **hear his voice** at Mount Sinai (Exod 33:11; Deut 4:36), **led him** into the cloud and **thick darkness** of his presence (Exod 20:21; 24:18), and personally **gave him the commandments**, including the Decalogue (Exod 20; 32:15; Deut 6:1), as part of his divinely revealed word, the Torah, which imparts **life and knowledge** to those who observe it (Sir 17:11; Lev 18:5; Deut 30:15–16; Ezek 20:11). The purpose of the Sinai revelation was **to teach Jacob**—a synonym for **Israel** (Ps 147:19)—God's **covenant** and **judgments** so they could live as his holy people.

Leaving Spiritual Egypt

Rabanus Maurus interprets the exodus from Egyptian slavery to the promised land †typologically as fulfilled in Christ and in the Christian life, leading from the slavery of sin to eternal life in heaven:

> Under the guidance of Christ, the Law freed the faithful from the spiritual Egypt and from the power of the true pharaoh by the waters of baptism, so that in the desert of this world, instructed and taught by the divine precepts, they would reach the promised land, the heavenly homeland, where they will have every good thing in abundance and will enjoy eternal life.[a]

a. Rabanus Maurus, *On Ecclesiasticus* 10.8 (Voicu, *Apocrypha*, 388).

VIII.C. (ii) Heroes of the Exodus: Aaron and Phinehas (45:6–26)

[6]He exalted Aaron, the brother of Moses,
  a holy man like him, of the tribe of Levi.
[7]He made an everlasting covenant with him,
  and gave him the priesthood of the people.
He blessed him with splendid vestments,
  and put a glorious robe upon him.
[8]He clothed him with superb perfection,
  and strengthened him with the symbols of authority,
  the linen breeches, the long robe, and the ephod.
[9]And he encircled him with pomegranates,
  with very many golden bells round about,
to send forth a sound as he walked,
  to make their ringing heard in the temple
  as a reminder to the sons of his people;
[10]with a holy garment, of gold and blue
  and purple, the work of an embroiderer;
with the oracle of judgment, Urim and Thummim;
[11]with twisted scarlet, the work of a craftsman;
with precious stones engraved like signets,
  in a setting of gold, the work of a jeweler,
for a reminder, in engraved letters,
  according to the number of the tribes of Israel;
[12]with a gold crown upon his turban,
  inscribed like a signet with "Holiness,"
a distinction to be prized, the work of an expert,
  the delight of the eyes, richly adorned.

¹³Before his time there never were such beautiful things.
  No outsider ever put them on,
but only his sons
  and his descendants perpetually.
¹⁴His sacrifices shall be wholly burned
  twice every day continually.
¹⁵Moses ordained him,
  and anointed him with holy oil;
it was an everlasting covenant for him
  and for his descendants all the days of heaven,
to minister to the Lord and serve as priest
  and bless his people in his name.
¹⁶He chose him out of all the living
  to offer sacrifice to the Lord,
incense and a pleasing odor as a memorial portion,
  to make atonement for the people.
¹⁷In his commandments he gave him
  authority in statutes and judgments,
to teach Jacob the testimonies,
  and to enlighten Israel with his law.
¹⁸Outsiders conspired against him,
  and envied him in the wilderness,
Dathan and Abiram and their men
  and the company of Korah, in wrath and anger.
¹⁹The Lord saw it and was not pleased,
  and in the wrath of his anger they were destroyed;
he wrought wonders against them
  to consume them in flaming fire.
²⁰He added glory to Aaron
  and gave him a heritage;
he allotted to him the first of the first fruits,
  he prepared bread of first fruits in abundance;
²¹for they eat the sacrifices to the Lord,
  which he gave to him and his descendants.
²²But in the land of the people he has no inheritance,
  and he has no portion among the people;
  for the Lord himself is his portion and inheritance.
²³Phinehas the son of Eleazar is the third in glory,
  for he was zealous in the fear of the Lord,
and stood fast, when the people turned away,
  in the ready goodness of his soul,
  and made atonement for Israel.
²⁴Therefore a covenant of peace was established with him,
  that he should be leader of the sanctuary and of his people,

that he and his descendants should have
the dignity of the priesthood for ever.
²⁵A covenant was also established with David,
the son of Jesse, of the tribe of Judah:
the heritage of the king is from son to son only;
so the heritage of Aaron is for his descendants.
²⁶May the Lord grant you wisdom in your heart
to judge his people in righteousness,
so that their prosperity may not vanish,
and that their glory may endure throughout their generations.

OT: Exod 28–29; Num 16; 18; 25; Ps 106:30–31; 1 Macc 2:54
NT: Heb 5:1–6; 7:11
Catechism: Old Covenant priesthood, 1539–43

45:6–7   The Lord **exalted Aaron, the brother of Moses**—both of whom were sons of
Amram and Jochebed (Exod 4:14; 6:20). Aaron was also **a holy man**, sanctified by
virtue of his priesthood (Ps 106:16), **of the tribe of Levi**, the fourth son of Jacob
(Gen 29:34; Exod 2:1–2; 4:14). God **made an everlasting covenant** with Aaron,
granting him and his sons **the priesthood**, which would remain in his genealogical
line (Exod 29:4–9, 44; 40:13–15). The Lord **blessed** Aaron **with splendid** priestly
vestments and **a glorious robe**, which Ben Sira describes at length (Sir 45:8–13;
Exod 28:1–4). Aaron's prominence in this chapter highlights the importance of
the priesthood for Ben Sira, given its central role in communicating God's wisdom
to Israel through the temple liturgy (Sir 24:10–12; 50:1–21).

45:8–9   The Lord **clothed** Aaron **with superb perfection** and beauty (50:11; Exod
28:2, 40), dignifying him with **symbols** of divine **authority** as represented by
the priestly garments, which included **the linen breeches** or undergarments
(Exod 28:42–43), **the long** blue **robe** (28:31–35), **and the ephod**—a decorative
apron of gold, blue, purple, and scarlet yarns that the high priest wore over
the robe (28:6–14). God **encircled** Aaron with decorative **pomegranates** knit-
ted of blue, purple, and scarlet stuff (28:33), alternating with **golden bells** on
the lower hem of the robe (28:34). These bells rang as the high priest **walked**
around **in the temple**, reminding the assembly that he was ministering inside
the sanctuary (28:35).

45:10–11   The **holy garment, of gold and blue and purple** likely refers to the em-
broidered ephod (Exod 28:6–14). The **oracle of judgment** is the breastpiece,
made from a piece of square cloth (28:15–30), in which were kept the **Urim
and Thummim** (literally, "the decider of truth"), small objects (perhaps similar
to dice) used to determine God's will (Sir 33:3; Num 27:21; 1 Sam 14:41). The
breastpiece was made of **twisted scarlet** (Exod 28:15) and featured twelve **precious stones engraved like signets**, arranged in four rows of three **in a setting
of gold**, representing the twelve **tribes of Israel** (28:17–21, 29).

Figure 11. The high priest ministering in the sanctuary

The high priest also wore **a gold crown** or plate **upon his turban** (Exod   45:12–13
28:36–38; 29:6), **inscribed like a signet** with a seal of **"Holiness"** (the inscrip-
tion "holy to the Lord," according to Exod 39:30). Wearing this crown was **a
distinction to be prized** and a high honor for the high priest, whose beautiful
ornament was a **delight** to the **eyes** of all who saw him. Ben Sira emphasizes
that before Aaron's **time such beautiful things** had never existed. Since the
garments symbolized his role as mediator between God and the people, **no
outsider ever put them on**; they were strictly reserved for Aaron's **sons** and
their **descendants perpetually** (Exod 29:29).

As for the high priest's liturgical functions, his **sacrifices** were to be **wholly**   45:14–15
burned twice every day continually—one lamb in the morning and one in the

The Garments of the High Priest

Although Ben Sira does not explain the symbolism of the high priest's garments, other †Second Temple texts from the two centuries after him shed light on what he likely intended. The Wisdom of Solomon asserts that upon Aaron's robe "the whole world was depicted" (Wis 18:24), suggesting that, for the Jews of that period, the high priest represented not only Israel but all of humanity and indeed the entire world before God. The Jewish philosopher Philo (ca. 20 BC–AD 50) depicts in detail the cosmic symbolism of the high priest's garments:

[117] Such was the vesture of the high priest. But I must not leave untold its meaning and that of its parts. We have in it as a whole and in its parts a typical representation of the world and its particular parts. . . . [131] In setting a turban on the priest's head, instead of a diadem, he expresses his judgement that he who is consecrated to God is superior when he acts as a priest to all others, not only the ordinary laymen, but even kings. . . . [133] Thus is the high priest arrayed when he sets forth to his holy duties, in order that when he enters to offer the ancestral prayers and sacrifices there may enter with him the whole universe, as signified in the types of it which he brings upon his person, the long robe a copy of the air, the pomegranate of water, the flower trimming of earth, the scarlet of fire, the ephod of heaven, the circular emeralds on the shoulder-tops with the six engravings in each of the two hemispheres which they resemble in form, the twelve stones on the breast in four rows of threes of the zodiac, the reason-seat of that Reason which holds together and administers all things. [134] For he who has been consecrated to the Father of the world must needs have that Father's Son [i.e., the world] with all His fullness of excellence to plead his cause, that sins may be remembered no more and good gifts showered in rich abundance. [135] . . . For, as he wears a vesture which represents the world, his first duty is to carry the pattern enshrined in his heart, and so be in a sense transformed from a man into the nature of the world; and . . . be himself a little world, a microcosm.[a]

a. Philo, *On the Life of Moses* 2.117, 131–35, in *Philo*, trans. F. H. Colson and G. H. Whitaker, vol. 6, Loeb Classical Library 289 (Cambridge, MA: Harvard University Press, 1935), 506–16. See also Josephus, *Antiquities* 3.7.7.

evening (Exod 29:38–42; Num 28:3–8). **Moses** instituted the priestly ministry when he **ordained** Aaron **and anointed him with holy oil** (Lev 8:12), establishing the **everlasting covenant** of the priesthood to last **all the days of heaven**—that is, as long as creation endures (Sir 45:7; Deut 11:21; Ps 89:29)—**to minister to the Lord** on behalf of Israel (Exod 28:41) **and bless his people in his name** with the solemn priestly blessing (Num 6:23–27).

45:16–17   The Lord **chose** Aaron, despite his flaws, from the entire human race **to offer** him **sacrifice**, the priests' primary role (Lev 1–7), with **incense** as a symbol of prayer. The grain offering consumed by fire, together with the incense, produced

a pleasing odor as a memorial portion that would symbolically "remind" the Lord of his people (Sir 35:7; Lev 2:2, 9, 16). The primary purpose of the sacrifices was **to make atonement** and obtain the forgiveness of sins **for the people** (Lev 4:20, 31; 16:32–34). **In his commandments** the Lord also gave Aaron and the priests **authority in statutes and judgments**: they were entrusted with the task of teaching God's **testimonies**, enlightening **Israel with his law**, making judicial decisions in upholding its observance (Lev 10:11; Deut 17:10–12; 21:5). The authority that God granted to the Aaronic priests prefigures the authority that Jesus would later give to his apostles (Matt 16:18–19; 18:18).

Aaron's priestly authority did not remain unchallenged. **Outsiders**, not from   45:18–19
his lineage and ineligible to be priests, **conspired against him** and sought to seize his priestly authority when they **envied him in the wilderness** (Num 16:1–35). **Dathan and Abiram**, along with **their men** from the tribe of Reuben, joined forces with **the company of Korah**—a Levite, but not a descendant of Aaron (Num 16:1)—to rise up against Aaron **in wrath and anger**. This rebellion against the priesthood greatly displeased the **Lord**, who **in the wrath of his anger** put an end to it by causing the earth to open up and swallow the rebels (Num 16:31–33); **he wrought wonders** against the other 250 men who had joined the rebellion by consuming them **in flaming fire** (Num 16:35).

After Korah's rebellion, the Lord **added glory to Aaron and gave him a heritage**   45:20–21
by increasing his priestly rights, privileges, and responsibilities (Num 18:1–7). He reserved the best portion of **the first fruits**, the first part of the harvest, for the priests (Num 18:11–13), and **prepared bread of first fruits in abundance**— possibly the bread of the presence that was kept in the sanctuary and eaten by the priests (Lev 24:5–9). The priests also ate part of **the sacrifices** offered **to the Lord**, which were reserved for Aaron **and his descendants** (Num 18:8–10).

Yet priestly privileges came at a cost. **In the land** of Israel the priest or Levite   45:22
had **no inheritance** or **portion** of territory **among the people** like the other tribes, **for the Lord himself** was their **portion and inheritance**. Serving God in his sanctuary was considered a higher privilege than owning land (Num 18:20; Deut 18:1; Josh 13:14).

Phinehas the son of Eleazar and grandson of Aaron (Exod 6:25) **is the third**   45:23–24
in glory after Moses and Aaron, **for he was zealous in the fear of the Lord**. Phinehas **stood fast** in faithfulness **when the people turned away** in rebellion at Shittim and committed sexual sin with the daughters of Moab (Num 25:1–5). With courageous resolve, he **made atonement for Israel**, opposing evil by killing an Israelite idolater and fornicator, along with his Midianite concubine, thereby averting God's wrath and halting a devastating plague. As a reward for his zeal, God established **a covenant of peace** with him, the "covenant of the perpetual priesthood" originally given to Aaron, appointing him **leader of the sanctuary and of his people**, and granting him **and his descendants** the **dignity of the** high **priesthood for ever** (Sir 45:7; Num 25:1–13; Ps 106:30–31; 1 Macc 2:54).

Zeal against the Flesh

Rabanus Maurus interprets Phinehas's godly zeal as a type of the zeal and intolerance of evil that Christians should demonstrate in combating the disordered desires of their flesh. If they do this successfully, they will share in Christ's eternal priesthood and kingdom:

> Whoever, moved by godly zeal, makes an effort to suppress the impulses of his flesh or reproves and restrains those under him, so as to not let them deviate from the truth out of lust and sexual desire, will have the dignity of the eternal priesthood in the church of God, which rightly belongs to that priest of whom it is written, "Like Melchizedek, you are a priest forever"[Ps 110:4]. He will possess, with him, the eternal kingdom in heavenly light.[a]

a. Rabanus Maurus, *On Ecclesiasticus* 10.10 (Voicu, *Apocrypha*, 391).

45:25–26   Just as the royal **covenant with David** is a hereditary covenant, where kingship is passed down through David's genealogical line **from son to son only** (2 Sam 7:11–16; 2 Chron 13:5; Ps 89:3–4), **so the heritage of Aaron**, the priesthood, is reserved **for his descendants**. Ben Sira concludes this section with a short prayer of blessing addressed to the priests of his own day. The first sentence appears only in the Hebrew: "And now bless the LORD who has crowned you with glory" (NRSV, ESV-CE, NABRE). Ben Sira prays that **the Lord grant** the priests **wisdom to judge his people in righteousness**, as stipulated by the law, **so that their prosperity may not vanish**, and their success, honor, and **glory may endure** for all generations to come (50:1–24).

VIII.D. From Conquest to Kingdom: Joshua, Caleb, the Judges, and Samuel (46:1–20)

> ¹Joshua the son of Nun was mighty in war,
>   and was the successor of Moses in prophesying.
> He became, in accordance with his name,
>   a great savior of God's elect,
> to take vengeance on the enemies that rose against them,
>   so that he might give Israel its inheritance.
> ²How glorious he was when he lifted his hands
>   and stretched out his sword against the cities!
> ³Who before him ever stood so firm?
>   For he waged the wars of the Lord.
> ⁴Was not the sun held back by his hand?
>   And did not one day become as long as two?

⁵He called upon the Most High, the Mighty One,
  when enemies pressed him on every side,
⁶and the great Lord answered him
  with hailstones of mighty power.
He hurled down war upon that nation,
  and at the descent of Beth-horon he destroyed those who
    resisted,
so that the nations might know his armament,
  that he was fighting in the sight of the Lord;
  for he wholly followed the Mighty One.
⁷And in the days of Moses he did a loyal deed,
  he and Caleb the son of Jephunneh:
  they withstood the congregation,
  restrained the people from sin,
  and stilled their wicked murmuring.
⁸And these two alone were preserved
  out of six hundred thousand people on foot,
to bring them into their inheritance,
  into a land flowing with milk and honey.
⁹And the Lord gave Caleb strength,
  which remained with him to old age,
so that he went up to the hill country,
  and his children obtained it for an inheritance;
¹⁰so that all the sons of Israel might see
  that it is good to follow the Lord.

¹¹The judges also, with their respective names,
  those whose hearts did not fall into idolatry
and who did not turn away from the Lord—
  may their memory be blessed!
¹²May their bones revive from where they lie,
  and may the name of those who have been honored
  live again in their sons!

¹³Samuel, beloved by his Lord,
  a prophet of the Lord, established the kingdom
  and anointed rulers over his people.
¹⁴By the law of the Lord he judged the congregation,
  and the Lord watched over Jacob.
¹⁵By his faithfulness he was proved to be a prophet,
  and by his words he became known as a trustworthy seer.
¹⁶He called upon the Lord, the Mighty One,
  when his enemies pressed him on every side,
and he offered in sacrifice a sucking lamb.
¹⁷Then the Lord thundered from heaven,
  and made his voice heard with a mighty sound;

¹⁸and he wiped out the leaders of the people of Tyre
and all the rulers of the Philistines.
¹⁹Before the time of his eternal sleep,
Samuel called men to witness before the Lord and his
anointed:
"I have not taken any one's property,
not so much as a pair of shoes."
And no man accused him.
²⁰Even after he had fallen asleep he prophesied
and revealed to the king his death,
and lifted up his voice out of the earth in prophecy,
to blot out the wickedness of the people.

OT: Num 13–14; Josh 8; 10; 14:6–15; Judg 1–16; 1 Sam 7–12; 28
NT: Acts 3:24; Heb 11:32–34
Catechism: fortitude, 1808

46:1 **Joshua the son of Nun**, also called Hoshea, was from the tribe of Ephraim (Exod 17:9–13; Num 13:8). He **was mighty in war** as he led the Israelites in the conquest of the promised land. As Moses's **successor** (Hebrew: "aide") **in prophesying** (Exod 24:13; 33:11), he came to be recognized as a prophet like his mentor. The book of Joshua is the first of the "former prophets" in the Jewish canon of Scripture. True to **his name**—Joshua means "the Lord saves"—he became **a great savior of God's elect**, the people of Israel, by defeating their **enemies**, the Amorites (Josh 10:6–14), and giving **Israel its inheritance**, the land of Canaan (Deut 1:38; 3:28; Josh 11:23).

46:2–3 Joshua was **glorious** when he **lifted his hands** as a signal for his army to attack the city of Ai (Josh 8:18–19, 26), and when he brandished **his sword against** the Canaanite **cities** that the Israelites conquered. No one could withstand him (Josh 1:5), **for he waged the wars of the Lord**—the true commander-in-chief who led Israel into battle (Josh 1:5; 10:14).

46:4–6 Ben Sira marvels at the miracle when **the sun** stood still at Joshua's command, so that **one day** became **as long as two**, enabling the Israelites to defeat the Amorite kings at Gibeon (Josh 10:6–14). Joshua **called upon the Most High** when his **enemies** threatened him **on every side, and the great Lord** delivered Israel by hurling devastating **hailstones** upon the Amorites. This occurred at **the descent of Beth-horon**—twin cities (Lower and Upper Beth-horon) between the territories of Ephraim and Benjamin, about twelve miles northeast of Jerusalem (Josh 10:11; 16:3, 5). There Joshua **destroyed** Israel's foes, **so that the nations might know his armament**—that is, the source of his military strength, that he was waging war on behalf of **the Lord**. Joshua's obedience was the key to his victory, **for he wholly followed the Mighty One**.

46:7 Returning to the wilderness period **in the days of Moses**, Joshua **did a loyal deed**, along with **Caleb the son of Jephunneh** from the tribe of Judah (Num

13:6), as two of the twelve spies whom Moses sent to scout the land of Canaan. When the people murmured and rebelled, Joshua and Caleb alone supported Moses in the plan to conquer the promised land: **they withstood the congregation** when everyone wanted to go back to Egypt, **restrained the people from sin** by exhorting them to trust in God, thereby averting his wrath (Hebrew, NABRE), **and stilled their wicked murmuring** against Moses and Aaron (Num 13:30–14:10).

Because of their faithfulness and courage, **these two alone**, Joshua and Caleb, **46:8** were spared among the **six hundred thousand people** who wandered through the wilderness **on foot** for nearly forty years (16:10; Num 11:21; 14:30; 26:65). They alone, as members of the first generation, survived the wanderings and were led by God into their promised **inheritance**, the prosperous **land** of Canaan, **flowing with milk and honey** (Exod 3:8; Deut 6:3).

Pleased with his servant, **the Lord gave Caleb strength** even into **old age**. At **46:9–10** eighty-five (Josh 14:6–11), Caleb conquered **the hill country** populated by the Anakim (Josh 14:12), and his descendants possessed it as **an inheritance** long after his death (Num 14:24; Josh 14:9, 13–15). The Lord made Caleb prosper **so that all the sons of Israel** would recognize in Caleb's enduring inheritance **that it is good** to obey, trust, and **follow the Lord**.

The judges who led Israel after the conquest, such as Othniel, Ehud, Deborah, **46:11–12** Barak, Gideon, Jephthah, and Samson, were key political and military leaders from the death of Joshua until the time of Samuel. However, Ben Sira acknowledges that several of them were not exemplary models of faith. He prays for those who did not succumb to **idolatry** or abandon **the Lord**, asking that **their memory be blessed** and that they may always be remembered and honored (35:7; 39:9). In a rare Old Testament allusion to the resurrection of the dead, Ben Sira wishes that **their bones** might **revive from where they lie** (49:10; Ezek 37:1–14) and that **the name** and memory of those **honored** in their lifetimes might **live again in their sons** (Sir 44:10–15; Tob 4:12).

Samuel is a transitional figure marking the shift between the judges and **46:13** the founding of the Israelite kingdom. He was **beloved by his Lord** for his irreproachable character and recognized as **a prophet** both during his lifetime (1 Sam 3:19–20) and after his death (2 Chron 35:18; Acts 3:24; 13:20). He **established the kingdom and anointed** Israel's first two kings, Saul (1 Sam 9:27–10:1) and David (16:3). This verse differs notably in the Hebrew, which emphasizes Samuel's unique consecration to God even before his birth: "Beloved of his people and dear to his Maker, pledged in a vow from his mother's womb, a Nazirite of the Lord in the prophetic office, was Samuel, judge and officiating priest. By the word of God he established the kingdom and anointed princes over the people" (compare NABRE).

In contrast to the often questionable leadership of many judges, Samuel ruled **46:14–15** **by the law of the Lord**, calling the people to return to God and his commandments

(1 Sam 7:3–6), thereby securing the Lord's protection over **Jacob** (Israel). **By his faithfulness** he earned an excellent reputation among the people as **a prophet** (1 Sam 9:6), and by the integrity of **his words** people recognized him as **a trustworthy seer**, whose visions were dependable (1 Sam 9:9, 11, 18–19).

46:16–18   Samuel was a powerful intercessor: like Joshua (46:5), he prayed to the mighty **Lord** when **his enemies**, the Philistines, **pressed him on every side** at Mizpah, and he offered a young **lamb** as a whole burnt offering (1 Sam 7:5–9) to God. In response, the **Lord** heard his prayer, **thundered from heaven** with a mighty voice, and routed **the leaders of the people of Tyre** (Hebrew: "the leaders of the enemy"[3]) and **the rulers of the Philistines** (1 Sam 7:10–14).

46:19–20   **Before the time of his eternal sleep**, near the end of his life, **Samuel called** a representative group of the people of Israel to testify **before the Lord and his anointed**, King Saul, that he had **not taken any one's property** during his time as judge of Israel. Aware of his irreproachable conduct, **no man accused him** of any wrongdoing (1 Sam 12:1–5). Even after his death Samuel **prophesied** when King Saul—in violation of the †Torah's prohibition against necromancy (Deut 18:9–14)—consulted him via the medium of Endor (1 Sam 28:3–19), revealing **to the king** that he would die the very next day. Samuel spoke prophetically after his death **to blot out the wickedness of the people**, perhaps in the sense that Saul's death and Israel's defeat on Mount Gilboa (1 Sam 31:1–6) atoned for their disobedience and sins.

Reflection and Application (46:1–20)

Ben Sira's survey of the conquest period under Joshua's leadership highlights the value of *fortitude* (also called courage, strength, or might). Fortitude is "the moral virtue that ensures firmness in difficulties and constancy in the pursuit of the good" (Catechism 1808). It is an essential virtue in situations of war, where soldiers, facing an enemy, risk serious injury or death. Without fortitude, an army would be doomed to defeat.

While many people today rarely, if ever, find themselves in such life-threatening situations, they are no less in need of fortitude, for it is the virtue that "strengthens the resolve to resist temptations and to overcome obstacles in the moral life." In a world filled with pressures tempting us to compromise with sin, Christians must exercise fortitude not only to follow God's commandments steadfastly but also to fearlessly resist evil in word and deed, even when this draws mockery or persecution. Fortitude "enables one to conquer fear, even fear of death, and to face trials and persecutions," even disposing one "to renounce and sacrifice his life in defense of a just cause" (Catechism 1808).

3. The Hebrew text is probably more accurate, given that Tyre is not mentioned in 1 Sam 7:7–14. The Hebrew words for "Tyre" and "enemy" are very close.

The Israelites' refusal to conquer the promised land, coupled with their desire to return to Egypt, stemmed not only from unbelief but also from a lack of fortitude, or cowardice (Num 13:25–14:10). Cowardice is not the same as fear. A coward is dominated and paralyzed by fear, allowing it to drive his actions and leading him to avoid difficulties at all costs. While there is much to fear in life—such as the prospect of losing one's health, job, financial security, a loved one, or many other things—a courageous person keeps fear in check and has the strength of character to take risks in pursuit of a higher good, serving God and neighbor.

While fortitude is an †acquired virtue that grows through practice (i.e., a person who repeats small acts of courage eventually becomes a courageous person), it is also one of the seven gifts of the Holy Spirit. This gift is a grace that perfects the virtue of fortitude in the soul (Isa 11:1–2; Catechism 1831), helping people to remain steadfast in the face of dangers while instilling in them a confident hope for eternal life.[4] Therefore, we should both practice the virtue of fortitude and also pray that God may grant us this great gift.

VIII.E. The Davidic Kingdom (47:1–11)

¹And after him Nathan rose up
   to prophesy in the days of David.
²As the fat is selected from the peace offering,
   so David was selected from the sons of Israel.
³He played with lions as with young goats,
   and with bears as with lambs of the flock.
⁴In his youth did he not kill a giant,
   and take away reproach from the people,
when he lifted his hand with a stone in the sling
   and struck down the boasting of Goliath?
⁵For he appealed to the Lord, the Most High,
   and he gave him strength in his right hand
to slay a man mighty in war,
   to exalt the power of his people.
⁶So they glorified him for his ten thousands,
   and praised him for the blessings of the Lord,
when the glorious diadem was bestowed upon him.
⁷For he wiped out his enemies on every side,
   and annihilated his adversaries the Philistines;
he crushed their power even to this day.
⁸In all that he did he gave thanks
   to the Holy One, the Most High, with ascriptions of glory;

4. Thomas Aquinas, *Summa Theologiae* II-II q. 139 a. 1.

he sang praise with all his heart,
    and he loved his Maker.
⁹He placed singers before the altar,
    to make sweet melody with their voices.
¹⁰He gave beauty to the feasts,
    and arranged their times throughout the year,
while they praised God's holy name,
    and the sanctuary resounded from early morning.
¹¹The Lord took away his sins,
    and exalted his power for ever;
he gave him the covenant of kings
    and a throne of glory in Israel.

OT: 1 Sam 16–17; 2 Sam 5–8; 11–12; 1 Chron 15:16; 16:4–6
NT: Matt 1:1; 17; 21:9; Luke 1:31–32; Rom 1:3
Catechism: Jesus, son of David, 437, 439, 559; David's envy and repentance, 2538; David's prayer, 2579

47:1–2   After Samuel, **Nathan rose up to prophesy in the days of David**. By proceeding from Samuel to Nathan, Ben Sira emphasizes the succession of prophets in Israel. Nathan announced God's covenant with David (2 Sam 7:4–17), rebuked him for his adultery with Bathsheba (2 Sam 12:1–15), and oversaw Solomon's accession to the throne (1 Kings 1:8–45). **As the fat** portions—considered the best, richest parts—were **selected from the peace offering** to be burned on the altar (Lev 3:3–5), **so David was selected from the sons of Israel** to be God's "choice portion" for royalty (1 Sam 16:4–13).

47:3–5   David demonstrated his courage and strength when **he played with lions as with young goats, and with bears as with lambs**—not literally, but he fought and killed them to protect his flock (1 Sam 17:34–36). Most notably, **in his youth** he killed the Philistine **giant** Goliath, removing the **reproach** and shame that Goliath had brought upon Israel when he defied their army (17:26). By hurling **a stone** with his **sling** and striking Goliath on the forehead, David silenced his **boasting** and restored honor to Israel (17:49–50). David defeated Goliath not by his own strength but by his faith in God (17:37, 45–47): because he called upon **the Lord**, he received the **strength** needed **to slay a man mighty in war** (17:33) and **exalt the power of his people** by securing victory for them.

47:6–7   After David's victory over Goliath, the young Israelite women **glorified him for his ten thousands** of slain enemies **and praised him** for the Lord's **blessings** (1 Sam 18:6–7) **when the glorious diadem**—the royal crown—**was bestowed upon him** and he became king. During his reign, David defeated **his enemies on every side**, winning military victories against **the Philistines** (2 Sam 5:17–25; 8:1; 21:15–22), as well as against the Moabites, Syrians, Edomites, and Ammonites

(2 Sam 8:2–14; 10:1–19). **He crushed their power** so thoroughly that the Philistines had virtually disappeared by Ben Sira's time.

In all his memorable deeds David **gave thanks** and **glory** to God. **He sang praise with all his heart**, as attested in the many psalms he authored, and **loved his Maker** wholeheartedly, fulfilling the great commandment of the †*Shema* (Deut 6:4–5). **He placed** musicians and **singers before the altar** of sacrifices to sing **sweet melody** to the Lord. David reformed and expanded Israel's liturgical worship by appointing the Levites as singers and musicians in the tabernacle service, which would later be succeeded by the temple of Solomon (1 Chron 15:16; 16:4–6).   **47:8–9**

Through his liturgical reforms and institution of liturgical praise (1 Chron 23:30–32), David added great **beauty** to the Israelite **feasts**, solemnizing these sacred **times throughout the year** as stipulated by the †Torah (Lev 23). As long as the Levites **praised God's holy name, the sanctuary resounded** with singing, giving glory to God **from early morning** until evening (Ps 57:8).   **47:10**

Because David humbly repented, **the Lord took away his sins,** most notably his adultery with Bathsheba and the ensuing murder of her husband Uriah (2 Sam 11:1–17; 12:13). Despite his faults, God **exalted** David's **power** by perpetuating the royal **covenant** with his descendants, establishing **a throne of glory in Israel** and ensuring that his royal dynasty would endure forever (2 Sam 7:12–16; Ps 89:28–29).   **47:11**

VIII.F. Solomon and the Divided Kingdom (47:12–25)

> ¹²After him rose up a wise son
>   who fared amply because of him;
> ¹³Solomon reigned in days of peace,
>   and God gave him rest on every side,
> that he might build a house for his name
>   and prepare a sanctuary to stand for ever.
> ¹⁴How wise you became in your youth!
>   You overflowed like a river with understanding.
> ¹⁵Your soul covered the earth,
>   and you filled it with parables and riddles.
> ¹⁶Your name reached to far-off islands,
>   and you were loved for your peace.
> ¹⁷For your songs and proverbs and parables,
>   and for your interpretations, the countries marveled at you.
> ¹⁸In the name of the Lord God,
>   who is called the God of Israel,
> you gathered gold like tin
>   and amassed silver like lead.

¹⁹But you laid your loins beside women,
    and through your body you were brought into subjection.
²⁰You put stain upon your honor,
    and defiled your posterity,
so that you brought wrath upon your children
    and they were grieved at your folly,
²¹so that the sovereignty was divided
    and a disobedient kingdom arose out of Ephraim.
²²But the Lord will never give up his mercy,
    nor cause any of his works to perish;
he will never blot out the descendants of his chosen one,
    nor destroy the posterity of him who loved him;
so he gave a remnant to Jacob,
    and to David a root of his stock.

²³Solomon rested with his fathers,
    and left behind him one of his sons,
ample in folly and lacking in understanding,
    Rehoboam, whose policy caused the people to revolt.
Also Jeroboam the son of Nebat, who caused Israel to sin
    and gave to Ephraim a sinful way.
²⁴Their sins became exceedingly many,
    so as to remove them from their land.
²⁵For they sought out every sort of wickedness,
    till vengeance came upon them.

OT: Deut 17:17; 1 Kings 3–6; 10–12; 2 Kings 17; Ps 89:29–38
NT: Matt 1:6–7; 12:42; Acts 7:47–49
Catechism: Jesus, greater than Solomon, 590; the temple of Solomon, 2580

47:12–13   **After** David came **a wise son** (1 Kings 5:7) who lived in security and prosperity on account of David's merits (11:12–13, 32–36). **Solomon**—whose name means "his peace"—**reigned** during a time of unprecedented **peace**, stability, and prosperity in Israel, as **God gave him rest** from his enemies **on every side** (4:20–21; 5:4). This enabled Solomon to **build a house** for the Lord's **name**— the Jerusalem temple (5:5; 6:1–38) or **sanctuary** (1 Chron 22:19)—which was hoped to endure **for ever**. Ancient Jews viewed the temple as a microcosm that sustained the existence of the world (Ps 78:69).⁵

47:14–17   Ben Sira addresses Solomon in the second person: **How wise you became in your youth**, at the beginning of your reign (1 Kings 3:9–12; 4:29–34; 10:1–8). Solomon **overflowed like a river with understanding**, reflecting wisdom herself (Sir 24:30–31; 39:22). His **soul** or understanding **covered the earth**, and his influence was far-reaching thanks to his many deep **parables and riddles** (1 Kings

5. See the commentary on Sir 50:1–21 below.

4:32). Solomon's fame extended even **to far-off islands**, making him renowned everywhere (10:1–13), and he was **loved for** his **peace**—a pun on Solomon's name, alluding to his peaceful reign. His **songs, proverbs**, and **parables** were known far and wide (4:32), and his **interpretations** of wisdom sayings (10:1–3) earned him the admiration of many nations (4:34).

In the name of the Lord, the God of Israel, Solomon became so rich that he **gathered gold** and **silver** as abundantly as cheap, ordinary metals **like tin** and **lead** (1 Kings 10:14–17; 27). Amassing such excessive wealth, however, violated the law of the king, which prohibited multiplying wives, silver, and gold (Deut 17:17). Even more gravely, Solomon abandoned himself to **women**, becoming notorious for having seven hundred wives and three hundred concubines (1 Kings 11:1–8). Through the misuse of his **body** and sexuality, he was **brought into subjection** to his passions (Prov 31:3).   **47:18–19**

By violating the law of the king (Deut 17:17), Solomon not only dishonored himself but also **defiled** his **posterity**, bringing divine **wrath** and punishment upon his **children**, who suffered much trouble because of his **folly**. Due to his sins, Israel's **sovereignty was divided**, with the kingdom split in two (1 Kings 12:16–20). **A disobedient kingdom arose** when the ten northern tribes—led by **Ephraim**—rebelled against Solomon's son Rehoboam, seceded from Judah, and formed the kingdom of Israel. This division began a long decline that ultimately ended with the exile of both kingdoms.   **47:20–21**

Despite Solomon's sins, **the Lord** pledged by covenant to never withdraw **his mercy** from his people, nor let **any of his works** or promises fail, nor **blot out the descendants of his chosen one**, David, **who loved him**. Because of David's faithfulness, the Lord provided a faithful **remnant to Jacob** (Israel) even amid the nation's decline, **and to David a root** and lineage through which the Davidic line would endure forever (2 Sam 7:14–16; 1 Kings 11:13, 39; Ps 89:29–38).   **47:22**

Solomon died and **rested with his fathers** (1 Kings 11:43), leaving **behind him one of his sons** to rule after him—a son who, in contrast to his father, was foolish and imprudent. This was **Rehoboam**, who by harshly increasing the yoke of servitude upon the ten northern tribes **caused the people to revolt**. In response, **Jeroboam the son of Nebat** led the northern tribes in their split from Judah (1 Kings 12:1–19) and then led **Israel to sin** by erecting two idolatrous golden calves in Bethel and Dan (14:16).   **47:23**

Over the next few centuries, Israel's **sins** multiplied **exceedingly**, until the Lord removed them **from their land** when the Assyrians deported the northern kingdom in 722 BC (2 Kings 17:20–23). Without restraint, they pursued **every sort of wickedness** (1 Kings 21:20, 25; 2 Kings 17:17), until divine **vengeance came upon them**. This fulfilled the warnings of the †Torah, which stated that the Lord would send Israel into exile if they persisted in rebelling against him (Deut 28:15–68; 2 Kings 17:20–23).   **47:24–25**

VIII.G. The Northern Kingdom of Israel: Elijah and Elisha (48:1–16)

[1]Then the prophet Elijah arose like a fire,
   and his word burned like a torch.
[2]He brought a famine upon them,
   and by his zeal he made them few in number.
[3]By the word of the Lord he shut up the heavens,
   and also three times brought down fire.
[4]How glorious you were, O Elijah, in your wondrous deeds!
   And who has the right to boast which you have?
[5]You who raised a corpse from death
   and from Hades, by the word of the Most High;
[6]who brought kings down to destruction,
   and famous men from their beds,
   and easily destroyed their dominion;
[7]who heard rebuke at Sinai
   and judgments of vengeance at Horeb;
[8]who anointed kings to inflict retribution,
   and prophets to succeed you.
[9]You who were taken up by a whirlwind of fire,
   in a chariot with horses of fire;
[10]you who are ready at the appointed time, it is written,
   to calm the wrath of God before it breaks out in fury,
to turn the heart of the father to the son,
   and to restore the tribes of Jacob.
[11]Blessed are those who saw you,
   and those who have fallen asleep in your love;
   for we also shall surely live,
   but our name, after death, will not be such.

[12]It was Elijah who was covered by the whirlwind,
   and Elisha was filled with his spirit;
in all his days he did not tremble before any ruler,
   and no one brought him into subjection.
[13]Nothing was too hard for him,
   and when he was dead his body prophesied.
[14]As in his life he did wonders,
   so in death his deeds were marvelous.

[15]For all this the people did not repent,
   and they did not forsake their sins,
till they were carried away captive from their land
   and were scattered over all the earth;
the people were left very few in number,
   but with rulers from the house of David.

¹⁶**Some of them did what was pleasing to God,
but others multiplied sins.**

OT: 1 Kings 17–19; 2 Kings 1–2; 13:14–21; Mal 4:5–6
NT: Matt 11:10–14; 17:10–13; Luke 1:17; James 5:17
Catechism: John the Baptist as Elijah, 718–19; Elijah's prayer, 2582–83, 2684

Elijah the Tishbite, who prophesied in the northern kingdom of Israel during   48:1–2
the reigns of Kings Ahab and Ahaziah (1 Kings 17–21; 2 Kings 1–2), **arose like
a fire, and his word burned like a torch**—an allusion to his calling down fire
from heaven (1 Kings 18:38; 2 Kings 1:10, 12), which foreshadows the fire of
the Holy Spirit (Catechism 696). The power of his words was manifest when
he **brought** a drought and **famine** upon the northern kingdom of Israel during King Ahab's reign (1 Kings 17); **by his zeal** (19:10, 14) **he made** the people
few in number, presumably because many perished in the famine, as God had
warned in the law of Moses (Deut 28:38–42, 62).

By the word of the Lord—that is, by God's authority—Elijah **shut up the**   48:3–4
heavens so that no rain fell on the land for three years (1 Kings 17:1; James
5:17). He also **brought down fire** from heaven, once to consume his burnt offering (1 Kings 18:38) and twice to burn up King Ahaziah's soldiers (2 Kings
1:10, 12). As with Solomon (Sir 47:14), Ben Sira addresses Elijah in the second person: **How glorious you were, O Elijah, in your wondrous deeds** and
marvelous miracles! No one else **has the right to boast** as he does, for aside
from his disciple Elisha, Elijah has no equal in the Old Testament in terms of
performing miracles.

Elijah even **raised a corpse**—the son of the widow of Zarephath (1 Kings   48:5–6
17:17–22)—**from death and from** †**Hades**, the realm of the dead (17:27; 21:10),
by the word and power **of the Most High** God. Elijah also **brought kings down
to destruction** when he prophesied that all the descendants of King Ahab would
be annihilated (1 Kings 19:17; 21:19–24), **and famous men from their beds**,
such as King Ahaziah, who died in his bed following an injury (2 Kings 1:1–17).
The †Vulgate adds that Elijah *easily destroyed their dominion* by bringing Ahab's
dynastic line to an end.

According to Ben Sira, when Elijah fled from Queen Jezebel, he **heard** God's   48:7–8
rebuke for his faintheartedness **at Sinai**, where he had become discouraged,
and judgments of vengeance at Horeb against the followers of Baal (1 Kings
19:8–18). Sinai and Horeb are synonyms for the mountain of God where Israel
received the †Torah (Exod 3:1; 19:11). There, God also commissioned Elijah to
anoint **kings**—Hazael of Syria and Jehu of Israel—**to inflict retribution** upon
Ahab and destroy his line. He was also directed to anoint **prophets** (Hebrew:
"a prophet") **to succeed** him (1 Kings 19:15–17)—namely, Elisha (19:19–21).

At the end of his life, Elijah did not die but was **taken up** to heaven **by a**   48:9–10
whirlwind of fire, in a chariot with horses of fire after passing on the mantle

of prophecy to Elisha (2 Kings 2:1–12). Elijah was expected to be **ready at the appointed time**, on the "great and awesome day of the Lord," as **written** in Mal 4:5–6, to return as the Messiah's forerunner who would **calm the wrath of God before it breaks out in fury** on the day of judgment. Malachi prophesied that the Messiah's forerunner would **turn the heart of the father to the son**, bringing reconciliation within the family (compare Matt 11:10–14; 17:10–13; Luke 1:17), and **restore the tribes of Jacob** through a new ingathering of Israel (Isa 49:6).

48:11   Ben Sira declares **blessed those who saw** Elijah in his lifetime—or perhaps those who will live to see him return (the Hebrew reads: "Blessed is the one who shall have seen you before he dies!"; NABRE). Blessed also are **those who have fallen asleep**—that is, those who have died—in his **love**, perhaps through experiencing Elijah's miracles that revealed God's mercy. The last part of the verse is obscure: the assertion that **we also shall surely live** may express a faint hope for life after death.

48:12   When **Elijah** was enveloped **by the whirlwind** and taken up to heaven (48:9), **Elisha**, Elijah's successor (1 Kings 19:16–21), **was filled** with a double portion of **his spirit** (2 Kings 2:9–12), so that he "performed twice as many signs, and marvels with every utterance of his mouth."[6] During his lifetime, under the reigns of Jehoram, Jehu, Jehoahaz, and Jehoash over the northern kingdom, Elisha **did not tremble before any ruler** but fearlessly opposed those godless kings, **and no one brought him into subjection** or intimidated him (2 Kings 2–13).

48:13–14   **Nothing was too hard for him**—as it is said of God (Gen 18:14)—and even after his death **his body prophesied**. Not that his corpse spoke, but it exercised prophetic healing powers: when a dead man was cast into Elisha's grave, the man was restored to life (2 Kings 13:21). Both **in life** and **death**, Elisha performed extraordinary miracles, manifesting God's power, which continued to work through him.

48:15–16   Despite the powerful miracles and ministry of Elijah and Elisha, **the people of the northern kingdom of Israel did not repent** of **their sins** but continued on the path of spiritual and moral decline until **they were carried away captive** by the Assyrians in 722 BC and **scattered** among foreign nations, as foretold in the Torah (Lev 26:33–35; Deut 4:25–27; 28:63–68). **The people** in the southern kingdom who were not deported—primarily the tribe of "Judah" (Hebrew, NABRE)—**were left very few in number** in the land, yet retained legitimate **rulers from the house of David**. In contrast to the rival dynasties in the northern kingdom, the royal Davidic line was preserved in the southern kingdom of Judah. Though **some** of the kings of Judah, such as Asa (1 Kings 15:11), Jehoshaphat (22:43), Joash (2 Kings 12:2–3), Azariah (15:3), Hezekiah (18:3), and Josiah (22:2), **did what was pleasing to God**, most of the **others multiplied sins** and were as wicked as the kings of the northern kingdom.

6. Hebrew and Syriac, NRSV, ESV-CE, NABRE.

VIII.H. The Southern Kingdom of Judah: Hezekiah and Isaiah (48:17–25)

> [17]Hezekiah fortified his city,
>   and brought water into the midst of it;
> he tunneled the sheer rock with iron
>   and built pools for water.
> [18]In his days Sennacherib came up,
>   and sent the Rabshakeh;
> he lifted up his hand against Zion
>   and made great boasts in his arrogance.
> [19]Then their hearts were shaken and their hands trembled,
>   and they were in anguish, like women with labor pains.
> [20]But they called upon the Lord who is merciful,
>   spreading forth their hands toward him;
> and the Holy One quickly heard them from heaven,
>   and delivered them by the hand of Isaiah.
> [21]The Lord struck the camp of the Assyrians,
>   and his angel wiped them out.
> [22]For Hezekiah did what was pleasing to the Lord,
>   and he held strongly to the ways of David his father,
> which Isaiah the prophet commanded,
>   who was great and faithful in his vision.
> [23]In his days the sun went backward,
>   and he lengthened the life of the king.
> [24]By the spirit of might he saw the last things,
>   and comforted those who mourned in Zion.
> [25]He revealed what was to occur to the end of time,
>   and the hidden things before they came to pass.

OT: 2 Kings 18–20; 2 Chron 32; Isa 36–38; 40–48
NT: Matt 3:3; 4:14; 8:17; 12:17–21; Acts 8:26–35
Catechism: Isaiah's prophecies, 497, 712–14, 1502

Hezekiah, one of the best kings of Judah (reigned ca. 715–687 BC), rebuilt and **48:17** expanded the walls of Jerusalem to defend it from the Assyrian invaders (2 Chron 32:5, 30). The fact that he **fortified** (or "strengthened") **his city** is a Hebrew pun on Hezekiah's name, which means "the Lord strengthened." Hezekiah **brought water into** Jerusalem by boring a tunnel from the Gihon spring to the Pool of Siloam, where his workmen **tunneled the sheer rock with iron and built pools for water** (2 Kings 20:20; 2 Chron 32:30; Isa 22:9–11). This underground water channel is still known today as "Hezekiah's Tunnel."

During Hezekiah's rule, **Sennacherib**, the king of Assyria (reigned ca. **48:18–19** 705–681 BC), invaded Judah, captured forty-six cities, and **came up** to besiege

343

Jerusalem (2 Kings 18:13–37; 2 Chron 32:1–23; Isa 36:1–22). He **sent the Rabshakeh**—his commander or high official—who threatened to attack **Zion** (Jerusalem) and arrogantly blasphemed God while defying Hezekiah's spokesmen (2 Kings 18:17–35; Isa 36:7–20). Facing the Assyrian threat, the terrified Jerusalemites **trembled in fear** of being overrun by the invaders and **were in anguish, like women with labor pains** (compare 2 Kings 19:3; Isa 37:3).

Figure 12. Hezekiah's Tunnel in Jerusalem

48:20–21   While in the original narrative King Hezekiah personally prays for deliverance (2 Kings 19:14–19; Isa 37:15–20), Ben Sira extends this prayer to the entire people, who **called upon the** merciful **Lord** while raising **their hands toward him**. Moved by this humble supplication, **the Holy One** promptly **delivered them** through the ministry of the prophet **Isaiah**, who reassured the people that God would protect Jerusalem (2 Kings 19:20–34; Isa 37:21–35). **The Lord** indeed acted according to Isaiah's words and **struck the camp of the Assyrians** by sending **his angel** to slay them, killing 185,000 soldiers that night (2 Kings 19:35).

48:22–23   Hezekiah's piety was the decisive factor in the routing of the Assyrians: he **did what was pleasing to the Lord**, faithfully following **the ways of David**, his ancestor, who despite his flaws was viewed as the ideal king (2 Kings 18:3–6; 20:3). Hezekiah's devotion was guided by **Isaiah the prophet**, who **commanded** the king to place his trust in the Lord, and whose prophetic **vision** proved true with the retreat of the Assyrians (2 Kings 19:1–7). During Isaiah's lifetime, **the sun went backward** when Hezekiah became sick and was at the point of death; the Lord heard his prayer and **lengthened** his **life** by fifteen years (2 Kings 20:1–11; Isa 38:1–8).

48:24–25   By his powerful **spirit**—that is, by a special inspiration—Isaiah prophetically **saw the last things**—future events—**and comforted those who mourned in Zion**. The second part of the book of Isaiah is sometimes known as the "Book of the

Consolation of Zion," in which the prophet comforts an exiled and afflicted Jerusalem (Isa 40:1–2). Isaiah **revealed what was to occur to the end of time**, including Israel's ingathering from exile (40:3–11), the name of Cyrus as the Lord's anointed one (44:28; 45:1; compare Ezra 1:1–8), and the rebuilding of Jerusalem (Isa 44:26–28; 62:6–7). Due to the accuracy of these prophecies, which had been fulfilled by Ben Sira's time, many modern biblical scholars believe that the book of Isaiah is the product of multiple authors and was not completed until sometime after the Babylonian exile. Ben Sira, however, believes that Isaiah foresaw **hidden things** in the distant future by divine inspiration, long **before they came to pass**, implying that he regards the entire book of Isaiah as the work of the eighth-century prophet.

VIII.I. King Josiah and the Prophets; Recalling Ancient Heroes (49:1–16)

[1]The memory of Josiah is like a blending of incense
    prepared by the art of the perfumer;
it is sweet as honey to every mouth,
    and like music at a banquet of wine.
[2]He was led aright in converting the people,
    and took away the abominations of iniquity.
[3]He set his heart upon the Lord;
    in the days of wicked men he strengthened godliness.

[4]Except David and Hezekiah and Josiah
    they all sinned greatly,
for they forsook the law of the Most High;
    the kings of Judah came to an end;
[5]for they gave their power to others,
    and their glory to a foreign nation,
[6]who set fire to the chosen city of the sanctuary,
    and made her streets desolate,
    according to the word of Jeremiah.
[7]For they had afflicted him;
    yet he had been consecrated in the womb as prophet,
to pluck up and afflict and destroy,
    and likewise to build and to plant.

[8]It was Ezekiel who saw the vision of glory
    which God showed him above the chariot of the cherubim.
[9]For God remembered his enemies with storm,
    and did good to those who directed their ways rightly.

[10]May the bones of the twelve prophets
    revive from where they lie,

for they comforted the people of Jacob
and delivered them with confident hope.

¹¹How shall we magnify Zerubbabel?
He was like a signet on the right hand,
¹²and so was Jeshua the son of Jozadak;
in their days they built the house
and raised a temple holy to the Lord,
prepared for everlasting glory.
¹³The memory of Nehemiah also is lasting;
he raised for us the walls that had fallen,
and set up the gates and bars
and rebuilt our ruined houses.

¹⁴No one like Enoch has been created on earth,
for he was taken up from the earth.
¹⁵And no man like Joseph has been born,
and his bones are cared for.
¹⁶Shem and Seth were honored among men,
and Adam above every living being in the creation.

OT: 2 Kings 22–25; Neh 2:1–7:3; Jer 1:10; 38:3–6; Ezek 1; Hag 2:6–9
NT: Matt 1:11–13; Heb 11:5
Catechism: Jeremiah, 220; kingdom and exile, 709–10

49:1 **The memory of Josiah**—the best and last of the good kings of Judah (reigned ca. 640–609 BC; 2 Kings 22:1–2)—is like blended **incense** (Sir 24:15; 45:16) **prepared** by a skilled **perfumer** for sacred use in the temple liturgy (Exod 30:7–9, 34–38). Josiah's righteousness is remembered as being **sweet as honey** (Sir 24:20) and pleasant **like music at a banquet of wine** (40:20). Although Josiah was not a priest, his righteous rule is described in priestly terms (Exod 25:6), with the same language used elsewhere to describe wisdom.

49:2–3 Josiah did what was right **in converting the people** back to God (Hebrew: "he grieved over our betrayals," NABRE). After the book of the law was found in the temple and read to him, Josiah tore his clothes in repentance and horror at how severely it had been neglected (2 Kings 22:11–13). He then launched a religious reform (ca. 622 BC), removing **the abominations of iniquity**—the pagan idols scattered throughout the land (2 Kings 23:1–20). Josiah earnestly **set his heart upon the Lord** (2 Kings 23:3, 25), and in those lawless times **he strengthened godliness** by his virtuous life. Although Josiah's reform turned out to be too little, too late in a time of sharp moral and spiritual decline, he was able to postpone God's judgment upon Judah until after his death (2 Kings 22:18–20).

49:4–6 While 1–2 Kings evaluates several kings of Judah positively (see the commentary on 48:15–16), Ben Sira's judgment is more severe: he views only **David, Hezekiah,** and **Josiah** as righteous kings; all others **sinned greatly**

Ezekiel Points to Christ

For Rabanus Maurus, Ezekiel's prophetic ministry during the Babylonian captivity foreshadowed Christ's own ministry, through which he offered humanity release from the captivity of sin.

Ezekiel, whose name is translated "confirmed by God" and who, in Babylon, predicted to the sinful masses the coming imprisonment, though promising forgiveness of sins to those who would turn and do penance, points in a mysterious way to the Lord and Savior, who is the power and wisdom of God and was called by the prophet the arm of the Lord. He has visited us, we who were in the prison of this world, foretelling future punishments for sinners and promising eternal healing to those who were repentant.[a]

a. Rabanus Maurus, *On Ecclesiasticus* 10.23 (Voicu, *Apocrypha*, 406).

because they either neglected or abandoned **the law of the Most High**, the standard by which Israel's loyalty to God was judged (Deut 28). Because of their transgressions, **the kings of Judah** and the Davidic line **came to an end**. This was due to their own actions, as **they gave their power to others** by pursuing political alliances with them, **and their glory to a foreign nation**, Babylon. Ultimately, King Nebuchadnezzar's army **set fire** to Jerusalem, **the chosen city** and home **of the sanctuary**, exiled the people to Babylonia (2 Kings 25:8–12), **and made her streets desolate, according to the word of Jeremiah**—the last great prophet of Judah, who ministered from around 627 to 586 BC and tirelessly warned the last kings of the impending destruction (Jer 36:29–31; 37:8–10; 38:3).

The kings, nobles, and people of Judah not only rejected Jeremiah's message; **49:7** they also persecuted and **afflicted him** (Jer 20:7–10; 37:13–16; 38:4–6). God had anticipated this, for he had already **consecrated** Jeremiah **in the womb as prophet** even before he was born, **to pluck up and afflict and destroy** by warning Judah of the coming judgment and exile, but also **to build and to plant** by promising the future restoration of the nation (Jer 1:10).

Ezekiel, the third major writing prophet of the Old Testament (after Isaiah **49:8–9** and Jeremiah), ministered during the Babylonian exile from 593 to 571 BC. God revealed to him a **vision of glory**—an awesome manifestation of the divine presence **above the chariot of the cherubim** (Ezek 1:4–28) that had previously rested in the temple's holy of holies (1 Chron 28:18). **God remembered** Ezekiel's **enemies** by punishing them **with storm**. This could be an allusion to Gog and Magog, symbolic names for Israel's foes destined to be destroyed by God's sovereign power at the end of history (Ezek 38–39). Yet God also **did good** to the righteous. The Hebrew of verse 9 reads: "He also referred to Job, who always persevered in the right path" (NABRE; see Ezek 14:14, 20).[7]

49:10   **The twelve** minor **prophets**—Hosea, Joel, Amos, Obadiah, Jonah, Micah, Nahum, Habakkuk, Zephaniah, Haggai, Zechariah, and Malachi—are preserved as a single book in the Hebrew canon. Ben Sira prays that their bones may **revive from where they lie**, expressing hope for the resurrection of the dead (46:12; Ezek 37:1–14). During their lifetimes, these prophets encouraged and exhorted **the people of Jacob** (Israel and Judah), warning them of the coming judgment and calling them to repent and return to the Lord. Even after disaster struck, the prophets continued to instill **hope** by assuring the people that the Lord had not abandoned them and would, in the future, restore them from exile.

49:11–12   **Zerubbabel**, a descendant of David, was one of the leaders who returned to Judea after the Babylonian exile. He became the governor of Judea under Darius I of Persia (Ezra 2:2; Hag 1:1). Ben Sira praises him for being **like a signet on the right hand**, referring to God's promise to restore to Zerubbabel the royal position that King Jeconiah (Jehoiachin) had lost before the exile (Jer 22:24; Hag 2:23). **Jeshua the son of Jozadak** was the high priest in Jerusalem at the time of the return from exile (Ezra 2:2). **In their days**, encouraged by the prophets Haggai and Zechariah (see Ezra 3:2; 5:1–2), Zerubbabel and Jeshua **built the house**—the second **temple**—which, like the temple of Solomon, became **holy to the Lord** and destined **for everlasting glory**. Haggai had prophesied that the second temple would surpass the first in glory (Hag 2:6–9).

49:13   **The memory of Nehemiah**—another major leader of the Jewish restoration after the exile (Neh 2:1–11)—**also is lasting**, as he was the chief architect of Jerusalem's reconstruction. He rebuilt the city **walls that had fallen** during the Babylonian conquest, restored the city's defensive **gates and bars**, and **rebuilt** the people's **ruined houses** despite facing considerable opposition (Neh 2:17–7:3).

49:14   Ben Sira concludes his praise of Israel's ancestors by returning to a few of the oldest patriarchs, working his way back to Adam. **No one like Enoch has been created** (Hebrew: "few like Enoch"), because God took him up **from the earth** to heaven before he died (44:16; Gen 5:24; Heb 11:5). The Hebrew "few" implies that at least another person, probably Elijah, was also taken up to heaven.

49:15–16   While Ben Sira skipped over Joseph in his survey of the early patriarchs, he briefly mentions him here. Like Enoch, Joseph was unique in that **his bones** were **cared for** by God (Hebrew: "his body was visited"), who ensured that they would be transported from Egypt back to the land of Israel for burial (Gen 50:25; Exod 13:19; Josh 24:32). **Shem**—the son of Noah (Gen 5:32; 6:10),

---

7. Compare NRSV. This variant reading likely derives from the fact that the Hebrew words for "enemy" and "Job" are very similar.

survivor of the flood (9:18), and father of the Semitic people (10:22–31)—**and Seth**—the third son of Adam and Eve (4:25)—were particularly **honored, and Adam above every** other **living being**, as he is the father of humanity. The Hebrew reads: "but beyond that of any living being was the splendor [*tipheret*] of Adam" (NABRE), linking Adam to Simon, who is called the "pride [*tipheret*] of his people" in the following verse.

VIII.J. Simon the High Priest (50:1–24)

> ¹The leader of his brethren and the pride of his people
> was Simon the high priest, son of Onias,
> who in his life repaired the house,
> and in his time fortified the temple.
> ²He laid the foundations for the high double walls,
> the high retaining walls for the temple enclosure.
> ³In his days a cistern for water was quarried out,
> a reservoir like the sea in circumference.
> ⁴He considered how to save his people from ruin,
> and fortified the city to withstand a siege.
> ⁵How glorious he was when the people gathered round him
> as he came out of the inner sanctuary!
> ⁶Like the morning star among the clouds,
> like the moon when it is full;
> ⁷like the sun shining upon the temple of the Most High,
> and like the rainbow gleaming in glorious clouds;
> ⁸like roses in the days of the first fruits,
> like lilies by a spring of water,
> like a green shoot on Lebanon on a summer day;
> ⁹like fire and incense in the censer,
> like a vessel of hammered gold
> adorned with all kinds of precious stones;
> ¹⁰like an olive tree putting forth its fruit,
> and like a cypress towering in the clouds.
> ¹¹When he put on his glorious robe
> and clothed himself with superb perfection
> and went up to the holy altar,
> he made the court of the sanctuary glorious.
> ¹²And when he received the portions from the hands of the priests,
> as he stood by the hearth of the altar
> with a garland of brethren around him,
> he was like a young cedar on Lebanon;
> and they surrounded him like the trunks of palm trees,
> ¹³all the sons of Aaron in their splendor

with the Lord's offering in their hands,
    before the whole congregation of Israel.
¹⁴Finishing the service at the altars,
    and arranging the offering to the Most High, the Almighty,
¹⁵he reached out his hand to the cup
    and poured a libation of the blood of the grape;
he poured it out at the foot of the altar,
    a pleasing odor to the Most High, the King of all.
¹⁶Then the sons of Aaron shouted,
    they sounded the trumpets of hammered work,
they made a great noise to be heard
    for remembrance before the Most High.
¹⁷Then all the people together made haste
    and fell to the ground upon their faces
to worship their Lord,
    the Almighty, God Most High.
¹⁸And the singers praised him with their voices
    in sweet and full-toned melody.
¹⁹And the people besought the Lord Most High
    in prayer before him who is merciful,
till the order of worship of the Lord was ended;
    so they completed his service.
²⁰Then Simon came down, and lifted up his hands
    over the whole congregation of the sons of Israel,
to pronounce the blessing of the Lord with his lips,
    and to glory in his name;
²¹and they bowed down in worship a second time,
    to receive the blessing from the Most High.

²²And now bless the God of all,
    who in every way does great things;
who exalts our days from birth,
    and deals with us according to his mercy.
²³May he give us gladness of heart,
    and grant that peace may be in our days in Israel,
    as in the days of old,
²⁴*that Israel may believe that the God of mercy is with us*
    to deliver us in our days!

OT: Gen 1:1–2:3; Exod 28:2–43; 29:38–42; Lev 16; Num 6:22–27; Sir 24
NT: Heb 8–9
Catechism: Old Covenant priesthood fulfilled in Christ's priesthood, 1539–45
Lectionary: 50:22–24: thanksgiving to God

50:1 The praise of Israel's ancestors culminates with a contemporary of Ben Sira who was the **leader of his brethren**—that is, of his fellow priests—and **the pride** or "splendor" (Hebrew *tipheret*) **of his people**—echoing the primeval "splendor" of Adam mentioned in the previous verse (49:16). This man is **Simon son of Onias** (Hebrew: "son of Yohanan" or "son of John"; see John 21:15–17), who served as **high priest** in Jerusalem from 219 to 196 BC. The many allusions to creation that follow suggest that Simon stands as a new Adam, representing not only Israel but all humanity. The phrase **in his life** (Hebrew: "in his generation") hints that Simon was no longer alive at the time of writing; yet Ben Sira's vivid description of his ministry indicates that he is recounting personal memories. Simon **repaired the house** of the Lord and **fortified the temple** (50:2–4). Since the temple was viewed as a type of microcosm in ancient Judaism,[8] Ben Sira seems to depict Simon's actions in the following verses as a "creation of the universe" in miniature, using hints and references to the Genesis account of creation.

    Simon **laid the foundations for the high double walls** (literally, the "double   **50:2** heights"), **the high retaining walls for the temple enclosure**. This verse is unclear in both Greek and Hebrew. While we do not know precisely which walls Ben Sira refers to, we do know that, by the first century BC, the Greek term for "retaining walls" (*analemma*) had taken on "a certain technical sense as a model or map of the cosmos, particularly the firmament."[9] Theologically, the temple served as the earthly counterpart of God's heavenly dwelling. On the second day of creation, God created the firmament, which separated the heavens from the earth (Gen 1:6–8), yet Ben Sira here depicts the temple as uniting them (see Ps 78:69).

    In Simon's **days a cistern** was dug to supply **water** to the temple precincts, **a**   **50:3–4** **reservoir like the sea**—alluding to the bronze basin in the temple's courtyard called "the molten sea," which was used for the ritual washing of the priests (1 Kings 7:23–26). This also evokes God's creation of the sea on the third day (Gen 1:9–10). Simon took steps to protect and **save his people from ruin**, defending them against brigands and plunderers; he also **fortified the city** and its walls so it could **withstand** an enemy **siege**.

    Ben Sira describes the high priest's ministry, possibly on Yom Kippur, the   **50:5** annual Day of Atonement, when he went into the holy of holies with the blood of sacrificial animals to atone for Israel's sins (Lev 16). Some think that the liturgy of the daily whole burnt offering is in view (Exod 29:38–42). Ben Sira's use of

---

8. Philo, for example, says, "The highest, and in the truest sense the holy, temple of God is, as we must believe, the whole universe" (*On the Special Laws* 1.66, in Philo, *On the Decalogue; On the Special Laws, Books 1–3*, trans. F. H. Colson, vol. 7, Loeb Classical Library 320 [Cambridge, MA: Harvard University Press, 1937], 137). On the temple as microcosm, see André Villeneuve, *Divine Marriage from Eden to the End of Days: Communion with God as Nuptial Mystery in the Story of Salvation* (Eugene, OR: Wipf & Stock, 2021), 64–69.

9. Crispin Fletcher-Louis, "The Cosmology of P and Theological Anthropology in the Wisdom of Jesus Ben Sira," in *Of Scribes and Sages: Studies in Early Jewish Interpretation and Transmission of Scripture*, ed. Craig A. Evans (London: T&T Clark, 2004), 35.

language from the poem on wisdom (Sir 24:1–34) suggests that he views the high priest as an embodiment of wisdom. Simon was **glorious**, like wisdom (6:31; 24:16–17), when **he came out of the inner sanctuary** (literally, "of the house of the veil")—either the inner veil as he exited the holy of holies on Yom Kippur, or the outer veil as he exited the temple building during the daily sacrifice.

50:6–7   The glorious appearance of Simon, like **the morning star, the moon**, and **the sun**, recalls the fourth day of creation, when God set the astral bodies to rule the day and night from the heavens (43:1–12; Gen 1:14–19). **The rainbow gleaming in glorious clouds** evokes God's covenant with Noah (Gen 9:13–16) and Ezekiel's vision of the divine glory (Ezek 1:28).

50:8–10   Ben Sira's depiction of the fruitful, life-giving ministry of the high priest, using imagery of **roses, lilies**, and **a green shoot on Lebanon**, recalls his depiction of wisdom in similar terms (24:13–17; 39:13–14), as well as God's creation of vegetation on the third day (Gen 1:11–12). The **fire and incense in the censer** carried by the priest, **like a vessel of hammered gold adorned** with **precious stones**, also evokes wisdom, which is portrayed as an offering of incense and as more precious than gold and precious stones (Sir 45:11; Job 28:16–19). The incense filling the sky may allude to the birds that filled the sky on the fifth day of creation (Gen 1:20–23), and the comparison of Simon to a fruitful **olive tree** and a towering **cypress** echoes the earlier description of wisdom (Sir 24:13–14).

50:11   Clothed in **his glorious robe**, with **superb perfection** (45:6–12; Exod 28:2–43)—for in his time the vestments of the high priest were believed to symbolize and represent the whole world (Wis 18:24)[10]—Simon **went up to the holy altar** where the sacrifices were burned (Exod 27:1–2; 2 Chron 4:1). There, he **made the court of the sanctuary** surrounding the bronze altar (2 Chron 4:9) **glorious** by his very presence.

50:12–13   When Simon **received the portions** of the sacrifices from **the priests** (Exod 29:17–18; Lev 1:6–8), standing **by the hearth of the altar** where the fire burned, with his fellow priests circling him like **a garland**, he again embodies wisdom, **like a young cedar on Lebanon**, with the others surrounding him **like the trunks of palm trees** (Sir 24:13–14). The priests, **the sons of Aaron** in their splendid garments, carried **the Lord's offering** before the gathered assembly, whom they represented. Ben Sira seems to depict Simon as a new Adam, clothed with "garments of glory" and restoring the image of God and the authority over every living creature given to Adam on the sixth day of creation (Gen 1:26–31).

50:14–15   As he completed the sacrificial **service at the altars** and arranged the pieces of the animal **offering** on the fire to be consumed for the Lord, the high priest **reached** for a **cup** that an assistant handed to him **and poured a libation** of wine as a drink offering (39:26) **at the foot of the altar**, as commanded by the

---

10. See the sidebar "The Garments of the High Priest," p. 328; Philo, *On the Life of Moses* 2.109–35; Josephus, *Antiquities* 3.7.7.

†Torah (Num 15:5–7; 28:6–8). The fact that this was **a pleasing odor to the Most High** indicates that God, **the King of all**, had favorably received the offering. At the conclusion of the service, **the sons of Aaron** (the priests) **shouted** and **sounded** the silver **trumpets**, as was customary on such solemn occasions, making **a great noise for remembrance before the Most High**. Having offered their sacrifice, with the resounding conclusion of the liturgical service, they solemnly called for his attention, as it were (Num 10:1–10). **Then all the people** prostrated themselves to join the high priest and **worship their Lord, the Almighty, God Most High**, who had so generously displayed his glory to Israel through the ministry of the high priest.   50:16–17

Ben Sira portrays Israel at the high point of the temple liturgy: **the singers praised** God **in sweet and full-toned melody**, as they had in the days of Hezekiah (47:9; 2 Chron 29:25–30), and offered their prayers (Hebrew: "shouted for joy") before **the Lord Most High**, the **merciful** one—a term reflecting a fundamental aspect of God's character (Exod 34:6; Deut 4:31; 2 Chron 30:9). This continued until **the order** (Greek *kosmos*) **of worship of the Lord was ended** (*synteleō*); and thus **they completed** (*teleiō*) **his service**. The use of the Greek   50:18–19

James (Jacques Joseph) Tissot / Public domain / The Jewish Museum

word *kosmos*, meaning both "world" and "order," and the repetition of the verb "to end" (*synteleō* or *teleiō*) echo the completion of creation in Genesis, when the heavens and the earth were "finished" (*synteleō*) and God "finished" (*synteleō*) his work (Gen 2:1–2). This confirms that Ben Sira is portraying Simon's liturgical ministry as the completion of God's creative work.

Then Simon came down from the altar of sacrifice **and lifted up his hands over the whole congregation of Israel**, just as Aaron did when he was inaugurated as priest (Lev 9:22–23), **to pronounce** the Lord's priestly **blessing** (Num 6:22–27) and **glory in his name**. On the Day of Atonement (Yom Kippur), the high priest would pronounce the ineffable name of God, YHWH (Exod 3:14), after sprinkling the mercy seat in the holy of holies with the sacrificial blood (Catechism 433). As Simon spoke, the people prostrated themselves **a second time, to receive the blessing from the Most High**. The †Mishnah records a similar ancient account of the priestly blessing on Yom   50:20–21

Figure 13. Priestly blessing

Kippur: "And when the priests and the people who were standing in the court-yard heard the fully pronounced Name [of the Lord] come from the mouth of the High Priest they would kneel, prostrate themselves, fall on their faces, and call out: Blessed be the Name of His glorious kingdom for ever and ever."[11] Simon's solemn blessing, concluding the liturgical service, also evokes God's blessing of the seventh day at the conclusion of creation (Gen 2:3).

50:22   Ben Sira now invites his readers to **bless the God of all** in response to the **great things** he has done throughout the history of salvation, from Adam to Simon. The Lord is the one **who exalts our days from birth, and deals with us according to** the same **mercy** he revealed in the history of Israel (Hebrew: "who fosters growth from the womb, fashioning it according to his will," NABRE).

50:23-24   Ben Sira blesses his readers, asking the Lord to grant them **gladness of heart** and **peace** upon **Israel, as in the days of old**—likely referring to the "golden age" of Solomon's reign, when Israel was a strong, independent nation. The RSV-2CE then follows the †Vulgate, where Ben Sira prays *that Israel may believe that the God of mercy is with us* to deliver us in our days! The Greek is similar: "May he entrust to us his mercy, and may he deliver us in our days!" (NRSV; compare ESV-CE). Yet the Hebrew is quite different: "May his goodness toward Simeon last forever; may he fulfill for him the covenant with Phinehas so that it may not be abrogated for him or his descendants while the heavens last" (NABRE).

The difference is easily explained: After Ben Sira wrote his original Hebrew text, the "covenant of Phinehas" (45:24) and the high priestly succession ended in Simon's family when his son Onias III was assassinated and his grandson Onias IV fled to Egypt. When Ben Sira's grandson translated the text into Greek (later followed by the Latin), he adapted it to better reflect the situation of his own day by removing the reference to Simon's priestly line.

VIII.K. Judah's Neighbors; Author's Postscript (50:25-29)

> [25]With two nations my soul is vexed,
>   and the third is no nation:
> [26]Those who live on Mount Seir, and the Philistines,
>   and the foolish people that dwell in Shechem.
>
> [27]Instruction in understanding and knowledge
>   I have written in this book,
> Jesus the son of Sirach, son of Eleazar, of Jerusalem,
>   who out of his heart poured forth wisdom.

11. Mishnah, *Yoma* 6:2. *The Mishnah: A New Integrated Translation and Commentary*, https://www .echok.com/mishnah/moed2/Yoma/6.pdf.

> ²⁸Blessed is he who concerns himself with these things,
> and he who lays them to heart will become wise.
> ²⁹For if he does them, he will be strong for all things,
> for the light of the Lord is his path.

OT: 2 Kings 17:24–41; Obadiah
NT: John 4:4–10
Catechism: participating in divine wisdom, 1950–54

Ben Sira concludes with a numerical saying expressing disdain for three **nations.**   50:25–26
Those who live on **Mount Seir**, south of the Dead Sea, are the Edomites—
descendants of Esau and longtime rivals of Israel (Ezek 25:12–14; 35:1–15;
Obad 1–4). The **Philistines,** subdued by David long ago, still symbolize the
pagan Hellenizers who threatened the Jewish faith in Ben Sira's day. The **foolish
people that dwell in Shechem** are the Samaritans, whose origins trace back to
the Assyrian conquest of the northern kingdom of Israel (2 Kings 17:24–41).
The Samaritans opposed the reconstruction of the Jerusalem temple and established a rival temple on Mount Gerizim, overlooking Shechem—an act the Jews
viewed as illegitimate and invalid (see John 4:20). They later allied themselves
with the Seleucids against the Jews. Ben Sira likely includes these two verses to
dismiss the religions of these nations as false counterparts to Simon's ministry.

Ben Sira's postscript summarizes the goal of his work: to communicate **in-**   50:27
struction in understanding and knowledge to all. He adds his author's signature: **Jesus the son of Sirach, son of Eleazar, of Jerusalem** (Hebrew: "Simon the
son of Yeshua [Jesus] the son of Eleazar the son of Sira"; see "Title, Author, Date"
in the introduction, pp. 17–19), **who out of his heart poured forth wisdom.**
From his own pursuit of wisdom, Ben Sira has become a source of wisdom for
others (16:25; 18:29).

Ben Sira concludes with a benediction: **Blessed is he who concerns himself**   50:28–29
with all the **things** he has taught throughout the book. One who meditates on
these teachings and takes them **to heart will become wise.** The key to wisdom,
however, is not only contemplating Ben Sira's teachings but also putting them
into practice: one who does so **will be strong** in every situation, **for the light of
the Lord is his path.** The Hebrew reads: "for the fear of the Lord is life." Many
scholars believe that the book originally ended here and that the last chapter
was added later.

The Epilogue of Sirach

Sirach 51

The book of Sirach ends with an epilogue that contains three sections: (1) a prayer of thanksgiving for deliverance, inspired by the Psalms (51:1–12); (2) a psalm of praise, included only in the Hebrew version and omitted from the RSV-2CE; and (3) an autobiographical poem on Ben Sira's search for wisdom (51:13–30).

A. Prayer of Thanksgiving (51:1–12)

[1]I will give thanks to you, O Lord and King,
and will praise you as God my Savior.
I give thanks to your name,
[2]for you have been my protector and helper
and have delivered my body from destruction
and from the snare of a slanderous tongue,
from lips that utter lies.
Before those who stood by
you were my helper, [3]and delivered me,
in the greatness of your mercy and of your name,
from the gnashings of teeth about to devour me,
from the hand of those who sought my life,
from the many afflictions that I endured,
[4]from choking fire on every side
and from the midst of fire which I did not kindle,
[5]from the depths of the belly of Hades,
from an unclean tongue and lying words—
[6]the slander of an unrighteous tongue to the king.
My soul drew near to death,
and my life was very near to Hades beneath.

⁷They surrounded me on every side,
 and there was no one to help me;
I looked for the assistance of men,
 and there was none.
⁸Then I remembered your mercy, O Lord,
 and your work from of old,
that you deliver those who wait for you
 and save them from the hand of their enemies.
⁹And I sent up my supplication from the earth,
 and prayed for deliverance from death.
¹⁰I appealed to the Lord, the Father of my lord,
 not to forsake me in the days of affliction,
 at the time when there is no help against the proud.
¹¹I will praise your name continually,
 and will sing praise with thanksgiving.
My prayer was heard,
 ¹²for you saved me from destruction
 and rescued me from an evil plight.
Therefore I will give thanks to you and praise you,
 and I will bless the name of the Lord.

OT: Pss 5:7; 27:1; 56:13; 89:26; 116:8; 136
NT: Eph 5:18–19; Col 3:16; Heb 13:15
Catechism: thanksgiving and praise, 2637–43
Lectionary: 51:1–8: Common of Martyrs; 51:8–12: Most Holy Name of Jesus

The Greek and Latin versions add a title: "A prayer of Jesus the son of Sirach."   **51:1**
By giving **thanks** to his **Lord and King**, Ben Sira acknowledges that everything
he has is a **gift** from **God**, his **Savior** (compare Luke 1:47; Hebrew: "God of my
salvation"). For this reason, it is fitting to **give thanks** to his **name**.

As his **protector and helper**, God delivered Ben Sira from dangers that could   **51:2–3**
have led to his **destruction** and death (34:12–17; Pss 56:13; 116:8), as well as
from **a slanderous tongue** and **lies** that could have ruined his reputation (Sir
28:13–26; Ps 109:2–3). While many **stood by** idly in times of need, God was
Ben Sira's **helper** who **delivered** him, in his abundant **mercy** (compare Pss 5:7;
106:7, 45). God saved him **from the gnashings of teeth** of enemies who, like
wild animals, were ready **to devour** him (Pss 17:12; 22:20–21; 35:16), as well
as from those **who sought** to end his **life** (Pss 35:4; 63:9).

The Lord also delivered Ben Sira from unspecified afflictions that, like a   **51:4–7**
choking fire, engulfed him **on every side** with no possibility of escape; from
close brushes with death that would have sent him into **the belly of** †**Hades**,
the underworld; and from malicious **slander** reported **to the king**, which could
have also cost him his **life**. As his enemies **surrounded** him, Ben Sira found **no
one to help**, and he remained utterly alone in his distress (Isa 63:5).

51:8–9   Having despaired of finding human assistance, Ben Sira **remembered** the Lord's **mercy** and kindness **from of old**, and how he delivers those who wait upon him (Ps 25:6; Isa 40:31) from the threats of **their enemies** (Hebrew: "from all evil"). Mindful of God's power to save, Ben Sira **sent up** his **supplication** to heaven **and prayed for deliverance from death** (Hebrew: "from the gates of Sheol I cried for help"; see Jon 2:2).

51:10   Ben Sira's final appeal to **the Lord, the Father of my lord** seems to suggest two lords in Greek, leading some commentators to interpret the phrase in a messianic sense (compare Ps 110:1). The Hebrew reads more conventionally: "I cried out, 'Lord, you are my Father,' for you are my mighty salvation" (see Ps 89:26). Once again, the author calls upon the Lord **not to forsake** him in **days of affliction**, when he is helpless and alone before **proud** and arrogant foes.

51:11–12   Because his **prayer was heard** and the Lord **saved** him from **destruction** and the **evil plight** that afflicted him, Ben Sira returns to his initial purpose—to **give thanks**, to **praise**, and to **bless the name of the Lord** for his great deeds of mercy (39:35; 51:1).

B. Psalm of Praise

The Hebrew adds the following psalm of praise between verses 12 and 13:

Give thanks to the LORD, for he is good,
for his mercy endures forever;

Give thanks to the God of praises,
for his mercy endures forever;

Give thanks to the guardian of Israel,
for his mercy endures forever;

Give thanks to him who formed all things,
for his mercy endures forever;

Give thanks to the redeemer of Israel,
for his mercy endures forever;

Give thanks to him who gathers the dispersed of Israel,
for his mercy endures forever;

Give thanks to him who rebuilt his city and his sanctuary,
for his mercy endures forever;

Give thanks to him who makes a horn to sprout for the house of David,
for his mercy endures forever;

Give thanks to him who has chosen the sons of Zadok to be priests,
　　for his mercy endures forever;

Give thanks to the shield of Abraham,
　　for his mercy endures forever;

Give thanks to the rock of Isaac,
　　for his mercy endures forever;

Give thanks to the mighty one of Jacob,
　　for his mercy endures forever;

Give thanks to him who has chosen Zion,
　　for his mercy endures forever;

Give thanks to the King of the kings of kings,
　　for his mercy endures forever;

He has raised up a horn for his people,
　　praise for all his loyal ones.

For the children of Israel, the people close to him.
　　Praise the Lord! (NRSV)

This psalm, which is modeled on Ps 136, borrows titles for God from various Old Testament texts. The Lord is the "God of praises" (Ps 109:1), "the guardian of Israel" (Ps 121:4) "who formed all things" (Jer 10:16; 51:19), "the redeemer of Israel" (Isa 49:7) who "gathers the dispersed of Israel" (Ps 147:2; Isa 11:12) and who "rebuilt his city and his sanctuary" (Ps 51:18; Isa 44:28). The psalm then associates God with five major figures of salvation history: King David (Ps 132:17); Zadok, the high priest during David's reign (1 Kings 1:38–39; Ezek 44:15); and the patriarchs Abraham (Gen 15:1), Isaac, and Jacob (32:9; 49:24). God is further praised as the one who "has chosen Zion" (Ps 132:13), the "king of kings" (a later term, Rev 17:14) who has "raised up a horn for his people" Israel (Ps 148:14).

C. The Author's Search for Wisdom (51:13–30)

[13]While I was still young, before I went on my travels,
　　I sought wisdom openly in my prayer.
[14]Before the temple I asked for her,
　　and I will search for her to the last.
[15]From blossom to ripening grape
　　my heart delighted in her;
my foot entered upon the straight path;
　　from my youth I followed her steps.

¹⁶I inclined my ear a little and received her,
> and I found for myself much instruction.
¹⁷I made progress therein;
> to him who gives wisdom I will give glory.
¹⁸For I resolved to live according to wisdom,
> and I was zealous for the good;
> and I shall never be put to shame.
¹⁹My soul grappled with wisdom,
> and in my conduct I was strict;
> I spread out my hands to the heavens,
> and lamented my ignorance of her.
²⁰I directed my soul to her,
> and through purification I found her.
> I gained understanding with her from the first,
> therefore I will not be forsaken.
²¹My heart was stirred to seek her,
> therefore I have gained a good possession.
²²The Lord gave me a tongue as my reward,
> and I will praise him with it.

²³Draw near to me, you who are untaught,
> and lodge in my school.
²⁴Why do you say you are lacking in these things,
> and why are your souls very thirsty?
²⁵I opened my mouth and said,
> Get these things for yourselves without money.
²⁶Put your neck under the yoke,
> and let your souls receive instruction;
> it is to be found close by.
²⁷See with your eyes that I have labored little
> and found for myself much rest.
²⁸Get instruction with a large sum of silver,
> and you will gain by it much gold.
²⁹May your soul rejoice in his mercy,
> and may you not be put to shame when you praise him.
³⁰Do your work before the appointed time,
> and in God's time he will give you your reward.

OT: 1 Kings 3:9; Prov 9:1–6; Wis 7:25–8:3; 9:1–4, 9–10; Sir 6:18–31; 24:10
NT: Matt 11:29
Catechism: the yoke of wisdom, 459; the beauty of wisdom, 2500

51:13–14   Ben Sira concludes his book with an autobiographical poem on his search for wisdom. His quest began early in life: while he was **still young** (6:18; Wis 8:2) and before the **travels** that were instrumental in his cultivation of wisdom (Sir 34:10–13; 39:4), he **sought wisdom** in **prayer**—for wisdom is not just a skill acquired through experience or study but a gift from God that one must ask for (1:19; 1 Kings 3:9; Wis 9:1–4, 9–10). Because she is most present in the sanctuary and in the context of Israel's liturgy (Sir 24:10; 50:1–21), Ben Sira sought her **before the temple**, and he intends to **search for her to the last**—for the rest of his life.

From blossom to ripening grape, which could mean either "from youth to   51:15
manhood" or "from the first blossoming of wisdom to its mature fruit," Ben Sira **delighted in her**. He pursued her wholeheartedly on **the straight path**, never straying from God's law. From his **youth** he **followed her steps**, not just as a set of teachings to learn but as a presence to follow and love (4:11–17; 6:26–28).

Putting in the effort to grow in wisdom by listening to her voice (6:23, 33,   51:16–17
35; 16:24) yields rich rewards: by inclining his **ear a little** and receiving her teachings with docility, Ben Sira gained **much instruction** (6:19; 51:27) and **made progress** in understanding her ways (Hebrew: "and her yoke was glorious to me," 6:24, 30; 51:26). Thus, **to him who gives wisdom**—whether God or human teachers—Ben Sira wishes to **give glory** (Hebrew: "and to my teacher I offer thanks").

Enamored with her, Ben Sira **resolved to live according to wisdom** by put-   51:18–19
ting her teachings into practice and being **zealous for the good**. This gave him confidence that he would **never be put to shame**. The idea of being shielded from shame by pursuing goodness casts wisdom as the antidote to Adam and Eve's fall in the garden of Eden (15:4; 24:22; Gen 2:25; 3:6–7). Ben Sira **grappled with wisdom** and fought for her (Hebrew: "longed for her") through self-discipline and **strict** conduct. He also **spread out** his **hands to the heavens** in a prayerful posture (1 Kings 8:22), and in humility **lamented** his **ignorance of her**.

Aware of his own limitations in wisdom, Ben Sira **directed** his **soul to her,**   51:20–22
and through purification of the heart, by avoiding sin and growing in virtue, he **found her**. By cultivating upright moral conduct and obedience to the law, he **gained understanding** (literally, "acquired a heart") through his knowledge of wisdom and gained assurance that she would not forsake him (2:10; 4:19; Prov 4:6). Once more, the primacy of love is emphasized: because his **heart was stirred to seek her**, Ben Sira **gained** wisdom as a prized **possession**. As a **reward** for his quest, **the Lord gave** him **a tongue**—that is, the ability to speak eloquently (Isa 50:4)—enabling him to teach effectively and **praise him** in return.

Ben Sira extends a final invitation to his readers, encouraging them to learn   51:23–24
from his wisdom (Prov 9:4, 16): **Draw near to me, you who are untaught** or uneducated, **and lodge in my school** to learn from my teachings. The Hebrew reads: "in my house of instruction" (*beit midrash*), the traditional Jewish term for the "house" where students gather to study the †Torah (compare Sir 14:23–27). He then asks, rhetorically, why they are still **lacking** in wisdom's teachings (Hebrew: "wisdom's food")—so essential for life—and allow their **souls** to remain **thirsty** by depriving themselves of the spring of wisdom (15:3; 24:19–21; Prov 9:5).

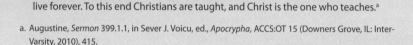

Lodge in My House of Instruction

LIVING TRADITION

St. Augustine extends Sirach's invitation to seek instruction and wisdom into the Christian life. While devout Jews from Ben Sira's time could find wisdom in his "house of instruction," Christians today find life-giving instruction in the Church of Christ:

> The Word of God was directed to us. It was proclaimed to exhort us, as the Scripture says: "Receive instruction in the house of instruction" (Sir 51:23, 28). Instruction is given so as to instruct, and the house of instruction is the church of Christ. Let us ask ourselves the object and purpose of this instruction: who is instructed, and who imparts the instruction. One learns to live well, and the purpose for which he learns to live well is so as to live forever. To this end Christians are taught, and Christ is the one who teaches.[a]

a. Augustine, *Sermon* 399.1.1, in Sever J. Voicu, ed., *Apocrypha*, ACCS:OT 15 (Downers Grove, IL: InterVarsity, 2010), 415.

51:25–26   Ben Sira therefore exhorts those who still lack wisdom: **Get these things** (Hebrew: "acquire wisdom"; see Prov 4:5, 7) **for yourselves without money**, for she is a free gift (Isa 55:1)—and Ben Sira apparently offers his own instruction at no charge. One must not be afraid of the sacrifices involved in pursuing wisdom: **put your neck under the yoke** of her teaching, **and let your souls receive instruction** or discipline (Sir 6:23–31; Matt 11:29), for wisdom is near and within reach. The Hebrew reads: "She is close to those who seek her, and the one who is in earnest finds her."

51:27–28   Ben Sira testifies that he has **labored little and found much rest**, for the effort required to seek wisdom is trivial compared to the rewards of obtaining her (6:19; 51:16). It is worthwhile to invest much to acquire **instruction** and wisdom, even **a large sum of silver**, as one can expect to **gain by it much gold**—that is, a significant return on one's investment.

51:29–30   Ben Sira expresses his heartfelt wishes for his readers, hoping they may **rejoice in** God's **mercy** and **not be put to shame when** they **praise him**, for shame is incompatible with wisdom (24:22; 51:18). He assures them that if they diligently seek wisdom throughout their lives, **before the appointed time** of death and judgment, God will, in his **time**, grant all wisdom seekers their **reward**—namely, wisdom herself and all the benefits that she brings. The Hebrew adds a final blessing: "Blessed be the Lord forever and praised be his name from generation to generation. Thus far the words of Simeon, the son of Yeshua [Jesus], who is called Ben Sira. The Wisdom of Simeon, the son of Yeshua [Jesus], the son of Eleazar, the son of Sira. May the name of the Lord be blessed from now to eternity."

Suggested Resources

From the Christian Tradition

Voicu, Sever J., ed. *Apocrypha.* ACCS:OT 15. Downers Grove, IL: InterVarsity, 2010. Selections from the Church Fathers on the Deuterocanonical books, including Sirach.

Scholarly Works

Box, G. H., and W. O. E. Oesterley. "Sirach." In *The Apocrypha and Pseudepigrapha of the Old Testament*, ed. R. H. Charles, 1:268–517. Oxford: Clarendon, 1913. Though dated, this technical commentary remains invaluable for its comprehensive, scholarly introduction and complete critical text detailing Sirach's many textual variants. Assumes knowledge of Hebrew and Greek.

Bullard, Roger A., and Howard A. Hatton. *A Handbook on Sirach.* UBS Handbook Series. New York: United Bible Societies, 2008. Focuses on exegetical, linguistic, and cultural issues related to the translation of Sirach, yet also serves as an excellent, nontechnical commentary. Follows the RSV and GNT, based on the Greek text with some insights from the Hebrew.

Kearns, C. J. "Ecclesiasticus, or the Wisdom of Jesus the Son of Sirach." In *A New Catholic Commentary on Holy Scripture*, ed. Reginald C. Fuller et al., 541–62. London: Thomas Nelson, 1969. Concise yet robust scholarly and theological Catholic introduction to Sirach, with some very brief notes on the text.

Oesterley, W. O. E. *The Wisdom of Jesus the Son of Sirach or Ecclesiasticus.* The Cambridge Bible for Schools and Colleges. Cambridge: Cambridge University Press, 1912. Older, technical, exhaustive scholarly commentary that details Sirach's textual variants and highlights some correlations with rabbinic literature. Similar to Box and Oesterley, above.

Phua, Michael. "Sirach, Book of." In *Dictionary of the Old Testament: Wisdom, Poetry and Writings*, ed. Tremper Longman III and Peter Enns, 720–28.

Downers Grove, IL: IVP Academic, 2008. Concise overview of Sirach's historical background, literary analysis, wisdom teachings, and connections with the New Testament. No commentary on the text.

Skehan, Patrick W., and Alexander A. Di Lella. *The Wisdom of Ben Sira*. AB. New York: Doubleday, 1987. A massive scholarly work; to this day the most comprehensive introduction and commentary on Sirach.

Wilson, Walter T. *The Wisdom of Sirach*. Eerdmans Critical Commentary. Grand Rapids: Eerdmans, 2023. A robust, extensive commentary that follows the NRSV translation. Although intended for nonspecialists and more readable than Skehan and Di Lella, it is heavily footnoted, drawing richly from ancient and modern works, and will appeal especially to more scholarly readers.

Midlevel Works

Coggins, R. J. *Sirach*. Guides to Apocrypha and Pseudepigrapha. Sheffield: Sheffield Academic, 1998. Useful, concise guide that topically surveys the major historical, linguistic, social, religious, and theological issues in Sirach. No verse-by-verse commentary.

Corley, Jeremy. *Sirach*. The New Collegeville Bible Commentary 21. Collegeville, MN: Liturgical Press, 2013. Light, readable, nontechnical Catholic introduction and commentary. Follows the NABRE, which is largely based on the Hebrew text.

Crenshaw, James L. "Sirach: Introduction, Commentary, and Reflections." In *The New Interpreter's Bible*, ed. Leander E. Keck et al., 5:601–867. Nashville: Abingdon, 1997. Comprehensive introduction and commentary by one of wisdom literature's foremost experts. Treats each section with a commentary on the text, followed by practical reflections.

Di Lella, Alexander A. "Sirach." In *The New Jerome Biblical Commentary*, ed. Raymond E. Brown, Joseph A. Fitzmyer, and Roland E. Murphy, 496–509. Englewood Cliffs, NJ: Prentice-Hall, 1990. A concise, nontechnical introduction and commentary by one of the authors of the Anchor Bible volume.

Popular Commentaries

Crenshaw, James L. "Sirach." In *Harper's Bible Commentary*, ed. James L. Mays, 836–54. San Francisco: Harper & Row, 1988. A brief introduction and commentary on each section of the text, rather than verse-by-verse; much more concise than Crenshaw's work in the *New Interpreter's Bible*, listed above.

Hahn, Scott, Curtis Mitch, and André Villeneuve, with Mark Giszczak and Dennis Walters. *The Books of Wisdom and Sirach: Commentary, Notes, and Study Questions*. Ignatius Catholic Study Bible. San Francisco: Ignatius, 2020. Introduction, text (RSV-2CE), and notes from a Catholic perspective.

Harrington, Daniel J. *Jesus Ben Sira of Jerusalem: A Biblical Guide to Living Wisely*. Collegeville, MN: Michael Glazier, 2005. Seeks to open up ancient

Jewish wisdom by focusing on Ben Sira and his book, its relationship to other wisdom books, content, literary forms, and social world, and how to read it as a handbook for personal and spiritual formation and "way of life."

———. "Sirach." In *The International Bible Commentary*, ed. William R. Farmer et al., 923–50. Collegeville, MN: Liturgical Press, 1998. A Catholic and ecumenical commentary addressed to the educated faithful, especially pastors and teachers. Comments on Sirach by section rather than verse-by-verse.

Reardon, Patrick Henry. *Wise Lives: Orthodox Christian Reflections on the Wisdom of Sirach*. Chesterton, IN: Ancient Faith Publishing, 2009. Unique Orthodox perspective focusing on the broad ideas and lessons taught in each chapter of Sirach.

Snaith, John G. *Ecclesiasticus or the Wisdom of Jesus, Son of Sirach*. London: Cambridge University Press, 1974. Brief introduction, full text (New English Bible translation), and simple, accessible notes.

———. "Sirach." In *Eerdmans Commentary on the Bible*, ed. James D. G. Dunn and John W. Rogerson, 779–98. Grand Rapids: Eerdmans, 2003. Very short introduction, followed by a readable commentary on the text.

Introductions to Wisdom Literature

Clifford, Richard J. *The Wisdom Literature*. Interpreting Biblical Texts. Nashville: Abingdon, 1998. Excellent, concise introduction to biblical wisdom, highlighting parallels with comparable ancient Near Eastern texts and examining the content and rhetoric of each wisdom book.

Crenshaw, James L. *Old Testament Wisdom: An Introduction*. 3rd ed. Louisville: Westminster John Knox, 2010. Perhaps the most comprehensive one-volume introduction to the Old Testament wisdom books; includes an analysis of the legacy of wisdom in the biblical canon and in other cultures.

Kealy, Sean P. *The Wisdom Books of the Bible—Proverbs, Job, Ecclesiastes, Ben Sira, Wisdom of Solomon: A Survey of the History of Their Interpretation*. Lewiston, NY: Edwin Mellen, 2012. A scholarly survey of the secondary literature on the biblical wisdom books, summarizing modern scholarship, Church Fathers, medieval authorities, and contemporary interpretations by artists and theologians.

Murphy, Roland E. *The Tree of Life: An Exploration of Biblical Wisdom Literature*. 3rd ed. Grand Rapids: Eerdmans, 2002. A standard introduction to the wisdom literature of the Bible, discussing aspects of wisdom such as "the fear of the Lord," moral formation, the universality of human experience, the mysteries of creation, and others.

Glossary

chiasm: a literary form and poetic device that involves a sequence of components repeated in inverted order (named for the crossover pattern of the Greek letter *chi*: X). A chiasm may include any number of terms, forming either a fully doubled scheme (A, B, C, C′, B′, A′) or a scheme with an isolated center (A, B, C, D, C′, B′, A′). For example, Sir 33:18 is a chiasm with a fully doubled scheme (A, B, B′, A′): "(A) Hear me, (B) you who are great among the people, (B′) and you leaders of the congregation, (A′) listen."

Decalogue: the Ten Commandments (Hebrew: "Ten Words") that God gave to Israel at Mount Sinai (Exod 20:1–17; Deut 5:6–21). The Decalogue, from the Greek for "ten words" (*deka-logos*), constitutes the moral foundation of the covenant between God and Israel (Exod 34:27–28; Deut 4:13). Jesus did not abolish the Ten Commandments (Matt 5:17) but affirmed that observing them remains necessary to gain eternal life (19:16–19).

Diaspora: the dispersion of the Jewish people or communities outside the land of Israel. Unlike the term "exile," which always implies a forced deportation, "diaspora" can refer to either a forced or a voluntary resettlement of the Jewish population. The term is used both in Second Temple Judaism (5th cent. BC–AD 70) and in the New Testament.

Hades: the dark and gloomy underworld and abode of the dead where it was believed that no one could praise God. *Hadēs* is the Greek equivalent of the Hebrew word *Sheol*. Generally, Old Testament writers did not have a clear idea of life after death and believed that all the deceased went to Hades (Ps 6:5; Sir 17:27; 21:10; Isa 38:18–19). The New Testament also refers to Hades (Luke 10:15; 16:23; Eph 4:9), while also teaching that Jesus has overcome it (Matt 16:18; Acts 2:27; Rev 1:18; 20:13–14).

Hellenism: the influence of Greek culture, language, and customs on the peoples ruled by the Greek Empire after the conquests of Alexander the Great

(333–323 BC). While most Jews could not entirely escape the influence of Hellenism, some rightly saw it as a threat to their cultural and religious identity and the Jewish way of life.

Hellenistic period: the period from the reign of Alexander the Great (356–323 BC) to the rise of the Roman Empire (31 BC), during which Greek culture flourished throughout the eastern Mediterranean world.

inclusio: a literary device in which a word or phrase appears at both the beginning and the end of a section, creating a strong sense of beginning and closure. All content between the repeated word or phrase is "included" in that unit (e.g., Sir 5:1–8).

Koine: the widely spoken form of the Greek language that became the lingua franca (common language) of much of the Mediterranean world from the fourth century BC to the sixth century AD. *Koine* Greek is a simplified form of classical Greek dialects such as Attic, Ionic, and Doric. It served as the language of the Septuagint and the New Testament.

Midrash: from the Hebrew verb *darash*, meaning "to seek or inquire"; plural "Midrashim." Refers to both rabbinic interpretative methods and collections of Jewish commentaries on the Hebrew Scriptures. Midrashim tend to bypass the literal meaning of the text, seeking instead its allegorical sense to enhance its meaning for the reader. A Midrash can be either *haggadic* (expounding on biblical narratives) or *halakhic* (expounding on legal texts). Important Midrashim include, from the Tannaitic period (first to third century AD): Mekhilta de-Rabbi Yishmael (Exodus), Sifra (Leviticus), and Sifre (Deuteronomy, Numbers); from the Amoraic period (third to sixth century): Genesis Rabbah, Leviticus Rabbah, Lamentations Rabbah, Esther Rabbah; from the sixth to the thirteenth century: Midrash Rabbah, Tanhuma, Pesiqta de Rab Kahana, Midrash Tehillim (Psalms).

Mishnah (Hebrew: "repetition" or "study"): a collection of oral traditions and laws compiled by Rabbi Judah the Prince ca. AD 200. Written in Hebrew, the Mishnah consists of six major parts or "orders": *Zeraim* (Seeds), on agricultural laws; *Moed* (Seasons/Festivals), on the Sabbath and festivals; *Nashim* (Women), on marriage, divorce, and family law; *Neziqin* (Damages), on civil and criminal jurisprudence; *Qodashim* (Holy Things), on sacrificial cult and dietary laws; and *Tohorot* (Purifications), on ritual defilement and purification. These orders are further divided up into sixty-three tractates. The Mishnah is the oldest postbiblical codification of the Jewish Oral Law.

numerical proverb or saying: a saying that highlights some feature of nature, society, ethics, or theology through a structured numerical pattern. It typically begins with a number, followed by a list of related items. Often the number is expressed as *x*, *x-plus-one* for emphasis; for example, Sir 23:16–18: "Two sorts of men multiply sins, and a third incurs wrath . . . " (see also 25:1–2, 7–11; 26:5–6, 28; 50:25–26).

parallelism: a stylistic device that involves two or more parallel lines of verse that complement each other in some way. In a synonymous parallelism, two lines repeat the same thought or a similar thought (e.g., Ps 19:1); in an antithetic parallelism, the lines stand in contrast to each other (e.g., Ps 1:6); in a synthetic parallelism, the second line completes a thought introduced by the first line (e.g., Ps 1:3). Parallelism is considered a central feature of Hebrew poetry.

postexilic period: the period following the return of the Jews from the Babylonian exile to the land of Israel. It is typically identified with the Persian period, beginning with the Persian conquest of Babylon (539 BC) and ending with the fall of the Persian Empire (331 BC). The books of Ezra and Nehemiah were written during this period. Although the years following the Persian period are also considered postexilic, they are usually referred to as the Hellenistic period.

Ptolemies: a Greek dynasty that reigned over Egypt from ca. 323 to 30 BC, also known as the Ptolemaic period. The Ptolemaic dynasty was founded after the death of Alexander the Great in 323 BC by his general Ptolemy I Soter (reigned 304–285 BC). The Ptolemies controlled Judah from 301 to 198 BC, after which the Seleucids took over the area.

sage (Hebrew *hakham*, "wise man"): a wise person, mentioned frequently in the biblical wisdom books, who possesses not only knowledge or skill but also the ability to apply experience intelligently to various situations in life. A sage acknowledges and reveres God, aware that wisdom is rooted in the fear of the Lord. Today, in modern Judaism, "sages" refers to the great rabbis of previous generations.

Second Temple period: the time between the building of the second Jewish temple in Jerusalem in 516 BC (Ezra 6:14–15) and its destruction by the Romans in AD 70. Some consider the period to begin with Cyrus's edict of 538 BC, which allowed the Jews to return to Jerusalem (Ezra 1:2–4). The events narrated in the Gospels and other New Testament books take place in the late Second Temple period.

Seleucids: a Greek dynasty founded after the death of Alexander the Great in 323 BC by one of his generals, Seleucus I Nicator. The Seleucid Empire encompassed Syria, Mesopotamia, and parts of Asia Minor. The Seleucids seized control of Judea from the Ptolemies of Egypt in 198 BC during the Fifth Syrian War. The severe persecution of the Jews by Seleucid king Antiochus IV Epiphanes led to the Maccabean revolt around 167 BC. Jonathan Maccabee negotiated peace with the Seleucids, gaining Jewish independence in 143 BC.

Shema (Hebrew: "hear" or "listen"): the Jewish creedal statement of faith in one God, which in its shortest form is expressed in Deut 6:4: "Hear, O Israel: The Lord our God is one Lord." The full passage includes a command to "love the Lord your God with all your heart, and with all your soul, and with all your might," along with instructions to teach God's commandments to one's children and reflect on them in all circumstances (Deut 6:4–9). The synagogue recitation of the *Shema* also includes Deut 11:13–21 and Num 15:37–41. Jesus referred to the *Shema* as the great commandment (Matt 22:36–38). It represents the most fundamental expression of the Jewish faith.

Talmud (Hebrew: "study" or "learning"): a vast collection of rabbinic teachings, discussions, and commentaries consisting of the Mishnah and the Gemara—an Aramaic commentary on the Mishnah. There are two Talmuds: the Palestinian (or Jerusalem) Talmud, compiled in the fifth century AD in the land of Israel, and the more extensive Babylonian Talmud, edited about a century later (mid-sixth century AD) in Babylonia. Both Talmuds are organized according to the orders and tractates of the Mishnah. The Babylonian Talmud is considered to be the most authoritative collection of rabbinic texts and the definitive compilation of Jewish Oral Law.

Torah: the Hebrew term for the Pentateuch, the first five books of the Bible (Genesis, Exodus, Leviticus, Numbers, Deuteronomy). Although commonly translated as "law," the term more accurately means "instruction" or "teaching." In a broader sense, Jews also use the term "Torah" to designate the body of ancient rabbinic writings known as the "oral Torah." They sometimes even call the entire body of sacred Jewish writings "Torah" (somewhat analogous to the Catholic concept of sacred Tradition).

Tosefta (Hebrew: "supplements"): a rabbinic compilation of teachings that supplement the Mishnah, completed in the third or fourth century AD. The Tosefta follows the same organizational structure as the Mishnah but is considered to hold lesser authority.

typology: the study of persons, events, or things in the Old Testament that symbolically prefigure and anticipate (as "types") the fulfillment of God's plan in the person of Christ.

virtue, acquired: a virtue developed through the repetition of certain human acts; for example, a person becomes generous by practicing repeated acts of generosity.

virtue, infused: a virtue or "power of the soul" directly imparted to or "poured into" the soul by God (compare Sir 15:5), in contrast to "acquired virtues" that are attained through the repetition of human acts.

Vulgate: the Latin translation of the Bible produced by St. Jerome (340–420), commissioned by Pope Damasus around AD 383. It soon became the authoritative Bible in the Catholic Church. The Council of Trent (1545–63) declared it to be the authorized Latin translation of the Church. A revised version, the Clementine Vulgate, was published in 1592. It was superseded by the *Nova Vulgata* (New Vulgate), published in 1979, which relies on more trustworthy manuscripts and modern critical methods.

Index of Pastoral Topics

almsgiving and charity, 3:30–4:10; 7:32–36; 12:1–7; 17:22–23; 18:15–18; 29:8–13; 34:21–22; 40:24
ancestors, 44:1–49:16
anger, quarreling, vengeance, 6:2–4; 8:1–3; 27:30–28:12
appearances, 11:2–13
begging, 40:28–30
business and trade, 26:29–27:3
counsel, 37:7–15
cowardice, 2:12–14
creation, 16:24–18:14; 39:12–35; 42:15–43:33
death and mourning, 14:11–19; 38:16–23; 41:1–4
discretion and moderation, 11:7–28
dreams, 34:1–8
duties to God and others, 7:18–36
fear of the lord, 1:11–2:18; 7:29–31; 19:20; 25:10–11; 34:13–15; 40:26–27
food, banquets, and table manners, 31:12–32:13; 37:27–31; 40:28–30
foresight and forethought, 18:19–29; 32:18–24
forgiveness, 28:1–7
free will, 15:11–20
friends and enemies, 6:5–17; 7:18; 9:10–16; 11:29–12:18; 19:13–17; 22:19–26; 27:16–21; 37:1–15
frugality and contentment, 29:21–28
God's power and mercy, 18:1–14
health and physicians, 30:14–25; 38:1–15

honor, 10:19–31
household management, 7:20–22; 33:19–31
human person, 17:1–24
humility, 3:17–25; 7:4–7, 16–17; 10:26–28; 11:1
independence, 33:19–23
joy, 14:11–19; 30:21–25; 40:18–27
law, 2:16; 9:15; 15:1; 17:11; 19:20; 24:23; 32:14–33:3; 35:1; 39:1–8
laziness, 22:1–2
leadership and rule, 7:4–7; 9:17–10:18
lending and borrowing, 29:1–20
lust, sexual immorality, 9:8–9; 18:30–19:4; 23:4–6, 16–27
lying and dishonesty, 7:13; 20:24–26; 27:22–24
parents and children, 3:1–16; 7:23–28; 16:1–4; 22:3–6; 23:14; 30:1–13; 41:5–10, 17; 42:9–14
prayer, example of, 23:1–6; 36:1–17; 50:22–24; 51:1–22
presumption, 5:1–7; 7:8–9
pride, 3:26–28; 10:6–18, 26–29; 11:2–6, 30–31; 13:1, 20; 21:4; 25:2; 27:28; 31:26; 32:18
professions, 38:24–39:11
providence, 11:14–28; 32:14–33:17; 39:12–35
prudence, 8:1–19
repentance, 5:7; 17:23–32; 18:21
reputation, good name, 6:1; 37:26; 39:9–11; 41:11–13; 44:8

rewards and punishments, 5:4–7; 11:14–28; 16:6–23; 17:15–24; 35:10–20; 40:1–17

sacrifice, 7:31; 34:18–35:13; 38:11

self-control, 18:30–19:3; 22:27–23:6; 37:27–31

shame, 4:21; 41:14–42:8

Sheol (Hades), 14:16–17; 17:27–28; 21:10; 28:21; 51:5–6

sin and folly, 16:6–23; 19:18–30; 20:13–23; 21:1–22:18; 27:12–15; 33:5–6; 41:15

speech and silence, 4:23–30; 5:9–6:1; 9:18; 19:4–17; 20:1–8, 13, 18–20; 22:7; 23:7–15; 27:4–7, 11–15; 28:13–26

travel, 34:9–12

trials, 2:1–11; 4:17; 27:5–8; 33:1

wealth and poverty, 5:1–3; 10:30–31; 11:10–28; 13:1–14:19; 25:2–3; 31:1–11

wisdom, 1:1–30; 4:11–19; 6:18–37; 14:20–15:10; 20:27–31; 24:1–34; 37:16–26; 39:1–11; 51:13–30

women (wives, daughters), 7:19, 24–26; 9:1–9; 22:3–5; 23:22–27; 25:1, 8; 25:13–26:27; 36:21–26; 40:19, 23; 42:6, 9–14

Index of Sidebars

The Anxiety of Riches, 241
Banquets in the Ancient World, 247
Beauty and Corrupt Will, 110
The Bitterness of Death, 299
The Body Reflects the Soul, 167
Climbing from Fear to Wisdom, 57
Courting Lady Wisdom through Salvation
    History, 205
Created and Uncreated Wisdom, 51
Death through Eve; Life through Mary, 211
Do Not Sin Presumptuously, 86
"Do Not Surrender Me to a Shameless
    Soul," 187
Enoch Walked with God, 321
The "Evil Tongue," 227
Ezekiel Points to Christ, 347
Five Vices That Dissolve Friendship, 184
The Fool, 181
From Natural to Divine Wisdom, 53
The Garments of the High Priest, 328
The Good and Evil Inclinations, 141
Honoring God by Honoring Parents, 66

Leaving Spiritual Egypt, 324
Lodge in My House of Instruction, 362
On Discerning Dreams, 261
On Sorrow and Grief, 282
Oral Law and Apostolic Tradition, 106
The Pleasures and Dangers of Wine, 248
Pride: The Cause of All Sins, 115
The Rainbow: Sign of Covenant and Judg-
    ment, 309
Repent and Return, 156
Rescued through Almsgiving, 232
Silent until the Right Moment, 170
Sinners Are Forgotten, 319
The Speech of the Fool and of the Wise,
    177
Testing the Potter's Vessels, 220
The Torah Exalts Her Followers, 139
Torah Study and Work, 98
Training One's Children, 237
Wisdom as Preexistent Torah, 203
Wounds of the Tongue, 228
Zeal against the Flesh, 330